HIGH STAKES

HAROLD RHODEN

HIGH STAKES

THE GAMBLE FOR THE HOWARD HUGHES WILL

CROWN PUBLISHERS, INC.
NEW YORK

Copyright © 1980 by Harold Rhoden
All rights reserved. No part of this book
may be reproduced or utilized in any form or by any means,
electronic or mechanical, including photocopying, recording,
or by any information storage and retrieval system,
without permission in writing from the publisher.
Inquiries should be addressed to Crown Publishers, Inc.,
One Park Avenue, New York, New York 10016
Printed in the United States of America
Published simultaneously in Canada
by General Publishing Company Limited
Library of Congress Cataloging in Publication Data
Rhoden, Harold.
High stakes.
1. Hughes, Howard Robard, 1905–1976–Estate.
I. Title.
KF759.H83R56   346.7305′4   80-13899
ISBN: 0-517-540673
Design by Camilla Filancia
10 9 8 7 6 5 4 3 2 1
First Edition

To my wife S H E I L A, *without whose love,*
and to my agent S H I R L E Y C O L L I E R, *without whose*
encouragement,
this book would still have been written.
But I don't know how.

And to
N O A H   D I E T R I C H,
with gratitude for his trust.

AUTHOR'S NOTE

This story is true.

Where events in the life and death of Howard Hughes are related by eyewitnesses, their words are quoted from court transcripts. Where the writings of Howard Hughes are printed, they are quoted from court exhibits. Although every event, in and out of court, took place as depicted, details were deleted, conversations and testimony were edited, literary license was taken, many participants were eliminated, and some names were changed.

HIGH STAKES

PROLOGUE

SALT LAKE CITY, UTAH, *April 27, 1976,* 4:50 P.M.

On the twenty-fifth floor of the Headquarters Building of the Church of Jesus Christ of Latter-day Saints, twenty-three-year-old information specialist Joshua T. Minever returned to his small office and picked up a bulky white envelope lying on his desk, one of the Church's Temple Square Visitors Center envelopes. It was unstamped, and handwritten in ink was:

President Spencer W. Kimball
Church of Jesus Christ
Salt Lake City, Utah

In the lower left corner was:

Personal.

Why did the mail boy leave a letter addressed to President Kimball on this desk? No one in the mail room could have mistaken this office for the president's. The envelope felt bulky—O Lord Jesus Christ in Heaven, it might be a plastic bomb to kill President Kimball! Minever dropped it on his desk and backed out of his office and ran down the hall to the uniformed security guard.

Security guard Bruce Todd followed Minever back toward the small office, and as Minever waited twenty yards down the hall, Todd gently pressed his fingertips to the envelope. He felt only paper inside, and walked out and offered the envelope back to Minever to deliver to President Kimball's secretary, Mrs. Applegate. But Minever shook his head and backed away and said that he would rather not, please. Todd grinned and said he would deliver it.

Rosemary Applegate opened the envelope and took out another envelope and a piece of white paper. On the piece of paper, handwritten in ink, was:

this was found by Joseph F. Smith's house in 1972
thought you would be interested—

The inner envelope was tan along the edges, the way paper looks when it's old, and the upper edge was a darker tan and brittle. On the front, handwritten in ink, was:

1

Dear Mr. Mckay

That was odd—David O. McKay, a past president of the Church, had died in 1972. She read on:

> *please see that this will*
> *is delivered after my death to*
> *Clark County Court House*
> *Las Vegas Nevada*
>
> *Howard R. Hughes*

The news for the past three weeks had been filled with stories about the death of multibillionaire Howard Hughes in a small jet racing him to a Houston hospital, and about the fact that no one had found his will. Could this—impossible! What would the will of Howard Hughes be doing on young Minever's desk? Oh, of course—it was still April! Inside, she would find *April Fool!* She slid her letter opener under the flap, and as she sliced it open, the brittle paper crumbled. She took out three folded pieces of yellow legal-size tablet paper, handwritten in ink. At the top of the first page was:

Last Will and Testament

The bottom of the third page was dated:

March 19, 1968

and signed:

Howard R. Hughes

Rosemary Applegate walked quickly with the papers to the office of D. Arthur Haycock, secretary to the First Presidency, stood quietly as Mr. Haycock examined the papers, and then followed Mr. Haycock to the office of First President Kimball and stood quietly next to Haycock as President Kimball examined the papers.

"Bring me the guard and Brother Minever! Get Brother Kirton on the phone, and until he gets here, I want these papers locked in my safe! Now, please, please! Not one word is to be said about this! Not one word! To anyone!

April 28, 1976, 8:12 A.M.

In President Kimball's office, General Counsel for the Church of Jesus Christ of Latter-day Saints, Wilford Kirton, tall and gaunt and in his early fifties, sat next to tiny Elder Elmer Yost of the Council of Twelve and examined the papers. President Kimball said, "Bill, do you think it's some sick soul's idea of a joke? Or do you think it's criminal?"

"I don't see anything in it that reads like a joke," Kirton said. "One fourth to a medical institute. One eighth to some universities. One sixteenth to our Church and—"

"What's the value of the entire estate?" Elmer Yost asked.

"I've read from two to ten billion," Kirton said, and looked back at the three yellow pages while Elmer bent over a message pad on President Kimball's desk and wrote some numbers.

Kirton said, "Here's a bequest of a sixteenth to a home for orphans, and another to the Boy Scouts. And a sixteenth to a William R. Lommis of Houston, and one to a Melvin Du Mar of Gabbs, Nevada. Ever hear of either of them?"

President Kimball shook his head.

Elmer was still writing zeros.

"Here's a sixteenth to his personal aides and one for a scholarship fund. The spelling in this is atrocious! Wouldn't you think a forger would take the trouble to spell correctly?"

President Kimball leaned forward. "Bill, surely you aren't considering a possibility that this is genuine!"

"From the way it was left here yesterday, I'd say it has to be a forgery. But there are things about it that just don't look like the work of a forger. If it turns out to be a forgery, we've got to be careful about how the Church will look filing it."

"Extremely careful! If we file it, we've got to make it abundantly clear that we're not sponsoring it."

For the next two hours, Wilford Kirton and Elmer Yost talked to every employee on the twenty-fifth floor and on the main floor. No one knew anything about the envelope except Inez Stanton, who sat at the information desk on the main floor. Inez said that that afternoon a tall woman in her forties, well dressed in black— or maybe it was her purse that was black— or it could be her hair that was black—was holding an envelope when she asked Inez where President Kimball's office was.

At 1:15 in his law office, Wilford Kirton opened the Yellow Pages to "Questioned Document Examiners" and found "Leslie King, Court Certified Expert in the Examination of Questioned Documents." Kirton wanted an opinion from someone not a member of the LDS Church. Leslie King was not a member, and was otherwise a lucky—if not a divinely inspired—choice. She had recently testified in the Federal District Court in Utah as an expert on the handwriting of Howard Hughes and still had photographs of exemplars of his handwriting, including one dated March 16, 1968.

At 2:20 Wilford Kirton escorted Leslie King into the library of his law suite and left her there to study the documents. At 4:10 Kirton's secretary told him that Miss King was ready, and he returned to his library for her opinion.

"It was written by Howard Hughes."

"But it—how certain are you?"

"It's possible to simulate a signature, but not three pages of writing."

"Perhaps you might want to examine it further."

"No, there's no need. I can show you dozens of points of comparison—pen lifts and line quality and idiosyncrasies in the letter forms. Even the spacing. Mr. Kirton, the man who wrote these three pages and signed the name *Howard Hughes* was Howard Hughes."

LAS VEGAS, NEVADA, *April 29, 1976,* 9:12 A.M.

At the filing window in the clerk's office, under blinding bright lights and surrounded by news reporters and cameramen, Wilford Kirton handed to the Clerk of Clark County, the envelope addressed to "Mr. Mckay," and the three yellow pages.

Within two hours, the wire-service story made headlines in newspapers throughout the United States and in London, Sydney, Paris, Mexico City, Quebec, Santo Domingo, and Shanghai. The *Los Angeles Times* printed:

HOWARD HUGHES "WILL" LEFT BY
MYSTERY WOMAN AT MORMON CHURCH

Last Will and Testament

I Howard R. Hughes being of sound and disposing mind and memory, not acting under duress, fraud or the undue influence of any person whomsoever, and being a resident of Las Vegas, Nevada, declare that this is to be my last Will and revolk all other Wills previously made by me—

After my death my estate is to be devided as follows—

first: one forth of all my assets to go to Hughes Medical Institute of Miami—

second: one eight of assets to be devided among the University of Texas—Rice Institute of Technology of Houston—the University of Nevada—and the University of Calif.

Howard R. Hughes

—page one—

Last Will and Testament

I Howard R. Hughes being of sound and disposing mind and memory, not acting under duress, fraud or the undue influence of any person whomsoever: and being a resident of Las Vegas Nevada. declare that this is to be my last Will and revolk all other wills previously made by me—

After my death my estate is to be devided as follows—

first: one forth of all my assets to go to Hughes Medical Institute of Miami—

second: one eight of assets to be devided among
the University of Texas—
Rice Institute of Technology
of Houston—
the University of Nevada—
and the University of Calif.

Howard R. Hughes

— page one —

third: one sixteenth to Church of Jesus Christ of Latterday Saints—David O. MaKay-Pre

Forth: one sixteenth to establish a home for Orphan Cildren—

Fifth: one sixteenth of assets to go to Boy Scouts of America—

sixth: one sixteenth: to be devided among Jean Peters of Los Angeles and Ella Rice of Houston—

seventh: one sixteenth of assets to William R. Lommis of Houston, Texas—

eighth: one sixteenth to go to Melvin Du Mar of Gabbs Nevada—

Howard R. Hughes

—page two—

third: one sixteenth to Church
of Jesus Christ of Latterday
Saints — David O. Makay Pre

Forth: one sixteenth to establish a home for Orphan
Cildren —

Fifth: one sixteenth of assets
to go to Boy Scouts
of America.

sixth: one sixteenth; to be
devided among Jean Peters of
Los Angeles and Ella Rice
of Houston —

seventh: one sixteenth of assets
to William R. Lommis of
Houston, Texas —

eighth; one sixteenth to go
to Melvin Du Mar of
Gabbs Nevada —

Howard R. Hughes

— page two —

ninth: one sixteenth to be devided amoung my personal aids at the time of my death—

tenth: one sixteenth to be used as school scholarship fund for entire Country—

the spruce goose is to be given to the City of Long Beach, Calif.—

the remainder of My estate is to be devided among the key men of the company's I own at the time of my death.

I appoint Noah Dietrich as the executer of this Will—

signed the 19 day of

March 1968

Howard R. Hughes

—page three—

ninth; one sixteenth to be
devided among my
personal aids at the time
of my death —

tenth; one sixteenth to be
used as school scholarship
fund for entire Country —

the spruce goose is to be given
to the city of Long Beach, Calif —

the remainder of My
estate is to be devided among
the key men of the company's
I own at the time of my
death.

I appoint Noah Dietrich
as the executer of this will —

signed the 19 day of
March 1968

Howard R. Hughes

— page three —

1. HOWARD WROTE IT

Joyce's jubilant voice on the phone squealed, "Hal, are you sitting down?" I wasn't, so I did. For nine years Joyce Harlan had been Noah Dietrich's devoted secretary. "You won't believe it! They've found Howard Hughes' will, and Noah's the executor!"

I didn't believe it. Hughes would never have named Noah Dietrich as his executor.

"But it's true! Noah just got a call from a wire service in Las Vegas. It's handwritten and it was just filed by the Mormon Church."

My first thought—as a lawyer concerned primarily with justice and the legal rights of my client—was of the millions in fees that would be paid out of the Howard Hughes estate to the attorney for the executor. Me! "Why would Howard Hughes leave a handwritten will? It must be a joke."

"It's no joke, Hal! Noah asked me to call you to take care of it."

Take care of it! How? When? Where? "Tell Noah I'll take care of it and call him back!"

After I hung up, I looked at the bookshelves forming the far wall of my Century City office. All I had on wills was an obsolete 1953 Probate Code; in my twenty-three years of practice, I had never handled a probate.

I walked to my couch, then back to my desk, then to the window, and I kept walking because I couldn't stay still. What do I do first? If a will is contested, does the executor named in it have a duty to defend it? Does he have a right to defend it? A will contest would cost thousands. Who pays for it? Noah couldn't. In what court do I submit it? And when? What if I don't when I should? Now, calm down and take one thing at a time! What's the first thing a lawyer does when his client is named as the executor in a will written by one of the richest men in the world? The lawyer asks somebody for some legal advice.

I walked fast to Stanley Fairfield's office, next to mine. Behind his Danish-modern desk, Stanley Fairfield, forty-one, a devoted lover of good mirrors, was looking at one in his hand. His tinted blond hair was brushed forward to hide a receding hairline and his blond mustache was trimmed to look like the kind in ads for Arrow shirts. As I told him the

15

news, his light blue eyes opened wide and his mouth spread into a faint smile as he saw God. "Do you think it could be true?"

"I don't know. First, what's that word in the law for a handwritten will?"

"Hal, you'll need help!"

"Plenty. What do you call a handwritten—"

"Do you know how big that estate is? Not hundreds of millions, but billions! Billions! Do you know what that means in attorneys' fees?"

"Yeah. Now, about that handwritten—"

"Where did it show up?"

"I don't know anything yet. First thing I want to—wait, I remember now—a holographic will."

"Why would Howard Hughes write a holographic will?"

"Maybe he couldn't afford a lawyer."

"Am I in? You'll need a lot of research and—"

"You're in! Stan, what are the duties of someone named as executor in a will when it first—"

"Millions in fees! No, hundreds of millions! That's in ordinary fees alone! Holy Shit! We'd run the casinos in Vegas! The whole fucking empire!"

At the door my secretary said, "Noah Dietrich is on the phone," and Stanley and I ran back to my office.

"Hal, forget it! It's a hoax."

"How do you know, Noah?"

"A newsman read it to me over the phone. It names the Spruce Goose, and Howard would never have used that name. And the spelling is childish. Don't waste your time."

Before the call had ended, Stanley no longer saw God, and after I hung up, he walked back to his office and I tried to go back to work, but I kept picturing myself standing before the court: *As attorney for the executor, I move to set aside Summa's sale of the Desert Inn for thirty million dollars, and I charge Summa's thieving board of directors . . .* playing a role about which I knew nothing in a financial world about which I knew less. It would have been fun.

An hour later, Noah phoned again, this time excited. "Hal, drop everything! Howard wrote it!"

"How do you know?"

"I have it right here! An AP reporter just flew in from Vegas with a Xerox copy. It's Howard's handwriting! I'd know it anywhere! Let's get in there and put those stealing bastards in jail and get rich. But let's get rich first. The television people are coming here in an hour to interview me. They want to know what legal steps I'm going to take. Brief me."

Oh, Christ!

"What do I tell them you and I are going to do?"

"Noah, it's very complex—it involves jurisdictional questions and the laws of domicile and—I'd better be there with you to keep you from looking as though you aren't thoroughly familiar with the procedures."

After the call, I ran back to Stanley's office. "Drop everything! It's Hughes' handwriting! Noah saw it! You and I are going to Noah's for a press conference! Give me your copy of Marshall's book on probate and I'll research as you drive."

Stanley rose and smiled as he again saw God. "Hundreds of millions in attorneys' fees!"

On the drive in Stanley's white Jaguar to Sunset Boulevard, I had a few questions: Who files what first to probate the will? Where? And why there? When? And why then? Stanley was experienced in probate matters. He didn't know either.

I learned in Marshall's book that we had to file a petition to probate the will in the state in which the testator was domiciled when he died. Howard Hughes' last domicile was the Desert Inn in Las Vegas, from 1966 to 1970. If after that he never acquired another domicile, Las Vegas would still be it, and since the old recluse had spent his last six years hiding out in hotel rooms around the world dodging process servers, the likely place to petition was Las Vegas.

We drove up the winding road in the Hollywood Hills north of Sunset, turned into Noah's grounds, past the rusted, sagging gate, and stopped in front of a gray stone mansion, built in the thirties to look like a Bavarian castle. Stanley adjusted the rearview mirror, combed his hair, turned his head to the right, then to the left, and liked what he saw.

The entrance was through the small, dingy kitchen. Noah's wife, Mary, once one of the stately Goldwyn Girls, now fifty and big, beamed and said, "How soon do we get our money?"

At the head of the long living-room table sat white-haired, white-faced eighty-seven-year-old Noah Dietrich bent forward in a plaid flannel robe, his arms braced on the table to hold himself up. In magazine articles about Noah Dietrich and Howard Hughes in the forties, Noah was called Hughes' "hatchet man," and Noah always chuckled at that. "When I had to fire someone, I fired him," Noah once told me. "Howard didn't have the balls to fire anyone. I always had to do it for him." Noah had been called the genius behind eighty percent of Hughes' wealth; the other twenty percent, they wrote, was luck. From 1925 to 1957 Noah had been not only the builder of the Hughes financial empire, but the brains of the emperor. "Hal, Howard wrote it!"

Stanley and I looked at Noah's Xerox copy of the will. Some of the letters were rewritten as though the writer didn't like the way he had done it the first time and kept going over it until he got it right. "Among" was spelled *amoung*, but six lines down, spelled correctly. "Las Vegas" was spelled *Las Vagas* on the envelope, but correctly in the will. "Revoke" was *revolk*, "divided" was *devided*, and there was a capital *M* on *My* in the middle of a sentence. Some of the writing was shaky, and some of the phrases were barely literate. Stanley winced and I must have, too. "Noah, did Hughes really write like this?"

"It's his handwriting! I'd know it anywhere!"

"This writing is lousy!"

"Howard was a lousy writer!"

A few minutes later, the press corps burst in: a reporter from CBS and his cameraman, two other television camera units, a UP reporter, someone from the *Los Angeles Times*, and two radio reporters.

"Mr. Dietrich, do you believe that this will is authentic?"

"No question about it, Howard wrote it."

"This morning, didn't you say you had some doubts?"

"This morning I said it was a goddam fake. But I hadn't seen a copy of it."

"What changed your mind?"

"A copy of it."

"But Mr. Dietrich, in view of your bitter court fight with Mr. Hughes in 1957, why would he have named you as executor of his will?"

"Because Howard knew that I was in the right in that suit! And he knew that I knew more about his business than anyone else did. A hell of a lot more than he did. He trusted me. He never trusted anyone else. He always respected my expertise in financial matters. And he respected my executive ability. And my integrity."

I had to add, "And your modesty."

A reporter asked, "Mr. Dietrich, what are you going to do about this will?"

"Turn the matter over to my lawyer."

"Mr. Rhoden, what are you going to do about this will?"

Panic if I don't get a crash course in probate. "On Mr. Dietrich's behalf, I'm going to petition the court to have it probated."

"Where?"

"Las Vegas."

"When?"

I selected, "Tomorrow."

"At what time?"

"Two o'clock." As good a time as any.

"Where in Las Vegas?"

"Where was the will filed?"

"Clark County Courthouse."

"That's where."

"Do you expect opposition?"

"I guarantee it."

"From whom?"

"From whoever would inherit Hughes' estate if he died without a will."

"Do you think it's genuine, Mr. Rhoden?"

"Well, I'm no handwriting expert, so —"

"I am," Noah said, "and that's Howard's handwriting!"

"What do you know about this Melvin Du Mar named to get one sixteenth on page two?"

"Never heard of him. You ever hear of him, Noah?"

"Never heard of him."

After the lights went off, the newsmen asked me to notify them of every step to be taken and where and when so that they could cover it, and I promised I would. As soon as they left, Stanley and I examined the copy of the will.

Noah said, "Hal, I can't cover the expenses for this."

"I know, Noah."

"Of course, when I'm in as the executor and you're my lawyer for the estate, there'll be millions in fees."

On our walk back to the car, Stanley said, "He doesn't look as though he's going to live to the end of the week. We could do all this work and if he dies, we're out! How long has he looked like this?"

"About fifteen years."

"What's he got?"

"Myasthenia gravis."

"Is it serious?"

"Terminal."

"Oh, no! How much more time does he have?"

"Ten years ago when I needed an early trial date for his libel case against Litton, Noah's doctor gave me an affidavit that although Noah had a fifty-fifty chance of living another year, he had only one chance in ten of living through a second year. That was ten years ago."

"What does his doctor say now?"

"His doctor is dead."

As we drove off, Stanley said, "Who pays for all this?"

"Right now, you and I. Are you still in?"

"I'm in!"

"Remember, Stan, it might be a fake. And it might cost a fortune and take many months to find out."

"This is that one chance in a lifetime. Can you picture the power? And the money? I tell you, it's that one chance in a lifetime!"

2. MELVIN DUMMAR

The next day at 1:00 in Las Vegas, a block from the Clark County Courthouse, on the third floor of the Nevada National Bank Building, Stanley and I entered the small reception room of the law suite of Alexander Morenus, where a grandmotherly secretary graciously greeted us as though we were rich clients. A minute later, in sauntered a short man, overjoyed and overstuffed in a light-blue suit, with a light-blue shirt, a light-blue tie, and shiny white shoes. Sixty, his head carried a stiff mahogany-brown toupee to make him look forty, but it didn't.

Alexander Morenus ushered us into his office, sat behind his desk, invited us to call him Alex, and lit a cigar. "Gentlemen, I'm ready to answer all your questions about our probate procedure here. They say that whatever Nevada probate law I don't know hasn't been written yet." He laughed at that. "And whatever judge I don't know on a first-name basis hasn't been elected yet." That he found even funnier. "All right, gentlemen, I guess you want me to brief you on my experience," but before we could tell him we didn't, he did, and the more he talked about the law, the more he displayed a mind uncluttered by too much knowledge of it. "Now, I know you agree, gentlemen, that we've got to have Mr. Dietrich appoint a Las Vegas bank in his place as executor."

"Why a bank?" I said.

"Because if not, when Mr. Dietrich passes away, the court appoints a relative and the relative picks his own lawyer. And we're out!"

"But suppose that after we work our balls off for years," Stanley asked, "our client, the executor bank, decides to fire us and pick its own lawyers?"

"It's a bank we can trust."

"No bank, Alex," I said.

"My bank may finance not only the costs but also the attorneys' fees!" His smile anticipated what surely had to be an enthusiastic acceptance of his proposal.

"No bank."

"Then what happens when our client dies?" Alex's impatience was ready to burst out of his blue outfit.

"No bank!"

Our host looked ready to tell me what to do with my petition, but instead sat back, puffed on his cigar and mumbled, "Whatever you say!" He didn't like me either.

Waiting for Morenus at the elevators, I whispered, "Where in hell did you get this guy?"

"He came highly recommended. But, so what? All we need for local counsel is someone who can point us to the clerk's office and the men's room. We don't need someone who can think."

"We've got him."

At 2:00 Morenus led Stanley and me into the courthouse and to the clerk's office on the second floor. The place was mobbed by the waiting press. The camera lights blasted on as we walked in, and a reporter asked, "Can you comment on the opinion of Bernard Bern?"

"Who's he?"

"Bernard Bern was one of the handwriting experts who examined Howard Hughes' handwriting during the Clifford Irving hoax, and it was his opinion that the forgery was a forgery. He was brought here by ABC and examined the Mormon will early today. It's his opinion that it was written by Howard Hughes."

A tall girl reporter shoved a long black cylinder almost into my mouth. "Mr. Rhoden, what will Mr. Dietrich do if he finds out that the Mormon will is a forgery?"

"Withdraw his petition to have it probated."

"Then you concede that it might be a forgery?"

"Of course. We're investigating that."

"How?"

How! "We're arranging for it to be examined by the best handwriting experts in the world." As soon as I can borrow the money to hire one.

As an historic event unequaled since the signing of the Japanese surrender, five cameras filmed my handing to the clerk our petition and a $75 check for the filing fee. After we left the clerk's office, Alex Morenus motioned for me to follow him. Away from the reporters, he said, "May I suggest something?"

"Anything, Alex—I need all the advice you can give me."

Alex fumed and didn't try to control it. "Don't ever say it! Don't even listen to the word 'forgery'! You've got to be positive with the press. This will is genuine! And you know it! If you have a doubt, they'll have a doubt."

"I have a doubt."

"But for God's sake, man, you can't admit it! I can't understand how you can use the word 'forgery' with the press!"

"'Forgery' is a word everybody's using when they talk about this will. And it's a word I'm going to keep using."

The dislike in Alex's tight lips had the potential of developing into something big.

Stanley and I were so elated about the expert hired by ABC that we decided to stay at the MGM Grand Hotel that night and celebrate and fly back in my Cessna 310 early the next morning. In my room, we turned on the 6:00 news to watch ourselves on television, and then we watched an interview with a gas-station attendant named Melvin Dummar.

Melvin Dummar, pudgy and young, dressed in a plaid sport shirt open at his thick neck, mumbled in a thin twang that he was "awful upset" by the news, and exhausted from all those questions from all those reporters who had flocked to Willard, Utah, to interview him from all over the United States. Asked where he lived in March 1968 and how he then spelled his last name, he said that in 1968 he lived in Gabbs, Nevada, and that his last name was always spelled the same way. Dummar's little eyes dripped tears down his chubby cheeks, and barely moving his lips, he whined, "I wish to God this never happened. It's a terrible nightmare."

Then Dummar was asked how he happened to be named in Howard Hughes' will.

"Well, I was drivin' down from Tonopah to L.A. an' I seen this old man. I thought he was a bum or somethin'. I gave him a ride an' dropped him off in Las Vegas. An' when he got out, he ast me if I could loan him any money, an' I gave him a quarter. He said his name was Howard Hughes. I din't believe him at the time. But I guess it really musta been him."

The reporter asked, "That was your only connection with Howard Hughes?"

"Uh-huh."

Stanley looked as sick as I felt. "What the fuck was that?"

"Who is this dummy?" I pulled out of my briefcase the Xerox copy of the will and looked at page two:

eighth: one sixteenth to Melvin Du Mar of Gabbs, Nevada.

And this was that *Melvin Du Mar?*

"Hughes left a hundred and fifty million bucks to this kid? For having done what? Oh, no!"

"Stan, let's not panic!"

"You believe one word of that shit?" Stanley paced the room. "Howard Hughes asking for a quarter? A quarter! Ten minutes ago I could see myself ordering that gray Rolls. Son of a bitch!"

"Don't cancel your order yet. Let's reason it out."

"You reason it out! It's a fucking forgery and that fat ass we just saw is the fucking forger!"

"The kid's a phony, but does it necessarily follow that the will is a forgery?"

Stanley sat down, and I took over the pacing. "If it's a forgery, who would the forger have to be?"

"That fat ass!" Stanley said.

"That's right! A forger unconnected with Dummar wouldn't have known about him. And if he did, he sure as hell wouldn't have put

Dummar's name in there. So if it's a forgery, Dummar's got to be in on it."

"He's in on it!"

"But for someone to try to pass off a forgery to rip off one of the biggest estates in the world—can you imagine the gall he'd have to have? The skill? The knowledge? Does that fit this kid we just saw?"

"Why couldn't this hillbilly have said he had seen Howard Hughes skipping out of a flying saucer? That would have made some sense! But Howard Hughes out in the desert hitchhiking?"

"If this were a forgery, that Melvin Dummar would have had to have been in on it, and I tell you it'd be impossible for Melvin Dummar to have been in on a forgery of a will of Howard Hughes."

"Why impossible?"

"Because Melvin Dummar is too dumb."

3. THE ROLLER COASTER

On May 5, 1976, on the 6:00 news, a short-haired lawyer stammered that he represented three second cousins of Howard Hughes, heirs under Texas law if there were no will. "Handwriting expert Spencer Otis examined the so-called Mormon will, and it's his opinion that it's a rank forgery."

If Otis were right, I wanted out. But if he were wrong and the case had to be tried, this publicity could hurt. It could influence other handwriting experts. It could stop the rich institutional beneficiaries from providing financial support for the case. And the effect of this publicity on potential jurors could be disastrous. I had to find out fast if that will was written by Howard Hughes or by Melvin Dummar.

The two top handwriting experts on the West Coast were Spencer Otis of San Francisco and Frederick Symington of Los Angeles. The morning after Otis' opinion was publicized, I phoned Frederick Symington. Symington said his fee would be $10,000 to go to Vegas for a look, and $50,000 to testify, and I said goodbye. Then I phoned handwriting expert Bernard Bern, who had examined the will for ABC. Mr. Bern wanted $2,000 to show me the report he had already written for the network. When I told him I would get someone else, his price shrank to $200. I accepted, and Mr. Bern agreed to be in my office at 9:00 the following morning to trade his report for a check and to state his expert opinion to the news media to counter Otis. I set up a press conference for 10:00.

At 9:00 the next morning, I greeted pint-sized, swollen-nosed, eighty-two-year-old Bernard Bern. He was wearing a black pin-striped suit with a large orange satin handkerchief sagging like a dead flower out of his breast pocket. Mr. Bern held tight to his report until I handed him his check, and then, spitting as he spoke, said, "First, I wanna point out what I wrote about them capital letters."

As I strained to decipher the single spaced report typed on a machine which had not been cleaned in decades, Mr. Bern pulled the sleeve of my coat, and still spitting, said, "Here's what I mean by consistent inconsistencies. Mr. Hughes wasn't consistent in nothin' he wrote. Here you'll notice how careful I point out not only them letters, but the links between them letters."

I looked at the wall and asked, What brainless bastard called this press conference without first interviewing this guy? You did, dummy!

"Mr. Bern, do you have an opinion about the age of the paper?"

"Sure. I studied it real careful like I always do on every job. You see, my philosophy is—"

"How old is the paper?"

"The first thing I done when I looked at it was—"

"How old is the paper?"

"At least ten years old."

"How do you know?"

"How do I know! That's what I been tryin' to tell you, 'cause I knew you was gonna ask me. To tell you how I know, I gotta tell you 'bout my background."

I walked to the window to avoid the spray.

"I been in psychic research for fifty years an' I done research in parapsychology an' metaphysics."

"Mr. Bern, about the age of the paper—"

"I ain't told you 'bout my background yet. You gotta hear 'bout my background. Don't you wanna hear 'bout my background?"

"Yes, but, first, about the age—"

"I began my study of psychic research—"

As Mr. Bern walked toward me at the window, I moved for protection to the chair behind my desk and said, "How do you know that the paper is ten years old?"

He walked behind my desk to be close to me. "I found them little specks o' dirt in them creases. Now, I gotta tell you 'bout my background. I was the only one listed. I know how they'll attack me. They do it every time, but I'll be ready for 'em 'cause there ain't nothin' I can't answer, an' nothin' I gotta be ashamed of, 'cause I was listed. An' if you was listed, you ain't got nothin' to be ashamed of, an' I was listed."

"All right! You were listed!"

"You act like you don't know what listed is."

"Mr. Bern, I do not know what listed is."

"You don't know what listed is?"

"Listed as what?"

"As a marriage counselor." He couldn't understand why I couldn't understand him.

"Listed where?"

"In the Yellow Pages."

The phone buzzed and my secretary told me that the press corps was on its way back. Oh, God, help your poor sinning son of a bitch now! In a few minutes, my office was packed with twenty-seven representatives of the local and national press with lights, cameras and microphones ready to record this momentous occasion. Mr. Bern sat at my right, and the NBC newscaster nodded for me to begin.

"This is Mr. Bernard Bern, a handwriting expert"—then I emphasized—"who was hired by ABC to examine the Mormon will. He is prepared—as was Spencer Otis yesterday—to give you his opinion of the authenticity of the will. Mr. Bern, did you examine the Mormon will in Las Vegas?"

"First I gotta explain this. I know what they was tryin' to do in them other cases, but I can prove I was listed."

"Sir, did you examine the Mormon will?"

"First, I gotta explain how I done it or you ain't gonna understan' nothin'!"

"Did you examine the Mormon will?"

"Why else am I here if I didn't examine it?"

"Did you compare it to any exemplars of Mr. Hughes' writings?"

"Now, that's a dumb question. How do you examine if you don't compare?"

"What was your conclusion?"

"First I gotta explain how my daughter an' me operate—"

"Mr. Bern, what was your opinion? Genuine or forgery?"

"I din't have no doubt, an' I said to my daughter, I said to her even before we went for coffee—you see, sometimes you ain't too sure, but my daughter an' me, we studied it real careful an' I'm sure—an' I says to her—"

"You mean it's your expert opinion that Howard Hughes wrote the Mormon will?"

"Ain't that what I just said?"

Thank you, God! "And thank you, Mr. Bern." I turned to the press. "Ladies and gentlemen, if you have any questions, please go ahead, and since you don't, thank you for coming—"

"Wait a minute!" Mr. Bern was indignant. "I ain't through yet. I got somethin' to say here." I was sprayed with another wash in my left ear as Mr. Bern went on. "You ain't gonna understan' nothin' if you don't understan' how we work, my daughter an' me."

One by one the lights mercifully went out, and the members of the press, some amused, some disgusted, picked up and packed up and thanked me for inviting them, and even after the last newsman left, Mr. Bern kept spitting at me about his daughter and his listing.

One of the attorneys who had volunteered to help me in the case was Eli Blumenfeld, a brilliant tax specialist. Eli phoned me the morning after the interview with Bernard Bern. "That was pitiful! How could you go on television with a shmuck like that for a handwriting expert?"

"It was easy. I made a mistake."

"Let's correct it. I've got someone who'll go to Las Vegas with you to examine that will. Adam Heller. He's an autograph dealer. He buys and sells famous autographs—Lincoln's, Thomas Jefferson's, the Marquis de Sade's. He makes a living knowing whether writing is genuine or not. Now, he's never testified, and in a way he's not exactly a handwriting expert."

"Then I don't want him."

"He's free."

"I'll take him."

At 9:30 the following morning, after the formalities in the courtroom of Judge Keith C. Hayes, Adam Heller and I were ushered by the big-bellied bailiff through the back door of the courtroom, down a narrow passageway, and into the stuffy jury room, followed by two television cameramen and a photographer from the *Las Vegas Sun*. A stocky detective leaned up against the wall with his fists on his waist, exposing a belted .38-caliber revolver. Next to him was the matronly court reporter ready to stenotype every word, and seated in chairs against the wall were the judge's plump court clerk and skinny, middle-aged law clerk. On the table were four sets of inch-thick plastic plates; each set sandwiched one of the three sheets of paper of the will, and one set protected the envelope.

When the cameramen finished filming our dramatic entrance, Adam Heller went to work. Heller was in his thirties, a balding man with an appearance not long remembered. After a half-hour examination he whispered that he wanted to speak to me privately. Outside the jury room in the passageway behind the judge's chambers, he said, "Hughes is probably the author of the will. Sixty-forty. Sixty he wrote it, forty he didn't. To be more sure, I'd need some original exemplars. My copies aren't good enough."

I asked Heller to continue studying while Alex Morenus drove me to the office of the *Las Vegas Sun* to see its publisher, Hank Greenspun. Alex had said that Greenspun had a collection of original memos handwritten by Hughes to Robert Maheu in 1968. Mr. Greenspun said that though he was convinced that the Mormon will was a fake, he would let me examine some of the Hughes memos locked in his safe. I selected eight dated around March 1968 and rushed them to the jury room and handed them to Heller. He moved the material around, studied it, and then asked me to look.

Heller had placed on each side of the first page of the will a memo, also on lined yellow legal-pad paper, handwritten by Howard Hughes, one in March 1968, and one in April 1968. The two handwritten memos obviously were written by the same hand. But the one in the middle— page one of the will— obviously was not! The appearance of that page of the will was conspicuously different from the appearance of the two comparison pages flanking it. The case was over.

"What's your opinion now?" I asked.

Heller motioned for me to follow him back into the passageway for another private conference. "It's still sixty-forty, but this time, it's sixty it's a forgery. It's probably a forgery."

After Heller finished, we left the jury room; in the hallway the lights shot on, the microphones poked at my face and the tall girl reporter asked, "What's your handwriting expert's opinion?"

"It's Heller's opinion that the Mormon will is probably a forgery."

"But he's your own—you must have meant— did you say forgery? Can we ask him directly?"

I said, "Of course," and she did, and Mr. Heller said what I had said he had said.

The girl reporter asked me, "What are you going to do now that it appears that the Mormon will is probably a forgery?"

"Fly back to Los Angeles. And cry."

On the flight back to Los Angeles with Adam Heller in the copilot's seat, the twin turbocharged engines of my Cessna 310 hummed us over scattered clouds at 10,500 feet with the DME indicating a ground speed of 216 knots, and I assured myself I was lucky I had found out early. All I had lost were a few weeks and a few hundred dollars. But if I were so lucky, why was my stomach so sick? What the hell, I wouldn't have liked a probate practice anyway. And those interviews on television were becoming a pain. And who needs a fee of $150 million?

On the flight back, I made plans to abandon the case.

On May 17, 1976, in my office, I greeted Mr. Jasper Ortega and three of his associates who had flown in to see me from Philadelphia. Mr. Ortega, slender, in a perfectly fitted black suit, smiled with nothing to smile at. "We've been following the developments of your case, and we know what you need. We'd like to offer our financial help."

"Why?"

"Our organization is equipped to offer the best service in the world in counterintelligence. We'd like to replace InterTel when Mr. Dietrich takes over as executor of the estate and manages Summa."

"Assuming that Summa needs counterintelligence, I couldn't promise to replace InterTel, because I don't even know what InterTel is."

"We know you don't." He walked to the window and looked out at the building that was a twin to the one we were in and said, "Right now, and for the past two weeks, you and this office have been under intensive, around-the-clock surveillance. They know everything you do and everything you say."

Bullshit! "Who do you mean by they?"

Mr. Ortega looked at his associates and smiled at my naiveté. "InterTel. Would you be willing to consider our organization?"

"Sure, I'd be willing to consider it, but—"

"Fair enough. Now you'll need a panel of the most renowned handwriting experts in the world. Obviously, the cost will be substantial, and we wanted to meet you to see what your attitude was. I think I can speak for my associates when I say I'm confident we can work with you."

I was not equally confident I could work with him.

"The first step," he said, "is to find out if the will is genuine."

"I don't think it is. I saw it compared to two—"

"On our staff we have a forensic handwriting expert, and we'd like to have him, under your auspices, go to Las Vegas to examine the will and compare it to our exemplars of Howard Hughes' handwriting."

"What'll it cost me?"

"Nothing."

"I accept."

"His name is Vladimir Wazencko. Sounds like a Russian spy, but he was born in Philadelphia and holds a master's degree from Northeastern University in police science. When do you want him?"

"Tomorrow morning, ten o'clock in Department 9 of the Clark County Courthouse in Las Vegas."

The next morning at 10:00 in the corridor outside Department 9 of the Clark County Courthouse in Las Vegas, I met Vladimir Wazencko, a huge man with thick black hair. As he told me about his experience as a handwriting expert in several hundred cases, I suffered the foul hunch that before he left Philadelphia, he had concluded that the will he was about to examine was genuine.

After the second hour, Mr. Wazencko grimly motioned for me to follow him back into the jury room. "First, no forger writes three pages when one would do. Second, no forger who makes a mistake in a stroke rewrites it in his finished work over and over again to improve it. That's idiocy! But all over the three pages of this will are these overwritings. See? Now, look here." He pointed out similarities between the will and the exemplars: letter forms that were identical, links between letters that were identical, breaks in letters and breaks in links that were identical, and slow, tremulous writing in the will and in the exemplars that were identical. "There's no doubt about it," he said. "The man who wrote those exemplars, Howard Hughes, wrote that will."

"Not so fast. I'd like to show you something." I took two of the handwritten memos I had again borrowed from Hank Greenspun, and placed one on each side of page one of the will. "Look at this! These two pages on the sides are obviously written by the same hand. But the will in the middle is obviously not written by the same hand as the other two."

"And you obviously don't know what the hell you're talking about!" Mr. Wazencko placed his Xerox copy of a memo handwritten by Hughes in 1968 next to one of the original memos loaned by Greenspun, also written by Hughes in 1968. "Look at these two! Do they look alike?"

They didn't! You'd swear that they could not have been written by the same hand!

"And yet, they were both written by the same hand," he said, "and in the same year. They don't look alike to you because the spacing is different. And the spacing is different because Hughes was inconsistent in his spacing. He was consistently inconsistent in his spacing, and this is true with every other feature of his writing. Nobody—absolutely nobody—judges the way you did, by a gross inspection! You'd do just as well making a comparison wearing a blindfold. In fact, you'd do a hellova lot better with a blindfold than with a goddam gross inspection!"

In the cab driving back to the MGM, I concluded that I had been unjustly suspicious of Mr. Wazencko, and I saw myself in the Cessna showroom looking up at a pressurized 340 and telling the salesman, "Deliver it in ten days with Collins radios," and I abandoned plans to abandon the case.

4. THE FROWNING MONKEYS

The news coverage of the developments of the case prompted a loan officer at the First Los Angeles Bank to not only extend my then overdue note for $30,000 but to increase it to $50,000 in the hope of having his bank become the depository bank after my client became the executor of the Hughes Estate, and on June 21, 1976, the news coverage brought me an invitation for lunch at Señor Pico's from Marvin M. Mitchelson. I had known Marvin for fourteen years as a fellow lawyer, fellow opera lover, and frequent client. Silver-haired, in his late forties, his face was still boyish, and he was only fifteen pounds overweight. During his first margarita, Marvin said, "All I want is to help. I'd give anything to take some part in all this. It's got to be the greatest will contest ever tried!"

"But what I need is heavy research into probate law, and research isn't your—"

"No, no, not research!"

"And I need money. I have only a few thousand left, and I've got to devote all my time to this case and that means closing my practice and shutting off all income. And I'll need a fortune for costs for depositions and—"

"I'll get you the money!"

Fat chance! Although Marvin earned $200,000 a year, he spent over $200,000 a year on pleasures such as shopping trips to Paris and Rome and on his two Rolls Royces and his new Mercedes. Because Marvin never paid his restaurant or laundry bills until legal action was threatened, or his office rent until eviction day, there wasn't one credit card company that would trust him with its plastic. To know Marvin was to know that accepting a lunch invitation from him meant picking up the check.

"Hal, isn't there some place for me in this? Christ, I'm fed up with those divorce cases and those nagging bitches. 'I want the house, I want both cars, I want both his balls!' I've had enough of that! I'd like to do something else for the rest of my life, something with class. And I thought that maybe you could find a spot for me somewhere with you up there on a policy-making level. I'd really work, Hal, I'd really work! Right now, what do you need other than money and some law clerk to do research for you?"

"I need a panel of the most competent, prestigious handwriting experts in the world."

"I'll go to Europe and get you your panel."

"Or, instead, I'll have another margarita."

"I'll really do it!"

"Sure, Marvin, sure."

"Give me some copies of the will and samples of Hughes' writing, and I'll leave for England right away."

"Before or after you pick up the check for lunch?"

"Hal, I'm a little short of cash today, do you—"

"Sure, Marvin, sure."

"I'm going to get you those experts!"

Three days later I received a phone call from Marvin in London. "I've got our first expert! He just told me it's genuine! He's all excited about it—he'll be famous! He's the top handwriting expert in England! Jeffrey Carroll. He does work for Scotland Yard. How do you like that? Scotland Yard! Now, his opinion is qualified until he sees the original in Las Vegas, but he's agreed to fly there to examine it."

"Marvin, you're beautiful!"

"The guy cost me five thousand dollars and it'll cost me another five for his expenses, but he's worth it. It's genuine! Hughes really wrote it!"

Two days later, from somewhere in Wales, Marvin phoned me that he was waiting for one of the best-known handwriting experts in Europe to finish his examination. The next day, Marvin told me that he would have the expert's answer by 5:00 P.M. Welsh time. Then I didn't hear from Marvin for four days. When his secretary told me she didn't know where to reach her boss, I told her to tell Marvin to cut the bullshit, get on the telephone, and give me the bad news. The following day, Marvin phoned and said, "The Welshman said it was a forgery, but I just saw the top expert in France, the man who runs the scientific lab in Marseilles for the police department. You'll love him!"

"What's his opinion?"

"Wait, let me tell you! Interpol sends him their toughest handwriting cases."

"Has he seen the will and the exemplars?"

"This man, you'll love! You'll love him!"

"Goddammit, Marvin, I love him! Did he see it?"

"He's studying it now. He'll know in a day or so. He's got his whole lab working on it. He's going to go for us—I feel it."

"What did you feel in Wales?"

"All right, one out of two isn't bad."

Two days later Marvin again phoned from Marseilles. "The old man's with us! Hughes wrote it! Ollivier's ready to come to Las Vegas to see the original, and he'll testify if it still looks good to him."

Two out of three wasn't bad either.

The next call from Marvin came a few days later from Mannheim, Germany. "This guy's name is Lothar Michel and he teaches forgery detection at Mannheim University! He's pretty sure that Hughes wrote it, but he won't give a final opinion until he sees the original. Three out of four! Not bad, huh? I'm on my way to Paris. I hear there's a famous expert there. Wish me luck!"

After three weeks Marvin phoned from his Century City office to assure me that he had left someone in Europe to finish his quest.

"Who?"

"Hal, trust me."

"I trust you. Now, who's working on this over there?"

"You misjudged him."

"For chrissakes, Marvin, who is it?"

"Herman Falitz. He has faith in the will and—"

"Well, I don't have faith in Herman Falitz! Why didn't you tell me you were turning this job over to that asshole?"

"Because I knew you weren't crazy about him."

I had never seen Herman Falitz, but about a year before, when Falitz phoned me and raised his shrill voice to lecture me on how to solve a legal problem for Marvin, I hung up on him.

"Hal, he's a genius in high finance, he's traded over fifty million dollars a day in the future's market—"

"He's an obnoxious, presumptuous, conniving—"

"I didn't say he was perfect."

The next morning, Marvin shouted on the phone, "Four out of five! Herman just called. The guy from Paris is for us," and a few days later, "Five out of six! A Dutchman named Hans Verhaeren! He was a handwriting expert for the Ministry of Justice in Amsterdam. He's one of the best handwriting experts in Holland! He's got to see the original in Vegas, but Herman said that the Dutchman told him it really looks good. What do you think of Herman now?"

"He's still an obnoxious—but you and he have done a remarkable job."

"What's next, boss?"

"Bring each expert to Vegas to see it."

"They're on their way. Anything more?"

"I need a couple of American experts."

"How many?"

"Three ought to be enough."

"I'll get you four. We'll keep one as a spare in case somebody gets sick."

Herman Falitz had spent several thousand dollars and three sweltering weeks running around Europe for the case, but I didn't want to see him. I didn't like him, and Marvin's pleading didn't change my mind. "You owe it to him to see him. And you owe it to me. Look at what he's done for you! For the case! He isn't asking for anything, he just wants to give you his ideas."

"I don't want his ideas."

"He wants to loan you money for your personal living expenses so that you can devote all your time to this case. And he wants to arrange for the costs."

"When am I to enjoy the pleasure of meeting this fine man?"

Two nights later, in the Hollywood Hills, Marvin drove us in his Rolls to Herman Falitz's house for dinner. As we turned up a steep curve I noticed a little creature—was it a man or woman?—standing at the curb in bare feet, wearing a calf-length white canvas gown. As we drove closer, I could see that it was either a man or a frowning monkey. "Marvin, surely that can't be—"

"That's him."

Herman Falitz was about five feet four and fifty, with dark kinky hair—he was bald across the top—worn in two pigtails tied at the back, yet protruding over his ears, giving him the appearance of a sphinx. He seemed pleased to usher us into his home. Outside, it was a small Hollywood modern guarded by two gray-painted plaster gargoyles; inside, it looked as though Herman had purchased all the merchandise of a bankrupt souvenir store in Tijuana. Herman asked me, "Are you into pre-Columbian art?"

I wasn't.

In the corner of the crowded living room was a large, brightly painted mummy case, which Herman assured me wasn't occupied. Next to the coffin were two large ornate coffee tables lined with ugly little stone statues with little potbellies, knock-knees, and big, ugly faces like frowning monkeys. On the floor behind the couch and lined up on each side were about two hundred of those works of art. Herman said that his collection was worth over $500,000 and pointed out the electronic devices of his intricate burglary-prevention system. He showed me piece after piece of his treasures for over an hour, and only then did I notice that all those little statues looked like Herman.

Mrs. Falitz, a lovely Peruvian lady, sat with us for dinner but dutifully refrained from speaking at the master's table in the presence of the master, and so I had to listen through dinner to Herman's stories about his brilliance in law school, the multimillion-dollar corporations he had managed, his Louisiana oil wells, his daily million-dollar stock transactions, the hippy ranch he had established in Arizona, and his first-name familiarity with most of Europe's royalty.

After dinner we returned to the museum for some brandy and, I hoped, to get down to amounts. "Harold, first, we've got to discuss settlement. I have some ideas about when I can settle this case."

Marvin walked behind Herman and motioned to me to calm down. I tried. "Herman, a settlement is impossible."

"It is not impossible! This case can be settled and I'm going to do it!" His voice was reaching that shrill pitch that had once made me hang up on him.

"Herman, the help I need is financial. Marvin said that you may be willing to consider a loan. I'll give you a promissory note secured by a deed of trust on my house and—"

"I'll handle the financial part of our case, just leave it to me. Don't worry about it, all right? And when I feel I'm ready, I'll negotiate a settlement."

"No, Herman, you will not."

Marvin said, "Maybe we could talk about settlement at another time. Herman, could you be a little more precise about the financial aspects?"

"What do you mean by precise?"

I explained it to him. "How much, and when, and under what terms will you help me? What I need is a trust account for costs, for travel and depositions, and fees for experts. And I need living expenses for myself and my family."

"I'll loan you enough each month for your personal needs at ten percent with promissory notes payable in one year. As for a trust account for traveling and depositions, I'll get to work on that as soon as I finish my inspection of a new well I'm bringing in in Louisiana. Have you ever seen them bring in a well?"

"No. Herman, what do you expect to get in return in addition to interest on your money?"

"You're rather blunt, Harold."

"That's one of my biggest faults. Now, here's the deal that Stanley Fairfield and Marvin have, and everybody else working with me will have. If it's a forgery everybody loses. If it's real and we get it admitted to probate, everybody gets only the opportunity to do a job in some capacity, and to share in what ought to be attorneys' fees of over a hundred million dollars. But no free ride. No matter what anybody does before the will is admitted to probate, if he goofs off after we win, he's out. And all fees'll be subject to court approval."

"I want to run the company."

"What company?"

"Summa. I want to be chairman of the board, and I want the power to run the company."

"No deal!" I got up.

"I don't expect a firm promise! I just want to be considered. Now sit down, for chrissakes! We'll talk about it more after it's admitted to probate. Which will be after I settle our case."

An hour later, when Marvin and I left, I felt like a whore.

5. THE TEXANS

I had no choice. I had to petition for the probate of the Mormon will in Houston, Texas. A few days after Hughes' death, a probate had been opened in Houston, as well as in Las Vegas and Los Angeles, by Summa's lawyers, representing Hughes' elderly aunt, alleging that no will had been found. If the Mormon will were not submitted to the Houston court, the estate could be depleted under the Texas laws of intestate succession before the validity of the will could be determined in Nevada. I phoned a friendly lady reporter on the *Houston Post* and asked her to recommend a competent Houston attorney, willing without any guarantee of a fee to be our local counsel in Houston. I told her that all I needed was someone who knew what the local rules were and where the courthouse was. She recommended Wilbur Dobbs. Wilbur Dobbs phoned and said that he knew what the local rules were and where the courthouse was, and that he would do anything for the opportunity to work in this case without any guarantee of a fee and at his own expense, and thanked me several times for allowing him to prepare the petition.

The evening of June 13, 1976, Stanley Fairfield and I walked out of the airport building and into the hot, wet oven that was Houston, and before we reached Wilbur Dobbs' Volkswagen, I was soaked. Despite the heat, Wilbur Dobbs wore a tie and a wool two-sizes-too-tight vested suit to meet us at the airport. He insisted on carrying my small suitcase and couldn't seem to stop grinning at his good fortune at having been selected to be unpaid local counsel in the Howard Hughes will case. In his mid-thirties, around six feet with dark eyes and Latin features, he would have been handsome if it had not been for what once was his hairline. Thick black hair bulged at the sides and back of his head and covered his ears, but only a few thin strands lay across the top, ready to leave him any morning. Wilbur drawled in a voice tied tight to the back of his throat as though it were a precious bird, which, if loosened, might fly away and be lost forever. He proudly told us about his plaintiffs' personal injury practice and his trial experience specializing in whip-lash rear-end collision cases settled without trial. By the time we arrived at our hotel, it was obvious that Wilbur Dobbs did not know what the local rules were, and that if he could find the courthouse it had to be because somebody was pointing at it.

Stanley and I dined at the Whitehall with Wilbur and his delicate, gray-haired wife. Before dinner, Wilbur chain-smoked through a double Chivas on the rocks, then two more, and during dinner just one more. After dinner, Wilbur chain-smoked through his second brandy and said, "Mr. Rhoden, Ah've been thankin' 'bout a plan since we talked. If y'all thank it's all right, Ah'd like to meet Melvin Dummar in Tonopah an' drive with him an' have him show me where he met Hughes, an' reenact everythin' he did."

"Great idea, Wilbur, but I don't have any expense money for you."

"That's no problem! No problem at all! Ah'll call Dummar's lawyers tomorrow. An' thank y'all for your confidence in me." Wilbur winked at his wife and celebrated his good fortune by ordering a third brandy.

That night in the bar, after Wilbur and his wife left, Stanley said, "I've been thinking a lot about Dietrich's age. He's got to substitute someone to be the executor in his place. And it's got to be someone you can trust not to change attorneys after the will is admitted to probate. Do you have anybody in mind?"

"Nobody. I know Dietrich, and it's got to be somebody he knows. The question is, whom does he know, whom he would appoint, whom we could trust to keep us in after we win?"

"Me."

I told him I would think about it. And I thought about it that night and while shaving the next morning. It boiled down to this: there was no one else. I didn't want to be the executor, I wanted to be the attorney for the executor. And I could trust Stanley not to bounce me. If not Stanley Fairfield, who?

At breakfast when I told Stanley I would recommend to Noah Dietrich that he substitute Stanley as the named executor, he beamed and shook my hand, and as he assured me for the third time that I could count on him to keep our legal team intact and that he would always listen to my advice, I felt a surge of confidence in this case that I had just made my first big mistake.

The next morning on the fifth floor of the Harris County Courthouse we were greeted by the cameras and microphones. "Mr. Rhoden, y'all really believe that Melvin Dummar picked up Howard Hughes in the desert?"

After the interviews, Wilbur pointed to a group of men walking from the elevator, led by a six-foot-three-inch, three-hundred pound gum-chewing mountain who Wilbur said was mighty Earl Yoakum, fat pillar of power of the Houston bar, the chief attorney representing Hughes' eighty-six-year-old aunt, Annette Gano Lummis. Wilbur said that Earl Yoakum was one of the senior partners of Yanks, Hamilton & Boswell, one of the two most prestigious law firms in Houston, a 112-man colossus that hired only Law Review graduates of Harvard-type schools. What was left of Earl Yoakum's red hair had grayed into pink and straggled over his ears and over his collar. He had a long pink mustache and a narrow pink goatee that would have made him look like Colonel Sanders if it had been white. To see Earl Yoakum once was to be impressed with his image forever.

Earl Yoakum pompously pushed his big belly down the hall, followed by a plump, well-scrubbed young man who looked as though his mother still tucked him in. This was Rex Clairbourne, Wilbur said, Yoakum's legal researcher, fact-digger, and briefcase carrier. Yoakum and Clairbourne were followed by four other assistants, and when the group approached us, Clairbourne mumbled something to Yoakum, and as Yoakum waddled by, he glared at me under his bushy pink eyebrows, and sneered as though I used perfume.

That evening, Stanley and I were the dinner guests of Ed Boyington at one of those elegant oak paneled clubs where all the waiters were black and none of the members were. Ed Boyington, a gracious Southern gentleman, was one of nineteen senior partners of the other of the two most prestigious law firms in Houston, representing Rice University, named in the Mormon will as a potential recipient of an estimated $100 million to $500 million. As soon as drinks were ordered, our host came to the point. "What do y'all think your chances are?"

"Good," I said. "Several of the world's top handwriting experts say that Hughes wrote it."

"What about this fella Dummar? Isn't there some question about his credibility?"

"I don't think there's any question about his credibility. He doesn't have any. But the important question is, whose handwriting is on that will? All the evidence points to Howard Hughes. Are you and the other beneficiaries coming in?"

"To be frank with you—an' Ah know you want me to be frank with you—counsel for the other universities an' for the Boy Scouts have been in contact with each other. An' our present policy is to sit back an' let you go ahead an' plow the field. We've been watchin' you on television an' in the press an' you seem to know where an' how to do the plowin'. If you dig up a good crop, then we'll sure be over to join y'all for dinner."

"Well, I've got a little problem. I don't mind doing the plowing, but I need more plows and I can't afford them."

"Ah understan' that. We all do. An' maybe after your case is more fully prepared an' it looks like a winner, we'll all give some thought to helpin' out in some way."

The morning after Stanley and I returned to Los Angeles, he burst into my office and asked me to walk with him down the hall, and as we did, he whispered that because of what he had just heard from Las Vegas, he believed that my office and his were bugged. "I've been contacted by some big people in Las Vegas. They flew in to have dinner with me last night at the Bistro. You know who I mean by big people?"

"Since you don't mean tall or fat, I suppose you mean rich."

"Mafia. This is what they told me to tell you. The Mormon will is going to be admitted to probate. You hear me? It doesn't make any difference who wrote it. It doesn't make any difference what jury we have. The verdict will be that it's genuine. It's a foregone conclusion, if you follow me."

"I follow you."

"All they want is control of the casinos for one year. Just one year. Right now, up front, they'll give us all the money we need for court costs and fees."

"Did you say fees?"

"I said fees! All we need! You hear me? All we need! As to the jury verdict, it's absolutely guaranteed."

The response I gave Stanley to relay to those big people was obscene, but as we walked back to my office I reconsidered my response. "Mafia? Forget what I said. Instead, tell those gallant gentlemen that it is with deep appreciation for their thoughtfulness that I must decline their generous offer of jury tampering."

6. A HIGH STAKES SEARCH FOR THE TRUTH

That sweltering summer morning in 1976, Judge Keith C. Hayes of the Nevada District Court, presiding in Department 9 on the second floor, moved to the larger courtroom of Department 2 on the main floor to accommodate the expected crowd of newspeople and attorneys for the first hearing of the petition for probate of the Mormon will.

I brought my wife Sheila on this trip because she thought it would be fun to watch the court proceedings, because she deserved a holiday, and because I didn't like sleeping in hotel rooms without her. Stanley Fairfield brought Doreen, whom he always introduced as his fiancée, and with whom he had been residing for several years. Doreen was a tall, regal lady in the dark half of her thirties who wore her shoe-polish-black hair hanging straight down her back six inches below her waist, trimmed to a sharp point in the center like an arrowhead. Doreen's stiff stance and studied movements, her eerie whisper, her pasty pale pancake-masked face and greasy red lips, always—when I was in her presence after the sun went down—put me on guard to protect my neck.

Inside the Courthouse, a crowd waited for us in a semicircle of bright lights; cameramen held minicams on their shoulders, and sound technicians stretched out those poles with black cylinders at the ends that looked like World War II German hand grenades, all eager to be the first to capture the sight and sound of what we were doing. We were doing nothing. The reporters wanted to know if Mr. Dietrich had a suspect for the forgery of the Mormon will; if there would be a trial by jury, and why by jury; and if I knew who killed Howard Hughes in Acapulco.

At the counsel table, flanked by Stanley and Alex, I sat as still as I could, pretending to be unaware of the artist in the jury box who kept looking at me and his tablet. I sat with my head turned and my chin jutting out, but after a few minutes that became uncomfortable, so to hell with it. When the bailiff said, "Everybody rise!" we all did, and after Judge Hayes took the bench, and the bailiff ordered us to sit down, we all did, and Stanley turned back, spotted Doreen, and responded to the smart smacking of her fingertips against her lips by blowing a kiss back at her.

Judge Hayes asked that each lawyer state his name and whom he represented. After Judge Hayes nodded at me, I stood up and introduced myself, Fairfield, and Morenus as attorneys for Noah Dietrich, proponent of the offered will. At the other table, big Earl Yoakum slowly strained to his feet. "Your Honor, mah name is Earl Yoakum of Yanks, Hamilton an' Boswell of Houston, Texas. Ah represent Mrs. Annette Gano Lummis, the rightful heir, as the sole survivin' aunt on the maternal side of the late Mr. Howard Hughes." A mellow, melodic quality in his bass drawl suggested that at one time Earl Yoakum must have had operatic aspirations. "It's our contention, Your Honor, that the three pages of this so-called . . ." He strained to bring himself to speak the word "will," and when he sputtered it, he winced as at a foul smell, and reached his empty hands out in front of his bulk, as though holding the corners of those invisible pages so as to get on his fingers as little as possible of what had been used in place of ink. "Ah say, these pages contain the filthiest forgery ever submitted to a court of the United States of America. The petition to have this garbage probated is an insult to the dignity of this most honorable Court. It's a perpetration of a fraud, an' as lead counsel for mah client, Ah intend to do everythin' in mah power to bring the forger to justice. Your Honor, never in mah twenty-five years as a trial lawyer in the great an' sovereign state of Texas have Ah seen anythin' so rotten as—"

"Thank you, Mr. Yoakum," Judge Hayes said, "but, right now, I'd like the record to reflect the appearances of counsel. Next?"

Next was Phillip Bittle of the New York firm of Littlejohn, O'Malley, Javitz & Littlejohn. Phillip Bittle, in his late forties, walked and sat with a stiff back; his healthy head of hair, clipped close in a military crewcut, was salt and pepper, mostly salt, and his salt-and-pepper mustache was clipped close under his small, ball-like nose. He wore honest horn-rimmed reading glasses, and when he wasn't reading, he would snap them off as though in obedience to an order. I recognized Phillip Bittle as the lawyer on television who had victoriously announced that Spencer Otis had found the will to be a rank forgery. The pinched expression on Bittle's face and the strain in his voice always gave the impression that he was wearing something too tight. By stammering his words in short bursts, he cut out of hearing about half of what he said, but I gathered that he represented three second cousins on Hughes' paternal side, potential heirs under Texas law if Hughes died without a will.

"Your Honor, my name is Thomas Post of Martin & Post, representing Miss Terry Moore, Howard Hughes' widow. My client married Mr. Hughes aboard his yacht in 1949. And, absent a divorce, she remained married to him at the time of his death."

Terry's lawyer didn't add that years after Terry had spent that night on the yacht with Mr. Hughes, absent any divorce from him, she married a football player. Then after she divorced the football player, while still a bosom friend of Mr. Hughes and still absent a divorce from him, she married Stuart Kramer, whose wife, movie actress Jean Peters, in a fair exchange, married Mr. Hughes. After several years of marriage and two children, Terry divorced Kramer and won substantial alimony and other wifely benefits on her contention that she had been legally married to Kramer those years.

"Your Honor, my name is Rulon Earl of the firm of Earl & Earl, representing the Church of Jesus Christ of Latter-day Saints. I am here to make clear to this Court my client's position on the offered will. The Church of Jesus Christ of Latter-day Saints does not take the position that the offered will is genuine. Nor does it take the position that the offered will is a forgery. Thank you." He sat down.

Judge Hayes leaned forward. "Then, counsel, what position is it that you wish to make clear?"

Mr. Earl rose again. "The Church of Jesus Christ of Latter-day Saints wishes to make clear its position that it takes no position."

After hearing from the Attorney General of Texas and several attorneys representing hopeful grandchildren of distant and deceased second cousins, Judge Hayes asked if there were any motions. I rose. "May it please the Court. I move that Your Honor request the Attorney General of Nevada to have the offered will examined in a law enforcement laboratory for fingerprints." I had in mind particularly the fingerprints of Howard Hughes.

"Your Honor, Ah object!" Earl Yoakum strained to his feet. "We don't want that so-called will examined by any so-called fingerprint experts unless we have our own fingerprint expert lookin' over his shoulder, an' we're not ready for that yet. Furthermore, a fingerprint examination might mean the use of chemicals which could affect the ink an' make it more difficult for us to prove it's a forgery."

Judge Hayes ruled, "Motion denied! But without prejudice, Mr. Rhoden, to your right to renew it at a later date. Anything further?"

Although I knew that my next motion would be denied at this early stage, I believed that the facts would excite the news media, and that this might stimulate the institutional beneficiaries named in the will to pay some of the costs of this case. "Your Honor, I move that the Court request the Attorney General of Nevada to have an examination made of the Pitney Bowes imprint on the back of the will envelope to ascertain the number of the machine that made the imprint. Since the envelope was not addressed for mailing, putting it through a Pitney Bowes stamp machine could have been only to have the imprint serve as a seal—since it overlaps both the closed lid of the envelope and the back of it—or to affix a date. Or both. Now, was the offered will written in Las Vegas, Nevada, in March 1968? The writing on it states that it was, and the Pitney Bowes imprint on the back of the envelope shows that the die of the machine had printed on it LAS VEGAS and then NEV. The date is clearly MAR for March. The day of the month and the year are obliterated. The imprint of the stamp charge is six cents. Our investigation disclosed that from January 7th, 1968, to May 16th, 1971, a first-class-mail stamp cost six cents." That investigation consisted of a phone call to the nearest post office. "Each Pitney Bowes machine has a different number. The number imprinted on the back of the will envelope cannot be read by the naked eye. But a technician in a police lab, such as the FBI's, might be able to read that number. Once we know the number on the imprint, it will be easy to find out from Pitney Bowes the location of the machine that made that imprint in March 1968. If the Pitney Bowes machine that made the imprint on the will envelope had been delivered to Howard Hughes, and on March 19th, 1968, was on the ninth floor of the Desert Inn, that might be of some interest. Even to Mr. Earl Yoakum, lead counsel from the great and sovereign state of Texas."

Yoakum and Bittle and six other attorneys sprang to object, but Judge Hayes gestured them to sit down, and turned to me. "Your motion is denied. Again, without prejudice."

Judge Keith Hayes, in his forties, a slight, pale man with a high forehead and a thin layer of ash-brown hair combed flat to the side, looked like an unhappy Bob Newhart. Alex Morenus had said that the judge had cancer, and he looked it, but his sharp voice and judicial demeanor gave him full command of his courtroom. "Gentlemen, the right of every interested party to a full examination of the offered will will be respected by this Court. At the same time, it is the duty of this Court to preserve the offered will in its present condition. If any interested party wishes any scientific examination of this document, he will present to this Court a qualified expert competent to represent that the examination will in no way change the condition of the document. This is a high stakes search for the truth. We are going to find it. And we are going to find it expeditiously. But at the same time, cautiously. We'll resume this hearing on August 27th, 1977, at nine-thirty A.M., at which time I want reports from counsel on your progress in discovery proceedings. Court is adjourned."

As soon as Judge Hayes left the bench, the press people rushed to my chair. My motion about the Pitney Bowes imprint, which I had expected to titillate them, titillated them. The first question was, "Does this Pitney Bowes imprint rule out a forgery?"

"No, but it does indicate that the writer of the will was in Las Vegas in the month of March in 1968 or in March of the next three years. And Howard Hughes was in Las Vegas in March 1968, 1969, and 1970."

After the last question, I joined Sheila at the back of the courtroom as gargantuan Earl Yoakum lumbered toward us. Unlike Phillip Bittle, whose only expression was discomfort, Earl Yoakum had two expressions: a Santa Claus grin or a contemptuous sneer. He was wearing the grin, and extended his hand, and when I introduced him to Sheila, he smiled at her the smile of a true Texas gentleman. "Real pleased to meet you, Ma'am." Then Earl Yoakum looked down at me. "Looks like you an' Ah are gonna be opponents."

I looked up at him. "You give up?"

That evening, despite Sheila's, "Oh, no, do we have to?" she and I went to dinner with Stanley and Doreen. In a curved booth in the Barrymore Room of the MGM, Stanley and Doreen sat hip to hip; their adoration for each other was demonstrated in their hand-holding when they walked and in their thigh-holding when they sat, and no matter who was at the table with them, when they felt the God-given impulse to kiss, they kissed. Stanley and Doreen frequently dined alone.

Sheila said, "Hal, if the will were a forgery, what would that Pitney Bowes imprint be doing on the envelope?"

"The will is dated March 1968 and a forger would want something to con people into believing that that was when it was written."

"Then a forger would want the Pitney Bowes imprint to show the year 1968, wouldn't he?"

"Of course."

"Since a forger would want it to show the year, doesn't the absence of the year indicate the absence of a forger?"

I turned to Stanley. "How come neither you nor I thought of that argument?"

Doreen said, "Hal, you really believe that Hughes wrote it, don't you?" Doreen's soft voice never varied from its softness, and her words, always spoken in a monotone, instilled the suspicion that she had been redone by some electric shock treatments.

"There are good reasons to believe it, and I believe it."

"Hal, if you and Stan are convinced, the two of you can convince a jury. And after you and Stan win, no matter what happens, you'll have a job for life." Doreen's head swung around toward Stanley as though something from his side had contacted her under the table. Doreen looked back at me. "What I meant was that you can count on Stanley's loyalty. After he's the executor, he won't forget you. And even when you decide to retire, he'll still see to it that you're taken care of."

7. YOU OR NO ONE!

After five phone calls to Pitney Bowes in three cities I learned that none of their machines had ever been installed in the name of Howard Hughes personally anywhere. Nor had any machine been installed in anyone's name on the ninth floor of the Desert Inn in Las Vegas, Nevada. But a Pitney Bowes machine had been installed in the Desert Inn in its name, and the Desert Inn still used it. It was installed June 1, 1967. The number of the machine was 841 862.

Since Vladimir Wazencko was a forensic expert familiar with the devices used in police labs, and had taken photographs of the front and back of the will envelope, I phoned and asked him if, by magnification or some special lights, he could read the number of the Pitney Bowes machine imprinted on the envelope. I told him what I had learned about the Desert Inn machine and explained that if 841 862 were the number on the will envelope, we would have powerful circumstantial evidence connecting Hughes with our will.

Two hours later, Wazencko phoned back and told me that he was able to read three of the six digits of the Pitney Bowes number imprinted on the back of the envelope. "The first digit is an *eight*. The fourth digit, an *eight*. And the fifth digit, a *six*. Your case is wrapped up!"

I compared the two sets of numbers:

Machine at Desert Inn:	8 4 1 8 6 2
Machine stamp on envelope:	8 ? ? 8 6 ?

With any two six-digit numbers, the odds against three pairs of digits in the same position, such as the first, fourth, and fifth in the two numbers, matching by pure chance were in the thousands. The matching of three digits in the two numbers meant that our will had been through the Pitney Bowes machine in the Desert Inn.

Noah and Mary Dietrich had moved in June 1976 from the decrepit castle off Sunset to a small house in Palm Springs, California, a short block from the Sunrise Hospital. Whenever I flew my 310 to Palm Springs, a thirty minute flight away, to confer with Noah, Mary would drive him to meet me in the coffee shop of the Palm Springs airport. I phoned Noah for a meeting in the coffee shop on August 7, 1976.

At the door, on time as always, Noah smiled and waved the hand that wasn't leaning on his cane and rasped, "Hi, Hal!" Other than his bright-red shirt, everything about Noah Dietrich was white: white pants, white shoes, white hair, and that almost-white face. This man, who one night twenty years before, in his late sixties, had helped me push my old Cadillac a half block to a gas station, now sluffed slowly, stooped, resting heavily on his cane, barely able to lift his feet for each step. "Are we winning again?"

I told him that we were winning again, and asked Mary to please leave us alone for a half hour, and she did.

"Noah, every lawyer with me on the case is working without a fee and paying his own expenses. They're all concerned because they have no guarantee of a job as attorneys for the executor."

"Tell them that you have my word that anybody you want on the legal staff stays on as long as you want him on. Now, what looks good to you for lunch?" He opened the menu.

"Noah, the lawyers are worried about your age."

"I am going to live to be at least a hundred."

"I know that, but the other lawyers in this case don't."

"Who's the youngest lawyer on your team?"

"Wilbur Dobbs. He's in his thirties."

"Tell him I'll guarantee in writing I'll outlive him."

"I did and he threw an actuarial table at me. Noah, I'd like you to please consider appointing someone in your place as the executor."

Noah put down the menu and stared at me.

"Please put yourself in the shoes of those lawyers. Noah, their futures hinge on your health."

"Bring your lawyers to see me. I'll sit down with each one at a table. And we'll arm-wrestle."

"Noah, you can't arm-wrestle the calendar."

"You think I'm too old to be the executor?"

"No, of course not!"

"I know that company and I can run it. You and I can run it together."

"Noah, we can still run it together. If you'll appoint someone to be the executor in your place, you can enter into a consultation contract with him and you'll have an income for life. And you'll be consulted on every major decision. You and I can still do it. I'll be the attorney for the estate and you'll be the executor's consultant. Noah, I need lawyers to be places where I can't be, and I need money for the cost of this litigation, and I can't get what I need unless you appoint someone who everyone can be sure won't change the legal team."

"Howard wanted me to do it. And I'm the only one who can do it. I know what's in the closet because I'm the one who put it there. But my own lawyer tells me I've got to appoint someone else. All right. If you say I have to step down, Hal, I will. I'll appoint someone else. Whom do you have in mind?"

"Noah, the man I'm going to suggest might not be perfect. The only perfect man for the job is Noah Dietrich. But other than you, anyone'll do who'll listen to you on matters of policy—"

"Who?"

"He did some work for you a few years ago on a real estate matter. You told me you found him to be competent."

"Who?"

"Stanley Fairfield."

Noah pointed his finger at me and snapped, "You or no one!"

"Noah, I could function better as a lawyer than an executor and I don't—"

"You or no one!"

"Noah, it would be bad for the case for me to be substituted in your place. Stanley'll listen to you and to me and—"

"You or no one!"

An hour later, flying back VFR to Los Angeles in my 310, as soon as I climbed out of the Palm Springs traffic pattern, I slid in an eight-track cartridge of Wagner's Greatest Hits and listened to the *Liebestod,* and climbing out of 7,200 feet for 7,500, flying up past cottony white clouds, I vowed to whatever God was listening in that I would be the best damned executor on earth.

I phoned Vladimir Wazencko in Philadelphia to find out why I had not received his promised written report, and while on the phone with him, I gave in to a suspicion that gnawed at me. I lied and said that I had made a mistake, that the number on the Pitney Bowes machine in the Desert Inn in 1968 was, instead of 841 862, really 841 222.

The next day, Vladimir Wazencko phoned from Philadelphia. "I took another look at my photograph of the Pitney Bowes imprint on the back of the envelope, and I'd like to revise the digits I gave you. I was mistaken in two of them. I told you that the last three digits were an *eight* and a *six* and one I couldn't make out. I was wrong. The fourth is a *two* and the fifth is a *two*. I still can't make out the last one."

"Mr. Wazencko, how positive are you that Howard Hughes wrote the will?"

"I'll testify to it. Is that positive enough for you?"

After I hung up I wondered what Wazencko would have found if I had told him the fourth and fifth digits on the Desert Inn machine were an omega and an omega.

On August 15, 1976, Vladimir Wazencko wrote that he would not send me his written report until I retained him with a check for $25,000. Adieu, Vladimir!

8. READY FOR TRIAL!

By midsummer I knew that I had to ramrod the case into an early trial. But to announce, "Ready for trial," I had to have at least one competent handwriting expert to support the will. I urged Marvin Mitchelson to arrange for Jeffrey Carroll to fly to Las Vegas to examine the will two days before our next court hearing.

The morning of August 25, 1976, in Las Vegas, Marvin and I drove thirty-five-year-old Jeffrey Carroll to the Courthouse. After examining and photographing the will in the jury room for four hours, Carroll told us that he wanted to go back to his room in the Hilton to develop his negatives in the bathroom and study his pictures before giving us his opinion. At 5:30 in one of the bars at the Hilton, Marvin said, "Why can't he make up his bloody mind?"

"Maybe he did make up his bloody mind in London and lied to you to get the five grand and the free trip to Vegas. Whatever his opinion is, I've got to know it before nine-thirty tomorrow morning."

"I'll have an answer for you by ten tonight. He's been up in that hotel room all day and I've had all I'm going to take from that limey shmuck!"

"Marvin, it isn't going to do any good to push him. If he thinks it's genuine, I don't want him antagonized, and if he doesn't, losing your temper isn't going to change his mind. Why don't you invite the jolly good chap to dinner?"

As Sheila and I walked across the lobby of the Hilton, toward the Bavarian Inn, there at the registration desk, facing us with outstretched arms, stood a little smiling monkey wearing a gray striped suit, shirt and tie, black shoes, and no socks. Since Herman Falitz had loaned me $25,000 I had to introduce him to Sheila. Herman had had a haircut; the braids in the back and the sphinx look were gone, and in their place, from an almost completely bald top, strands of black curls hung like loose wires down the sides of his face and over his ears. Having heard from Marvin that the court session the following morning could be important, Herman had flown in for moral support. He graciously invited us to be his guests for dinner, and since I couldn't think up an excuse fast enough, I accepted.

Before we ordered, Herman said that he wanted to contribute a tactical plan for our case, and after my assurance that it would be safe to talk in front of Sheila, he lowered his voice, which was itself a contribution. "Melvin Dummar is a danger area in our case. Right? Right! They're going to argue that his story about having picked up Howard Hughes in the desert is bullshit, that Hughes didn't know Dummar, and that therefore, the will naming Dummar must be a fake. Right? Right! Now, can they force Melvin Dummar to testify in our case in Nevada?"

"No."

"Right! Melvin lives in Utah! So what'll they do? Take his deposition in Utah. Since Melvin's story stinks, we don't want his deposition taken. Right?"

"Wrong! They have a legal right to take his deposition."

"Look, I've sunk a lot of money into this case! That trip to Europe, the loan to you—"

"We want all the facts out in the open. Right? Right!"

"Of course we do, but we also want to use our heads! If they don't get Melvin Dummar's deposition, what's their case?"

"Handwriting experts to call it a forgery. Maybe some of Hughes' aides to testify that he never wrote a will."

"Without the testimony of Dummar, their case is shit! They can't get into evidence what Dummar said about picking up Hughes if Dummar doesn't give a deposition. It would be hearsay, right?"

"Jesus Christ, right! So what?"

"So, Dummar's deposition must not be taken. Right?"

"Wrong! Herman, what the hell've you got in mind?"

"I have a contact I can trust. He runs a lamasery in Tibet. I help support it. We can ship Melvin there and stash him away until the case is over. Well? Why are you staring at me? Say something!"

"Herman, you have a unique sense of humor."

"I mean it!"

"No, you don't, Herman, no you don't. Tell me you don't."

"I do! Melvin Dummar is a danger area."

"I don't care if he's a doomsday bomb, we're not going to hide him!"

"Why not?"

"Why not!"

"What troubles you? Tibet? All right, I have an alternate suggestion."

"We have Dummar shot and bury him in the desert."

"No, I have this ranch in Arizona outside of Phoenix. Timothy Leary used to be my guest there in the sixties. It's still occupied by young people who have problems with drugs and our Fascist police force. We could keep Melvin at the ranch. It wouldn't be as good as the lamasery, but I think it'd be safe. What about it? Well? What do you say?"

Not only did Herman Falitz hold my promissory notes, which he could call in at any time, but I counted on him for future financial help, and so I strained to hold back the words that fought to burst out of my vile mouth. "Herman, my answer is no! Not in the lamasery in Tibet! Not at your hippy ranch in Arizona! Not in your Egyptian mummy case! Not anywhere!"

"Harold, you seem rather short-tempered. I realize that you're under a strain."

"A terrible strain, Herman, just terrible, you have no idea!"

"What if we ship him to a place outside of Helsinki near—"

"No!"

"You're stubborn!"

"That's another one of my faults."

That night at 10:30, Marvin sounded exhausted on the telephone. "Carroll has a problem! He found a lack of motor control in the will that indicates some kind of illness and he didn't find the same thing in the exemplars. He's no longer convinced that Hughes wrote it. But he's not convinced that Hughes didn't. He's still working on it."

At 12:20 A.M. that night, Marvin phoned again. "Carroll's with us! He's one inch away from a statement to the press tomorrow morning."

"What did you do, offer him a bonus?"

"No, I found a doctor. He's in the room with Carroll now. He's going to take care of Carroll's problem."

"What doctor? What problem?"

"Hughes died of kidney disease. So I got a doctor who explained that the disease affects motor control in handwriting, but it has this effect only at times. That explains the bad motor control in the will. Carroll said his problem is no longer a problem. We'll meet you for breakfast at eight o'clock in the coffee shop. Carroll'll be with us by then."

The next morning after breakfast at 8:30 in the coffee shop, when Eli Blumenfeld, Stanley Fairfield, and I were ready to leave for court, Marvin walked fast to our table. "Carroll's still working on it! He says he needs about an hour more. You guys go on to court and as soon as he's ready I'll bring him there."

"Marvin, I've got to know by nine-thirty whether we have a handwriting expert or we don't."

"I explained that to the son of a bitch, but he's still studying those fucking photographs!"

In Judge Hayes' Department 9, the courtroom was again packed with lawyers and the press. At 9:30, waiting for Judge Hayes to take the bench, Alex Morenus didn't try to hide his irritation as he shook his head at me. "I told you before, there's no way you can get a trial date today! A trial can't possibly be set within two years. Why don't you listen to me?"

Stanley said, "A trial date today'd be great, but we still don't even have one expert! How can you say ready for trial?"

"I can say ready for trial, because we have Verhaeren in Holland, the two Frenchmen, and the German from Mannheim—that's four in Europe who'll testify that Hughes wrote it. That's our whole case, along with anything I get from Hughes' aides and his doctors, and I can take all those depositions in two months."

Bulky, broad-faced Eli Blumenfeld was soft-spoken and usually a patient man, but he wasn't patient this morning. "What about the Englishman in the hotel room? In England he was sure that Hughes wrote it. Here in Vegas, he isn't so sure. What if every one of those European experts gets the free trip here and the fee for looking at the original, and then decides he isn't so sure?"

"Gentlemen, we need money to take the depositions of Hughes' aides and his doctors. We need money for experts. This money can come from the universities named in the will, but until we get a trial date, nobody is going to write any checks."

Eli said, "But we're not ready! It may be two years before we get all the facts."

"That could happen, if we let it. But we won't let it. I can't afford to spend two years preparing this case. I need pressure for fast discovery proceedings and that pressure is a trial date."

Eli said, "What are you going to ask for?"

"Sixty days."

Eli said, "That's ridiculous!"

"What?" Alex shouted. "A trial date at the end of this year? This year? Don't you ever listen to me?"

I walked to the contestants' table. "What do you fellows think about a trial date?"

Earl Yoakum's chuckle bounced his big belly. "Y'all gotta be kiddin'! Ask me in a year or two, an' Ah'll talk to you. Maybe."

Phillip Bittle said, "The setting of a trial date now is out of the question. I won't even consider it."

Judge Hayes took the bench. "Gentlemen, first I want a progress report on discovery proceedings."

Earl Yoakum grunted and rose. "Discovery is comin' along with dispatch, Your Honor."

Bittle stood at attention and said, "I concur, Your Honor."

I rose and said, "I don't, Your Honor. The one thing that discovery is not coming along with is dispatch."

"What's the problem, Counsel?" Judge Hayes asked.

"To take the depositions of Mr. Hughes' aides I must serve them with subpoenas. To serve them, I must learn where they're hiding. To learn this, I must obtain answers to interrogatories from the contestants who have access to this information from the aides' employer, Summa Corporation. Even though Mr. Hughes has been dead for several months, his body servants are still on his company's payroll."

Yoakum shouted, "Ah take offense at the callin' of Mr. Hughes' executive staff assistants 'body servants!' That's an insult to a fine group of loyal an' dedicated executives!"

"Whatever we call those middle-aged messengers, those mindless members of Howard Hughes' toilet-paper platoon, Summa personnel know where they're hiding. And in trying to pry this information out of Summa, I've been paralyzed by their rigid policy of procrastination."

Judge Hayes asked, "What can I do about it?"

"This, Your Honor. These potential witnesses, on Summa's payroll, are controlled by Summa. Special Administrator William Lummis, as trustee of all the shares of Summa, recently voted himself in as chairman of the board of Summa. And Mr. Lummis, a member of Mr. Yoakum's Houston law firm, is represented by Mr. Yoakum who also represents Mr. Lummis' mother as a contestant. Your Honor can order Mr. Yoakum to require Mr. Lummis to give me the names and addresses of those witnesses and to instruct each one to stop dodging long enough for my exhausted process server to catch him and hand him a subpoena."

"Ah object!" Yoakum was on his feet again, and this was not easy. "Ah resent the insinuation that these executive staff assistants are hidin' out! Ah'm informed that they're all on extended vacations."

Judge Hayes said, "Gentlemen, I want discovery expedited, and I expect counsel to cooperate fully in making all potential witnesses under their control available for depositions. Next?"

I again moved the Court for an order that the will be examined for fingerprints, counsel for the contestants again objected, and the Court again denied my motion without prejudice to my renewing it at a later time. "Anything more, Mr. Rhoden?"

"The proponent can be ready for trial sixty days from now, around November 1st." I sat down.

Yoakum chuckled. "Your Honor, a trial date within a year an' a half would be impossible! Nobody could be ready!"

Back on my feet, I said, "On November 1st, proponent will be ready."

Phillip Bittle stood at his table like a stiff stick of dynamite about to explode and stammered, "Your Honor, Mr. Rhoden can't be ready—he can't look at this Court and say it."

I rose again and looked at Judge Hayes and said, "Your Honor, ready for trial!"

The clamor at contestants' table as they consulted with each other and with the row of assistants behind them suddenly stopped as Judge Hayes banged his gavel for order.

Yoakum said, "Surely, Your Honor can't seriously consider Mr. Rhoden's absurd position that he's gonna be ready for trial in a couple of months." Earl Yoakum smiled a broad, confident smile exuding an expectation that no one could be cruel enough to disappoint.

Judge Hayes ruled, "The will contest is set for trial to commence before a jury at ten A.M. on Monday the 10th of January, 1977."

9. THE FIFTH

In the lobby of the Hilton, the evening Judge Hayes set our trial date, Marvin Mitchelson and I waited with Jeffrey Carroll for the bellman to bring him his luggage. Mr. Carroll said to us, "I can tell you one thing for certain. It isn't a rank forgery as your American expert Spencer Otis has said."

"That's great!" I said. "It isn't a rank forgery, it's a good forgery, is that what you're telling us?"

"Oh, no, not at all, not by any means!"

"Mr. Carroll, if you don't think that Hughes wrote it, please say so now, so that we can know where—"

"No, I can say no such thing. I think he did write it. But there are some aspects that trouble me, and I must be absolutely certain in my findings. You see, unlike a lawyer, an examiner of questioned documents in my country can never make a mistake. Never. Once he's wrong, he's through. If ever I make a mistake, I'll leave the profession."

One way, I thought, to avoid making a mistake is to avoid making a decision. With his briefcase of clippings from Las Vegas newspaper stories about him and pictures of him examining the will, and with Marvin Mitchelson's check for $5,000, Jeffrey Carroll left us and Las Vegas. In the bar, Marvin ended his staring at his brandy snifter, looked at me and let it burst out. "Hal, do you really think it's genuine?"

"Yes, I do. You don't?"

"No."

"Why not?"

"First, that expert in Wales. He wanted the trip to Las Vegas. But he had to tell me it was a fake. Then there's that autograph dealer you took to Vegas. And now, the hotshot from Scotland Yard who can't make up his mind."

"Then why are you in this, Marvin? Why waste your time? And your money?"

"Because I think you're going to win."

"You think this is a forgery but that a jury is going to be fooled into —"

"Not fooled! Persuaded! They're going to be persuaded because they're going to want to be persuaded. If this is a fake, at least seventy-seven percent of those billions goes to taxes, and the rest is split between some forgotten old aunt and some second cousins Hughes never heard of. But if it's admitted to probate, hundreds of millions go to medical research, and for orphans and for scholarships. They'll beg to be persuaded!"

Three days later, on August 30, 1976, Marvin Mitchelson and I returned in my 310 to Las Vegas, this time to the MGM Grand to meet Dudley Woodcock, the dean of American handwriting experts. Marvin had met Woodcock in his New York office two weeks earlier to show him a photograph of the will and a batch of exemplars of Hughes' handwriting. Woodcock examined the documents but refused to give even a tentative opinion until he had examined the original in Las Vegas. His fee was $5,000 plus his expenses.

Dudley Woodcock had written the most authoritative book on questioned document examination used in the United States, and if he were with us, his prestige would cloak our position with a respectability which would surely bring in the institutional beneficiaries with financial support for our case.

At 6:30, the evening before he was to examine the will, Dudley Woodcock met Marvin and me for dinner outside the Barrymore Room in the MGM Grand. Woodcock, white-haired, in his sixties, in a dark blue suit, tie knotted tight under a starched white collar, looked like an old movie version of a floorwalker in a men's department store, and glared at me when we were introduced as though I were a clerk he had caught pocketing a pair of shorts. At our table, Woodcock—no longer the floorwalker—was a heroic seventeenth-century European king about to be beheaded, eating his last dinner and not liking his company.

"Mr. Woodcock," I said, "all Marvin and I want is the benefit of your expert opinion. If you find that this will is not genuine, then we certainly want—"

"Sir, the opinion I will give you is the opinion I will give you, and I don't see any point in discussing it further."

The next morning at 9:30 in the courthouse Woodcock began examining and photographing the will, and at 12:00 noon he packed his equipment and left the courthouse, Marvin and I following him a step behind because he didn't seem to want to be seen with us. At 1:30 P.M., Woodcock checked out of the MGM, leaving Marvin and me with his hotel bill and his assurance that we would receive his written opinion within two weeks. Marvin asked, "Can you tell us, Mr. Woodcock, if you have any leaning one way or the other?"

It was obvious that Dudley Woodcock never leaned; he was either straight up or down flat. Woodcock winced at Marvin. "Sir, I just told you that you'll have my written opinion within two weeks."

As Woodcock walked away, Marvin said, "If this guy comes out for us, how are we going to know it isn't because he loves us?"

The setting of a trial date had one of its intended effects. Bittle and Yoakum began noticing depositions. Bittle led off with the deposition of Linda Dummar Diego, Melvin's ex-wife; it was taken in the Los Angeles office of the law firm used by Bittle's New York firm in the Los Angeles probate proceedings; twelve lawyers attended.

Linda Diego, small, around twenty-seven, perhaps pretty in her teens, testified that she thought she had spent New Year's Eve, December 31, 1967, with Melvin in Los Angeles. No, she had no recollection of Melvin's telling her that New Year's Eve about having picked up a man who had said he was Howard Hughes. But she did overhear a conversation between Melvin and her father, Wayne Sisk, in which Melvin had said something like that. "My father just kinda laughed at Mel. You know, kinda needlin' Mel, like Mel was makin' up the whole thing. An' my father says, why din't Mel take a pitcher a the man. An' Mel says he din't have no camera an' din't think it was Howard Hughes anyway, an' why would he take a pitcher of an old bum, you know?"

The deposition lasted two full days, approximately thirteen hours, during which Phillip Bittle explored those matters which he insisted supported his contention that the Mormon will was a forgery:

"How many television game shows did you appear on?"

"Three or four."

"On any of them did you wear a costume?"

"Oh, sure, all."

"Did Melvin Dummar design the costumes you wore?"

"No, he just took me to this place where they rent costumes an' wigs."

"You mean, Melvin Dummar used his artistic imagination to select your costumes?"

"We sorta done it together."

"Did Melvin Dummar select the wigs you wore?"

"He just said I oughta wear one."

"Did he tell you why?"

"He said it'd make me look silly, so I oughta wear it, which I wore it."

"Did Melvin tell you that by this pretense you were to deceive the producers of the game show?"

"He just said to act silly 'cause them was the kinda people who got on them game shows."

During a recess, Eli and I asked Bittle for his theory of the relevance of those game-show questions. Without looking up from his notes, Bittle disdainfully stammered, "Artful deception."

I asked, "Artful what?"

"Artful deception. In case you don't know, that's one type of fraud. Deception, which is artful."

"You mean that in getting his wife to make an ass of herself on some game shows, Melvin practiced the same deception that—"

"That's my theory and I don't care whether you like it or not."

"Then, Mr. Bittle, we won't tell you whether we like it or not. Will we, Eli?"

"No, Hal, we won't tell him."

Most of the three hours of the afternoon were devoted to the prizes Linda had won on those game shows.

"And what did you win on the third show?"

"A piano. A hunnerd dollars, a weekend for two in Catalina, an' an electric toaster."

"What did you do with the piano?"

"I sold it."

"Why did you sell it?"

"'Cause I couldn't play it."

"How much did you sell it for?"

"This was more than ten years ago! Jesus!"

"What did you do with the money you got from the sale of the piano?"

"I paid bills."

"What bills?"

"Hey, do you remember what bills you paid ten years ago?"

"Let's take the next item, the hundred dollars. What did you do with it?"

"I don't remember what I done with it no more than I remember what I done with the money I got from the piano. Jesus!"

"Did you go to Catalina?"

"No."

"Why not?"

"I been to Catalina before, an' it's the pits."

"It's the what?"

Mrs. Diego rolled her eyes up, sat back in her chair, and spoke slowly to assist Mr. Bittle. "A place where you don't like it is the pits. Like a hole in the ground, see? It's bad as you go down, an' then it gets worse, an' at the very bottom it's the pits."

"Did you sell the two tickets for the weekend in Catalina?"

"Probably. You wanna know to who?"

"Yes, if you please."

"I don't remember."

"Now, about that toaster—"

"Oh, my God! You wanna know whether it toasted two slices or four slices? I don't remember. I don't have it no more. You wanna know what I done with it? I don't remember what I done with it an' how long are you gonna go on askin' questions like this?"

One more day. 9:00 A.M. to 5:00 P.M.

A week later, Phillip Bittle took the deposition of Melvin's aunt Erma Dummar. Erma married Melvin's uncle, Richard Dummar in 1973, met Melvin at the wedding and never saw him again. Erma's son Willy met Melvin in 1973 at the wedding and worked with him in Melvin's father's lath and plastering business in Los Angeles, but Willy did not see Melvin in 1976 until after news of Melvin's name in the Mormon will. When Melvin was to appear on television, cousin Willy dashed to Willard to take charge of the press conference as agent for Melvin in his future career as a recording artist and writer of country-western songs and as exclusive distributor of Melvin's name and likeness on T-shirts. But the evening after the press conference, Melvin's wife, Bonnie, ordered Ron to leave because she suspected that he was an opportunist.

Phillip Bittle's theory was that Aunt Erma and her son Ron were co-conspirators with Melvin in the forging of the Mormon will. Bittle's evidence of this conspiracy was that Aunt Erma had had an article published in the June 1972 issue of *Millionaire Magazine* entitled "Millionaire Spotlights Kay Alls." In the same issue was an article on Howard Hughes written by someone whom Erma didn't know. The Hughes article required research, and Phillip Bittle reasoned that because Aunt Erma was connected with *Millionaire Magazine,* she must have had access to the research material used by the writer of the Hughes article. Bittle concluded that from this research, Aunt Erma learned what to put in a will supposedly written by Howard Hughes, and along with her opportunist son, connived with Melvin to rip off the Hughes estate.

Since I was working on a brief I would soon need, I asked Eli to attend Aunt Erma's deposition for me.

After the noon recess, Eli phoned me and chuckled as he reported that Bittle had spent the three morning hours trying to find out from Aunt Erma where her son Willy was. It seemed that Aunt Erma didn't know where Will was, and to Phillip Bittle, that Aunt Erma didn't know where Willy was was evidence of a plot to thwart Phillip Bittle in his effort to slap Willy with a subpoena for his deposition, and this plot was further evidence of a conspiracy between Aunt Erma, Willy, and Melvin Dummar to defraud Bittle's clients of their rightful share as heirs in the estate of their beloved second cousin, Howard Hughes.

At 3:10 P.M. that afternoon Eli phoned again, this time in panic. "Hal, you won't believe this! She took the Fifth!"

"She took the what?"

"The Fifth! The fuckin' Fifth! She took it on the advice of her attorney! She declined to answer questions on the ground that her answers might tend to incriminate her!"

"You can't be serious!"

"Bittle adjourned the deposition! He's already phoned the press here and in Houston to tell them that Melvin Dummar's aunt is hiding behind the Fifth Amendment!"

"To what question?"

"To a dozen questions!"

"Give me one, for chrissakes!"

"Bittle asked her if she knew who forged the Mormon will."

10. THE DUTCHMAN

That Aunt Erma had taken the Fifth was announced by grimacing Phillip Bittle on the 6:00 news. At 9:00 that evening, I phoned Erma's lawyer at his home. "Why did you have her take the Fifth?"

"I had to! This lawyer Phillip Bittle accused my client of conspiracy to forge the will."

"Did your client have anything to do with the writing of it?"

"Of course not!"

"Does she know who did?"

"Of course not!"

"Then why in hell did you have her take the Fifth?"

"Because she was accused of being involved in a forgery!"

The next morning I requested the court to order Erma to answer the questions she had declined to answer. Her attorney reconsidered and promised that upon a resumption of his client's deposition she would answer the questions. Erma's deposition was resumed and she testified that she knew nothing about the writing of the will, nothing about any forgery, that she had no agreement of any kind with Melvin Dummar or with anybody else to forge anything anywhere at any time.

In late September, as soon as I learned that John Holmes and Roy Crawford, two of Hughes' personal aides, and Dr. Lawrence Chaffin, one of the doctors with Hughes at the time of his death, were Los Angeles residents, I rushed my process server out with subpoenas. My server's reports showed a thundering lack of enthusiasm on the part of these witnesses to be witnesses:

> Process server went to address. Housekeeper said Dr. Chaffin was in backyard. Server saw him watering lawn. Description checked. Housekeeper returned, said Dr. Chaffin wasn't in. Server went in backyard. Dr. Chaffin ran. Server ran after him. Before server reached Dr. Chaffin, he ran into small tool shed, refused to come out. Server waited one hour. Server informed doctor he was leaving papers on door step of tool shed. Dr. pretended he wasn't in tool shed.

When my server was told by Mrs. John Holmes that her husband was expected home for dinner at 6:00, he sat in his parked car four houses down and watched the Holmes house. At 10:00 that evening, having seen no one enter, my server again rang the Holmes doorbell and was told by Mrs. Holmes that she no longer had any idea when her husband would return home, if ever, nor where he was or why. My server said he would try again next week, moved his car one block away and waited. At 9:30 A.M. the next morning, as John Holmes confidently strolled toward his house, he saw my server's car approaching and ran for the door. The car screeched to a halt, my server jumped out, dashed for the door, and reached it the instant Holmes did and announced, "We tied!"

After Holmes, Crawford, and Chaffin were served, they made a joint motion before the Los Angeles Probate Court for a protective order that their depositions not be taken. Their motions were denied. I set the deposition of John Holmes for October 6, 1976, at 9:30 A.M. in my office, and on October 5, 1976, at 4:30 I received a call from Horace Cummings who said he had been retained by Mr. Holmes, Mr. Crawford, and Dr. Chaffin to represent them in their depositions. "My clients feel that they need a lawyer to be protected from abusive treatment."

"By whom?"

"By you. As for your deposition set for tomorrow morning for Mr. Holmes—it's inconvenient for him to attend."

"What's inconvenient about it?"

"Mr. Holmes has previous plans to be out of town tomorrow."

"Mr. Holmes was served with a subpoena. A subpoena is not an invitation to dinner. If he doesn't show up, I'll get a warrant for his arrest."

The next morning in my office at 9:30 A.M. Mr. Holmes did not show up, and at 2:00 that afternoon a Judge in the Los Angeles Probate Court issued a warrant for the arrest of John Holmes. Two hours after the news was on the radio, Mr. Holmes appeared in the Probate Court with his attorney, and the warrant was withdrawn on Holmes' promise that he would show up for a deposition in my office on November 8, 1976.

I told Marvin Mitchelson that it was imperative that we know if any reliable American handwriting experts were going to be with us. In Atlanta, Georgia, at a convention of examiners of questioned documents, Marvin contacted Polly Jean Pfau of Detroit. After a $1,000 examination of a photograph of the will and some exemplars of Hughes' writing, her tentative opinion was that the will was genuine. For an additional $3,500 fee and her expenses, Mrs. Pfau agreed to fly to Las Vegas to examine the original will. I met Polly Jean Pfau at lunch with Marvin at the Four Queens in Las Vegas. The stout blond lady in her late forties—because of thirty extra pounds she looked to be in her late fifties—said that she was almost convinced that the will was written by Howard Hughes. "There are just a few things I need to firm up my opinion," she said. "Samples of the handwriting of Noah Dietrich and of Melvin Dummar. And samples of Mr. Hughes' writing where he misspelled simple words."

"Polly, if it's your opinion that Hughes wrote it," I said, "it follows that Dietrich didn't and Dummar didn't. Why do you want samples of their handwriting?"

"I still have to satisfy myself that neither Noah Dietrich nor Melvin Dummar could have written it."

I still had to satisfy myself that this lady was competent. "I can show you dozens of memos where Hughes misspelled simple words, and one in which he even misspelled his last name. But what has this to do with handwriting?"

"You have his last name misspelled? I'm becoming more convinced every minute."

I was becoming more convinced every minute that I needed another American handwriting expert.

By the middle of September there was still no word from Jeffrey Carroll in London. But on September 15, 1976, I received five pages of words from Dudley Woodcock in New York, ending with: "Unquestionably a forgery."

"Sheila, I don't know whom I can call as an expert. Ninety days before trial and I don't have one I can believe in!"

"What are you going to do in front of the jury in January?"

"I don't know. As of now, all I can do is stand up before them at attention and sing, 'God Bless America'."

On October 1, 1976, Hans Verhaeren of Amsterdam, Holland, checked into the Hilton in Las Vegas. Since I had to be in Houston to argue my motion to see the autopsy report, Marvin Mitchelson and Herman Falitz escorted Mr. Verhaeren in Las Vegas to the courthouse and back for two days. Falitz had agreed to pay Verhaeren's fee, and invited him to spend a few days at Falitz's other home in Palm Springs after his examination was completed. After a two-day examination of the will in the courthouse in Las Vegas, Verhaeren wanted to go to Los Angeles to examine the original of the 1970 letter handwritten by Howard Hughes and addressed to "Dear Chester and Bill" on file in the Federal Courthouse. Marvin flew Verhaeren to Los Angeles and checked him into the Century Plaza Hotel opposite my office in Century City. After nine more days of study, Verhaeren was ready and Marvin brought him to my office.

Hans Verhaeren looked as though he had just walked off the top of a box of Dutch Masters Cigars, and was masquerading in modern clothes. Short, round, balding, in his late sixties, he bowed slightly when he shook my hand. His smiling face was distinguished by a brown, rectangular goatee, and his soft, mellow voice was distinguished by impeccable English. Verhaeren's smile dropped as he walked slowly to a chair, and from the way he sat solidly back in it, I sensed that he was getting set to recite his reasons for no longer being able to say that the will was valid.

"Gentlemen, when I first looked at the photographs of the questioned testament in Amsterdam, I was certain that it was a forgery. The indications of forgery were quite numerous and quite obvious. For example, tremulous strokes, blunt-ended pen lifts in most unnatural places, and superfluous little strokes tacked on to letters. All indications of copying. Then after examining the testament for a fortnight in comparison with the known writings of Mr. Hughes, I stated my tentative conclusion that they were written by the same person. I reached this tentative conclusion because the numerous indications of forgery in the questioned testament were also to be found in the known writings of Mr. Hughes. Therefore, what first appeared to be indications of forgery became counterindicative—that is, became indications of genuineness. This opinion was tentative because I had to examine the original of the questioned testament. I have now completed my examination and I am prepared to give you my firm opinion. The hand that wrote the known writings of Howard Hughes and the hand that wrote the three-page testament dated March 19, 1968, is the same hand.

To give you all the reasons upon which I base my opinion would take several days and would require projection equipment and slides and enlargements. My reasons will be explained to you in considerable detail in my written report."

"Mr. Verhaeren, how certain are you?" I asked.

"It would be utterly impossible for any person other than the writer of the exemplars to have written the questioned testament."

"But, if a forger has sufficient skill, couldn't he—"

"No, no, no!" Verhaeren smiled and shook his head. "Let me explain. If a trained handwriting expert—and that is what a forger must be to fool an expert—practiced for at least two hours a day, each day for a year, he might be able—assuming a high degree of skill, a superior intellect, and years of experience—to write in the Hughesian style two or three words. But he could not forge a text of three pages. To write such a lengthy text in another man's style, he would have to unlearn his own way of writing completely, and this, is impossible. It is impossible, because of the extreme automation of the movement patterns that constitute a person's handwriting. With three words or so, I might, yes, be fooled by a talented professional forger who practiced each day for a year. But to fool me with the writing of three pages, that same professional would have to practice each day for about one hundred years. And, sir, I doubt that many professional forgers would elect to devote so much of their valuable time to so precarious an enterprise."

Verhaeren agreed to return to Las Vegas to testify in January. After he and Marvin left, I carefully studied his credentials. Hans Verhaeren became a forensic handwriting expert in 1951 in the Ministry of Justice in Holland, was made the head of the Document Section in 1965, and held that title until he retired in 1975. In addition to advising the Courts of Justice as to the authenticity of the handwriting of questioned documents, he instructed police detectives. He had examined about two thousand questioned documents a year for fourteen years, and had testified as an expert in over two hundred criminal trials and in over one hundred civil trials in courts throughout the Netherlands and in Germany. Verhaeren was a participant in the International Meeting of Forensic Sciences, and was invited to deliver papers to that group in 1966, 1967, and 1972 on problems of statistical analysis in the detection of forgeries. And he had written numerous articles for publication in the leading periodical on handwriting in Holland, *Acta Graphologa*.

The following morning, before he was to leave Los Angeles for his visit with Herman Falitz in Palm Springs, Verhaeren returned and asked my receptionist if he could see me. Standing stiffly in my reception room, he asked in a whisper if he could talk to me alone. As I escorted him back to my office, I knew I was about to hear from my little Dutch expert that he would remain steadfast in his opinion upon my promise that after we won, he would be paid, say, a million dollars. In my office, Verhaeren told me that he wanted my advice concerning what he said was a "very delicate matter." I knew it!

"I spent over two weeks of intensive work on this case in Holland, sir. Two days in Las Vegas, and nine days here in Los Angeles. Because of its worldwide importance, I gave this matter my utmost concentration. My report to you will probably be over a hundred pages. As I understand it, you are the lawyer who will present the case in court, but Mr. Mitchelson and Mr. Falitz are the ones to whom I am to look for my fee."

"That's correct."

"They told me that they will pay me a reasonable fee for my services. The problem is, I do not know what in your country a reasonable fee is. So I have come back to ask your advice. Because of the time I have spent on this case, and the enormous responsibility in giving an opinion on a matter of this import, is a fee for my work to date reasonable in the amount of eight hundred dollars?"

"No, Mr. Verhaeren, a fee for your work to date would not be reasonable in the amount of eight hundred dollars. Your fee ought to be five thousand and expenses."

"Oh, no, sir, no, that would be utterly out of the question!"

"An absolute minimum would be two thousand five hundred and—"

"Under no circumstances would I accept such a fee. But you have told me what I wanted to know. A fee of eight hundred would not be excessive."

After Verhaeren left, I phoned Falitz in Palm Springs and told him of my talk with Verhaeren.

"Harold, it's generous of you to be generous with my money! But I still have to bring those two Frenchmen and the German over here."

"Herman, I urge that you force the Dutchman to take at least twenty-five hundred."

"And I urge that you let me handle the financial aspects of our case."

In Palm Springs Herman Falitz gave Hans Verhaeren a check for $1,000. The following day, after he cashed some traveler's checks, Hans Verhaeren handed back to Herman Falitz two $100 bills. Herman Falitz declined them.

11. THE JUDGE PAUL GRANT MATTER

A week after Hans Verhaeren left for Holland, Herman Falitz phoned to tell me that he had almost convinced Simon J. McIntosh to put up the money for part of our costs.

"That's great! How much will he put up, what does he expect in return, and who is he?"

"You don't know who Simon J. is? He's one of the most influential bankers in the country! He's made loans of hundreds of millions to governments! He advised two Presidents! His is one of the most famous names in the fuckin' financial world! Now, surely, you recognize his name?"

"Never heard of him. Why is he doing this?"

"Simon J. lives in Salt Lake City. Therefore, he's a Mormon." Herman's words became garbled.

"Herman, take your time and swallow what you're eating, and when you're through, continue talking."

He stopped talking for a few seconds and I heard only the biting and slurping. "But you have to fly to Salt Lake City to close it. McIntosh's lawyer is Wilford Kirton, who happens to be general counsel for the Mormon Church—" and then another mouthful of something made it difficult to understand him.

"Herman, what are you eating?"

"Nuts."

"Call me back when you're finished eating the nuts."

"All right, all right, wait a minute! Better now? McIntosh listens to Kirton. If Kirton feels that you've got a good chance to win, McIntosh'll supply the money. It's up to you to convince Kirton." Another mouthful of nuts was chewed in my ear, again muffling Herman's words. "You can see Kirton in Salt Lake City tomorrow morning."

"Thanks, Herman. And to prove my appreciation, when I get to Salt Lake City, I'll send you a can of nuts."

The next morning at 10:00 in the unpretentious law offices of Kirton, McConkie, Boyer & Boyle in Salt Lake City, Wilford Kirton agreed that with handwriting experts such as Verhaeren, we had a winnable case. He explained that because the LDS Church officials were sensitive to accusations in the press that they were avaricious, they would not support the will, but he would advise his client, Simon J. McIntosh, to arrange for his bank to transfer funds to Falitz to be used for certain costs. At this stage, McIntosh would commit no more than $30,000, none of which could be used for travel expenses or as a fee for any handwriting expert or any lawyer. "You can use the money for deposition costs, process serving, and the like—everything backed by receipts and vouchers, of course. If this case is won, Mr. McIntosh will expect Mr. Falitz to earn enough in fees working for the executor to be able to repay these advances."

I thanked Mr. Kirton and rose to leave. "By the way, what's your theory," I asked, "as to who left the will on the twenty-fifth floor that day?"

"I don't have one. I'm anxious to hear yours."

"I don't have one. I don't know who had the will after Hughes wrote it. And I can't imagine why whoever had it would have sneaked it into the Church Headquarters."

"The circumstances surrounding the delivery don't support the conclusion that the will is genuine, do they?"

"No, they don't." I thought of the $30,000. "But, on the other hand, those circumstances don't support the conclusion of forgery either. Remember, the instruction on the envelope was to deliver it to the Clark County Courthouse in Las Vegas. Not to the LDS Church in Salt Lake City. Why would a forger forge an instruction and then violate his instruction? A forger wouldn't."

"The surrounding facts seem inconsistent with both the theory of genuineness and the theory of forgery, don't they?"

"True. But which theory is more likely? Would a forger have his product delivered in such a way as to make it look suspicious? Of course not. But Hughes was eccentric."

"When you present your evidence in Las Vegas two months from now, what are you going to use to show where the will was and who had it from the time Hughes wrote it until the time it showed up here in Salt Lake City?"

"If I piled all the evidence I have on that subject on an empty table, I'd still have an empty table. Instead of evidence of who had it, I'll have to use arguments that it couldn't have been forged. Arguments the contestants can't answer. For example, they contend that Dummar forged the will in April 1976 after Hughes died on April 5th. But since Dummar was in Willard, Utah, at all times in April 1976, how could he have got on the back of the will envelope a Pitney Bowes stamp imprint made by a Las Vegas, Nevada, machine?"

"You know, don't you, that someone saw that will envelope addressed to 'Dear Mr. McKay' in 1972?"

"What! No, I didn't know that. Who saw it? Where?"

"Oh, I thought you knew." Kirton opened a drawer and said, "There's a city judge here who's well respected, an upstanding member of the Church. Paul Grant. After I delivered the will and its envelope to the court in Las Vegas, I received this letter from him. Why don't you just read it?"

May 5, 1976
Salt Lake City, Utah

Dear Mr. Kirton:

Enclosed is a brief statement of an incident which occurred in 1972. The facts are clear to me.

I received a telephone call requesting my advice. The caller said that he had in his possession a packet which included an envelope addressed to a Mr. McKay, whom he believed referred to David O.

McKay, purporting to contain a will with instructions to file it upon the writer's death, and signed Howard Hughes.

The materials had been acquired a short distance south of West High School on 300 West Street in Salt Lake City.

The man wanted to know what to do with the will since President McKay had died about two and a half years before. I expressed skepticism about the authenticity of the document, and suggested to the caller that to avoid embarrassment, he could hold on to the letter until Howard Hughes died and then turn it over to the authorities.

The content of the will was not discussed. The conversation was short. I remembered the incident from time to time because I was amused by the suggestion that a Hughes will would be handled in such an informal manner. I did not take the incident seriously until the death of Mr. Hughes and the unusual manner in which a purported will appeared in the Church Office Building in Salt Lake City.

The phone call occurred between late spring and early fall of 1972.

I am willing to testify concerning this but do not desire to be examined by any media personnel.

Respectfully yours,
Paul G. Grant
City Judge

I was elated. "What do you suppose the caller had said to Grant to cause him to write 'The materials had been acquired a short distance south of West High School on 300 West Street in Salt Lake City'? Acquired how? In a burglary? Found on a sidewalk or a lawn? Did somebody just walk up to this guy and hand it to him? Where is this high school?"

"Oh, then there's something else you don't know. Remember what was written on that note that accompanied the will when it was dropped off at our church last April? 'This was found by Joseph F. Smith's house in 1972.' The location that that caller described to Judge Grant—this 'short distance south of West High School on 300 West Street'—do you know what that location is near?"

"No."

"That location is near the house of Joseph F. Smith."

"Jesus Christ!" The news sat me back down. "Mr. Kirton, I apologize." Kirton smiled, and his waving gesture dispensed forgiveness.

"What could the connection be between the two?" I said. "There must be one."

"What two?"

"The 1972 caller to Judge Grant and whoever wrote that note. There must be some connection between them. Each had handled the same will envelope. And each had the same story about where it was found. And about when it was found. By the way, who was Joseph F. Smith?"

"He was the president of our church after President David O. McKay died."

"When Joseph F. Smith took office as president, would he have taken possession of anything his predecessor had been holding for safekeeping as president?"

"I suppose so."

"Where's the original of that note?"

"An investigator for the Attorney General of Nevada asked to borrow it and the Visitors Center envelope, and I gave them to him about a week ago. You look the way Galileo must have when the little one and the big one both landed at the same time. What is it?"

"That phone call to Judge Grant means that our will could not have been forged in April 1976!"

"But, if it's a forgery, what difference does it make whether it was forged in 1976 or in 1972?"

"The only forgery theory that makes any sense—the only one the contestants have—is that the will was forged after Hughes died in April 1976. But now here's evidence that the will envelope was in existence more than four years earlier. If you have only one theory consistent with forgery, and the evidence disintegrates your theory, what's left?"

12. THE AIDES

On November 6, 1976, a shorthand reporter, twelve attorneys, and I waited in my office for Roy Crawford to appear under subpoena for the first deposition of one of the personal aides of Howard Hughes. I knew that Roy Crawford would be a vicious, thick-necked, frowning three-hundred-pounder, a devoted ape who had been ready for twenty years to crash his massive fists into the face of anyone who attempted to invade the privacy of his beloved boss, and who was still ready to protect that privacy after his boss's death. In the top right-hand drawer of my desk, I kept a loaded .38 Colt Cobra. Just to display. To avoid bloodshed. Mine.

Ten minutes late, Horace Cummings of the Los Angeles firm of Wyatt & Blankanhorn stomped into my office. An ex-UCLA quarterback, around forty with short gray hair, Cummings had the kind of face they used in recruiting posters. Behind him was Roy Crawford. Crawford looked like a retired jockey: sixty-five years old, tiny, almost shriveled, neatly dressed in a cadet-sized banker's suit. His dyed brown hair was combed straight back and flat as he had worn it in the thirties. He meekly extended his hand and squeaked, "How do you do, sir?" I was glad nobody knew what I had in my top right-hand drawer.

Roy Crawford took the oath and sat with his back straight so as not to look like a retired jockey.

"When is the last time you saw Mr. Yoakum before today?"

"Two or three months ago, sir."

"Try again, sir."

"Yesterday."

"Did you discuss with Mr. Yoakum yesterday the testimony you expected to give today?"

"Yes."

Mr. Cummings said, "I was present and we didn't discuss any testimony to be given today."

"Counsel, I'm not asking you!" The session was not destined to be long, pleasant, or productive.

Roy Crawford testified that in 1950 he began working out of the Hughes Productions office in Hollywood as a personal messenger for Mr. Hughes. In 1955 he became supervisor of the team that made security arrangements in advance of Mr. Hughes' arrivals at hotels, ensuring that Mr. Hughes occupied an entire floor on which not even hotel employees would be allowed, and arranging for the elevator mechanism to be set so that the elevator could not stop at Mr. Hughes' floor unless a passenger used a specially made key.

In 1957, when Mr. Hughes lived in the Beverly Hills Hotel, Crawford became his personal aide with the title of Executive Staff Assistant. Crawford lived in Bungalow 7, Mr. Hughes lived in Bungalow 9, and the newly wedded Mrs. Hughes lived in Bungalow 12. Crawford's executive duties, which he shared with John Holmes, included delivering to Mr. Hughes daily newspapers, boxes of Kleenex, and yellow legal pads.

In 1960 Mr. and Mrs. Hughes moved to Rancho Santa Fe, and in 1961 to a French Regency house in the elegant hills of Bel Air. There Mr. Hughes ordered his aides to work, eat, and sleep in the same bedroom he used to work, eat, and sleep. Mrs. Hughes slept elsewhere. But after a few months, the aides gently persuaded Mr. Hughes to allow them to sit in waiting in the dressing-room area in the hallway entrance inside the bedroom. Although they were in the same room, whenever Mr. Hughes wanted one of his executive staff assistants, he would ring a little bell. Crawford testified that not once in the next five years did Mr. Hughes step outside that bedroom suite.

From Thanksgiving 1966 until Thanksgiving 1970, Crawford lived on the eighth floor of the Desert Inn Hotel in Las Vegas, Nevada, and worked on the ninth floor, twelve days on, four off. Crawford accompanied Mr. Hughes in the move out of the Desert Inn to the Britannia Beach Hotel in the Bahamas on Thanksgiving 1970, but in February 1971, Crawford was ordered by Kay Glenn, the Hughes Tool Company executive to whom the aides reported, to return to Los Angeles. Crawford did, and never again saw, spoke to, or heard from Howard Hughes.

Back in Los Angeles, Kay Glenn told Crawford that he had been pulled out as an aide to work on a special project for Mrs. Hughes. But there never was a special project for Mrs. Hughes.

"You have no idea why you were removed?"

"No."

"Did you ask anyone why?"

"You don't ask."

Crawford was kept on the Hughes Tool Company payroll with an increase in salary, and at the time of his deposition he worked in the office that arranged for the transportation of executives in small corporate jets. Three months after Howard Hughes' death Crawford was rewarded by Summa with a new employment contract guaranteeing him several more years of employment, and with a second contract to take effect when the current one terminated, guaranteeing him payment for life as a consultant. Both contracts provided that if, without Summa's permission, Crawford told anybody anything about Howard Hughes, he would lose the money and all medical and other benefits under his contracts.

Crawford could not recall the last week of December 1967, nor the first few days of January 1968. Nor did he have or know of any records to refresh his memory. Crawford testified that during Mr. Hughes' four-year stay in the Desert Inn, prior to the day he left, Mr. Hughes did not once leave the ninth floor. Mr. Hughes was physically able to leave. He had clothes. He was in no way restrained. He did not leave because he did not choose to leave.

Crawford said that there was no difference in the way Mr. Hughes appeared at the end of December 1967 and during the next three years in the Desert Inn.

"In late December 1967, describe Hughes' hair."

Mr. Cummings said, "Objection! What has Mr. Hughes' hair got to do with this case?"

"Counsel, Melvin Dummar claims that in late December 1967, he picked up a man who said he was Howard Hughes. Contestants claim that Hughes was not picked up by Dummar, that Hughes never knew Dummar, and therefore, that Hughes could not have written a will naming Dummar. Now, Dummar has described the appearance of the man he picked up in the desert, and we've got to know how Howard Hughes appeared at the time in question. Mr. Crawford, at the end of 1967 how long was Howard Hughes' hair?"

"A little longer than average."

"Was his hair long enough to reach his shoulders?"

"No! Never!"

"Are you certain of that?"

"Mr. Hughes' hair never reached his shoulders."

"Mr. Crawford, other people who saw Mr. Hughes at that time have said that Howard Hughes' hair was below his shoulders."

"Yes, Mr. Hughes' hair was below his shoulders."

"Why did you tell me a few seconds ago that his hair never reached his shoulders?"

"Well, his hair went below the shoulders in the back. I didn't know that you were asking me about where his hair was in the back."

"You thought I was asking you how long his hair was when it hung down over his face?"

Mr. Cummings barked, "You're abusing the witness!"

"Mr. Crawford, did Howard Hughes' beard look the same during his entire four-year stay at the Desert Inn?"

"About the same."

"Describe it."

"Grayish. Down from his sideburns and covering the sides of his face and his jaw."

"How long was it?"

"Possibly two inches."

"What about five inches long?"

"Yes, I'd say about five inches long."

"It was never as short as two inches was it, sir?"

"No, sir."

"Describe Howard Hughes' fingernails during the Desert Inn period."

"Quite long."

"Did Howard Hughes wear shoes anytime during the Desert Inn period?"

"No. Mr. Hughes had a pair of brown oxfords in his closet, but he never wore them."

"How do you know he never wore them?"

"Because Mr. Hughes' toenails were too long. So long that it would have been impossible for him to have worn shoes at any time in the Desert Inn."

"During the Desert Inn period, did you executive staff assistants keep any written record of Hughes' activities?"

"Yes. We kept logs."

"Are those logs still in existence?"

"I believe they were destroyed when they had no further purpose."

"Did you keep them throughout the entire Desert Inn period?"

"We began keeping them early in 1967 and until we left in 1970."

"What type of entries did you make in those logs?"

"Business transactions, conversations, what Mr. Hughes ate, when he went to bed, what he watched on television, and entries of that sort."

"During those four years in the Desert Inn, other than carrying messages, what were your duties?"

"Whatever Mr. Hughes wanted done, we did."

"What did he want done that you did?"

Horace Cummings growled, "I instruct him not to answer and I adjourn the deposition to obtain a court order to protect him from this abuse! We're leaving!" He walked out and Roy Crawford obediently followed his quarterback.

On November 8, 1976, Horace Cummings was again in my office for a deposition, this time with John Holmes. Holmes, the only non-Mormon among Howard Hughes' aides, resembled Roy Crawford, but was a few inches taller, a few pounds heavier, and a few years younger. Like Crawford, John Holmes was humble and stiffly courteous, weighed his words carefully, and spoke them slowly.

John Holmes began working for Hughes Productions in 1949 as a driver and chaperone of starlets in Los Angeles and Lake Tahoe with fellow driver-chaperone, Kay Glenn. In 1957, with the title of Staff Executive, Holmes became a personal aide to Howard Hughes. "My duties were secretarial. I took messages."

Away from his wife and four children, Holmes lived in Bungalow 8 and served Mr. Hughes in Bungalow 9 of the Beverly Hills Hotel for the next three years. Holmes would be ordered to report to Bungalow 3 to wait for a call—sometimes he would wait several hours—to tell him what was to be in the sandwich he was to bring to Bungalow 9 for Mr. Hughes' next meal. Holmes and Roy Crawford worked together each night on a fourteen-hour shift, serving Mr. Hughes for those three years without one night off.

"But, surely, you had Christmas Eve off?"

"No."

"Didn't you get a night off on your wedding anniversary?"

"No."

"Not on Thanksgiving?"

"No. Mr. Hughes always did something on Thanksgiving."

"No point in my asking you about St. Valentine's day."

After Christmas 1960, when Mr. Hughes and his wife moved out of the Beverly Hills Hotel to Rancho Sante Fe south of Los Angeles, Holmes accompanied Mr. and Mrs. Hughes in a limousine driven by Mr. Hughes himself; this, Holmes testified, was the last time in his life that Mr. Hughes drove. In Rancho Sante Fe, the twenty-four-hour duty began and Mr. Hughes had an aide within arm's reach at all times from the day he arrived until the day he died.

At Rancho Sante Fe, Holmes and Crawford alternated twelve-hour shifts. On only two occasions did Howard Hughes leave his bedroom; he went to another bungalow both times, and both times Holmes was with him. During the Sante Fe year, still not one day off.

In 1961, Mr. and Mrs. Hughes moved into the French Regency house in Bel Air where, with the addition of George Francom and Levar Myler, the four aides worked eight-hour shifts. Holmes always worked the night shift, and during the five years in the Bel Air house, still not one night off. Holmes testified that Howard Hughes never once left his Bel Air house bedroom until the day he left in 1966. Mr. Hughes wore clothes when he arrived and clothes when he left for his private train to Boston, but not once during those five years in the Bel Air house did Mr. Hughes wear any clothes.

In 1966, Mr. Hughes, his aides, and a platoon of security guards rode a private train to Boston. Mr. Hughes did not once leave his car on the three-day trip. In Boston, Mr. Hughes and his entourage stayed at the Ritz Carlton, and Mr. Hughes never left the Ritz between the day he checked in and the day he checked out six months later. Mr. Hughes was visited by no one during his stay there, except for his wife, who flew to Boston for one thirty-minute afternoon visit.

On Thanksgiving 1966, Howard Hughes, his aides, and the security guards left Boston on another private train, and at no time did Hughes leave his compartment before they arrived in Las Vegas. On the train, Hughes would summon his aides by clanking a knife on a pipe along the wall. In Las Vegas, Mr. Hughes was secretly whisked to the ninth floor of the Desert Inn, and there he stayed until the night he left, Thanksgiving 1970.

Holmes could not recall if, on December 29, 30, and 31, 1967, he was on or off duty.

"Then you can't tell us what Mr. Hughes was doing or where he was between December 29th and the 31st, 1967?"

"No, but if he had been out, I would have heard about it, and I didn't hear about it."

"Wasn't there a fire-escape door Hughes could have used without being seen by the Desert Inn guard?"

"Yes, but if Mr. Hughes had left by the fire-escape door any aide on duty would have heard him, because that back door had a noisy bolt. We tested the door to see how it worked, and it made quite a racket."

At no time during his four-year residence on the ninth floor of the Desert Inn was Howard Hughes visited by his wife, Jean Peters. Nor by any other woman. Nor by any of his executives. Not even by Robert Maheu. Mr. Hughes' only contact was with his aides.

"During those years in the Desert Inn, did Hughes frequently walk around naked in front of his aides?"

"Of course not!"

Throughout the Desert Inn period Hughes looked the same, with minor variations in the length of his hair and beard.

"Mr. Holmes, in the Desert Inn did Howard Hughes have long hair reaching down his back below his shoulders?"

"No, certainly not!"

"Did his hair reach his shoulders?"

"That's ridiculous! Never!"

"Describe the length of his hair."

"An inch or two longer than mine." Holmes' hair was cut scalp-close above his ears and combed straight back on the top, short and neat.

"Was Mr. Hughes' beard the same throughout the Desert Inn period?"

"Yes."

"Describe it."

"A Vandyke about two inches long at the chin."

"Did he have his beard under his sideburns, and covering the side of his face, and covering his jawline?"

"No, I said it was a Vandyke. The sides of Mr. Hughes' face were clean-shaven. He had no beard under his sideburns or around the jawline."

"Was there any time during the Desert Inn period when Howard Hughes had a beard that was about five inches long?"

"Never!"

"Mr. Holmes, during that Desert Inn period, were Mr. Hughes' fingernails quite long?"

"No, they were not, as you put it, quite long. There was nothing unusual about his fingernails."

"Anything unusual during the Desert Inn period about Mr. Hughes' toenails?"

"More nonsense! Nothing unusual about his toenails."

"Not so long that he couldn't wear shoes?"

"That's silly! And it's false."

"Mr. Holmes, during Hughes' stay in the Desert Inn Hotel, did he ever wear shoes?"

"Constantly! When he walked from his bed to the bathroom and from there back to his bed, he always wore that same pair of old brown shoes."

"In that suite on the ninth floor of the Desert Inn, where was Hughes most of the time?"

"In bed. When he wasn't in bed, he was in the bathroom."

"Did he ever sit in a chair during those four years?"

"I would say he was either in bed or the bathroom."

"During the Desert Inn period, did you make any log entries of Mr. Hughes' activities?"

"Never."

"Did any of Mr. Hughes' other aides, such as Roy Crawford, make entries in any logs?"

"Absolutely not. I didn't keep any logs and neither did Mr. Crawford or anyone else."

"Have you ever heard of any logs having been kept by any of Mr. Hughes' aides during the Desert Inn period?"

"No, I have never heard of any such logs. Except from you."

"If any logs had been kept by any of the other aides, would you have known about it?"

"Absolutely."

"Did you ever hear Howard Hughes say anything about a will?"

"Yes."

"What?"

"That he had written a holographic will."

"When was the last time you heard him say this?"

"1975."

"What did Mr. Hughes say in 1975 about a holographic will?"

"He told me again that he had written it on a piece of yellow paper that had lines on it."

"Did Mr. Hughes tell you if you were in the will?"

"He said that he provided for us by job description rather than by name."

I opened the file on my desk and took another look at the holographic will, page three:

ninth: one sixteenth to be devided amoung my personal aids at the time of my death—

"When Mr. Hughes told you he had written a will, did he use the word 'holographic'?"

"Yes, he did."

"You testified that Mr. Hughes said that he wrote his holographic will on a piece of paper. Now, did he say 'a' piece or 'one' piece or—"

"Several pieces of paper."

"How many pieces?"

"He didn't tell me."

"Did he say, a hundred pieces of paper?"

"He said he couldn't remember how many it was."

"Did you ask him?"

"No."

"What prompted him to tell you that he couldn't remember the number of pages?"

"I don't remember."

"Did Mr. Hughes tell you when he had written this holographic will?"

"He said he wrote it at the gray house near the tenth tee of the Bel Air Golf Course in Los Angeles, California."

I knew that Howard Hughes had lived in a gray-painted house near the Bel Air Golf Course in the late 1940s. But in the late 1940s, Howard Hughes could not have written a holographic will providing for his personal aides. In the late 1940s Hughes didn't have any personal aides.

"Did he tell you where that holographic will was?"

"No."

"We've heard from Mel Stewart, Mr. Hughes' barber, that Mr. Hughes had back sores—the bone actually protruding from the skin on his shoulder—when he was in the Desert Inn. During the Desert Inn period, did Mr. Hughes have any sores on his back that needed draining or irrigation?"

Phillip Bittle shouted, "I protest! Details like that ought not to be brought into this record! It's disgusting."

Earl Yoakum said, "Ah join in Mr. Bittle's most appropriate objection."

Bittle added, "Your questions are designed to annoy this witness, who I understand has a great affection for Mr. Hughes."

"Gentlemen, these questions are designed to help us determine whom we can believe. Hughes may have had those bedsores because he stayed in bed for four years, and if so, this would support the contestants. But it might be that the barber is mistaken about when Hughes had those bedsores."

Bittle said, "Mr. Rhoden, you are utterly insensitive! If you persist in this line of inquiry, I'll take the matter up with Judge Hayes!"

"Mr. Holmes, answer my question!"

Cummings said, "I instruct my client not to answer!"

"Did you buy any drugs for Mr. Hughes during the Desert Inn period?"

Cummings said, "The witness refuses to answer on the ground that his answer may tend to incriminate him, and he invokes the Fifth Amendment."

"Mr. Holmes, since the death of Mr. Hughes, have you been kept on as an employee of Summa?"

"Yes."

"What have you been doing for the money Summa's been paying you?"

Cummings objected, instructed his client not to answer, motioned for his client to follow, and walked out.

I called after him, "Aren't you even going to wave goodbye?"

Horace Cummings reconsidered the advisability of having walked Roy Crawford out of the deposition on November 6 and agreed to return him on November 10 to finish his deposition. Crawford described his duties for Howard Hughes during the Desert Inn period. He answered the telephone, wrote messages, handed them to Mr. Hughes, took messages from Mr. Hughes, and read them aloud in return telephone calls.

During Hughes' three-year stay at the Beverly Hills Hotel and his five-year stay in the Bel Air house and his four-year stay in the Desert Inn, Howard Hughes walked around most of the time stark naked.

"Mr. Crawford, you testified last week about logs which you and the other aides typed and filed during the Desert Inn period. Did Mr. John Holmes have anything to do with those logs?"

"He wrote them the same as everyone else."

"Did he also file the logs in the cabinet as you did?"

"Yes."

"How do you know that Mr. Holmes did those things?"

"I saw him doing them."

"During that Desert Inn period did Howard Hughes have a Vandyke?"

"No, he did not."

"What is your idea of a Vandyke?"

"A small beard, pointed, covering the chin. It's where the sides of the face under the sideburns are clean-shaven. I know what a Vandyke is, sir, and Mr. Hughes did not have a Vandyke during the Desert Inn period."

"Was Howard Hughes ever in Tonopah, Nevada?"

"Yes. But I was not with him."

"How do you know he was in Tonopah?"

"From his pilot's log book. He was there more than once."

"Where is that pilot's log book?"

"I don't know."

"When was the last time you saw it?"

"I saw a few sheets of it this year."

"Where did you see them?"

"At Romaine Street."

"Who has that log book now?"

"I don't know."

"When you saw that pilot's log book in the building on Romaine Street, who had the log book?"

"I don't know. I just walked into a room and saw a table and the log book was on it."

"You testified that Howard Hughes could not have left the ninth floor of the Desert Inn because he couldn't have worn shoes, and that he couldn't have worn shoes because his toenails were too long. Are you positive that at no time during that four-year period did Howard Hughes walk around that Desert Inn suite wearing shoes?"

"Mr. Hughes never once wore shoes in the Desert Inn. He couldn't have."

"Mr. Crawford on the ninth floor of the Desert Inn was there a back door leading to a fire escape?"

"Yes."

"Could anyone on that ninth floor have used that back door to leave without the Desert Inn guard stationed at the elevator seeing him?"

"Yes."

"Was there a bolt on that back door?"

"Yes."

"Did you ever work the bolt?"

"Yes."

"Can you tell us anything about the sound of the bolt? Noisy or quiet?"

"There wasn't anything noisy about it."

"How do you know it wasn't noisy?"

"I tried it myself. It wasn't noisy."

13. THE MAN FROM PARIS

On November 11, 1976, Herman Falitz screamed on the phone from Las Vegas that after examining the will, Pierre Faideau's tentative opinion reached in Paris was confirmed. The next day Falitz brought Faideau and his wife to my office. Faideau, tall, stooped, forty, wore a brown tweed jacket that showed that at one time he had been at least twenty pounds heavier. Combing his gray streaked flowing hair was of no interest to him and he didn't appear to have the strength for it. His cadaverous-gray skin, slow walk, and slow murmuring speech when we first saw him in the reception room prompted Stanley Fairfield to whisper to me as the Faideaus walked ahead to my office, "What good is he? He isn't going to be alive to testify in January."

In 1957, after a seven-year apprenticeship in Geneva, Pierre Faideau qualified as a handwriting expert before the Court of Appeal of Poitiers, and in 1965 in Paris he received the title of Court Designated Expert. In 1972 he was appointed by the Cour de Cassation, the highest court in France, as one of only twelve experts qualified for this post. Faideau was currently assigned over three hundred cases a year, mostly criminal, some involving two or three hundred documents.

I asked Monsieur Faideau how certain he was. His wife, a gracious Algerian Arab, spoke to him in French, and he smiled as he replied to her in French in a soft, musical voice. She said, "He say it is the work of his life that he know a forgery, and the testament he examine was not a forgery."

"Madame Faideau, please tell your husband that I mean no offense, but I must ask this question. Could he be mistaken?"

After the Faideaus spoke to each other in French, she answered, "He say, yes, he could be mistaken. But, he will say before God, that he is not mistaken."

Two days after Pierre Faideau returned to Paris, Herman Falitz and Marvin Mitchelson flew to Las Vegas to arrange with Alex Morenus for the examination of the will by Lothar Michel of Mannheim, Germany. After his examination, Herr and Frau Michel were brought to my office by Mitchelson and Falitz. As with the last team, Frau Michel interpreted for her husband. For fifteen years, Lothar Michel had been a detector of forgeries for the German government. He had testified thousands of times and took credit for the conviction of thousands of forgers. He was a professor at Mannheim University, teaching forgery detection to other court-appointed handwriting experts. He had written many articles and several books on handwriting comparison, was the editor of the *Mannheim Review*, and president of the World Symposium held under his auspices.

"My husband vill testify in your American court zat ze qvestioned zree-page testament he examine in Las Vegas, und all off ze samples off handwriting by Howard Hughes vere written by ze zame hand, yah."

Herman Falitz learned that the expert who had set up the handwriting lab for the CIA, Rupert Ingersol, lived near Houston, Texas, and arranged for me to meet him. I met Ingersol at the Whitehall Hotel for dinner the next time Stanley and I were in Houston and gave him a photograph of the will and a packet of exemplars. Ten days later, I received a letter from Ingersol stating that his opinion had to be tentative until he could examine the original of the questioned document in Las Vegas: The various characteristics favor the conclusion that the will is genuine.

A week later, Herman Falitz phoned from Las Vegas to report that we now had a second American on our side, although Falitz had some difficulty understanding Ingersol's opinion.

"Herman, what do you mean, some difficulty understanding him? It's either genuine or a forgery or he isn't sure. Which?"

"It's genuine, but—" Herman slurped and said something I couldn't understand.

"Herman, why do I imagine that you are eating?"

"Because I am eating."

"But, Herman, it's most unpleasant to be at the other end of the telephone when you are eating."

"It's more unpleasant to be at my end when I feel like eating and don't."

"I'll phone Ingersol and find out why you can't understand him. Maybe he, too, eats nuts when he talks."

I phoned Ingersol. He said, "I'm ninety-five percent sure that Hughes wrote it."

I was reluctant to call an expert who would testify that he had a five percent doubt. "Mr. Ingersol, would you please tell me what aspect of the handwriting gives you that five percent doubt?"

"I see that you don't know much about handwriting examinations. It's not an exact science. Ninety-five percent is as certain as any expert can possibly be if he's honest about it."

"O.K., I'll designate you as an expert to testify for us, and please, Mr. Ingersol, excuse my ignorance of the way you handwriting experts express yourselves."

"Teaching you lawyers is one of the most difficult aspects of my profession."

The four universities named as beneficiaries in the will hired two handwriting experts to examine it: Grace Kemp of Memphis, Tennessee, and Montgomery Bagby of northern California. The newspapers reported that both experts had branded the will a forgery, and that as a consequence, the universities would not allow themselves to be further contaminated by the will offered for probate by Noah Dietrich.

In mid-November, Marvin Mitchelson brought Jan Beck, a handwriting expert from Seattle to Las Vegas to examine the will. A friendly pipe smoker in a suede jacket, Beck met Marvin and me in the hallway after his one-hour examination, shook his head, and whispered, "Sorry, you guys, there's no use my spending any more time with it."

"Sheila, you keep asking me if it's a forgery. All right, I'm now finally able to give you my decisive conclusion. I'm not sure."

Herman Falitz contacted another handwriting expert, Daniel Casey of Atlanta and arranged for him to fly to Las Vegas to examine the will. Casey had worked for thirty years as a handwriting expert for the U.S. Postal Department. In Casey's letter to me he wrote:

Howard Hughes is the probable author. There is good similarity in writing habit throughout all of the documents. The writing in the will was not made at the slow speed expected in a simulation attempted by a forger.

Casey's report pointed out numerous similarities which supported his conclusion, including the writing of the word *of,* the formation of *p*'s, *t*-crossings, and ending strokes which:

are not characteristic of simulation attempts. And in my opinion, a forger copying another person's handwriting would not allow misspellings of words and retraced letters.

In late November, Marvin Mitchelson brought Lon Thomas, an expert from Gilroy, California, to Las Vegas to examine the will. Marvin phoned me from Las Vegas. "Thomas has some compliments for Melvin Dummar. You might want to pass them on to Melvin. He said that the writer of the will obviously studied hard and made a diligent attempt to copy Hughes' handwriting. Diligent, he said. He said that the forgery was good enough to fool a lot of experts. Melvin ought to like that."

Polly Jean Pfau wrote, "It is my final, definite, firm conclusion that the writer of the questioned will was Howard R. Hughes."

By the end of November there was only one more handwriting expert still to examine the original will for our side: Henri Ollivier of Marseilles. By this time, Mitchelson and Falitz had brought to Las Vegas five American experts to examine the will. Three—Pfau, Ingersol, and Casey—found it to be genuine. Two—Beck and Thomas—found it to be a forgery. I found it to be confusing.

14. THE RIDE IN THE DESERT

When Yoakum and Bittle scheduled the deposition of Melvin Dummar in Salt Lake City on December 7, 1976, the time had come for me to meet Melvin Dummar. The initial question was: Is Melvin Dummar telling the truth?

If so, would his story hold up under the stress of a pressured cross-examination? Could a domineering examiner push dumb Dummar into changing his story, and make him look like a liar even though he weren't one?

Since Melvin Dummar was a resident of Utah, he could not legally be compelled to testify in Nevada, but if he did not, the contestants could read his deposition testimony to the jury. Therefore, the probate of the Mormon will could hinge on the quality of the testimony of Melvin Dummar in his coming deposition.

The issue was clear. If Howard Hughes had never met Melvin, the will had to be a forgery.

Roger Dutson, Dummar's lawyer, working for a contingent fee, stood to earn $10 million to $20 million if Dummar received his one sixteenth, and so Dutson wanted his client properly prepared for his deposition. But Dutson knew the risk in bringing his client to me. I owed no duty to his client, and I had warned Dutson that I would try to break Dummar, and if Dummar were lying, I would not only withdraw the petition for probate, I would inform the court that Dummar was involved in the forgery.

One examination technique I planned to use with Dummar was to pretend that I wanted him to add a false detail to his story to support it. If a liar believes that the detail will help his story, he is likely to add it. If Dummar added the detail, we would know that he was either a liar or that he could be persuaded to embellish his story and made to look like a liar. And I planned to pretend that I wanted him to eliminate some detail he claimed he remembered. If he eliminated the detail, he would be either a liar or weak enough to be pushed into looking like one.

I asked Stanley Fairfield and Eli Blumenfeld to sit in on this crucial interview with Dummar. Roger Dutson, in his early forties with thinning light brown hair, wore frameless glasses, spoke softly and slowly, and you just knew that he ate a lot of fruits and vegetables. Roger Dutson was the kind of man who, if it meant a prize of a million dollars upon his producing one person who didn't like him, would lose.

Dutson introduced his client as though he were presenting us to the crown prince. Melvin Dummar, five feet ten, fifty pounds overweight, fat bulging above and below his beltline, was thirty-five years old but looked twenty. He wore an open-necked blue sport shirt and spoke in a nasal twang never moving his lips more than necessary and usually less. Melvin sat back tensed in the center chair in front of my desk, and as I lit my pipe, I looked at this boyish blob of blubber and thought, If this hick thinks he can lie to me, he's crazy!

"How do you feel, Mr. Dummar?"

"Fine."

"Are you relaxed?"

"Yes, sir."

"You're lying! You're scared shitless that your phony story is going to be cracked and that you're going to be dragged off to jail! Now, when I ask you a question, am I going to get a truthful answer?"

"Yes, sir."

"Let's start again. How do you feel, Mr. Dummar?"

"Real lousy."

"That's better. Why, Mr. Dummar, do you feel real lousy?"

"I dunno."

"Now, listen carefully! If this will is a fake and you tell us today when and where and how it was written, and by whom so that this case can end without the waste of any more time or money or energy— especially mine—I'll inform the court that you've repented, and I promise you'll get straight probation. What about it?"

I looked at him and waited for an answer. He looked at me and waited for a question. I said, "What's your answer?"

"To what?"

"Are you ready to confess?"

"To what?"

"To what! To your involvement in the forgery of the Mormon will!"

"I din't have nothin' to do with writin' that will."

"Do you expect us to believe that Howard Hughes wrote it?"

"I never said who wrote it."

"Did you pick up Howard Hughes in the desert and give him a ride to Las Vegas?"

"The old man I picked up said his name was Howard Hughes, but I din't think it was him."

"You never had any other contact in your life with Howard Hughes?"

"No."

"If Howard Hughes wasn't the old man you picked up in the desert, Howard Hughes would never have known your name, would he?"

"I don't see how he could've. Who would've told him my name?"

"Let's start at the beginning of your trip from Gabbs the night you say you picked up an old man in the desert. When did you make the trip?"

"Around the end of December 1967."

"Where were you going?"

"To Los Angeles."

"Why?"

"My wife, Linda, an' me, we lived in Gabbs with our daughter, Darcy. An' my wife an' another guy an' Darcy, they went to Los Angeles. An' I went down to get Darcy an' Linda back."

"Anybody with you in the car?"

"No."

"After you left Gabbs, did you stop anywhere?"

"At Tonopah."

"What time did you leave Tonopah?"

"Around midnight."

"Melvin, for you to be believed by the jury, it's essential that you remember certain details. You now recall looking at your watch. Was it five to twelve? Two minutes after twelve?"

"I don't remember lookin' at my watch. I don't remember if I had a watch, even."

"After you left Tonopah, what was the next thing that happened?"

"I drove down toward L.A. an' decided to stop an' drive off the highway to go to the bathroom."

"How far did you drive off the highway?"

"About a hunnerd yards."

"Why that far?"

"I din't want nobody watchin', you know."

"Yes, I know, but you didn't have to drive a hundred yards to avoid an audience."

"Well, this little side road started goin' away from the highway, but then it turned an' it kept goin' along with the highway."

"What happened next?"

"I stopped my car. My lights was on an' I seen a man layin' on the road. He was face down an' his arms was out. I thought he was dead. I got outa my car an' walked over to him. When I seen he was movin' I figured he wasn't dead."

"How was the man dressed?"

"He had on pants an' a tan shirt."

"What color were his pants?"

"I don't remember."

"Yes, you do! If you can remember the color of his shirt, you can remember the color of his pants. If a jury's going to believe you, Melvin, we've got to have the color of those pants. What color?"

"I jest don't remember."

"I'll help you, Melvin. You stand to clear over fifty million dollars after taxes if the jury believes you. Now, what was the color of his pants? Any color, Melvin—use your head—any color!"

"I sure wish I could remember. But I jest cain't picture his pants."

"Was there a jacket near the man?"

"I don't remember seein' one."

"This was in December around midnight. What would you say the temperature was?"

"Maybe twenny degrees."

"Above or below?"

"Above or below what?"

"Jesus Christ! Zero!"

"Above."

"You say you found a man lying on this road, wearing only a shirt, around midnight with the temperature around twenty degrees above zero and you expect us to believe that?"

"That's what happened."

"Melvin, your story has to be believable. It's not believable that a man would be on that road wearing only a shirt at midnight with the temperature twenty degrees above zero. Now, Melvin, the man was wearing a jacket over that tan shirt, wasn't he?"

"No, sir, the man wasn't wearin' no jacket. An' I cain't say he was. I jest cain't."

"What did you do when you got to the man?"

"I bent down an' I says somethin' like, 'Are you all right?' An' he says somethin' like, 'I'm all right.' I put my arms under his an' helped him get up. Then I walked him to the car."

"I'm going to tell you something very few people know. At the end of December 1967, Howard Hughes weighed close to two hundred pounds. Now, what was the weight of the man you lifted up?"

"This old man was real skinny. It was like liftin' up bones with real soft flesh. He wasn't no two hunnerd pounds."

"Howard Hughes was about six feet three inches tall. How tall was the man you picked up?"

"I dunno. He was stooped over an' shakin' real bad an' his arms was crossed over his middle an' he din't stand straight up."

"What did the two of you say to each other?"

"I kept sayin, 'Do you wanna go to a hospital? Are you all right? What happened?' An' 'Do you want me to call the police?' An' he kept sayin',

'No, I'm all right.' He din't want to go to no hospital an' he din't want me to call the police. I says, 'I'm on my way to Los Angeles,' an' he says would I drop him off in Las Vegas. An' I says, 'Sure, it's on the way.' So, we got to my car an' he sat in front with me an' I drove to Las Vegas."

"Did you do anything else before you left the scene?"

"I din't go to the bathroom."

"Why not? Are you going to tell us you didn't go to the bathroom because you couldn't find a bathroom?"

"If I had went to the bathroom, I'd tell you. But I cain't tell you that, 'cause I don't remember doin' that."

"Do you expect us to believe that you stopped to do something and then drove off without doing what you stopped for?"

"I know it don't sound so good, but I gotta tell it like it was."

"What did the man look like?"

"He was kinda old. An' I remember blood had came down from behind his left ear. They was bloodstains on the collar of his shirt, I remember that. The bloodstains was dry—it wasn't drippin' down in the car or nothin'."

"And you remember a detail like that after nine years?"

"I remember it."

"No, you don't! You think you remember it. To be believed by a jury, you've got to be flexible on a detail like this. Fifty million after taxes, Melvin! Now, you aren't sure you saw those bloodstains, are you?"

"I'm sure I saw 'em."

"What else did you notice about the man?"

"He had a scar or somethin' discolored under his left eye."

"Was it a scar or not?"

"I think it was a scar. I ain't real sure."

"You've got to be sure! If you're not sure about this, that jury isn't going to be sure about you. Melvin, tell me you're sure."

"I ain't sure."

"Did you stop the car after you picked up the man and before you got to Las Vegas?"

"No."

"As you were driving, you were looking straight ahead, weren't you?"

"Yeah."

"Then when was it that you observed on your passenger's face the scar that maybe wasn't a scar and the dried bloodstains?"

"Well, when I was drivin' I'd look at him every now an' then an' this is what I seen. I remember he made me real nervous."

"Why?"

"'Cause every time I looked at him, I seen him starin' at me. I figured I got a real nut in the car, probably a wino, an' I din't know what he might do."

"Did the man appear to be hurt?"

"When I first picked him up he was shakin' real bad, but later when we was drivin' he wasn't shakin' no more."

"Did you say anything to the man during the drive?"

"I told him I was goin' down to Los Angeles to try to get my little daughter back an' I told him about the job I had in Gabbs."

"What was your job in Gabbs?"

"Baggin' magnesium for Basic Industries. An' he ast me about my other jobs, an' I told him I worked for the milk company in L.A. an' for my dad in his lath an' plasterin' business. An' I told him I wanned to get a better job an' I tried different places in L.A. like Hughes Aircraft Company an' I couldn't get no job there. Then the man says he knew a lot about Hughes Aircraft Company 'cause his name is Howard Hughes."

"Did you believe the man?"

"A course not. What would Howard Hughes be doin' out there in the desert?"

"Did you wonder why he would lie to you?"

"All I remember is, I thought he was drunk or crazy or somethin' an' I wished he wasn't in my car."

"When he told you his name was Howard Hughes, what did you say to him?"

"I don't remember that I said nothin'. All I remember is that I felt real uncomfortable-like. He kept starin' at me when I was talkin' to him, an' it's night an' we wasn't near no town or nothin' an' I wished we was in Las Vegas an' I could get this old guy outa my car."

"Did the man ask you your name?"

"Yeah, he wanned to know my name, an' I told him."

"Did he write it down?"

"No. He jest ast me many times what my name was."

"Why did he keep asking you?"

"I dunno."

"What happened when you got to Las Vegas?"

"He says, will I take him to the back a the Sands Hotel an' let him out. So I let him out at the Sands, an' that's all."

"No, Melvin. At that time, Howard Hughes lived in the Desert Inn. Wasn't that the hotel that the old man told you to drive him to?"

"No, it was the Sands."

"Melvin, you're describing an event that occurred nine years ago. Surely you can't be that positive about the name of the hotel."

"But I am positive."

"Melvin, listen to me! The name 'Desert Inn' suggests the Sahara Desert and sand. And the name 'Sands' suggests the Sahara and desert. Couldn't you easily confuse one of those names with one of the others?"

"Yeah, I could easily confuse the names."

"Now, what was the name of the hotel that the old man told you he wanted to go to?"

"The Sands."

"How did the two of you say goodbye to each other?"

"I don't remember sayin' goodbye. Oh, yeah, I do remember that when he got outa my car, he says to me, did I have any loose change on me I could loan him. I had some coins in my pocket an' I give him a coin or two."

"Did the man say something like, 'Thank you, son, I'll remember you in my will for your kindness'? Come on, Melvin, it would help us a great deal, if he said that. He did, didn't he?"

"No, he din't say nothin' like that."

"What did you do next?"

"I drove away to get outa there an' back on the highway."

"Describe his hair, if any."

"Kinda straggly-like. Sorta gray an' real mussed."

"Was the man clean-shaven?"

"He had some kinda whiskers, but I don't remember that real good."

"Then, how is it you remember the dried blood down his left ear?"

"I dunno. I remember the blood. I don't remember much about his whiskers."

"Melvin, that man wasn't Howard Hughes, was he?"

"I din't think so at the time. But now that this will has my name in it, that old man musta been him. How else could my name be in a will of Howard Hughes if that old man wasn't him?"

"After this incident, did you tell anybody about it?"

"Yeah, I think I did. But except for my father-in-law, I don't remember tellin' nobody about it. But I guess I did."

"What do you mean you guess you did?"

Dutson said, "We've interviewed dozens of people that Mel had contact with about that time, both in Gabbs and in Los Angeles. We have statements from several people who recalled that Mel told them that he picked up an old bum in the desert who said that his name was Howard Hughes. Mel didn't believe that he really picked up Howard Hughes and the story was told as sort of a joke."

I turned back to Melvin. "Melvin, did you save this man's life by picking him up and taking him in your car and driving him back to Las Vegas?"

"No."

"Do you feel that what you did would warrant your being named as a beneficiary in a will to take possibly a hundred and fifty million dollars?"

"No."

"Melvin, there are four lawyers in this room. We'd all like you to admit the truth, but we don't need your admission. We know the truth. We all know that the will was forged and that your name is in it because either you are the forger or you're in a conspiracy with the forger." I stared at Melvin for an indication that he wanted to deny it. No indication.

"Melvin, there is no way that Howard Hughes could have been out in the desert at the time you claim to have picked up an old man. His personal aides have given us documentary proof that Howard Hughes was in the Desert Inn at the time you say you picked him up. Those aides have logs in which they recorded Howard Hughes' every movement twenty-four hours a day! Those aides are all ex-FBI agents. They're also all Mormons, and therefore, highly credible. And they've shown us those logs. That's how we know this will is a fake. If you leave this room without confessing, we're going to see to it that you rot in prison until you can't get it up anymore." I waited for Melvin to speak.

"I don't know nothin' about who wrote that will if Howard Hughes din't." Melvin's eyes watered and he looked as though he were telling us that he didn't have enough money to bury his cat.

"Melvin, do you know anything about the delivery of this will to the Mormon Church Headquarters Building on the 27th of April, 1976?"

"I don't know nothin' about it."

"Would you submit to a lie detector test?"

"Sure, I would."

Dutson said, "Now wait a minute! I have a duty to my client. There are some Fifth Amendment problems. And I'm not confident that that machine is reliable. I'd have to look into the qualifications of the expert. And I think I ought to talk this matter over with my partner. I'll let you know in the next day or two."

I looked at Eli and Stanley and asked, "Anybody have any questions for him?" Nobody did.

I turned back to Melvin. "I apologize for the unpleasantness. I lied when I told you we had evidence that the will is a forgery. We have a great deal of evidence that it's not a forgery. And I'm sure I speak for everyone in this room when I tell you that we believe you, Melvin."

Melvin relaxed in his chair for the first time since he had come into my office, and tried to smile, but he couldn't because he had to cry.

15. THE MAN FROM MARSEILLES

After Melvin Dummar and Roger Dutson left my office, Stanley said, "I believe him! He held up every time you leaned on him. But how in hell are we going to get a jury to believe him?"

Eli said, "He picked up an old man in the desert. I believe that. The part of his story that troubles me is that that old man was Howard Hughes."

"No," I said, "that the old man was Howard Hughes isn't part of Dummar's story. Dummar never said that the old man was Howard Hughes."

Stanley said, "Why would Howard Hughes be alone out in the middle of the Nevada—wait! Could he have been in a fight and dumped there?"

"Dumped from where?" Eli said. "Some old drunk could have had a problem in a nearby whorehouse and been dumped out in the desert, but Howard Hughes?"

I walked to the west window and looked down at the cement of Century City and across the Avenue of the Stars at most of West Los Angeles, and at the pale-blue strip of Pacific Ocean. "But, what liar would make up a story as unbelievable as that?"

During the week after my interview with Melvin Dummar I phoned Roger Dutson three times to ask him if he had made up his mind about submitting his client to a lie detector test, and each time Roger told me that he and his partner were still gathering information on the reliability of the polygraph. I asked Eli to get me the names of the top polygraph experts in the country.

By early December there was still no report from Jeffrey Carroll in London.

The last of our European experts to come to Las Vegas to examine the original will was Henri Ollivier of Marseilles. Henri Ollivier, a doctor of medicine as well as doctor of police science at Marseilles University, was the director of the Laboratoire Interregional. He had specialized for over thirty years in the detection of forgeries, had testified as an expert countless times, and was a prolific writer and lecturer on forensic handwriting. Interpol had referred its difficult cases to Ollivier for a decade, and called him the most competent handwriting expert in Europe. In 1956, Henri Ollivier was awarded the highest medal given by France, the Légion d'Honneur for his expertise in the detection of forgery.

In my office, Marvin Mitchelson proudly introduced me to the rotund sixty-eight-year-old Henri Ollivier and to his chunky fifty-year-old traveling companion, Madame Coulet. Since neither of our visitors spoke English, Marvin had hired an interpreter, Honoré Comet, a French instructor in one of those learn-to-speak-it-now language schools. Monsieur Ollivier, wearing gray flannel slacks and a dark-blue double-breasted blazer, was as volatile as his Parisian countryman Pierre

Faideau was subdued. The translator said for Ollivier, "I am positive! Absolutely! It is indisputably the same hand! Monsieur Howard Hughes wrote the will I examined in Las Vegas!"

Then Ollivier said something more, and as we heard the translation— "If anyone can prove me wrong, I will place my head on the guillotine!"—Ollivier gestured like an Italian tenor after the last high C, with his arms up high, the backs of his hands facing out, and a look that asked, How did you like that one?

One week after my interview with Dummar, I phoned Roger Dutson a fourth time to ask if he had made up his mind about submitting his client to a lie detector test. Roger told me he was still unable to convince his partner that the test was reliable, that he was looking into the qualifications of several polygraph experts, and that he would give me an answer in a few days. That same day, Eli reported back that he had talked to polygraph experts in six police departments and had phoned his friends in Washington, D.C., and that everyone named the same man as the top expert in the country: Dr. David Raskin, who had recently been given a $100,000 grant by the Department of Justice for research in deception-detection techniques. Dr. Raskin had written extensively in this field and had testified in many cases throughout the country. By coincidence, Dr. David Raskin's office was in Salt Lake City. I suggested to Eli that he phone Dr. Raskin to ask if he would give a polygraph test to Melvin Dummar, and, if so, what his fee would be.

Two hours later, Eli phoned back. "Dr. Raskin said he would not give a polygraph test to Melvin Dummar because—Hal, are you ready for this?—because Dr. Raskin already gave a polygraph test to Melvin Dummar! Four days ago!"

"Did you ask him what the result was?"

"He said he couldn't give me this information without Roger Dutson's permission. Now, if you'll look down at the front of your suit, you may notice what your Mormon buddy Roger Dutson has been shoveling at you from Salt Lake City all week."

I looked. Then I phoned Roger Dutson. "Roger, are you still trying to convince your partner to allow Melvin to take a lie detector test?"

"Yes, we're still arguing about it."

"Would you please stop arguing about it long enough to pull Dr. David Raskin's report out of your desk and read me the last paragraph?"

"How did you—well, I don't—you see, this may be a confidential matter and it may not be right for me to—look, I'm sorry I couldn't tell you about it."

"Roger, everything I've got is riding on this case, and this case depends on whether your client is telling the truth, and if he's a lying forger, I want to know it, and now! Melvin flunked the test, didn't he?"

"No."

"You're not going to tell me he passed it."

"Well, he didn't exactly pass it, either."

"Did he take it?"

"He took it."

"Roger, please read me the last paragraph of Raskin's report!"

"All right, here's what it says. 'For these reasons, the subject cannot be tested.' You see, the test showed that Melvin was being deceptive on every question. When he was asked if he picked up an old man in the desert, his reaction showed deception. When he was asked if he knew anything about the delivery of the will, again the graph showed deception. But when Melvin was asked if he lived in Utah and Melvin said yes, the needle also showed deception. Melvin has a driver's license, and when Raskin asked him if he had a driver's license and Melvin said yes, Melvin's reaction showed this same crazy deception with the needles going almost off the graph!"

16. THE UPDIKE DEAL

"Hal, I've got a witness who can put Hughes out of the Desert Inn!" Phoning from Chicago, Marvin Mitchelson said that he had just met a writer from *Playboy* magazine who had recently interviewed Billy Joe Updike in Mexico City.

During Hughes' four years at the Desert Inn, Billy Joe Updike worked for Howard Hughes purchasing abandoned mines in Nevada, several around Tonopah. Before Hughes died, Summa brought a multimillion-dollar suit against Updike alleging that he had used only a paltry portion of the millions drawn by him from Hughes Tool Company for those purchases, stashing the rest in foreign bank accounts under fictitious names. When Updike failed to pay an income tax on the allegedly pilfered millions, the Internal Revenue Service took offense and indicted Updike for income-tax evasion. When Updike failed to show up for a court hearing, the judge took offense and issued a bench warrant for Updike's arrest. To avoid arrest in the United States, Updike fled for refuge to Mexico City.

Updike admitted having deposited in foreign bank accounts those millions he had received from Hughes Tool Company for the purchase of those mines, but he said he did so under orders of Howard Hughes personally. Updike's story was that Hughes wanted quick access to cash without having to burden his busy executives with knowledge of what he wanted it for. To accomplish this, Hughes instructed Billy Joe to locate some mining claims which could be bought for a few hundred dollars each, but to tell Hughes Tool Company that the price was a few hundred thousand dollars each. Hughes would approve the purchases and instruct a corporate officer to advance the hundreds of thousands to Updike; Updike would buy the mining claims for a few hundred and secrete the balance in foreign banks. Then, whenever Hughes wanted some ready cash, he could simply instruct Billy Joe to withdraw a million or two and do what Hughes wanted done with it. Later, when Hughes denied that he had made any such arrangement with Billy Joe, the corporation (its name changed to Summa in 1972) ordered Billy Joe to return the millions in those foreign banks. But Billy Joe contended that as the agent for Mr. Hughes, his duty was to Mr. Hughes and not to Summa executives, whom, he said, Mr. Hughes did not trust. Updike insisted on written proof that Mr. Hughes had changed his mind and really wanted the millions returned to Summa, but instead of signing a demand for a return of the money, Howard Hughes died.

"Hal, maybe I was wrong. Maybe Hughes did get out of the Desert Inn and was picked up by Dummar! This guy at *Playboy* told me that Billy Joe Updike told him that Hughes got out and that he can prove it."

As a favor to Marvin Mitchelson, the *Playboy* writer set up a meeting between Updike, Marvin, and me in a hotel selected by Updike in Mexico City. In Marvin's hotel room in the Camino Real, Billy Joe Updike, tall and flabby, in his thirties, cautiously worded his answers, even though he had been assured by the *Playboy* writer that we were not secret agents for Summa, the IRS, the CIA, or the Mormon Church, and that we would not tape our meeting. Yes, he said, he did have evidence—eyewitness and documentary proof—that while Howard Hughes lived in the Desert Inn, he was frequently out of it. There were times, he said, when Hughes visited his Krupp Ranch, about twenty minutes west of Las Vegas, and on a few occasions Hughes was in the Tonopah area.

I asked, "May we please see the documentary evidence?"

"You'll have to talk to my attorney in Los Angeles. I have problems, you know."

I knew but I didn't care, and didn't understand what his problems had to do with the evidence he had and I wanted. "Would you at least describe the documentary evidence? Signed statements? Letters?"

"Not unless my attorney in Los Angeles gives me the okay."

"Would you tell us the names of these eyewitnesses?"

"I don't think I ought to tell you nothing unless my attorney tells me we've got a deal."

"What deal?"

"I'll give you my attorney's name in Los Angeles."

"How could we possibly make any deal with you? I know you have some dispute with the IRS, but there's no way—"

"My lawyer's name in Los Angeles is Felix Culpepper."

Since Felix Culpepper was a tax attorney with whom Eli Blumenfeld had dealt in past years, I asked Eli to join me in meeting Culpepper for lunch in Century City. In Harry's Bar, Eli and I found Felix Culpepper alone at a table. He was a short, fat man chewing on a short, fat cigar. As soon as we sat down, I asked, "Mr. Culpepper, what evidence does Billy Joe Updike have, and what does he want for it?"

Felix Culpepper took a long drag on his cigar. "Don't you want to order lunch first?"

"No, I'd like to talk about your client's evidence first."

"What's in it for my client?"

"Why should there be anything in it for your client? It's his duty and it's your duty to make evidence available when—"

"I don't need you to tell me what my duty is!"

Eli interrupted to save the meeting. "Felix, what Hal means is, we've been having trouble getting at the truth, and if your client has any evidence that can help us, we're naturally very anxious to see it."

Culpepper looked at me. "I want your word—nothing in writing—that when the will is admitted to probate, Summa's lawsuit against my client will be dismissed."

"Summa's lawsuit against your client is an asset of the estate. The executor of the estate must preserve all its assets, including that lawsuit. Whether that lawsuit is pressed or dismissed must depend on its merits. If I were to agree to let go of a multimillion-dollar asset, which do you suppose would happen to me first? Disbarment or jail? No deal."

"You're not being practical." He leaned forward and whispered, "If you want this will of yours admitted to probate, you're going to need the help that Mr. Updike can give you. And he's not going to give it to you without a deal." Culpepper looked at Eli with pretended amusement. "Eli, when did Rhoden get out of the nursery?"

"Mr. Culpepper," I said, "I may simply depose your client in Mexico."

"Try it and he'll take the Fifth. And if you subpoena me, I'll take the attorney-client privilege. Are you ready to consider a deal?"

I got up.

"Now, wait a minute," Culpepper said. "Sit down! And calm down! I have an alternative."

I sat down.

"The Summa lawyers negotiated a settlement with us a year ago. Half of all the money in those accounts was to go back to Summa. And we accepted. But Summa backed out. Now, I think that Mr. Updike would consider giving you the evidence you need in exchange for your word that after the will is admitted to probate, you'll go back and keep the settlement agreement Summa made last year."

"What happens to the other half of the embezzled money?"

"I don't like the word 'embezzled.' It's money my client holds as an agent for his principal, Howard Hughes."

"What happens to the half your client doesn't give back?"

"He keeps it."

"As what? A Christmas bonus?"

"As fair compensation for having been harassed by Summa! For having been forced to leave the country! For the expenses he's incurred in defense of a phony lawsuit! For the injury to his reputation! Do you know what this has done to his family? It's made them fugitives!"

"How much money would he be keeping?"

"Around five million."

"No deal." I got up and walked out and Eli followed me.

17. HOAX

In the notary's large deposition room in Salt Lake City, the morning of December 7, 1976, the house was packed. Phillip Bittle, angry as usual, had flown in from New York with his assistant; the Attorney General of Nevada had sent his chief deputy; the attorney appointed by the Houston Court to represent absent heirs was there to earn a fee; and Yoakum chuckled with Rex Clairbourne and with the senior partner of Yoakum's Las Vegas firm, Theodore Andropolis.

Theodore Andropolis, tall, bony-faced, in his early sixties, hadn't lost a strand of his thick white hair, and was a handsome figure even though his chalky skin made him look embalmed. He was always courteous to everyone else, but whenever he saw me, his face strained to hold back his loathing. When Andropolis took his seat next to Yoakum at the long table in the deposition room, he gave me one of those you-despicable-bastard! looks, and I smiled back and waved and said, "Nice to see you again," and he got madder.

Melvin Dummar sat between Roger Dutson and his partner, George Handy. Handy, a good six feet six with thin gray hair, in his mid-fifties, looked as if he were in his mid-seventies; despite a deep voice and the appearance of a field marshal, he had the ferocity of a well-fed kitten.

After Melvin Dummar took the oath, Earl Yoakum began the questioning. "Here's a copy of the so-called Mormon will. Have you ever seen the original?"

"No, sir."

"Did you participate in the writin' of it?"

"No."

"The envelope with this three-page will inside it was found in a Mormon Church Visitors Center envelope. Inside the church envelope was a note referrin' to the home of Joseph F. Smith. Did you address the Visitors Center envelope or write the note?"

"No."

"Did you ever see that Visitors Center envelope?"

"No."

"You ever touch it?"

"No."

"Do you have any idea how this so-called will ended up on the desk of one of the Mormon Church employees on the twenty-fifth floor of the Church Office buildin'?"

"No."

"Mr. Dummar, do you understand that the answers you're givin' are under penalty of perjury?"

"Yes."

Melvin Dummar was questioned for an hour and ten minutes about his pickup of the old man in the desert sometime between December 28, 1967, and the middle of January 1968.

Then Dummar testified that he had never read any magazine article or book about Howard Hughes. He had never read anything about Clifford Irving, who had been sent to prison for forging Hughes' handwriting. Nor had he read *Hoax,* a book about Irving's fraud.

"You never even once had your hand on the book *Hoax* in Weber State Library?"

"No. I was never in the library at Weber."

"Mr. Dummar, your fingerprints are on file in Hawthorne, Nevada, aren't they?"

"I guess so."

"Mr. Dummar, if Ah told you that your fingerprints have been lifted from the Visitors Center envelope, would you have any explanation for this, if you never touched that envelope?"

"No."

"Mr. Dummar, would you be willin' to give us a set of your fingerprints here an' now?"

"It's all right with me."

Theodore Andropolis, ready with his ink pad and fingerprint card, took smiling Melvin's fingerprints.

At a table at Big Boy's restaurant for lunch, I sat opposite Roger Dutson. On my left was George Handy, and on Handy's other side was Melvin Dummar. As soon as we were seated, I said to Melvin, "I don't want to talk to you about this case. The first question they're going to ask after lunch is, 'Were you told what to say.' So, Melvin, tell the truth and watch the calories."

After we ordered, Handy asked me quietly in that low rumble, "What do you think they're trying to pull with those questions about Mel's fingerprints on that outer envelope?"

"They're bluffing. They don't have any evidence. Yoakum's pretending he has Melvin's prints on the Visitors Center envelope on the outside chance that Melvin did touch it and will be scared into confessing. Now, what's this about Melvin's fingerprints on file in Nevada?"

"It's nothing," Dutson said. "Melvin was involved with a bad check, and there was some fuss about it, but he was never convicted of anything."

Handy said, "If they really do have Mel's fingerprints on that Visitors Center envelope, is it possible that someone got Mel's fingerprints and put them there so that it looked as though he had touched it when he really didn't?"

"I don't know," I said, "but I'd rather not talk about this in front of your client."

"Mel's reading the menu," Handy said. "He can't read and listen at the same time."

After the noon recess, Phillip Bittle's first question was, "What did Mr. Rhoden say to you during lunch?"

"He said he din't wanna say nothin' to me."

Bittle asked Melvin to write, "Mr. Spencer Kimball, Latter-day Saints, and Spruce Goose." Melvin wrote *Spencer Kimble* and *Later Day Saints*. He spelled Spruce Goose correctly.

When Bittle asked Roger Dutson for the samples of Melvin's handwriting Roger had promised him, Roger supplied us all with copies of Melvin's handwriting of the first Ten Amendments to the U.S. Constitution, and with pages of answers to an examination Melvin had handwritten for a class in management at Weber State College in 1975.

Bittle then showed Melvin a Xerox copy of each page of the book *Hoax,* and handed me a copy. "When you testified this morning that you never touched this book in Weber State Library, you were committing perjury, weren't you?"

"No."

"From April 5th to April 29th, 1976, what were you doing?"

"I was at my gas station. Or in school. Or workin' on my rental units in Ogden."

"Do you have any records that show where you were durin' the month of April 1976?"

"Yes. We have a cash register with a tape. Whenever we was on duty we put in letters. Like I used *A* for myself, an' Bonnie used a *B*. Our initials are on the tapes."

"Would you let us look at those tapes?"

"Sure."

I noticed Theodore Andropolis staring at me. I looked away, and when I glanced back he was still staring at me.

"Where did you pick up this old man with reference to the Cottontail Ranch?"

"About four or five miles south of the Cottontail."

"That's a house of ill repute, is it not?"

"Huh?"

"Is it a whorehouse?"

Melvin grinned. "I guess it is."

I glanced back at Theodore Andropolis, still staring at me with that cold look on his gray stone face. I said, "Off the record! Hold it, everybody! I'm sorry to be the one to tell you, but you might want to pause for a moment of prayer. I think that Mr. Andropolis is dead."

Everybody turned to him, and Andropolis looked up at the ceiling in disgust, and this was refreshing, because who feels comfortable sitting opposite a cadaver?

"Mr. Dummar, did you ever make a costume?"

"Yes."

"For what?"

"'Let's Make a Deal.'"

"Have you ever worn a wig?"

"Yes, on 'Let's Make a Deal.'"

"What kind of wig?"

"Afro with a lotta colors."

"Was it to depict yourself as a male or a female?"

"I dunno."

"On your first game show, 'Truth or Consequences,' did you win a prize?"

"Yes."

"What did you do on that program?"

"I had to sweep in a little cardboard house. An' they blew smoke up around the cardboard house. An' they had some women from the audience dressed as firemen turn a fire hose on me."

"For that you won a prize? On 'Let's Make a Deal' in 1970, did you wear a costume?"

"Yes. It was some oranges."

"Describe it."

"I had on orange pants, an' an orange sweatshirt, an' a string of oranges around my neck an' a hat shaped like an orange."

"What was the next game show you were on?"

"'The Dating Game,' I think."

"Did you have to date someone?"

"No. I din't win the prize."

"That was the prize?"

"Yes, the date was the prize. I din't get to go on the date." Melvin seemed to remember something sad.

"What was your next game show?"

"I think it was 'Let's Make a Deal' again."

"Describe the costume this time."

"I had the same hat on I had the first time with a duck on top with a sign that said, 'Quacking up for a deal.'"

"Who was the designer of the hat?"

"Me."

It went on like this, it seemed for days; but it was only two hours and twenty minutes more.

Then Yoakum took over the examination again. "Mr. Dummar, Ah'm gonna tell you flat out. We have your fingerprints on the outside of the Visitors Center envelope. You touched it. Now, are you gonna admit that you touched it?"

"I never touched it."

Melvin denied that his fingerprints could have been on a copy of *Life* magazine in the Weber State Library. But about the book *Hoax,* Melvin said, "I don't know whether I touched it or not."

"This mornin' you testified that you had never touched it in that library. Where else could you have touched it if you had touched it?"

"Somebody maybe handed it to me, I'm not real sure. I seem to remember somebody showin' me a book an' they said it was about Howard Hughes an' I remember takin' it into my hands an' then handin' it back to him."

"When was this?"

"Right after the will was found."

"Did that book have anything cut out of it?"

"I dunno."

At the end of the day, it was my turn. "Mr. Dummar, you've been asked for hours about wigs and costumes. Now, did you show up at the Mormon Church in drag?"

"Huh?"

"Did you ever disguise yourself as a woman to drop a will off at the Mormon Church?"

"No."

"Did you make a wig or a costume for anybody else to do that?"

"No."

After Melvin Dummar's deposition ended, we quit for the day. The next morning we were to take the deposition of Melvin's wife, Bonnie. That evening in my room at the Hotel Utah, I looked through my Xerox copy of *Hoax* supplied by Bittle. In the center of the book was a section of photographs of Howard Hughes, his two ex-wives, some actresses, Noah Dietrich, and others. There were references to William Lummis, the son of Howard Hughes' maternal aunt, Annette Gano Lummis. In the will, the name was spelled *Lommis.* If Melvin had copied the name from his research material—this book—wouldn't he have spelled it correctly?

On the other hand, if Howard Hughes had written the will, wouldn't he have spelled his family name correctly? Not necessarily. Hughes' spelling was atrocious; he misspelled the name of the executive who replaced Dietrich after having spelled it correctly for ten years; in one memo written in the late 1960s he misspelled his own last name. Could Hughes have meant the second letter in *Lummis* to be a *u* but mindlessly closed the top, turning it into an *o* for some strange reason? What strange reason? The same strange reason that made him write an *a* instead of an *e* in *Las Vagas* on the envelope, and that made him keep overwriting the *o* in *follows* on page one and the top of the *G* in *Gabbs* on page two.

There were no references in the book to the University of California, the University of Texas, or the University of Nevada, other beneficiaries named in the will. Nor was there any reference to the Boy Scouts. Nor to anything from which any forger would guess that Howard Hughes would have wanted to provide needy students with scholarships, or that he had any concern for orphans.

The next morning when I showed up at the same place for Bonnie's deposition, Roger Dutson and George Handy were waiting for me at the front door and quietly asked me to follow them to a room for an urgent private talk. George Handy said, "Last night, after the deposition ended, I went to the Weber State Library to see their copy of *Hoax*. The librarian said that their one copy, along with a bound volume of *Life* magazine, had been taken out of the library by the Attorney General of Nevada. I drove to see Mel and asked him to dig into his recollection. He told me he couldn't remember ever touching that book in the library, although, as he said in the deposition, he might have touched it when someone showed it to him. But he didn't read it. Then, this morning, I got a call from Mel. He said that in the middle of the night, he suddenly remembered. He did go into the Weber State College Library. He did get the book *Hoax*. He did touch it and he did glance at it. What do we do?"

"We get your client back here under oath and right now!"

Roger Dutson said, "If Mel comes back, they're going to work him over with this contradiction and try to make it look like something it isn't."

"I want to hear your client's answers to Yoakum and Bittle's questions. And I want to hear them now! Not on the witness stand in front of a jury in Las Vegas a month from now! Gentlemen, do you want this case to go to trial this coming January?"

Dutson said, "Of course we do."

"Then, get that lying lardass back here this afternoon!"

18. AT WEBER STATE

On December 8, 1976, at 9:00 A.M. in the notary's deposition room, Bonnie sat at the long conference table ready to answer the accusation that she was involved with Melvin in the forgery of the Mormon will. Bonnie, around twenty-five, short and dumpy with small shoulders and broad hips, had hands that had done work. Earl Yoakum began the questioning.

Bonnie Dummar testified that she had dropped out of high school after her first year to take a three-month course to become a dental assistant. She met Melvin in the spring of 1973 and married him in October of that year. She had three children from a prior marriage.

"Have you ever seen the original of these three xeroxed pages of this so-called will?"

"No."

"Do you believe this to be the authentic will of Howard Hughes?"

"In my heart, yes."

"Why?"

"'Cause I don't see no way in the world it could have my husband's name in it, if Mr. Hughes din't write it."

"Unless, of course, your husband wrote it."

"I know that's not true."

"How do you know?"

"I've had almost a twenny-four-hour observation on him since we got married."

"From last April 5th to the 29th, what was Melvin doing?"

"Workin' in our station or on our property."

"What about Sundays an' holidays?"

"Mel always worked Sundays an' holidays. Except when we closed early 'cause we had ran outa gas."

"What about the evenings?"

"Mel went to college three nights a week. An' I always seen him when he got back."

"Did he leave the Ogden area at any time last April?"

"He couldn't have."

"How do you know?"

"'Cause I seen him all the time."

Phillip Bittle asked Bonnie to write the words he dictated. She wrote "divided," *devided*. In the will, it was spelled *devided*.

She wrote "revoke," *revolk*. In the will, it was spelled *revolk*.

He asked her to write the plural of "company" and she wrote *companys*. In the will, the plural of company was spelled *companys*.

She spelled "University" and "Las Vegas" correctly.

Bittle asked her to write "one fourth" and she wrote *one-furth*.

He asked her to write "executor" and she wrote *exutor*.

"Are you a good speller?"

"Average."

"Is Melvin a good speller?"

"He tells me he's a poor speller. He usually has a dictionary with him when he writes anything. He doesn't like to spell words wrong."

"Do you know anything about the Pitney Bowes mark on the reverse side of the inner envelope?"

"A what mark?"

"The Pitney Bowes postal meter mark on the back of the inner envelope."

"A what mark?"

On December 8, 1976, at 2:15 P.M. Melvin Dummar returned for a resumption of his deposition. Phillip Bittle said, "Mr. Dummar, we were told this morning that you wish to change your testimony. Go ahead."

"Well, all last night I been tryin' to retrace my footsteps to see if I could recall where I had went an' who I talked to. I think it was the second week after the will came out, that some of the reporters kinda hinted that the will was a forgery an' that I forged it. An' a couple of 'em said to me, 'You better get the book *Hoax* an' see what happened to some guy when he tried forgin' Hughes' handwritin'.' They was houndin' me, askin' if I read this or read that, an' I was about ready to go insane almost. One day I went into the library an' ast if they had any books about Howard Hughes. An' the librarian gave me two books. One was *Hoax*. I sat down an' leafed through the books for maybe five minutes, but my mind was spinnin' around so much I couldn't read 'em or nothin'. So I left 'em on the desk, an' walked out."

"Yesterday you swore that you did not touch the book *Hoax* in the library. Now you tell us you did."

"Yesterday I said that maybe somebody gave me a book an' maybe I touched it, an' I thought maybe it was a newsman. But in thinkin' it over, I think it was the librarian that handed me them books."

"Did you cut anything out of the book *Hoax*?"

"I din't cut nothin' out of no books."

"Did you talk to Mr. Handy last night?"

"Yes. He said I oughta try to retrace my steps, an' recall if I ever been in that library an' touched that book."

"Mr. Dummar, isn't it true that Mr. Handy told you last night that he had just gone to the Weber State Library an' found that the book *Hoax* had been picked up by the Attorney General of Nevada?"

"Yes."

"Isn't it true that you then realized that we had your fingerprints on that book, and that you had better run back here an' admit that you touched it in Weber State Library?"

"My memory was triggered by what Mr. Handy said about retracin' my steps at the library."

"Mr. Dummar, you remembered all along that you had handled the book *Hoax* in the Weber State Library and you lied when you swore you didn't!"

"No."

"What about the Visitors Center envelope? Do you also now remember that you touched that envelope and left your fingerprints on it?"

"No. I never touched that envelope."

"Mr. Dummar, do you realize that if your fingerprints are on the Visitors Center envelope, it means that you were involved in its delivery and committed perjury?"

"I never touched it."

"Mr. Dummar, on the thirteenth of October, two months ago, that inner note and the Visitors Center envelope were turned over to the Chief Investigator for the Attorney General of Nevada. Now, are you ready to admit that your fingerprints are on that Visitors Center envelope?"

"No, 'cause I never touched it."

"Mr. Dummar, in Hawthorne, Nevada, in 1968, did you stand trial before a jury accused of a criminal offense?"

"Yes."

"What was the charge against you?"

"Well, they said that this check was handed to the lady to be cashed an' that I done it an' I din't, an' I was acquitted."

"No, you weren't! The jury was unable to agree and the case against you was dismissed! Am I correct?"

"I guess so."

"What was the charge against you, Melvin, with regard to that check?"

"That I was the one who handed over the check."

"Let me refresh your memory. The charge was that the signature on the back of the check was not the signature of the payee, isn't that true?"

"I guess so. It was a long time ago."

"What were you charged with, Melvin?"

"I don't remember the details."

"Melvin, you were charged with the commission of a crime. That crime has a name. What was the crime named in the charge against you, Melvin?"

"Forgery."

19. THE THUMBPRINT

Although Melvin Dummar's credibility was punctured by his deposition testimony, his credibility could survive that wound. But if his fingerprints were on that Visitors Center envelope, didn't he have to be involved in writing what was inside it. I made several copies of the photograph of the Visitors Center envelope and of the inner Smith note and copies of Melvin Dummar's handwriting used as exhibits in his deposition, and sent a set of each to Hans Verhaeren in Amsterdam, Henri Ollivier in Marseilles, Polly Jean Pfau in Detroit, and Rupert Ingersol in Houston. I wrote the same letter to each one:

Is the handwriting on the Visitors Center envelope and on the inner note, the handwriting of Melvin Dummar?

Please phone me collect.

To learn if it were possible to falsify fingerprints, I asked Eli Blumenfeld to call experts west of the Mississippi while I made calls to the east. From police-department experts in Chicago and in New York, we learned that it was impossible to fool a competent fingerprint expert with an artificially planted fingerprint. From a police department expert in St. Louis we learned that it was quite possible to fool a competent fingerprint expert with an artificially planted fingerprint, and he said he could demonstrate this. But before proceeding further into artificially planted fingerprints, I had to know if Yoakum and Bittle really had Melvin's fingerprints on that Visitors Center envelope. Since the Attorney General of Nevada had obtained that envelope from Wilford Kirton, I phoned Kirton and asked him to find out the results of the AG's examination of it. Kirton said he would try.

Four days after I had rushed my letter to Hans Verhaeren, I received a phone call from him in Holland. "The writing on the envelope addressed to President Kimball is disguised. And it is the same writing as that on the note concerning Joseph F. Smith. I have compared this writing with the exemplars of the handwriting of Melvin Dummar, and I must say that it is quite probable that this Melvin Dummar is the one who wrote the Kimball envelope and the Joseph F. Smith note."

"Mr. Verhaeren, does this affect your opinion as to who wrote the three-page will?"

"Why, of course not."

The day after I heard from Hans Verhaeren, Polly Jean Pfau phoned me. "I think that Dummar wrote the Mormon Church envelope and that little note about Smith."

"Polly, I don't see how that's possible. Study it some more."

Polly Jean Pfau studied it some more and phoned me at my home the following evening. "I can't be positive because the handwriting on the Church envelope and on the Smith note is obviously disguised. But the more I study it, the more it looks to me as though Dummar is the one who wrote both of them."

Four days after I sent my letter to Rupert Ingersol, I phoned Herman Falitz to press Ingersol for an answer. Herman Falitz phoned back the following morning. "Ingersol said that Melvin Dummar did not write the Visitors Center envelope or the Joseph Smith note. And he's certain of it. Don't I always bring good news, Harold?"

That same afternoon I received another call from Herman Falitz. "Ingersol said that after more study, he's no longer certain that Dummar didn't write the Church envelope or the Smith note. He's still working on it."

That evening, I received a third call from Herman Falitz. "Ingersol now says that the Church envelope and the Smith note were both written by Melvin Dummar."

I phoned Rupert Ingersol. He said, "This Melvin Dummar wrote the Church envelope addressed to President Kimball and the note concerning Joseph F. Smith's house in 1972."

"Do you still say that you're ninety-five percent certain that Howard Hughes wrote the will?"

"Who said that?"

"You did."

"I never said that."

"Yes, you did! I designated you as one of our expert witnesses based on that."

"All I ever said to you was that it was possible that Hughes could have written that will. Possible he could, possible he couldn't. I said it was fifty-fifty."

"If you had said fifty-fifty, that would mean that you didn't have any opinion and I certainly wouldn't have designated you as a witness!"

"That's the trouble with you lawyers! You hear what you want to hear. All I ever said was fifty-fifty, and that's all I say now. Fifty-fifty!"

Henry Ollivier in Marseilles phoned Honoré Comet, our interpreter in

Los Angeles, to relay his answer to me. Comet phoned and said, "Dr. Ollivier told me to tell you that the Visitors Center envelope handwriting and the handwriting on the note concerning Joseph F. Smith are disguised. He cannot be absolutely certain, but he believes that the same person who wrote the envelope and the Smith note wrote the words of the First Ten Amendments to the Constitution, and the other exemplars that you said were written by Melvin Dummar."

I told Eli that there was no longer any need for further investigation into artificially planted fingerprints.

I anguished over the opinions of Verhaeren and Ollivier and Pfau. Could they be wrong in their opinions that Melvin Dummar probably wrote the Visitors Center envelope and the Smith note? If they were wrong in that, couldn't they be wrong in their opinions that Hughes wrote the will?

If they were right in their opinions that Melvin Dummar wrote the Visitors Center envelope and the Smith note, didn't that mean that they were wrong in their opinions that Hughes wrote the will? Either way, the handwriting evidence on which I had intended to base my case was crumbling.

On December 9, 1976, on the 11:00 news, ABC showed an interview in Salt Lake City with Roger Dutson and Melvin Dummar. Melvin drawled in his bland monotone, "I never touched that envelope. If they say my fingerprints are on it, then somebody put 'em on it without my knowin' it, 'cause I never touched it."

Roger Dutson stated to the camera. "We appeal to the woman who delivered the Mormon will to the Church Headquarters last April 27, to come forward. We assure her that she has committed no crime, and that if she admits that she made this delivery, and tells us how she came into possession of Howard Hughes' will, no harm will come to her."

On December 10, 1976, during a recess of the resumed deposition of John Holmes, I sat in a phone booth in a corridor of the Los Angeles County Courthouse and returned Wilford Kirton's call to my office. Kirton said, "This morning I heard from the Nevada Attorney General's investigator that they had sent the Visitors Center envelope to the FBI. The FBI reported that they found one fingerprint on it. The left thumbprint of Melvin Dummar. You understand that I must advise my client to shut off the flow of funds to your case."

"Of course."

After the call, I stayed seated in the phone booth. It was all over. All wasted. Well, it was better than finding out in front of a jury in Las Vegas a month or two from now and even deeper in debt.

Stanley walked over. "Hal, what the hell's the matter?"

"Dummar's fingerprint is on the outer envelope!"

"I knew it! I knew it all along! I knew it the first time we saw that lying fat ass on television that night in Vegas!"

Back in the courtroom I announced that the deposition could continue without us, and as Phillip Bittle growled, "You can't leave," Stanley and I left and walked across the street to the Curtain Call, exchanging obscene comments about Melvin Dummar.

Stanley said, "We called that blubber-belly dumb! He tried to pull off the biggest heist in history and used us to front for him. He used us, and we called him dumb!"

At a table in the Curtain Call, when our manhattans arrived, we clanked our glasses and I toasted, "To the end of the Hughes case! May the abortion rot in an uncoffined grave on Melvin Dummar's fat gut!"

"When do we dismiss the petitions and apply to Texas for good-faith fees?"

"As soon as we have proof that it's a fake."

"You're kidding!" Stanley banged his glass on the table and stared at me. "What do you need, a motion picture of Dummar writing it?"

"I know Dummar wrote it, Stan, but knowing it isn't proof."

"Proof! Dummar's print on that Church envelope means that he was involved in delivering the will, and if he was involved in delivering it, he was involved in writing it."

"That's probably true, but your conclusion doesn't necessarily follow from your premise. We need conclusive proof."

"We've got conclusive proof! What do you say we go into court tomorrow? We inform the press that there'll be a big news break. We tell the court that we withdraw, then we go to Texas for fees for our good-faith efforts and our good-faith withdrawal!"

"As soon as we tie up a few loose ends."

"What'll it cost you every week you're tying up those few loose ends? When we got that trial date, I began farming out every case in my office. You know what it's done to my income? How long are you going to go on tying up those loose ends?"

"Stan, I've got to be absolutely certain!"

"You're still hoping for a miracle! Dummar wrote that fucking thing and you know it, but you're hoping for a miracle that he didn't!"

"I can't walk out until I'm positive!"

Stanley tossed four dollar bills on the table and stood up. "The drinks are on me. I'm out of the case! As of now! I'm not going to spend another dime on it! Not another fucking minute on it! I'll see you around."

Alone with my manhattan, I stared at it and asked, Hey, stupid, why don't you withdraw tomorrow?

I can't.

Why not?

Don't I owe it to those beneficiaries to make sure it's a forgery before I dump it? Don't I owe it to medical research and to the orphanage and the scholarships?

Bullshit!

What do you mean, bullshit!

That isn't the reason you won't withdraw!

Fuck you!

Over my left shoulder the waiter asked, "Did you say something?"

"I hope not."

20. THE THREE HORSEMEN

The day after I heard the clincher from Wilford Kirton, I flew my 310 to Palm Springs to meet Noah Dietrich in our usual booth in the airport coffee shop. I told him about Melvin Dummar's handwriting and fingerprint on the Visitors Center envelope, and about his perjury. "Noah, I expect to have conclusive evidence any day now that it's a forgery. When I get it, I'll want your permission to withdraw your petitions for probate."

"Howard wrote it! I don't give a damn who had it after that, or why he lied about it. Hal, Howard wrote it!"

"Noah, I have to either withdraw the petitions or withdraw from the case."

"If ever you're completely satisfied it's a forgery, withdraw the petitions. But I still say Howard wrote it. I'd know his handwriting anywhere."

On December 13, 1976, in Department 12 of the Los Angeles Probate Court, I stood before the Judge. Phillip Bittle had flown in from New York, expecting me to withdraw the petition for probate in California, to be followed by withdrawals in Nevada and Texas, and he was ready to stammer his victory speech to the press. A jovial Earl Yoakum was there with his staff, and the attorney generals of Texas and Nevada had their deputies present to witness the surrender.

"May it please the Court, I move at this time that all discovery proceedings in this case be suspended. I have reason to believe that the will I have submitted for probate is probably a forgery."

Phillip Bittle interrupted. "What does Counsel mean by 'probably'?"

"What is your intention, Counsel?" the Judge asked.

"I intend to make certain that the purported will is a forgery and then withdraw the petition for probate."

"Motion granted!"

As soon as the judge left the bench, Bittle stomped over to me and ranted, "It's a forgery and you know it! If you don't immediately dismiss your petitions for probate, I'm going to have you cited before the California bar for unethical conduct!"

"Mr. Bittle, since you and I are experienced trial lawyers, I'm going to reply to you in the language we both understand. I invoke that legal doctrine known for hundreds of years in the English common law. I'll translate for you from the Latin: If displeased, go fuck thyself!"

That night on television they ran the tape of Phillip Bittle interviewed outside the courtroom after our hearing that morning. "Mr. Earl Yoakum and I uncovered conclusive evidence that the Mormon will is a forgery. Dummar swore that he had never touched the Church envelope, and we found his fingerprint on it. Therefore, Melvin Dummar is a perjurer and a forger. And the refusal of the proponent to withdraw this forgery from probate is an obstruction of justice!"

The next interview was with Earl Yoakum. "Despite positive proof that this will is a fraud, the proponent still refuses to do the ethical thing of removin' it from the court!"

The news commentator had a few words of his own. "Why do our courts tolerate the continued perpetration of this hoax? Two fine lawyers, one in Houston and one in New York, each a credit to the legal profession, have proved that the Mormon will is a forgery, and yet, that forgery is still before the courts in three states. How long are our courts going to allow themselves to be abused by this conspiracy?"

When I phoned Sam Mayerson and said that I wanted him to invite Sheila and me for dinner, he did, and after dinner in his small home in Encino, Sam and I went into his den for some brandy and for the reason I was there. A lanky, Jewish Abe Lincoln from Corpus Christi, Texas, Sam's graying curly black hair was cut short the way he had worn it as a P-38 pilot in World War II. Sam was a good friend; whenever I came to him for advice, he never gave me any.

"I ought to withdraw," I said. "There's nothing left of the case. Dummar's a perjurer. Since he was involved in delivering the will, he almost certainly had to be involved in writing it. Sam, tell me to bail out."

"Ah can't tell you that."

"Why not? As the proponent of the Mormon will, I'm in the cockpit of an airplane with its wings broken off and its engine on fire, diving straight down. Nothing drastic has happened to me yet, but I sense that disaster is imminent, and my best friend won't tell me to bail out."

"You tell me. Why don't you bail out?"

"I'm afraid."

"Of what?"

"That I might be wrong."

"How could you be wrong? They've got Dummar dead-bang! Surely you don't think that after Hughes wrote his will he gave it to this Utah gas station attendant for safekeeping?"

"Ridiculous! Why would Howard Hughes give his will to Melvin Dummar?"

"You want to tell me it's possible that Hughes gave it to someone else and that that guy decided on his own to search for Melvin Dummar in Willard, Utah, and—"

"Ridiculous!"

"Then why don't you bail out?"

"Sam, there're too many facts which simply don't fit a forgery."

"Like what?"

"Like that Pitney Bowes imprint. Like the obvious overwritings in the will. And the misspellings — especially of words spelled correctly in other places in it. Sam, you've been a DA for twenty-four years. Have you ever known a forger to turn out a piece of crap like this? This isn't a ten-dollar check. Wouldn't you think that in a job of this size, a forger would rewrite a page if he made a mistake? And why would he spell a word correctly in one place and incorrectly in another?"

"So the forger's a bad speller."

"Then, wouldn't you think that to steal a hundred and fifty million dollars, a forger would invest ninety-eight cents in a drugstore diction-ary? Sam, a forger wouldn't overwrite letters and misspell like this, but do you know who did? In dozens of handwritten memos? Howard Hughes."

"Coincidence."

"Then there are the letters in the will written with the same idiosyncrasies found in memos written by Hughes—memos no forger could possibly have seen. Each similarity, another coincidence? And there's that phone call to Judge Grant in Salt Lake City in 1972. And the fact that the will wasn't delivered the way a forger would have delivered it. A forger would go for the safety of mailing it in. That is, after he had wiped off his fingerprints. But here, a dummy drops it off in broad daylight holding it in his bare hands. Sam, these facts just don't fit a forgery!"

"But what about Dummar's story of how he happened to be named in the will? The old man out in the desert has to be the real Howard Hughes. Couple that fact with the fact of the will winding up in the hands of Dummar and tell me what those facts fit."

"I know, I know! Those facts do fit a forgery, I know that! But what the hell do I do with the facts that don't fit a forgery? Forget them? I'd like to. But I can't. I want to—Christ, I need to—this goddamned case is bleeding the financial hell out of me. But I can't! I've got to be absolutely certain it's a forgery before I dump it."

"Why do you have to be so certain?"

"You want to hear a reason? I've got one. If this will is probated, the hundreds of millions to go to medical research might be used to find a cure for cancer. I'm the only proponent of this will, and if I drop it, it stays dropped. Now, what if it turns out that the will I dropped was real? That cure for cancer that doesn't get found, doesn't get found because I dropped that will! And there are the children. Countless children yet unborn will grow up in shitty orphanages, and hundreds of millions that would have provided scholarships get eaten up in taxes—all because I dropped that will! Before I can let this happen, I've got to be absolutely certain that what I drop is a forgery. How do you like that reason? It's noble. Even heroic in a nonphysical way. But it isn't mine."

"Now tell me yours."

"Oh, you want the truth? That's different. My reason? My real reason? Sam, the truth is, I'm not sure I know what my real reason is."

"What do you think it is?"

"It may be the headline ABANDONED HUGHES WILL FOUND TO BE GENUINE. The article goes on to say: *The lawyer entrusted with proving the genuineness of the Hughes will panicked and ran out of the courthouse and from his responsibilities after jumping to the fallacious conclusion that just because someone named in the will lied when he denied having possession of it, it necessarily followed that the will written by Howard Hughes wasn't written by Howard Hughes.* The disgrace would be even worse than submitting a fake will for probate and losing."

"After the case is closed, how could anyone ever find the will to be genuine?"

"What if next year one of those investigative reporters makes a study of all the evidence about the will and discovers that Howard Hughes really wrote it? There are a lot of mistakes I could live with, but a mistake based on sloppy reasoning—a mistake that would cost so much—Sam, I just don't have the balls to risk making a mistake like that!"

I finished my drink and stared at the empty snifter while Sam waited for me to get it all said. "But maybe my real reason for holding on is even worse. But for that one, I'll need another brandy."

Sam poured a second one for me.

"I want that fee. I want the fame. And I want the fun. The three horsemen: the fee, the fame, and the fun. Another chance like this will never come again. Not to me. I'd hate like hell to wake up one morning a year from now after I dropped that will to find out that Hughes really wrote it, and that I had had this one chance in my life to do something great—to make it big, but that I blew it. I had stopped thinking! I just plain blew it! Sam, I've got to be absolutely certain!"

"Then, be absolutely certain."

In Las Vegas on December 16, 1976, in Judge Hayes' courtroom, growling Earl Yoakum and his entourage, furious Phillip Bittle, the young deputies of the Attorney General's offices in Nevada and Texas, and attorneys appointed in both states to represent absent heirs opposed my motions.

"May it please the Court," I said, "my first motion is that the trial date in this will contest, January 7th, 1977, be vacated, that the matter go off calendar, and that all discovery be stayed. It now looks as though the will I've been proposing for probate is a forgery."

Bittle said, "Then, Your Honor, why doesn't Mr. Rhoden have the decency to withdraw his petition?"

"Your Honor I would be happy to withdraw my petition. Today. If only I could be positive that the will is a forgery. Melvin Dummar was involved in its delivery and in all probability was involved in writing it. But I must be absolutely certain."

"Your Honor," Yoakum said, "what Mr. Rhoden really wants is time to create some phony evidence that Dummar's fingerprint on that outer envelope was faked on it. Ah don't think the Court ought to allow Mr. Rhoden time to falsify evidence an' to—"

I sprang to my feet and shouted, "Your Honor, this lying—"

But the crack of Judge Hayes' gavel and his sharp "Mr. Rhoden, be seated!" stopped me.

"Ah ask that Your Honor order Mr. Rhoden to either withdraw the petition right here an' now or go to trial on January 7th."

Judge Hayes said to Yoakum, "You want me to order the proponent to present a case which he believes is not well founded? Or in the alternative, order him to withdraw a petition which he is not yet satisfied he is justified in withdrawing? Proponent's motion that the trial date be vacated is granted! Proponent's motion that all discovery proceedings be suspended until further order is granted! Anything more, Mr. Rhoden?"

"Yes, Your Honor. Now that all handwriting experts for both sides have examined the purported will, I again urge that Your Honor order that the offered will be examined by a police lab, preferably the FBI, to determine if there are fingerprints on the offered will. Next, I move that this Court order that the offered will and its envelope be examined by competent experts to determine the age of the paper. If the paper on which the offered will, dated March 19th, 1968, is no more than, say, two years old, that evidence of forgery would be conclusive, and we wouldn't need Dummar's confession. Last, I move that Your Honor order that the ink on the will be examined. If experts can tell us that the ink on it was put there less than eight years ago, we'd have conclusive evidence that the will is a forgery. What we need, if the Court please, is evidence—not of a high degree of probability—but concrete evidence of

forgery such that it would be absolutely impossible for the will to have
been other than a forgery."

"Proponent's motions are granted! This Court orders that the offered
will be taken into custody by the Attorney General of Nevada and
delivered by him to the Federal Bureau of Investigation in Washington,
D.C., to be examined by experts to determine the age of the paper, the
age of the ink, the presence of fingerprints, and the identity of the
handwriter."

On December 19, 1976, I received a letter from Hans Verhaeren:

> I have read the newspaper accounts of fingerprint evidence that
> the will I examined was written by a forger.
>
> I do not know how to apologize to you, to Mr. Mitchelson, and to
> Mr. Falitz for my disgraceful error. It saddens me greatly to have to
> confess to you that despite my many years of studies and experi-
> ence, I was wrong. I do not know how I could have been wrong in
> concluding that the will was written by Howard Hughes, but from
> what I have read in the newspapers, it appears that as a matter of
> scientific fact, I was wrong.
>
> It is most difficult for me to have to admit to you, but perhaps,
> even more difficult for me to have to admit to myself, that my pride
> in my learning and in my judgment and in my competence was,
> after all, misplaced all these years.
>
> Please forgive me, sir.

Two days later I received a letter from Lothar Michel of Mannheim,
Germany. Michel made no mention of having heard the same news that
Verhaeren had heard. Instead, Lothar Michel wrote that he had
suddenly developed new insight into the handwriting question:

> Since I last saw you, I have given the matter further study. In
> reviewing my photographs of the handwriting of Howard Hughes in
> the various exemplars, and the questioned handwriting on the
> testament, I now conclude that my opinion given to you in
> California was in error and that, in fact, the questioned testament
> was not written by Howard Hughes. There is no point in my
> discussing with you the reasons for my opinion, because I no longer
> wish to testify.

That same week I heard from Daniel Casey of Atlanta:

> Further reflection requires that I downgrade the opinion I gave
> you in my letter where I stated that Howard Hughes was *probably*
> the author of the purported will. I now wish to change that to read
> "Howard Hughes was *possibly* the author of the questioned will."

In view of this, I am sure that you will no longer require my testimony.

I put in eight calls to Polly Jean Pfau. Her housekeeper said that Mrs. Pfau was out of town, visiting a relative in Vermont and could not be reached by telephone.

"Hello, Herman, what can I do for you?"
"Are you working on the affidavit for us to get fees from the court in Texas?"
"No."
"Why not?"
"Because I don't feel like it right now."
"Listen, I've paid out over twenty thousand dollars in expenses and I've loaned you thirty thousand. I want it back!"
"I don't blame you, Herman."
"I want you to tell me that you'll withdraw that fucking will from Texas and that you'll immediately prepare an affidavit that you're sorry you believed in it, that you acted in good faith, and that for all the work we've done, fees ought to be paid to you and Marvin and me."
"I'll do it when I'm ready."
"When are you going to be ready?" Herman screamed.
"Who in hell do you think you're screaming at?"
Herman screamed something more and I hung up.

Honoré Comet phoned me. "Dr. Ollivier called me to relay this message. He read about the fingerprint of Melvin Dummar and about the opinion in the United States that Dummar wrote the will. I wrote down Dr. Ollivier's words, and I'll give you a word-for-word translation. 'In the Louvre, Melvin Dummar may have left his fingerprints on the *Mona Lisa*, but that is not indisputable evidence that he painted it. Howard Hughes wrote the will I examined in Las Vegas. I have no interest in whose fingerprints are found on anything, but I suggest that you investigate the possibility that since this Dummar apparently had possession of the will before it was delivered to your court, he stole it from the living quarters of Howard Hughes. Most respectfully yours, Dr. Henri Ollivier.'"

On Christmas Eve, after Sheila and the children went to bed, I sat alone on the floor of our den, looking at the blinking lights on our Christmas tree and listening to the crackling fire and to "O Holy Night" on our eight-track. How can anyone be sure that he knows his true reason for what he does? A man tells others what he wants them to hear; doesn't he also tell himself what he wants himself to hear? One thing I knew: I had to be certain, and whatever it was that made me stay in until I was certain was expensive. The monthly loans from Herman Falitz had stopped, and every day I waited was another day closer to bankruptcy. And when I walked across the Century City mall or into restaurants or down the escalators to the parking levels, I seemed to see more every day the glares of people thinking, There's the guy sponsoring that phony Mormon will. Is he in with the forger or just plain stupid? This, I told myself, was the stuff paranoia was made of.

There was nothing to do except wait for the FBI report that would give me the absolute certainty I needed to back out. The chilling thought was, what if the FBI's report is inconclusive on the age of the paper? And on the age of the ink? What do I do then? How could I pull a confession out of Melvin Dummar? Dummar's lawyers owed him a duty, no matter how guilty he was, to protect him from criminal prosecution. They couldn't allow their client to incriminate himself by statements to the police, and for the same reason they couldn't allow their client to incriminate himself by statements to me, because I could, and would, testify in a forgery trial against him. There was no way that Dummar's lawyers could allow me to question him now.

On January 10, 1977, I received a call from Roger Dutson. "Hal, George and I have been talking it over. We can't get Mel to tell us the truth. We've tried pleading with him, we've tried praying with him—we don't know what to do to get him to tell us the truth."

"Have you tried swinging a hammer into his lying mouth?"

"We've given a lot of thought to something else. George and I are rather easygoing. George isn't used to trial work and I'm not really suited to what we need here. What we need here is someone to press Mel a little bit to squeeze the truth out of him. Mel knows that even though we're irritated with him for what he's done, we're still fond of him, and he knows that we're really—I don't know how to put it—"

"That you're really two nice guys."

"Yes, and what we need is someone who isn't. I mean—"

"Let me see if I can help word it for you, Roger. You mean you'd like to have Melvin questioned by some son of a bitch callused enough to coerce a confession out of him."

"You state it rather crudely, but that is what George and I were talking about."

"Tell me, Roger, this son of a bitch to do the questioning—whom did you have in mind?"

21. THE BLUE MERCEDES

In Ogden, Utah, on January 11, 1977, at 10:30 A.M., in George Handy's office, he and I watched Roger Dutson walk Melvin in for the inquisition. Roger took the leather chair in the corner and pointed for Melvin to sit on the hard chair four feet in front of me. Melvin grimly grabbed the ends of the armrests as he faced me.

"Hello, Melvin. Glad to see me?"

"No, sir."

"That's refreshing! A truthful answer out of Melvin Dummar. Melvin, are you ready to tell us about how you delivered that forgery to the Mormon Church last April?"

"I din't deliver it. If my fingerprints're on that envelope, I don't know how they got there."

"Before I ask you some questions, Melvin, I want to give you a little news. Next Tuesday you're going to be arrested."

Melvin's eyes watered and his lips tightened.

"You're going to be arrested next Tuesday because next Monday Phillip Bittle and Earl Yoakum and I are going to testify before a Federal Grand Jury to help the United States Attorney get an indictment against you. The charges are forgery, perjury, obstruction of justice, falsification of evidence, and a few other assorted felonies. When the indictment is returned, the U.S. Attorney is going to have the Federal Court in Salt Lake City issue a warrant for your arrest. However, I also have some good news. You can be freed on bail pending your trial. Bail is going to be set at fifty thousand dollars."

Melvin stiffened and looked at Dutson and then at Handy and then back at me. "I don't see how I can make that kinda bail."

"That's too bad, Melvin. I don't think you're going to like jail. From what I've heard, it's most uncomfortable in jail for celebrities. Particularly boyish-looking celebrities. And you are a boyish-looking celebrity, Melvin. But I'm sure you'll agree that you've got it coming. What you've been doing to your lawyers and to the press, you're now going to have done to you. Do you understand me, Melvin?"

"Yes, sir!"

"Now, the sentencing judge is going to take into consideration not only the number of lies you've told, but to whom. That you lied to the press and to your lawyers and to me isn't going to upset the courts too much, but when you lied in your deposition you were lying to the court, and courts get real touchy—you have no idea how touchy—when they are the ones lied to. I don't mean that your sentences on each count are going to run consecutively—if that happened, you'd get something like two hundred and thirty-seven years—no, I don't think that any court'll give you more than forty-two years. Now, the reason I'm here is to persuade you to help me and thereby help yourself to avoid serving a day in jail. Are you interested in listening to my proposition?"

"Yes, sir."

"Melvin, everybody's out for your ass. But we're also out for things far more important to us than your ass. The attorneys for the contestants want me to withdraw my petitions for probate of your phony will. And I want to stop paying for depositions and airline tickets in this case, and I want to get back to earning a living. But before I can pull out, I've got to know when it was forged, where, how, and by whom. If I get this information from you, I'll withdraw my petition. And, if I do, Yoakum and Bittle won't appear before the Grand Jury, and neither will I. And there'll be no indictment. And no arrest. Now, are you ready to tell me what I want to know?"

"Yes, sir."

"Good! Melvin, yesterday, before Roger Dutson and I arranged for this meeting today, I had a long talk with"—I looked at a name I had made up and written on my yellow pad on the airline to Salt Lake City—"Francis W. Sagmaster, Jr. He's the FBI chief fingerprint expert, the one who conducted the examination of the Visitors Center envelope, your Joseph F. Smith note, the inner McKay envelope, and the three pages of your phony will. He found a lot of fingerprints. On all the pages of the will. As well as on the two envelopes. Guess whose fingerprints he found. Your fingerprints, Melvin. Now, I'm not going to ask you if you handled those papers—I know you did. What I want to know first is this. When did you last have that three-page will in your hands?"

Melvin stared at me, stiffened, and sobbed. George Handy poured a glass of water, handed it to Melvin, and Melvin drank it and gave the glass back to Handy. Melvin wiped his eyes with both his hands, then looked at me and said, "The day I delivered it to the Church."

"Who addressed the Visitors Center envelope to President Kimball?"

"I did."

"Who wrote that note about finding the contents in 1972 near the home of Joseph F. Smith?"

"I did."

"Who wrote the will?"

"I don't know."

"Where did you get it?"

"In Las Vegas."

"When?"

"In 1968."

"How?"

"A man gave it to me."

"What man?"

"I don't know his name."

"You mean some guy just walked up to you and handed—all right, tell us how you got it."

"Well, it was after I picked up this old man in the desert. My wife Linda, she went to Las Vegas an' got a job in one a the casinos. She had took my car, an' I went there to get my car outa the parkin' lot, an' I seen a note on the windshield. The note said, 'Hello, Melvin. I've been lookin' for you. Where have you been?' An' then the note told me to go to one a the hotels, an' to talk to the manager in the casino, that he had somethin' for me to pick up."

"What hotel?"

"I don't remember."

"Go on."

"So, I went to see this guy. An' he says for me to wait. Then he came back an' gave me a big envelope. He told me to open it when I got home, an' that I better not tell anybody about it. Then he gave me instructions."

"Written instructions?"

"No, they was told to me."

"Did you follow the instructions?"

"Yes."

"You followed them in 1976?"

"Yes."

"You remembered those instructions for eight years?"

"Yeah, I got a pretty good—an' also, they was written. I forgot. They was in the envelope. An' I reread 'em."

"When did you first read them?"

"When I got back to Gabbs."

"When did you get back to Gabbs?"

"The next mornin'."

"No, Melvin, you must have opened that envelope as soon as you got into your car, because you never could have waited that long to open the envelope to see what was in it."

"Well, I don't remember for sure where I read 'em—maybe I read 'em in my car."

"Those instructions were written on how many pages?"

"About ten."

"Where are these instructions?"

"I hid 'em."

"Get them."

"I forgot where I hid 'em."

"How could you have reread the instructions if you had forgotten where you hid them?"

"I got 'em in 1968 an' I read 'em the first time, an' that's also when I reread 'em."

"You mean, you read them the night you got them, and then you reread them the next morning?"

"I think so."

"And for eight years you remembered what you had read on those ten pages of instructions?"

"Uh huh."

"What did the instructions say?"

"That I would be killed if I told anybody I had the will of Howard Hughes."

"What else did the ten pages of instructions contain?"

"I don't remember."

"After Hughes died, why did it take you so long to turn the will over to the authorities?"

"Because for about three weeks I forgot where I hid it an' I kept lookin' an' I couldn't find it."

"Melvin, I have a daughter who's fifteen months old. If you were to try to persuade her to swallow your story, she'd choke with laughter. I'm going to give you some free advice. Give up lying and instead take up robbing banks."

Melvin didn't move; he stared at me; his eyes watered and his thin lips trembled, and after a minute he whispered, "You mean, you don't believe me?"

At 12:00, Roger suggested that we break for lunch, that he talk to his client alone and that we resume at 2:00. After lunch, Melvin admitted that his 1968 Las Vegas story was a lie, and he said he was ready to tell the truth. And for the next two hours, Melvin continued lying.

At 4:30 I told Melvin Dummar that I had had enough, and I accepted Roger Dutson's offer to drive me to the airport. We all walked into the large lobby, we three lawyers walking together and Melvin following about twenty feet behind. Melvin sniveled like a schoolboy who walked alone because none of the other kids liked him, and I sensed that he was ready to break. As I slowed our walk, Melvin passed us and reached for the outer door before we did. He put his hands on the door and when he didn't push it open, I knew that he wanted another chance. At the door, I motioned for Melvin's lawyers to stand back, and I walked up to whisper to Melvin.

"Melvin, you want to tell the truth. I know that. You want us to hear it. And you want God to hear you tell the truth, don't you, Melvin?"

"Yes, sir, I do. I really do, sir."

It took Melvin a few minutes more to stop sniveling. Then he said, "I'm ready now."

Dutson and Handy quietly moved closer and we stood still at the door while Melvin mumbled that on April 27, 1976, the date he delivered the will to the Mormon Church Headquarters, a man whom he had never seen before drove up to his gas station.

"He was drivin' a blue Mercedes. He ast me if I was Melvin Dummar, an' when I told him I was, he handed me the will an' some instructions an' told me I was to take it to the Mormon Church Headquarters Building in Salt Lake City. When Bonnie relieved me, I drove to Salt Lake City an' done like he told me."

"Did the man leave you at your gas station in Willard?"

"No, he followed me in his Mercedes all the way to Salt Lake City to be sure I went there like he told me. He followed me in his car so close we was almost bumper-to-bumper an' I thought we was gonna have an accident 'cause he drove so close."

"What were the instructions?"

"They said that if I ever told anybody about gettin' the will or takin' it to the Church, I'd be killed."

"What else?"

"I don't remember."

"Did the instructions tell you to open the envelope and read the will inside it?"

"No. But that's what I did anyway. That's how my fingerprints got all over it."

"Where are the instructions, Melvin?"

"I lost 'em about two months later."

"Why did you keep the instructions?"

"I din't keep 'em. I remember now, I burned 'em the night I got 'em."

"Why did you burn them?"

"'Cause I din't want nobody to find 'em."

"Melvin, do you think if you looked hard enough you might be able to find those instructions?"

"Well, maybe I could, if I had a couple a days to look."

"Melvin, you're not really a bad liar. You're pitiful."

Melvin looked straight up in anguish and whined, "Why don't nobody believe me?"

As we walked in the snow to Dutson's car, Melvin whimpered, "I musta got it somewhere."

22. THE GRANT DEPOSITION

The morning after my failure in Salt Lake City, I phoned the Associated Press and said I would hold a press conference in my office at 11:00 A.M. I felt that any minute Dummar's squirming lawyers might inform the press that their client had admitted that it was he who had delivered the will to the Mormon Church. I had to beat them to it or face the charge that I had withheld the truth and admitted it only after it was told by the honest Mormons. And this could be bad when I appeared before Judge Gregory in Texas on a motion that I be paid for my good-faith work in this case.

At the news conference I said, "Melvin Dummar admitted last night that he delivered the purported will to the Mormon Church. Dummar said first that he had been given the will by one of Hughes' managers in a Las Vegas casino in 1968. Then that on April 27th, 1976, a stranger delivered it to him. If you believe either of those, you'll believe that you own a piece of the rock."

"What's your next step?"

"I'm going to make a motion before Judge Hayes to allow me to put Melvin Dummar on a witness stand under oath in open court subject to cross-examination by all counsel."

"What good'll that do? If Dummar didn't tell you the truth in Utah yesterday, why would he tell it in a courtroom?"

"It's one thing to lie in a lawyer's office. He can't be prosecuted for perjury. But in a courtroom, he can."

"Is there any procedure in the law for this sort of thing before a trial?"

"No."

"Then how can Judge Hayes allow it?"

"Judge Hayes has called this a high stakes search for the truth. What I suggest is legally impossible, but Judge Hayes may do it anyway."

After the press conference, Alex Morenus in Las Vegas phoned me. "Judge Hayes is in a hospital in Houston for his chemotherapy treatments, and he saw you on television from his bed and granted your motion."

"From his bed?"

"From his bed."

The morning after the press conference, I received a call from Phillip Bittle in New York to apologize for having lost his temper in court the week before. "And we appreciate your exposure of Melvin Dummar. Now that you've got Dummar's statement that he delivered the will, do you need anything more?"

"Damned little, but I'd like a full confession from that lying son of a bitch. If I can't get one, the FBI report ought to let me out."

"I hope it won't take you too long. For your sake, too!"

"So do I. For my sake, too."

That same afternoon I received a call from chuckling Earl Yoakum in Houston. "Ah wanna congratulate you on switchin' over an' joinin' our team. How does it feel to be on the winnin' side of this case?"

"I'm enthralled."

"Ah've been tellin' you all along it was a fake."

"If you had told me about that damned fingerprint as soon as you'd found it, we might've brought this case to an end a lot sooner."

"Well, we had a lot of arguments about whether to show our hand before trial. One plan was to go to trial in January without tellin' you anythin' about Dummar's fingerprints, an' lettin' Melvin get on that witness stand an' swear he never touched it, an' then presentin' the FBI fingerprint expert." He chuckled again. "What would you've done then?"

"Pass out."

"You never could've recovered from a blow like that. Ah want you to know that Ah've really enjoyed workin' on this case with you. Now, don't be too unhappy about it. Like they say, you cain't win 'em all."

Roger Dutson phoned from Ogden. "There's no way we're going to allow Mel to set foot in Las Vegas, let alone get on a witness stand! We can't let him incriminate himself. We want Mel to tell the truth and we want out of this case as much as you do, but the Deputy Attorney General in Nevada said that if Mel steps one foot off an airplane in Vegas, he's going to be handcuffed before he gets the other foot off. We can't walk our client into Las Vegas unless we have a guarantee that he won't be arrested. If you can get us some kind of immunity, we'll think it over."

I phoned Judge Hayes in the Houston hospital and told him about the problem Dummar's lawyer had with the threatened arrest of his client in Las Vegas. Judge Hayes agreed that a quick end to this case with a confession from Dummar was far more important than arresting Dummar, and said that he would do what he could with the Attorney General of Nevada and with the Las Vegas District Attorney to work out some type of safe-conduct pass for Dummar. I told Judge Hayes that I would be in court in Houston in a few days, and asked if I could see him on this procedural matter with opposing counsel before I left Houston. Judge Hayes said he would welcome a visit from us.

I had enough difficult dilemmas. I didn't need any more, I didn't want any more, but I had one more. Once the forgery was established as a certainty, would I have a moral obligation to expose the incompetence of the handwriting experts who had given me their positive—and well-paid-for—opinions that the will was genuine? Particularly Pierre Faideau of Paris and Henri Ollivier of Marseilles, handwriting experts who, every year, handled hundreds of criminal cases as officers of the court. In France and Holland in criminal cases handwriting experts are appointed by the court, and, disinterested financially, their opinions are often decisive. If an expert in this exalted position is incompetent, that incompetence could put an innocent man to death. If the French experts could be wrong in my case, they could be wrong in a case in which a defendant's life hinged on whether he had written a ransom note. What if the defendant didn't write it, but Faideau in Paris or Ollivier in Marseilles testified that he did?

If it were known to the Paris and Marseilles courts that the opinions of Faideau and Ollivier were unreliable, could it be that an innocent defendant might be spared from a guilty verdict based on the testimony of a pretentious fake?

On the other hand, exposing those two Frenchmen might ruin their lives. And whether some Frenchman lost his head or not was none of my business. The hell it wasn't! What if that Frenchman were one of my three sons?

The next morning in Houston before Judge Gregory, I moved that all proceedings in this case be suspended. "Your Honor, I believe that within thirty days I'll have sufficient evidence of forgery to warrant the withdrawal of proponent's petition."

Judge Gregory said, "Counsel, I understand that you have a confession from Melvin Dummar. What more do you need?"

"Your Honor, what I have from Melvin Dummar is an admission. Not a confession. Melvin Dummar admitted that he delivered the will to the Mormon Church. This means that he committed perjury when he denied in his deposition that he had had anything to do with that delivery. But Melvin Dummar has not admitted that the will is a forgery."

Without rising, Earl Yoakum said, "May Ah make a comment, Your Honor? Ah thought a couple of days ago that Mr. Rhoden was on the right track when he finally stated that Melvin Dummar was a perjurer. But now Ah find out that Mr. Rhoden wants to have another examination of Melvin Dummar. This time in open court. Why? The only reason is to try to resurrect Melvin Dummar's credibility. Melvin Dummar is utterly destroyed as a result of the deposition Ah took in Ogden, Utah, but now Mr. Rhoden has a trick up his sleeve to rehabilitate Melvin Dummar! In askin' for this delay, Mr. Rhoden is seekin' to perpetrate a fraud on this Court just like he's tryin' to perpetrate a fraud on the court in Las Vegas!"

After Judge Gregory granted my motion for a stay of all proceedings for thirty days, I stormed out of the courtroom and went alone to the Houston Medical Center.

Judge Hayes, sitting on his bed in street clothes, invited me in. "Since I spoke with you, I've been on the phone with the Attorney General and our District Attorney, and I've had my law clerk research it, and the bottom line is this. I don't have the jurisdiction to initiate a grant of immunity. Either the Attorney General or the District Attorney must ask for it, and neither of them will. But, I have a gentlemen's agreement with the DA and the AG that if Melvin Dummar voluntarily walks into my courtroom in Las Vegas, he'll be allowed to get on an airplane to leave Las Vegas when he finishes. That is, if he does nothing on that witness stand to warrant my holding him in contempt. If he lies and it's obvious, I will hold him in contempt and put him in jail."

"I think that his lawyer will agree to that. But I'd like to stop acting as a go-between in this. Do I have your permission, Judge, to have Roger Dutson phone you directly?"

"If you like. Now, I have an idea I want to discuss with you. I'm a bishop in the Mormon Church. I understand that Melvin Dummar is a Mormon, although apparently a jack Mormon. Before Melvin gets on the witness stand to testify, what if I were to have a private talk with him in my chambers? Perhaps I could appeal to him as a bishop of his Church and ask him to join me in prayer. What do you think the chances are of getting a confession out of him that way?"

"May I please disagree? I want Melvin Dummar to be afraid of the judge. If he has a session with you in chambers in which you try to pray the truth out of him, he's going to look upon you as a kindly father and he's not going to be afraid of you on that bench."

"You think I ought to play the role of the stern judge?"

"Very stern."

"All right, that's the way we'll do it. I'll give you this crack at him. You know, it's quite unusual to see an advocate for one side switch over and become an advocate for the other. You seem to be of considerable help to the contestants."

"I'm not trying to help them. I'm trying to stop my losses. That thing's got to be a forgery and I want out of this case. Judge, I'm trying to help myself."

I wanted whatever confession I would receive from Melvin Dummar to account for what Judge Paul Grant knew, and to do that, I needed the testimony of Judge Grant before I took the deposition of Melvin Dummar on January 25. I phoned Phillip Bittle in New York and told him why I wanted Judge Grant's deposition and when and where it would be taken.

"This is a trick, and you're not going to get away with it! Earl Yoakum was right! You want Judge Grant's deposition to rehabilitate Melvin Dummar in the eyes of the public!"

"You can't be serious! Grant doesn't say the will is genuine. He doesn't corroborate Dummar!"

"You know it's our theory that Melvin wrote this in April 1976!"

"And Grant's testimony would indicate that it was written sometime before July of 1972, but might it not be that Melvin Dummar or some other forger he's in with wrote it before that call was made to Judge Grant? Whatever the truth is, surely you—"

"This case is about to close and I don't intend to let you reopen it. I'm going to call Judge Hayes right now and put a stop to this!"

At the scheduled time and place, Phillip Bittle, Earl Yoakum, a Salt Lake City stenotype reporter, and I were seated in Judge Grant's small office in the Salt Lake City courthouse. Judge Grant was about six feet seven, young and courteous and, like his fellow Mormons of Salt Lake City, in no hurry to finish anything he said.

As soon as the witness took the oath, Phillip Bittle and Earl Yoakum began their objections for the record, taking fifteen minutes and sixteen pages of transcript, repeating the arguments they had made to Judge Hayes—Bittle on the telephone and Yoakum in a personal meeting in Judge Hayes' hospital room—that the deposition ought not to be taken.

In answers to my questions, Judge Grant testified that he could place the phone call in July 1972 because it was near the time of the death of Joseph Fielding Smith. The caller sounded like a sixty-year-old man. The conversation lasted two to four minutes. Grant did not recall asking the caller's name, nor if the caller gave it.

In cross-examination, Phillip Bittle asked, "Within the past year, have you made any payments on the mortgage on your home, other than the usual monthly payments?"

"No."

"Our investigation disclosed that you had a loan of one hundred and forty-four thousand dollars with the Zion Bank of Salt Lake City, and that it was recently paid off in cash."

"Fire your investigator. I've never had any loan with the Zion Bank. Never any loan near that amount with any bank. And I haven't paid off any loans in the last year."

"Well, we've had to do this in a hurry, and mistakes might have been made. Judge Grant, have you transferred any cash to friends or relatives within the past year?"

"No, I haven't transferred any cash to anybody. Friends, relatives, or conspirators."

"Judge, do you have any safety deposit boxes?"

"No."

"Judge, isn't it true that you've been in need of cash recently because of some unfortunate business investments? Didn't a recreational loan of yours of ninety-seven hundred dollars go delinquent?"

"Oh, yes, a ski resort investment went sour. In 1973."

"Judge Grant, do we have your permission to have our investigator examine the records of your accounts with the banks and savings and loan associations that you deal with in Salt Lake City?"

"Well, if I don't give my permission, you'll get those records anyway, won't you? Sure, go ahead and search all you want. Apparently you've been at it for some time now."

"Only a few days, Judge."

Earl Yoakum continued the cross-examination, and when he, too, went into Judge Grant's financial transactions, I objected. "Mr. Yoakum, I don't have the time to seek a protective order that your offensive examination end, but unless you have something substantial along this line, I'm going to adjourn this deposition."

"Mr. Rhoden, Ah'm gonna ask whatever questions Ah want an' take as long as Ah want an' there's nothin' you're gonna do about it!"

"This deposition is adjourned!" I said. "Miss reporter, please have it delivered to Judge Hayes' courtroom in Las Vegas, Nevada, no later than January 24th."

Bittle stammered, "I object to that and instruct the reporter not to type this deposition! Mr. Rhoden wants to use it to support Melvin Dummar's perjury!"

Yoakum said, "Ah object to its being delivered to the court in Las Vegas, an' Ah want to make a few statements in the record an' to this witness concernin' Mr. Rhoden's unethical conduct. Judge Grant, you may want to know that Mr. Rhoden is the proponent of a will which he and everyone knows is a forgery. Instead of withdrawin' from the case—"

"That's enough!" I said. "This is a deposition proceeding and no place for you to make speeches!"

"For you to stop me, you're gonna have to grow about four inches taller real fast."

I got to my feet. "I can't stop you, but I sure as hell can stop listening to you shoot off your big mouth! This deposition is adjourned and I'm leaving!" I left, and Yoakum continued.

23. ROCKVIEW BLUES

On January 25, 1977, the corridor outside Judge Hayes' Department 9 was packed with spectators, cameramen and sound technicians, and news reporters from New York, Houston, Salt Lake City, and Los Angeles, as well as the Las Vegas contingent. Smoking alone in a corner was long haired, bearded Larry DuBois, the *Playboy* interviewer who looked like a too tall, too lean Jesus Christ, and near him the District Attorney of Clark County and his Chief Deputy conferred with two deputies of the Attorney General of Nevada. The line of spectators went back from the door of the courtroom to the stairs, down into the lobby, and outside to the street, and parading along the sidewalk were groups of young girls with banners:

MELVIN, WE BELIEVE YOU.
WE LOVE YOU, MELVIN.

I wanted a full confession: where Dummar forged it and when and what he copied from. And how he got the Pitney Bowes imprint on the envelope. And who phoned Judge Grant in 1972. After Dummar's confession, I would withdraw the will. For days I had daydreamed of what it would be like: Melvin would tell another version packed with easy-to-puncture lies and would finally break down and mutter, *"All right, all right, yes, I admit I wrote it!"* And after I tied up the last loose end, I would turn from the sobbing witness and, oblivious to the spontaneous applause of the cheering spectators, I would walk back to the counsel table like a triumphant matador after the kill.

By 9:40 the three seats directly behind me reserved for Melvin Dummar and his two lawyers, were still empty. From contestants' table Earl Yoakum asked, "Where's your star, Mr. Rhoden? Still studyin' his lines?" And as his big belly bounced with his laugh, Melvin Dummar and his two lawyers entered the courtroom. Melvin was wearing his new country-western outfit: denim pants, a big-buckled belt, and a blue flowered satin sportshirt opened wide at his chubby neck. Judge Hayes in his black robe took the bench and ordered me to proceed. I called Melvin Dummar to the stand. He walked to it, turned to the clerk, and I prayed, Please, God, help me to break him!

Judge Hayes addressed the witness. "Mr. Dummar, under the Fifth Amendment of the United States Constitution, a person may refuse to answer any question which may tend to incriminate him. Do you wish that protection?"

"I don't see no reason to take the Fifth Amendment on anythin'."

"Then, anything you say here may be used against you in any criminal prosecution. Are you still willing to testify?"

"Yes, sir."

"Mr. Rhoden, examine the witness."

I showed Melvin Dummar a copy of the Visitors Center envelope and the Joseph F. Smith note. "When did you write the words on the original of this envelope and on this note?"

"The day I left 'em in the Church Headquarters Building."

"Where did you do the writing?"

"There."

"Did you put anything into the Visitors Center envelope?"

"I put that note in it. An' I put in it the other envelope with the will inside it."

"You were asked in your deposition last month in Salt Lake City, if you had ever seen the Visitors Center envelope and the Joseph F. Smith note, and your answer was 'No.' You were lying, weren't you Mr. Dummar?"

"Yes, sir."

"In that same deposition you testified that you had never seen the original of the purported will and its envelope. When you gave that answer you were again committing perjury, weren't you?"

"Yes, sir."

"Mr. Dummar, before I ask you about that will, I want you to know that if you lie in this courtroom the way you lied in your deposition, you're going to feel the wrath of this Court, and wrath means an order straight to jail! Now, where did that will come from?"

"It was left at my service station in Willard."

"When?"

"April 27th, 1976. About ten in the mornin'."

"Where in your station was it left?"

"I first saw it layin' on the bar."

"Who left it there?"

"A man who had came in musta put it there. I din't see him put it there, but he musta put it there. After he left, I walked back to where my schoolwork was an' there was that envelope. I read it an' I read the will."

"Was the envelope sealed or unsealed when you first saw it?"

"Sealed."

"How did you open it?"

"I steamed it open."

"After you read the will, what did you do with it?"

"I put it back in the envelope an' sealed it back up."

"After you resealed it, what did you do with it?"

"When my wife came back about three-thirty, I drove to Salt Lake City an' to the Church Office Buildin' an' I got to thinkin' I jest din't want nobody to know I had anythin' to do with it. So I took the envelope that I picked up from the Visitors Center an' put the will in it, an' wrote the note an' put the note in it, an' set it on a desk an' left."

"Mr. Dummar, as you sit here on this witness stand, are you afraid of anyone?"

He paused and I felt I had him. We were going to get the names of the instigators!

Melvin said, "Yes, I guess so."

I knew it! I had done it! "Who, Mr. Dummar? Now, you don't have to be afraid, you'll be protected!"

"Him." Melvin kept looking at me but pointed toward his left and up.

"You mean, Judge Hayes?"

"Yes, sir."

"No, no, I mean did anyone warn you that if you testified about his involvement in the writing of this will, you'd be harmed in some way?"

"Oh, no!"

"Mr. Dummar, isn't this true? Someone told you about a scheme to forge a will for Howard Hughes. You didn't really want to be part of it, but this person persuaded you to allow your name to be used. And you're sorry. Mr. Dummar, nobody here wants to see you go to jail. Now, don't you want to tell us something along that line?"

"No. 'Cause that's not the case."

Strike one.

"Mr. Dummar, let's go back. About ten o'clock, the morning of the 27th of April, 1976, a man walked into your service station in Willard, Utah, is that it?"

Dummar explained that the man drove up, but Dummar wasn't sure in what make of car. The man didn't buy any gas. The man was around fifty, about Dummar's height, five feet ten, medium build, without a hat. Dummar couldn't remember the color of the man's hair, nor if he wore glasses, nor if he smoked. Dummar couldn't remember whether the man wore a suit or sports clothes, but "he looked fairly neat. He ast me if I was Melvin Dummar."

"Was your name on a sign in front of your station anywhere?"

"There was a sign that said 'Dummar's.' It din't say my first name."

"Did you ask the man how he knew your first name?"

"No."

"Why didn't you ask him how he knew your first name?"

"I din't care how he knew my first name."

"What else did he say?"

"He said he had been lookin' for me."

"Did you ask him why he had been looking for you?"

"No."

"Why didn't you ask him why?"

"I din't care."

"What else did the man say?"

"I cain't remember exactly, jest that the conversation led to what did I think of Howard Hughes' dyin'."

"What did you answer?"

"Everybody has to go sometime—somethin' like that."

"How long was he there?"

"Maybe around ten minutes. Maybe a half hour."

"Did you stand in one place talking to the man all that time?"

"Oh, no, I waited on customers."

"What was this stranger doing while you waited on customers?"

"He followed me around."

"Did you ask him why he followed you around?"

"No."

"Why didn't you—I know, you didn't care."

"I din't care."

"After he asked you how you felt about the death of Howard Hughes, did he say anything else?"

"Somethin' like wouldn't it be nice if someone like me was in a will of Howard Hughes? An' I can remember him tellin' me somethin' about a will of Howard Hughes bein' found in Salt Lake City."

"When I saw you in your lawyer's office about two weeks ago, you didn't tell me anything about a stranger telling you that a will was found in Salt Lake City, did you?"

"No."

"Why didn't you tell me that then?"

"'Cause I din't think you'd believe me."

"Do you think I believe any of this stuff you're giving us now?"

"It doesn't matter."

"When this stranger told you that a will had been found in Salt Lake City, did he tell you where in Salt Lake City?"

"I think he said it was found somewhere around Joseph Smith's house or in his house. I cain't remember exactly."

"Did this man tell you when it was found?"

"He told me in 1972."

"Did he tell you who found it?"

"I'm not sure."

"Did this man give you any instructions about what to do with the envelope?"

"No, he never said nothin' about no envelope."

"Tell us how the man left."

"I din't see him leave."

"You said that you steamed the envelope open. Why didn't you take a knife or letter opener or use your finger and open it the way everybody else opens an envelope?"

"'Cause I din't want nobody to know I opened it."

"How did you do the steaming?"

"I had an electric fryin' pan on my counter, an' I put water in it an' turned it up."

"Had you ever before steamed open an envelope?"

"Yes. Letters my ex-wife got, an' some she had wrote to her boyfriend before she mailed 'em."

"After you steamed the envelope open, what did you find inside?"

"The will."

"Here's the will that was deposited in this Court last April 30th. Were those smudge marks on it when you took it out of the envelope?"

"I cain't remember."

"Did you notice anything unusual about the will?"

"Yes."

"What?"

"That I was named in it."

"After you read it, what did you do with it?"

"Put it back in the envelope. I took the will out again 'cause I couldn't believe what I read. An' I read it again. An' I done that several times."

"How did you reseal the envelope?"

"I took some other envelopes an' got some glue off an' sealed it back up. An' I put it in the little electric oven that we used to heat sandwiches in."

"Why did you put it in the little oven?"

"Because I was frustrated on how to seal it up. There was some places where it wouldn't stick down. I thought maybe the oven heat would help loosen the glue."

"Did the envelope reseal?"

"Yes."

"When you took the envelope out of the oven, did you see anything unusual about it?"

"It was scorched kinda around the edges."

"You'll notice on the back of this envelope a Pitney Bowes imprint. Was this imprint on the back of the envelope when you were doing this resealing job?"

"Yes."

"How were you able to get the lid of the envelope lined up with the Pitney Bowes imprint?"

"I jest did."

"Mr. Dummar, listen to me! It is scientifically simple to tell if the lid of an envelope contains only the original glue or added glue. The FBI will finish its examination in a day or two. Now, you didn't add any glue from any other source to that lid on the back of the envelope, did you?"

"Yes, I did."

Strike two.

"What did you do after you resealed the envelope?"

"I decided to take it to the president a the Church."

"When your wife Bonnie arrived, did you tell her the good news?"

"No, I din't tell her nothin' about it."

"Why not?"

"Because I din't know if it was real or someone was pullin' a joke on me, or what. An' she had been kiddin' about Howard Hughes, an' not to worry. 'Someday he's gonna leave us somethin' in his will,' an' stuff, an' when I seen it I got concerned."

"When did your wife first say this about your being left something in a will of Howard Hughes'?"

"Several times since we was married."

"What did she say?"

"'One of these days Uncle Howie is gonna leave us somethin' in his will.'"

"Did she tell you Uncle Howie's last name?"

"Uncle Howie Hughes is what I assumed."

"Did you ever tell Bonnie about your picking up an old man who said his name was Howard Hughes?"

"Not that I remember."

"What did you say to her when she told you about Uncle Howie providing for you in his will?"

"I told her she was crazy once."

"What did you plan to tell the president of the Church?"

"The truth."

"Didn't you expect that within hours after you told him that you had Howard Hughes' will in your possession, the whole world would know that you were not only mentioned in the will but the one to whom it was delivered?"

"I din't think about what would happen after I gave it to him."

"Mr. Dummar, I again offer you the opportunity to recant. Do you want to recant?"

"Do I wanna what?"

"Do you know the meaning of the word 'recant'?"

"No."

"While you're still on the witness stand, if you admit that you've been lying, your perjury may be wiped out. Is there anything in your testimony you would care to voluntarily change before we continue?"

"No, sir."

Strike three.

"Mr. Dummar, you say that after your wife returned to your station, you drove to Salt Lake City. What did you do in Salt Lake City?"

"I went into the Visitors Center to ask where I could find the president. I went down some stairs to a basement an' talked to a bishop, an' he told me in the office buildin' across the street. So I went there. Then somebody told me to go to the twenny-fifth floor. So I went up."

"What happened on the twenty-fifth floor?"

"A secretary said I had to wait. Then I ast another secretary where the men's room was. She told me an' I went in. An' while I was in there I decided not to wait. I wrote the note an' made out the envelope."

"Where did you get the envelope and paper to write the note?"

"At the Visitors Center."

"When you first arrived at the Visitors Center, did you anticipate needing an envelope?"

"No. I was gonna take it home as a souvenir. I never been there before. So I jest picked up an envelope an' a piece a paper."

"And by odd coincidence, just a few minutes later, you had need for that envelope and that piece of paper?"

"Uh huh."

"After you addressed the Visitors Center envelope in the men's room, what did you expect to do with it?"

"Leave it with the president."

"You had no intention of mailing it?"

"No."

"Then, why, after you wrote the president's name, did you go on and write *Church of Jesus Christ, Salt Lake City, Utah*? What was the purpose of adding the city and state, addressing an envelope for mailing which you had no intention of mailing?"

"So that they would know that that is where it was supposed to go."

"You felt that if you just wrote *President Spencer Kimball* and left it on his floor, nobody would know where it was to go?"

"I guess I could have jest put his name on there. I don't know why I put the whole address there."

"You deliberately disguised your handwriting, didn't you?"

"Yes. But I planned on comin' back an' explainin' it to him the next day."

"You mean you intended to come back the next day and say, 'President Kimball, I'm the fellow who left that envelope here yesterday, and when I addressed it to you, I disguised my handwriting because yesterday I didn't want you to know who I am, but today, I'm here to show you who I am.' Is that what you're telling us?"

"Yes."

"What did you expect to accomplish by disguising your handwriting if the disguise was to last for only one day?"

"I don't know."

Judge Hayes said, "Mr. Dummar, turn your chair around and face me! It's obvious that you are a liar! Mr. Dummar, your soul is in jeopardy, but I am not concerned about your soul. Right now I'm concerned about your hide, and you had better be concerned about your hide, because if you persist in lying, I will make it my special duty to have a piece of your hide! I will direct the District Attorney to bring a criminal prosecution against you for any untruth that you speak in this courtroom from here on out. And Mr. Dummar, the Nevada State Prison is not a country club. On the other side of it, if you will now give us the truth, you will have my sympathy. Now, you have raised your hand in a sacred oath. You have sworn before this Court and before God that you will tell the truth. Brother Dummar, I want the truth! Where did that will come from?"

"A man brought it to my station."

"You persist in the answers you gave this morning?"

"I do, Judge."

Judge Hayes looked at the attorneys for the contestants and then at me. "I have done my best, gentlemen. Proceed, Mr. Rhoden."

"After you left the bathroom on the twenty-fifth floor, what did you do?"

"I walked across the hallway an' into an office an' laid the envelope on a desk an' left."

"When you got home, did you tell your wife about all this?"

"I wanned to, but I jest wasn't sure if it was real or not. An' if she was involved in some way, I din't want her to know that I knew."

"Mr. Dummar, are you protecting your wife?"

"I don't think she had anything to do with it, now."

"For a while you did?"

"Yes."

"Until when?"

"Recently. I ast her if she was involved an' she said no."

"After the news media questioned you about your one contact with Howard Hughes, you said you were deeply disturbed. Why?"

"'Cause I din't know whether it was real or not, an' I din't wanna be accused if it wasn't."

"Mr. Dummar, if you had nothing to do with writing it—if someone left it at your station—why did you feel that you would be accused, if it turned out to be a forgery, of being the forger?"

"'Cause I had been in trouble before for somethin' like that that I din't do, an' that's what scared me so bad."

"You felt that the mere fact that it was in your possession would make it look as though you were the forger?"

"Yes."

"Then, Mr. Dummar, why did you walk into the Mormon Church Headquarters with it in your bare hands in broad daylight?"

"'Cause I was gonna explain to the president a the Church an' have a word of prayer with him an' tell him the story an' let him handle it an' advise me, because I could trust him."

"When you went to the Church that day, did you feel you were doing something wrong?"

"Not that day."

"Do you now feel that you did something wrong?"

"Yes."

"What?"

"I lied to everybody about it. I lied to my lawyers. I lied to my wife. I lied to the reporters. I din't tell the truth to nobody."

"The day after you left the will at the Mormon Church, why didn't you go back there?"

"I jest couldn't get away."

"What about the day after?"

"The day after is when the news broke an' all the gravediggers started throwin' it at me, an' sayin' it was a forgery, an' I din't wanna tell anyone I ever seen it or had anythin' to do with it."

The second day, I tried again. "Mr. Dummar, whether that will is genuine or not, can you give us any reason why that stranger would have left it with you?"

"I don't know why. I've wondered a million times about that."

"Mr. Dummar, if it meant the next fifty years in the Nevada State Prison, would you still say it happened that way?"

"Yes, I would."

"It may mean exactly that, Mr. Dummar!"

"If I have to go to jail for tellin' the truth, then there's nothin' I can do about it. If that's the way God wants it, then that's the way it's gonna be."

"Mr. Dummar, there are over a hundred people in this courtroom. Don't you know that not one believes you?"

"I know that."

"Mr. Dummar, if you don't withdraw this story you've been telling us, you may leave this courtroom in handcuffs. Won't you tell us the truth?"

"That's the way it happened. That's the way I got it."

I gave up when we broke for lunch. Next it would be Bittle's turn. When we adjourned, the tall *Playboy* interviewer showed me a Xerox copy of a memo he had obtained after Hughes' death. He said that the memo was written to Howard Hughes by John Holmes in 1975, and was found among the boxes of papers left at the Acapulco Princess after Hughes' death. The typed portion read:

Re: Your will.

While we were in Las Vegas, Nadine sent you a note. You told me that the note was about your will.

Evidently, Nadine believes the will she has is the true will and she must have been given instructions in the past by you to keep it secure. If the handwritten will is the real will, it could be that you had it updated later to the one Nadine has.

At any rate, wouldn't it be prudent to have Nadine send you the one she has under sealed cover and then have whoever holds the handwritten one send it to you in the same method?

The handwriting at the bottom of the memo, by John Holmes was:

Reply—will get down to constructing new will as soon as possible. We'll use Boswell and Strauss to draft it.

Phillip Bittle opened the cross-examination for the contestants. "Mr. Dummar, while it's my intention to discredit this so-called will, I do not intend to injure you personally. Please understand that. Now, were you discharged from the Air Force because of emotional problems?"

"Yes, sir."

"I understand that it's not uncommon for people to have trouble telling the truth. Sick people called psychopaths. These unfortunate people have a disability given to them by God. I believe that in this area, you have a measure of admirable respect." When Dummar winced, Bittle added, "Do you understand what I'm talking about?"

"You mean, do I have respect for sick people who cain't tell the truth?"

"No! Respect for God!"

"Oh. Yes, I have respect for God."

"Mr. Dummar, do you feel that you have a psychopathic or sociopathic disability which affects your veracity?"

"Huh?"

"Mr. Dummar, you are perpetrating a fraud upon this court. And my clients are the victims of your fraud. My clients respected Howard Hughes and are proud that they were related to him. They consider him a great man. A genius. And they are thoroughly disgusted with the way his bones have been picked over, bedsores and disgusting details mentioned—all because you have encouraged the thought that this will is genuine. It's been a spectacle! A shame to that great man's memory! The news of this will was received by my clients on the radio on April 29th. One of my clients, Barbara Cameron in Los Angeles, had experienced breast cancer. Yet, she greeted the news with equanimity." Bittle stammered on for ten minutes, describing his client's afflictions and dreams. "And then they saw you on television, as I did. You were in a deep, heavy mood. You choked as you spoke. I was kind of caught by it, and suddenly my wife said, 'My God, it's just like the women on the game shows.' I later found out what she meant."

Spectators and members of the press began leaving. Several minutes later, in the same question, Bittle said, "I'm going to suggest that you and I make a deal. Not exactly like the deal on the television game show that you appeared on illegally so many times, 'Let's Make a Deal,' but a deal nevertheless. I was a child in New York during the depression and I can remember, sir, kind of hoping one of those trucks going by at night would have a box of chewing gum on it, and it would fall off. I fantasized about that. So I can understand you, Mr. Dummar, and I think I can speak very effectively for you. And I pledge to you that I would speak a whole day on your behalf to try to get you probation if you will now tell the truth. That is my pledge and that is my deal."

When Bittle finished his oration, Melvin looked up at Judge Hayes. "Am I supposed to say somethin'?"

Judge Hayes said, "You may reply to Mr. Bittle's comments, if you wish."

Melvin said, "I don't know whether that will is a forgery or not. I know I din't forge it, if it is. That's all I got to say."

Bittle began the afternoon session. "Mr. Dummar, I'm going to appeal to you in the concept of a neighbor or a friend. And I would like to call you Melvin, if I may. May I do that?"

"Fine."

"Melvin, did you remarry your first wife, Linda, knowing she was pregnant by another man?"

"Yes."

"But you nevertheless shrouded that child with your name and adopted it. You took care of it and you protected that child beautifully, haven't you?"

"Yes."

"That was a fine thing you did. And there are a lot of other good things I could say about you. You've helped bums and hitchhikers. You've been a very nice person to a lot of people. But, I believe you have been a captive of your imagination. You have a very romantic and creative imagination, haven't you, Melvin?"

"I don't know."

"You don't? Didn't you write a ballad entitled 'Rockview Blues'?"

"Yes."

"What was 'Rockview'?"

"The name of the dairy I worked at in Los Angeles."

"Let me read that ballad to you." And Bittle did. The whole thing. All ten stanzas:

> "Well, I know it's the middle of the night
> "But heck, that's all right,
> "'Cause I'm a milkman for Rockview,
>
> . . .
>
> "So everything's okay,
> "But us poor milkmen don't get no raise in pay.
> "Well, I think I'll ask old Pete what he has to say,
> "But, I guess in another hundred years, it won't matter anyway.
> "'Cause I'm a milkman for Rockview."

Melvin tried to hold back his grin of pride that his poem had been read to the public.

"Mr. Dummar, there's a Pitney Bowes imprint on the back of the envelope. Do you realize that if it should be proved that the Pitney Bowes mark has not been disturbed, it would mean that you did not steam it open after the imprint was put there? Do you understand me?"

"Yes."

Judge Hayes interrupted. "Is it your position, Mr. Bittle, that it would be difficult to steam the envelope open and reseal it with a perfect alignment of that Pitney Bowes impression?"

"Precisely!" Bittle answered. "I will add, Your Honor, that Mr. Spencer Otis, a questioned-document examiner, has informed me that there has been no break in the Pitney Bowes imprint on the back of the envelope, and no sign of any excess mucilage that would suggest that this thing was opened by a steam process and then resealed. We anticipated this fabrication. We expect that the FBI's scientific evidence will thoroughly discredit Mr. Dummar and will prove that he committed perjury."

By the end of the second day, it was obvious that Dummar would not confess, and each time a reporter walked out, Bittle glared at him as though the reporter's back was an insult to Bittle's showmanship. That evening at dinner in the Barrymore Room of the MGM with worried Roger Dutson, gloomy George Handy, a sympathetic network newscaster, and the *Playboy* writer, Larry DuBois, DuBois was silent while the rest of us speculated about Dummar's possible imprisonment for perjury. After the rest of us had exhausted our exasperations, DuBois— every time I looked at him, I pictured the Last Supper—turned to

Dutson and said, "Would you please pass the bread? I believe him."

We all looked at DuBois, who was focusing on buttering his bread. "I believe him," he said again.

No one asked DuBois why. "Here's why," DuBois said. "If Dummar commits perjury, it's jail. And it'd be simple to prove him a perjurer, if he were one, on all this about the steaming and the added glue. Since Dummar knows he could be contradicted by scientific evidence on its way from the FBI, why would he lie?" DuBois gave everyone time to answer. Nobody did. "And what about Dummar's wife and her 'Uncle Howie' remarks? He comes here and tells something nobody else knows about, something that goes far to cripple his chance of becoming a millionaire. Something that enhances his chance of going to jail. Would a liar do that? No. Dummar did. Ergo, he's not a liar."

The next morning in the half empty courtroom, Earl Yoakum, slowly chewing gum, began his cross-examination with a prolonged stare at the witness. Finally, he snarled, "You make me sick!" After another long pause, Yoakum said, "Mr. Dummar, I have only a few questions for you. Maybe you wonder why I have only a few questions for you. Has that entered your mind?"

"No."

"Then let me review with you some of the reasons why I have only a few questions for you." For the next two hours and ten minutes Yoakum reviewed Dummar's lies, and by the time Yoakum said, "Ah'm not gonna waste any more of mah valuable time with you," there were only two reporters and three spectators left.

Judge Hayes looked down at me and said, "Anything further, Mr. Rhoden?"

I rose. "No, Your Honor. I apologize to the Court. I failed to get what we came here for. Thank you for letting me try."

24. THE MAN IN ALASKA

Outside the courthouse after Melvin Dummar's pitiful performance, a *New York Times* reporter suggested that I submit to Melvin, a far more believable story to see if it refreshed his memory. The story was that a few weeks after Hughes had died, a bi-plane flown in *Hell's Angels* landed in the backyard of Melvin's gas station in Willard. Out of the rear seat climbed Jean Harlow, wearing a leather helmet, a white scarf, and nothing else. As she swayed toward Melvin, holding an envelope where decency demanded, she said, "Mel honey, Howie Baby wants you to deliver his little ol' will to the Mormon Church in Salt Lake City. Howie selected you for this errand because there just isn't anyone in the whole world he respects like he does you." And when Melvin looked behind Jean at the plane, whom do you think he saw in the front seat, wearing a felt hat and goggles, grinning and waving?

Back in Los Angeles after the Dummar fiasco in Las Vegas, I plunged into a flurry of inactivity waiting for the FBI report. Surely the FBI would find either that the will's paper was not manufactured in or before 1968, or that the ink had not been on that paper for eight years, and I could withdraw my petitions and apply to the court in Houston for good-faith fees. On Sunday night, February 6, 1977, at my home, I received a telephone call from Roger Dutson. "I just had a phone call from someone who said that he was the one who dropped the will off at Mel's station."

"What's his name?"

"He wouldn't give it to me."

"Forget it. Goodbye, Roger."

"Wait! What if he's telling the truth?"

"What's his phone number?"

"He wouldn't give it to me."

"Goodbye, Roger."

"What reason could he have for lying? He didn't ask for any money."

"Where was he calling from?"

"He wouldn't tell me."

"Goodbye, Roger."

"I got him to agree to call me again tomorrow night at seven o'clock."

I didn't give the matter another thought. During the past ten months, I had received dozens of phone calls and boxes of letters and telegrams from people—swindlers or psychotics or both—wanting to know where to get in line to collect their shares of the estate. One claimed to be Howard Hughes' illegitimate son who communicated with Dad through a transmitter-receiver implanted in each of their mouths under a rear molar. Another was a sick old lady in Louisiana who claimed to be Hughes' mulatto daughter. A belligerent screamer from Arkansas claimed that she was an ex-mistress whose name had been erased from Howard Hughes' will by the CIA. Many of the claimants demanded that they be written into the will because they had picked up Howard Hughes hitchhiking, one in the Mohave desert in 1972, one in Harlem in 1940, one in the parking lot of Disneyland—that idiot didn't know when, but was open to suggestions—and one hopeful claimed heirship because in 1975 he had given Howard Hughes a ride on his motorcycle in downtown Los Angeles.

The next night I received another phone call from Roger Dutson. "He still won't give me his name or his phone number and he won't tell me where he's calling from."

"Then why waste your time with him?"

"Well, he told me again that he dropped the will off at Mel's station.

He doesn't want anything. Why would he say it if it weren't true? I pleaded with him to let me meet him someplace and he finally agreed to the lobby of the Captain Cook Hotel tomorrow night at eight-thirty. Want to go?"

"Where's the Captain Cook Hotel?"

"In Anchorage, Alaska."

"Goodbye, Roger."

"Let's go up there. We can't just ignore this."

"Roger, this is February. It's cold in Alaska in February. I remember that from geography in the seventh grade. I'd freeze my Los Angeles ass off in Alaska. And for what? What do we do up there? Run in those tennis-racket snowshoes chasing some crazy Eskimo around the igloos? Goodbye, Roger."

"Hold on a minute. I recorded my conversation with him tonight. Will you listen to the tape?"

"Did you warn him that you were recording him?"

"No."

"Roger, I'm shocked! And you a Mormon! That was sneaky, Roger. Are you suggesting that I listen to a surreptitiously recorded phone conversation?"

"Will you listen to the tape?"

"Of course."

The recorded voice was nasal and gruff and sounded as though it belonged to someone who had studied speech under Damon Runyon. But the man didn't seem to have anything loose. He didn't want publicity. He didn't want money. He didn't want to be involved in this case. What the hell did he want? I was curious, but it would be frivolous to fly to Alaska. I agreed to fly to Alaska.

After the phone call, I opened my atlas to see where in Alaska Anchorage was. "Sheila, I'm flying to Anchorage, Alaska, tomorrow morning."

"Why?"

"I don't know why."

"You're flying to Alaska, and you don't know why?"

"To see a potential witness."

"Who?"

"I don't know who."

"What does this witness claim to know?"

I was reluctant to say it out loud. "He claims he's the one who—I don't know how to tell you."

"Just tell me."

"The one who dropped off the will at Dummar's gas station."

"You can't be serious!"

Every possibility had to be examined. First was that the voice in Alaska belonged to a paranoid. If so, Dutson and I would turn around and fly back. Second was that this Alaskan liar wanted money to support Dummar, and possibly, if an agreement were made with him, he planned to follow up with blackmail to keep quiet about the agreement. But if so, why was he playing so hard to get? And how could he expect anybody to use, let alone pay for a lie like that? A third possibility was that he was lying in a conspiracy with Dummar. If so, I might get something from him to prove it and close the case! That possibility made the trip worthwhile. But why would Dummar in Utah conspire with someone in Alaska? A fourth was that I was being lured into a trap by Summa's InterTel agents. The man in Alaska could be a plant to tape a conversation in which he would offer for a price to lie to support Dummar, and if I agreed to it they would threaten me with the tape to force me to withdraw the will. But why use a plant in Alaska? The last possibility was that the man in Alaska was telling the truth. A razor-thin possibility. No, thinner than that.

From Los Angeles I arranged with an Anchorage law firm to have three investigators stationed at the doors of the Captain Cook Hotel at 8:30 the next night. If somebody showed up with some concocted evidence and wouldn't identify himself, I wanted him followed to his car to get his license number and from that, his name and address for a subpoena.

In cold, slushy Anchorage, at 7:00 the next night, I shivered into the law office, met the eager, young investigators, arranged for signals, and laid out the plan. With the intrigue and my old hat and battered trenchcoat, I felt like Humphrey Bogart. At 8:30 I met Roger Dutson in the lobby of the Captain Cook, and at the appointed time at the house phones, we met a scowling, stocky man with a bulging belly. Though he was in his mid-fifties there was no gray in his wavy brown hair, which needed trimming over the ears, or in his drooping brown mustache, which needed trimming over his mouth. Standing next to his taller, silver-haired friend, the scowler looked at a piece of paper and, in a nasal and gruff voice said, "Who's Dutson?"

"I am."

"An' who are you?"

"Rhoden."

That seemed to be the other name on the paper, and our unhappy host motioned for Roger and me to follow him to the bar. The scowler and his friend sat opposite Roger and me. The scowler and his friend and I ordered drinks, and when Roger ordered milk the scowler looked at his friend and snickered, then turned to me and asked if I knew Dan Harper. I told him I didn't. The scowler lit a cigarette. "You don't, huh?" He waited for me to again deny that I knew this Harper and when I didn't, he said, "Threats piss me off, you know what I mean?"

"I didn't threaten you. And I didn't have anyone else threaten you. I don't even know who you are, and I don't know what the hell I'm doing in Anchorage, Alaska."

"How come this Dan Harper gave me your name?"

"Who's Dan Harper?"

The scowler reached inside his heavy leather jacket, took that same piece of paper out of the pocket of his plaid shirt, looked at the paper, and said, "Your name's Rhoden, right?" I nodded and the scowler put the paper back, looked at me, and leaned forward. "You tell that motherfucker Dan Harper that I done what he wanned an' that's the end of it! I ain't doin' no more! I ain't talkin' no more an' I don't want no more phone calls, you know what I mean?"

I thought of the cost of the air fare and the overpriced hotel room for the night. "I don't know what you're talking about. I don't even know your name. By the way, what is your name?"

"Why do you wanna know my name?"

"What am I going to do as we sit here, call you 'Hey, you'?"

"Oh, you just want my name to be polite, is that it? Bullshit! You want my name so that you can find me an' slap me with a fuckin' subpoena."

"That's right. But only in the most unlikely event that I'd have any reason to subpoena you."

"Well, I don't want no fuckin' subpoena. Now look here—" He reached back and took out that piece of paper again and looked at it. "Let's see, you're Rhoden, right? Rhoden, I just wanna mind my own business, you know what I mean?" He put the paper back. "All I'm gonna tell you is, I knew the old man. I knew him real good, you know what I mean?"

"What old man?"

The scowler looked around and then back at me and lowered his voice. "Hughes. Who do you think I mean?"

"When did you meet him?"

"Around 'Forty-six. Maybe 'Forty-seven."

"Where?"

"At the Corrigan Ranch in Ventura. Whicha you two guys is the lawyer for Dummar an' which one for Dietrich?"

"I represent Dietrich."

"Ask Dietrich about the Corrigan Ranch in Ventura."

"Did you ever meet Noah Dietrich?"

"Never. The old man used to say to me, 'I want you to stay away from everyone in my organization. I don't want nobody to know about you, an' especially keep away from Noah Dietrich.' An' I done my job, you know what I mean? An' I never once fucked up. Now, about this dummy Dummar, I done my job good an' it's all over. When're you two guys leavin' Anchorage?"

"Tomorrow morning," I said. "Look, whatever your name is, Roger and I made a long, expensive trip up here because of your call to him. Please let me ask you a few questions. Roger told me that you said that you were the one who delivered Howard Hughes' will to Melvin Dummar last April. Where—"

"Wait a minute! I din't say it was a will. I din't open it an' look in. I said I think it was a will 'cause that's what Hughes said it was when he gave it to me. You have a few questions, have you?" He looked at his silver-haired friend, then back to me and lowered his voice. "What's in it for me?"

"Nothing is in it for you. Not one dime. Not now, not later. No job and no promise of a job."

"A job? Who's lookin' for a job? Do I look to you like a guy who's lookin' for a fuckin' job? I got a million-dollar construction business up here. A job! Jesus!"

The scowler's friend said, "Why should he talk to you if there's nothing in it for him?"

"Because he's a lover of humanity."

Dutson broke in. "I represent Melvin Dummar. Now, I know that no one cares about Melvin Dummar, but in this will there are some really worthwhile charitable bequests. There's a gift of a great deal of money to the Mormon Church."

"You a Mormon?"

"Yes."

"That explains the milk."

"This will is in serious trouble now," Dutson said. "My client denied having ever touched it. Later he admitted that he delivered it. Throughout, he's been somewhat evasive."

"You mean he lied his fuckin' head off."

"That is perhaps a more apt description," Dutson said, "and because of that, the will may not be admitted to probate. Now, if we could prove that someone really did deliver that will to him, if we had someone's testimony—"

"I ain't givin' no testimony to nobody, nowhere!"

"You may be the only one who can corroborate Melvin Dummar."

"I ain't corroboratin' nobody!"

"Without your testimony," Roger said, "this will can never be admitted to probate. With your testimony, a great deal of good can be done."

"Good for who? I don't care nothin' about no fuckin' probate. What's in it for me?"

"Grief," I said.

"What's your name again?"

"Rhoden."

"Fuck you, Rhoden! If there ain't nothin' in it for me, I ain't doin' nothin' for nobody."

After two hours in the bar, the scowler said, "All right, I'll give you one thing. You can find me anyway if you work hard enough at it. I'm well known up here. I'll save you the trouble an' the cost a them stupid assholes you got planted at the doors—Jesus Christ, I seen 'em the minute I walked in. I'll give you my name. LeVane Forsythe." He gave us his business phone number and the name and address of his company. "And this is Dick Sears, the chief architect on our project."

I asked, "Would you be willing to tell us this much? What did you do for Howard Hughes?"

He looked at me and blew smoke out the side of his mouth. "I made deliveries, you know what I mean?"

"Of what?"

"Envelopes. Sometimes packages."

"Envelopes and packages containing what?"

"I never opened one, so I don't know what was inside, you know what I mean?"

"To whom did you make the deliveries?"

"Holy shit! Do I have to draw you a pitcher? People in politics."

"When you handled those envelopes, did it feel to you as though there was cash inside?"

Forsythe grinned. "You might say that that suspicion may've crossed my mind."

I had learned years ago from Noah Dietrich that bribing politicians with cash delivered in envelopes had been one of Howard Hughes' hobbies since the late 1930s. I asked, "The envelope that you dropped off at Dummar's gas station—where did Hughes give it to you?"

"The Bayshore Inn. Vancouver, Canada."

"What were you doing there?"

"I got a message to meet Hughes there. So I went there. An' when I got there, I went where I was supposed to go an' I seen him."

"When was this?"

"It was some time—I think in the summer an' I think it was 1971."

"Did Howard Hughes give you anything more than this envelope on that occasion?"

"He gave me a large envelope an' he said there was three envelopes in it. The one I delivered was one of 'em."

"How did you know where to deliver it?"

"Later someone for Hughes phoned me an' gave me instructions about where I was to deliver it if Hughes died."

I knew that Howard Hughes was not at the Bayshore Inn Hotel in Vancouver, Canada, in 1971. But he was there from March to September in 1972. I asked, "Can you tell me the names of any of the politicians to whom you delivered cash?"

"I ain't givin' no names—an' who said I delivered cash? I said I delivered envelopes an' packages."

"What did you think you were delivering in the packages? Homemade cookies?"

"No. I knew I wasn't deliverin' no homemade cookies. Hey, you're a real smart-ass, ain't you? Look, I never opened no package or no envelope an' if I din't see what's in it, I don't know what's in it. An' you ain't puttin' no words in my mouth! Hey, are you recordin' this talk?"

We ended the conversation at 2:30 that morning with Forsythe reluctantly agreeing to see us the next day if he found anything on paper to support any part of his story. As Roger and I waited at the elevator, I asked him, without expecting an answer, why Forsythe had agreed to look for records that would support his story. Forsythe had to know that if he found any, he would be dragged into a courtroom. If he didn't want to be dragged into a courtroom, why would he look for records? If he looked for records, didn't that mean that he wanted to be dragged in and that when he said he didn't, he was lying? I felt that Forsythe was lying about the whole thing. But I was not certain. Dutson felt that Forsythe was telling the truth. But he was not certain.

25. DELIVER THIS ONE

The next day, Forsythe phoned me at the Captain Cook and said that if Dutson and I went to his office he would show us what he had found. In his upstairs office in a newly constructed two-story building, LeVane Forsythe showed us his 1976 Month-at-a-Glance calendar. For the month of April, a handwritten entry in the rectangle numbered 26 read:

Leave for Utah today

The entry for the 27th read:

Delivered will to Dummar's Gas Station

Forsythe also showed us a card that had printed on it "INVITATION," then "HOLIDAY CHRISTMAS PARTY, 24 December 1975," and on the back of it, written in pencil, was:

Deliver to Melvin Dummar. Ogedon, Utah. Gas station and groc. 1-7-76. Can't miss it. Check. Make sure Melvin is there. Vent.

Forsythe said that he had written the message as he heard it over the phone. Our host had his secretary make Xerox copies of the April sheet of his calendar and of the front and back of the card, and then asked, "How about you doin' me a favor in return? I'd like a copy of that will." I gave his secretary my photographs of the three pages of the will and its envelope.

I asked him if he had kept a copy of the airline ticket for his trip to Salt Lake City the day he delivered the will to Melvin Dummar.

"I don't know. Maybe."

"Would you be kind enough to look?"

"When I get around to it. I'm busy, you know? I'm workin' on a hospital project—a twenny million dollar deal an' I ain't got time to look for no airline ticket. You think that's all I gotta do, look for an old airline ticket?"

"It would mean a great deal to us to have that ticket. We'll stay in Anchorage and wait."

"How do you like that! Here I find two pieces of evidence for you, an' you want more. If I had that ticket, you'd still want more. Now, when I get around to it, I'll look, but—what was your name again?"

"Rhoden."

"Rhoden, I ain't gonna spend the resta the fuckin' winter breakin' my ass for your client Melvin Dummar."

"I represent Noah Dietrich."

"Well, I ain't breakin' my ass for Dietrich, neither."

"Mr. Forsythe, if we bring Melvin Dummar up here, would you give us a few minutes of your time? I'd like to see if he can identify you."

"Why not? Is that kid a Mormon?"

"Yes."

"Okay, I'll even buy him a glass a milk. Now, if you fly him up here, tell him to remember to bring his brains along."

In the cab on the way back to the Captain Cook I urged Dutson to fly Dummar up to Anchorage. "I want to see those two lay eyes on each other."

"What do you think about that calendar and the writing on that card?"

"I think he faked them."

"You think he might be in this with Mel?"

"Let's find out."

"I'll have George Handy fly Melvin up here."

"Why do we need Handy?"

"Well, Mel isn't too sharp. He could never get up here alone."

In the hotel I phoned Noah Dietrich. Noah had never heard of LeVane Forsythe, and the description meant nothing to him.

After dinner that evening I received another phone call from LeVane Forsythe. He said he had found something. "I ain't sayin' nothin' on the phone. If you wanna see it, get your ass in a cab."

In the living room of Forsythe's new house, his gracious, hefty wife brought a brandy for me and a milk for Roger as we waited for Forsythe to come in with what he had found. If he had that airline ticket—but how could he? He couldn't have delivered Hughes' will to Melvin Dummar. But Forsythe might show us something that connected him with Dummar. I pictured myself in court: *Your Honor, I now have conclusive evidence that Melvin Dummar, along with another illiterate thief in Anchorage, Alaska, conspired to forge this will and to steal the estate from its rightful heirs!*

Forsythe walked in holding a small brown paper envelope so as not to leave fingerprints on it, and dropped it on the coffee table in front of me. The surface of the paper had been damaged by what appeared to be the removal of scotch tape in two places, and between the damaged spots were the pencilled words:

deliver this one

"That's the envelope that had the other envelope with the will in it."

"Where did you get this envelope?"

"From the old man. At the Bayshore, like I told you. He gave me this large envelope, an' in it, he says, is three smaller envelopes. This is one of 'em. Later I got instructions where to deliver it an' that's where I delivered it. Dummar's gas station."

I took a photograph of the will envelope out of my briefcase and compared the writing to the writing on Forsythe's envelope. The writing on the will envelope appeared larger, but the letters of the word *deliver* on both envelopes were written with the same breaks separating the letters, and, other than a difference in size, the writing on the two envelopes was conspicuously similar. This son of a bitch had used the writing on the copy of the will envelope that I gave him yesterday as a model to forge those three words! But, if he had forged them, why did he make them so much smaller than the writing he copied?

"Mr. Forsythe, how did you happen to keep this envelope?"

"I just did."

"Did you keep the larger one?"

"I don't know."

"Did you keep either of the other two envelopes that were with this one?"

"Maybe I did, maybe I din't. Christ, I find you one an' you wanna know why I din't find all three. Shit!"

"Did you have any reason to keep this envelope?"

"No. I just din't get around to usin' it, that's all."

"Using it? For what?"

"For mailin'. What else do you use an envelope for?"

"You mean, you would use this envelope to mail something to somebody else?"

"Why not?"

Mrs. Forsythe smiled. "Lee always does that. When he receives an envelope or one of those cardboard cylinders, he saves it and then reuses it to mail something to someone else."

Forsythe said, "There some law against that?"

"No, but—this envelope has some writing on it. Who do you think did the writing?"

"Probably Howard Hughes. So?"

"And you'd use an envelope that had on it the handwriting of Howard Hughes to mail a letter to your brother-in-law?"

"I ain't got no brother-in-law."

"Would you use it to mail anything to anybody?"

"Why the shit not? Somethin' about that seems to bother you, Rhoden. What the fuck's wrong with that?"

Forsythe agreed to allow me to take his envelope to a professional photographer the next morning to have it photographed in true size for examination by our handwriting experts.

"Mr. Forsythe, would you please tell me what you remember about Dummar's gas station the day you were there to drop off that envelope?"

"You wanna know what I remember about it? I'll tell you. You can take notes. I don't remember nothin' about it."

"Can you remember what kind of gas was sold there?"

"Nope."

"Whether the building was stone or wood or what it was?"

"Nope."

"The color of the building or the color of any part of it?"

"Nope."

"Can you recall if there was a building there at all?"

"Sure, there was a building there. I went in it. So there had to be a building there for me to go in it. I remember one thing about it. It was off the side of the road."

"Most gas stations are."

"Your name is Rhoden, right?"

"Yeah."

"Rhoden, do you get along good with that smart-ass way you got?"

"No."

"No wonder. All right, all I remember is that it was kinda crappy, you know? It wasn't a new operation, let's put it that way."

"You mean it was dilapidated?"

"That's beautiful. I like that. Dilapidated. That's what the shithouse was, it was dilapidated."

"Did anybody other than Melvin Dummar see you there that day?"

"How do I know? I ain't been back askin' nobody if they seen me."

"You were there only ten months ago. Could you please explain why it is that you can remember so little about the place?"

"Who remembers so little? I remember enough. I was there, I seen this kid an' I talked to him an' I left the envelope there like I was told. Now what's so little about that?"

"But you can't seem to remember the surroundings."

"Why should I remember the surroundin's? I wasn't there to appraise the dump, for chrissakes! Who says I'm supposed to remember all that shit about what kinda gas they sold an' what color the walls was." He glared at me. "I ain't really crazy about your questions, Dutson."

"My name is Rhoden. When you talked to Melvin Dummar that day, did you say anything to him about this will having been found near the home of Joseph F. Smith in 1972?"

"Who?"

"Joseph F. Smith."

"I don't know no Joseph F. Smith. An' I don't know nothin' about nothin' being found in 1972, an' I din't say nothin' like that. If the kid says I said that to him, he's lyin' his fuckin' head off, because I din't."

"How tall was Melvin Dummar?"

"About my height." Forsythe was around five feet six. "I don't know what problem you two guys've got. You're holdin' the goods. I got it from Hughes, an' I gave it to the dummy. What more do you need?"

"The lawyers for the other side will not readily believe this. They're going to contend that you're in a conspiracy with Melvin Dummar to back up his lies to help him in a forgery plot to rip off the estate."

"They're gonna say that? Really? That's shit! That's what it is, shit, you know what I mean?"

Before driving us back to the Captain Cook, Forsythe let us borrow a brochure put out by Modern Construction Company, where he had worked as an estimator before forming his own company. In it was a picture of Forsythe when he did not have a mustache, and, according to Forsythe, the way he looked in April 1976 when he visited Melvin Dummar. On the cover of that brochure was a picture of the president of Modern, a man in his mid-fifties who bore a faint resemblance to Forsythe, and throughout the brochure were pictures of other employees.

Escorted by George Handy, Melvin Dummar arrived at the Captain Cook late the next afternoon. In my hotel room, Dummar's lawyers and I watched him thumb through the brochure and look several times at the face on the cover and at the picture of Forsythe. Finally Melvin selected the face on the cover. "I think maybe that's him. But I ain't sure." He looked back again at Forsythe's picture and said, "You know, I ain't sayin' this was the man in my gas station, but I seen this one somewhere. Maybe I seen him in the service."

We put Melvin in a crowded bar and then asked Forsythe to pick him out. Forsythe walked to Melvin as though drawn by a magnet. Melvin stood up and took Forsythe's outstretched hand, and I heard Dutson mumble behind me, "Glory be to God!" as Forsythe said, "Kid, you sure did fuck it up!"

I asked Melvin, "Have you ever seen this man before?"

"I cain't say I reconize him. Cain't say I don't. I know I seen him somewhere. But I'm not sure where I seen him. Or when I seen him."

In the dining room, Melvin's lawyers, Forsythe, Sears, and I returned with our plates from the buffet to the long table, and several minutes later, Melvin, slowly and carefully as though walking on a wire, returned to the table with a mountain of food piled on his plate. As Melvin plowed into the mountain, stuffing his mouth, Forsythe grinned and said to Melvin, "Hey, kid, it's a buffet. You don't have to take it all at one time.

You can go back for more as many times as you want." With a mouthful of food, Melvin tried to say, thank you, but couldn't. After the rest of us were finished eating, Melvin again slowly and carefully returned to the table with a second mountain of food topped with three desserts, and later, with his cheeks puffed with one of the desserts, Melvin stared at Forsythe and said, "If you was in my station, how long was you there?"

"Shit, I din't use no stopwatch, how do I know how long I was there?" Forsythe leaned toward me and mumbled quietly, "Hey, do you really think I'd ever be in on anythin' with a dummy like that?"

26. HURT CITY

After Melvin finished his third dessert, Roger and I thanked Forsythe and Sears for their time, and I told Forsythe that I might have to contact him again. Dutson, Handy, and Dummar retired early, and I went to the bar on the top floor to talk to a couple of Martels.

Who was this guy? A lying forger?

Or an ex-bagman for Howard Hughes forced out of retirement to save his old boss' will? Little chance of that.

A nut looking for publicity? Publicity was the last thing he wanted.

That he was telling the truth didn't make sense.

That he was lying didn't make sense.

If Forsythe had faked that calendar and that card, he went to a lot of trouble, but forging that *deliver this one* envelope had to take far more trouble. Why would he go to that trouble?

Over a second Martel I thought of the bombshell it would be if Forsythe were telling the truth. If he were lying to back up Dummar's story, why wouldn't he have lied to back up what Dummar had said about Joseph F. Smith's house in 1972? If Forsythe and Dummar were in it together, why would Dummar have failed to identify Forsythe? And why would Forsythe have failed to recall anything about Dummar's gas station? Surely, a liar would have learned something about the place he was going to lie about having visited.

But Forsythe's story had to be phony. That Howard Hughes wanted his will delivered to Melvin Dummar was ridiculous! There must be some connection between Forsythe and Dummar to explain Forsythe's story. I needed a team of investigators with unlimited expense accounts to delve into Forsythe's background, his credit card charges around April 27, 1976, his hotel bills, airline tickets for that date, and any connection with Melvin Dummar or with anyone the two of them knew. But I didn't have the money to hire one investigator, let alone a team. And I didn't have the money for—yes, I did! I suddenly realized that I had it all! I could use my opponents' investigators and their fat expense accounts to help me! If I noticed Forsythe's deposition, Yoakum and Bittle would turn their investigators loose to do the job for me and get me the hell out of this case. I congratulated myself on a great idea.

But how could I con Forsythe into sitting still for a deposition? And where? Legally, I could not force him out of Alaska to testify. If I subpoenaed him for a deposition in Alaska, his lawyer could delay the proceedings for months, and I could not afford to wait that long. I had to persuade Forsythe to go to Los Angeles or Las Vegas for a quick deposition, giving the other side just enough time to investigate him and expose him for me.

I was fumbling in my wallet to pay the check when I looked up and saw LeVane Forsythe and Dick Sears walking to my table. Forsythe said, "When you wasn't in your room, we figured you'd be up here. We'd like to talk to you alone without them Mormons around."

I invited them to sit down. Forsythe lit a cigarette, and both men leaned forward. Here it comes, I thought, these bastards are going to tell me that if I want Forsythe to keep lying, I had to promise him a piece of the action.

Forsythe said, "Rhoden, you're bein' took."

"What?"

"You're bein' took by them Mormons. Me an' Dick've been talkin' it over since we met Melvin Dummar, an' we got it figured out. I made a bum delivery."

"Huh?"

"I delivered it to the wrong Melvin Dummar. This Dummar I gave it to, that dummy downstairs, ain't the right one. I think somebody gave me the wrong instructions an' I got the wrong Dummar. This kid we seen tonight can't be the Melvin Dummar Hughes knew. I knew Hughes—he wouldn't have nothin' to do with a jerk like this. This kid lives in Utah. When was Hughes in Utah? I don't know of Hughes ever bein' in Utah."

"It's the right Melvin Dummar under the will."

"It's the wrong Melvin Dummar an' them Mormons know it. They think they're pullin' a fast one on you, Rhoden. Them Mormons are all alike—they drink their fuckin' milk, an' they don't use no dirty words, an' they walk around like a buncha angels, but they'll steal your ass off if you ain't watchin' it. You listen to me, Rhoden, that's the wrong Melvin Dummar down there!"

"Gentlemen! The will refers to a Melvin Dummar of Gabbs, Nevada. The Melvin Dummar downstairs now lives in Willard, Utah, but in 1968 he lived in Gabbs, Nevada. How many Melvin Dummars do you think there were in 1968 in Gabbs, Nevada?"

They looked at each other and sat back. Forsythe ordered a brandy and Sears ordered a scotch and said, "We really thought we had somethin' there for you."

"Mr. Forsythe—"

"Call me Lee."

"What did Howard Hughes call you?"

"He mispronounced my name—he always called me Levan. But I din't never correct him. I don't correct nobody."

"How did you get the call from Dan Harper?"

"Wil Painter at Modern Construction got the call. He's the manager there. He called me an' said that a guy named Dan Harper called me, an' Wil gave Harper my new number."

"What did Harper say to you?"

"First he said, 'What's Ventura?' Since he din't know, I wasn't gonna tell him. So he said, 'I figured it out an' I think you was the one who dropped off the will to that kid in Utah.' So I says, 'You figure whatever you want, I don't give a shit.' An' then he says that the will is in trouble in Las Vegas because the kid I left it with says he never seen it, an' they caught him lyin'. An' he tells me, the will's in Shitsville."

"Where?"

Forsythe spoke slowly. "Shitsville! That means it ain't in no sweet-smellin' place doin' good. Now, that wasn't his exact words, but, you get the idea. So I says, 'I don't give a fuck, farewell.' An' he says—an' here's where I got real pissed off—he says, 'Your son's got a good job at Hughes Aircraft.' So I knew he knew somethin'. Then he says, 'If you don't cooperate in doin' this one little favor, your son's gonna be thrown out on his ass,' or words to that effect. Now, my son's got a family in L.A. an' a good deal down there an' I don't go for this, you know what I mean?"

"How long has your son been working for Hughes Aircraft?"

"Since around 1972, when the old man got him a job there. So this son of a bitch says, 'You got a pencil, I want you to copy this down,' an' he gives me the name of your buddy—what's his name again?"

"Roger Dutson."

"That's right. Harper says that this guy is Dummar's lawyer, an' then he gives me your name, an' he tells me you're Dietrich's lawyer. Then he gives me two numbers. Both are area code 801. Then he tells me all I gotta do is call one a the two a you, an' say I dropped it off at Dummar's gas station. So I figured, shit, what's one lousy phone call? I don't hafta give my name or nothin'. So I called what's-his-name." Forsythe put out his cigarette and lit another one. "I should never've called him. I gut-reacted too fast. An' I should never've talked to you two guys up here. It's takin' up too much a my time. Rhoden, if you really don't know who this Harper is, would you like to find out?"

"I'd like to find out."

"Here's what you do. You go back down to the Lower Forty-eight an' sit on your ass an' do nothin'. Now, that ain't too hard for a lawyer, is it?"

"And in nine months, Dan Harper hatches out from under me, right?"

"If you do nothin' like I tell you, an' there's nothin' in the press, Harper won't hear nothin', so he'll call me and wanna know if I done like he said. Then I'll record the son of a bitch an' nail him for you."

"No, I can't just sit back and wait."

"You're makin' a mistake, Rhoden. I'm tellin' you to make no noise an' wait."

"Lee, just one more question, please. How did you get from Anchorage to Melvin Dummar's gas station?"

"How do you think? By bicycle?"

"What airline?"

"Do you remember what you took when you flew somewhere a year ago? Maybe I took two airlines. Maybe I transferred in Seattle. Sometimes I go from here to Seattle on Airwest an' change in Seattle to Western to go down to L.A. Maybe United. All I know is I went from here to Seattle an' then to Salt Lake City an' then back to Seattle. Then from Seattle I went with some friends a mine to 'Frisco on a business trip."

From the way LeVane Forsythe would look to his left and then to his right before answering a question, as though to be sure that no one had sneaked up behind him, and from the way he would draw on his cigarette for time to select an answer, if you were standing next to him soaking in a rainstorm, and you heard him say, "It's raining," you wouldn't believe him.

"Lee, it may be necessary for me to take your deposition."

"I ain't givin' no deposition!"

"Then I may have to serve you with a subpoena."

"I don't advise that, Rhoden! I got a bad memory, an' it can get worse, you know what I mean?"

"You mean you're going to forget that you delivered that envelope to Melvin Dummar?"

"Shit, no! I don't care about that. But I do care about the resta what can come out."

"Like what?"

Forsythe said quietly, "Like them deliveries I made. Look, Rhoden, I got a family here. I got a big business with partners like Dick. I owe 'em not to fuck it all up. I don't want no noise about my knowin' the old man, an' them deliveries. I'm gonna have a bad memory about them deliveries or I'm gonna take the Fifth, you know what I mean? An' I got IRS problems. If I say one fuckin' word about anythin' I done, I'm in Hurt City. I ain't gonna do it. Not for nobody!"

"What about people who could benefit from the hundreds of millions that would go to medical research if this will is admitted to probate?"

"Put down the shovel, Rhoden! What's in it for me?"

"Nothing you can put in a bank."

"Then what?"

"Knowledge that you've helped others."

"What others? You mean dumb Dummar an' them Mormons?"

"No, people who'd benefit from medical research. Kids who'd get scholarships. Orphans who'd get a decent place to live in—"

"An' all them sick people an' all them little orphans is gonna send me a thank-you note, is that it?"

"No. I doubt that you'd get even one thank-you note. Most of the good under this will would come long after you're gone. And no one is going to bother looking back at a court record fifty or a hundred years from now to read about what you did."

"Christ, Rhoden, you give me the chills talkin' about what's gonna happen after I'm dead."

"Lee, the only personal benefit that you can get out of testifying in this case is that people who know you are bound to think that you did a decent thing. Everyone would know that you took a lot of heat at the exposure of your past life with Hughes, but that you took it to help people you didn't know. People you would never know. People who would never thank you. People who would never know your name."

Forsythe said nothing for a minute, and then stared at his cigarette as he put it out. I could see that he was thinking over what I had said. Forsythe leaned forward, and I looked for tears in his eyes. "Rhoden," he said slowly and with a new softness in his voice, "you are full of more bullshit than any other lawyer I ever heard, an' I heard a lot of 'em."

27. THE DEPOSIT SLIP

The next step was to lure Bittle and Yoakum into assigning their investigators to nail Forsythe for me. To accomplish this I had to schedule Forsythe's deposition, but first, I had to persuade Forsythe to submit to it. I phoned him the morning after I returned to Los Angeles.

"Rhoden, I ain't goin' into no courtroom in Vegas or nowhere else. Why should I?"

"You have a choice, Lee. A deposition in Anchorage or a deposition down here. If we do it in Anchorage and you refuse to answer questions, there'll be motions before a judge up there. That'll mean publicity in Anchorage. If you come to L.A. or Vegas, I can set up a hearing before a judge who can rule on your objections on the spot, without publicity."

Several days and several phone calls later, Forsythe agreed to give a deposition. But only in Anchorage and only if I paid his lawyer's fee and expenses.

"Why do you need a lawyer?"

"In case I gotta take the fuckin' Fifth."

"About what?"

"About them deliveries, for chrissakes! I ain't tellin' nobody about no deliveries, you know what I mean? An' I ain't sayin' nothin' about no payments I got. Nothin' about how much or when I got 'em, or what I done with 'em."

"Lee, if you feel you need a lawyer, you'll have to pay him yourself."

If Forsythe were lying about his bagman relationship with Howard Hughes, I wondered, if he didn't have this past, why the anxiety over its exposure? He was pretending. Why?

Forsythe's Los Angeles lawyer, Bradley Marcus, agreed to represent him in Las Vegas for $2,500 plus expenses, but if he had to go to Anchorage his fee would be $5,000 plus expenses, and the same for each return trip if there were any court hearings on objections. Forsythe elected to go to Las Vegas for his deposition. But on condition that the courtroom be closed to the press, and "there ain't nothin' in no newspapers about nobody bein' a bagman, you know what I mean?"

In Judge Hayes' courtroom, with Theodore Andropolis there for Earl Yoakum, I requested Judge Hayes to allow a deposition in his courtroom of LeVane Forsythe, a resident of Anchorage, Alaska. "Since this witness may claim the Fifth, the matter could be expedited if the deposition could be taken in this courtroom where Your Honor could settle the issue with an immediate ruling."

Andropolis asked, "The Fifth about what?"

"Your Honor, this witness has indicated some reluctance to disclose the details of a past occupation which he says he engaged in as a confidential courier for Howard Hughes."

Andropolis took out of his file a Xerox copy of a page of a court transcript. I had told no one about Forsythe, other than Alex Morenus, who had to set up the hearing for me, and the lawyers who had been working with me on this case in Los Angeles. Andropolis said, "We oppose the motion. Mr. LeVane Forsythe is not unknown to the courts in Las Vegas. In 1970, during the protracted hearings in the dispute between Robert Maheu and Summa over the departure of Howard Hughes from the Desert Inn, this same LeVane Forsythe testified that he was present at the time of that departure. Judge Babcock, who heard the matter, said of Forsythe, and I quote, 'This man is a fanciful fabricator, utterly unworthy of belief.'"

Judge Hayes granted my motion for the unusual deposition, and set it for March 10, 1977.

I was interested in how opposing counsel knew, before they heard my motion in open court concerning Forsythe, that I was going to make a motion concerning Forsythe. But I was much more interested in Forsythe's prior participation in litigation involving Howard Hughes.

When I phoned Forsythe that we had a March 10 date for his

deposition in Las Vegas, he reneged. "I've been thinkin' it over. I don't wanna go before some judge who'll throw my ass in jail if I don't answer those fuckin' questions, which I ain't gonna answer."

"You don't have to worry about this judge in Vegas."

"Why don't I?"

"He's a Mormon. Naturally, he wants the will admitted to probate. Christ, he'll welcome you with open arms! So, please, Lee, reconsider! A lot of us are counting on you."

"Rhoden, I ain't sure I like you, you know what I mean?"

Forsythe finally agreed to fly down to Las Vegas for a deposition. The last week of February, when he and I were in daily telephone contact, he insisted that he could prove that he was in Salt Lake City by his airline ticket from Seattle. "Now, move your lazy ass an' find it!"

"But you don't even remember what airline you took!"

"So, check 'em all!"

"What name do I look for?"

"I made maybe fifty trips for Hughes an' each time I used another name. How am I gonna remember what name I used on each trip?"

"Then, how am I going to find your damned ticket?"

"Check the records the airlines keep of everybody in every seat from Seattle to Salt Lake City on the 26th. Maybe the 27th, but I think it was the 26th. So check both days!"

Because he was so insistent, there might actually be a ticket to be found. If so, it could have been planted by Forsythe last April to back up his phony story, and a planted ticket could be a big step toward proof that Forsythe was in with Dummar. But, if he had planted a ticket by buying one in April 1976 for this purpose and wanted it found, why didn't he simply show me his copy? There it was again: What if Forsythe really did fly to Salt Lake City that day last April? What if he really did deliver that envelope to Dummar? What if, in Canada, in 1972, Forsythe really did get that envelope from Howard Hughes?

On March 7, 1977, I received a phone call from Anchorage. "Rhoden, I want you to listen to this. I recorded it about an hour ago."

A voice I didn't recognize said, "Are you LeVane Forsythe?"

Forsythe's voice answered, "Yeah."

The other voice said, "I'm gonna tell you this only once. If you get on that witness stand in Las Vegas and shoot off your fuckin' mouth about any deliveries you made to the capital, you ain't gonna get out of Las Vegas alive!" Then a click and the sound on a telephone when there's no one at the other end.

"Lee, are you still going to testify in Las Vegas?"

"Yeah. I said I would an' I will. But I'm tellin' you Rhoden, I don't want no questions about no deliveries!"

"About that reference to deliveries to the capital, did that mean the capital of a state, or Washington, D.C.?"

"I ain't sayin' nothin' to you or nobody about no capitals, you know what I mean?"

On March 9, 1977, Bradley Marcus phoned me and laid it out. "I want your promise that you won't ask Forsythe about any deliveries he made for Howard Hughes. And no questions about any payments he got from Hughes."

"What if the contestants ask him?"

"Then he takes the Fifth, but you won't argue against it. That's what Lee wants, and I have your word or it's no deposition."

"You have my word."

Stanley Fairfield and Eli Blumenfeld volunteered to go with me to Las Vegas to help catch a detail that could blow Forsythe's story and make us all heroes. On March 10, 1977, the corridor outside Judge Hayes' courtroom reverberated with the reporters' moans at being closed out of the hearing. When I arrived, Yoakum was grinning before an ABC camera. "Ah tell you, this Forsythe is a kook! He heard about those jokes Melvin Dummar was tellin' here last January an' he decided to come down an' give us a few of his own."

"Then, you don't believe that he was a confidential courier for Howard Hughes?"

"He was a confidential courier for Howard Hughes like Ah was a prima ballerina for the Bolshoi."

"Then, what's his purpose in coming here?"

"He's a kook, Ah tell you! If he were tellin' the truth, why would he've waited so long?"

"But, Mr. Yoakum, if he were lying, why would he have waited so long?"

Yoakum glared at the reporter. "Because it just occurred to the kook last January, that's why! He heard what Dummar said about someone droppin' off a will at his gas station, an' this guy decided that he'd be just right to play the part."

Five minutes before we were to start, LeVane Forsythe arrived, scowling and tight-lipped at the questions coming at him from the press. As we walked into the courtroom, Bradley Marcus whispered, "If he takes the Fifth, you pass. Do I have your word?"

"I gave you my word yesterday."

"Lee wants it again."

"He's got it again."

Judge Hayes ordered the courtroom cleared of all spectators, called Forsythe to the stand, and ordered him to remain in town until the deposition was completed, no matter how many days it might take. "Gentlemen, I'll be in my chambers if you need me for a ruling." Judge Hayes left the bench and Forsythe was mine.

LeVane Forsythe testified that for the past year, with two other partners, he had been an owner of Arctic Metal Structures engaged in constructing a hospital in Anchorage. Before that, in Anchorage, he was the chief estimator for Modern Construction.

I showed him the McKay envelope which had contained the will when it was found in the Mormon Church Headquarters Building on April 29, 1976. He said he last saw that envelope on April 26 or April 27, 1976— he wasn't sure which—the day he left it at Melvin Dummar's gas station outside Ogden, Utah. He received it in the Bayshore Inn Hotel, Vancouver, Canada.

"What brought you to the Bayshore Inn?"

"I brought myself."

"Why?"

"I got a call from Mr. Hughes."

"Did you recognize the voice on the telephone?"

"Sure. It was Mr. Hughes' voice."

"Where in the Bayshore Inn did he tell you to meet him?"

"He gave me a floor an' a room number."

"What were the numbers?"

"I think the floor was the seventeenth. Or the nineteenth, maybe. I don't remember the room number. Jesus, this was 1972."

"When you told me about this in Anchorage last month, didn't you tell me it was 1971?"

"If I did, I made a mistake. I know where I was when I got the call. In Paulsbo, Washington. I ast my wife when this was an' she says it had to be 1972, so I say it was 1972."

"When you arrived at the Bayshore Inn and went to the room, what happened?"

"He said to come in. The door wasn't closed, an' it wasn't exactly opened. It was sorta ajar."

"Anybody in the room?"

"Only Mr. Hughes."

"Had you met Mr. Hughes before?"

From behind me, I heard Bradley Marcus say, "Objection, Fifth Amendment!" Dammit, this wasn't our agreement!

"Describe the man you saw in the hotel room."

"Hughes? His hair was gray an' he was skinny."

"Can you describe the length of his hair?"

"No."

"Why not?"

"I wasn't there to look at his hair an' I just ain't sure, that's why not."

"How was he dressed?"

"In a bathrobe. I remember he had a towel on his lap."

"What was said when you went in?"

"He ast me how I was. I told him my back was botherin' me from the trip."

"What else did you talk about?"

"He told me why I was there. He said he had a brown envelope that was layin' on the table, an' he wanned to entrust me with it. He said I would probably be retainin' it for some time. He wanned to know if I would accept that responsibility because the brown envelope contained instructions in case of his death. I told him I would."

"What else did Howard Hughes tell you about the brown envelope?"

"He said there was three envelopes in it. One I was to mail. One I was to deliver. And the other was self-explanatory, you know what I mean?"

"Did he say anything about opening the large envelope which contained the three smaller ones?"

"On no occasion was I to open that envelope until he passed away. He said he may call for it back, an' if he did, he din't wanna find it open."

"Did Mr. Hughes tell you where the envelope had been before he gave it to you?"

"He told me somebody had it before myself who no longer wanned the responsibility to hold it."

"How long were you in the room with him?"

"Twenny minutes, maybe a little longer."

"When you left, did anyone escort you out?"

"I went out the way I came in, on my own."

"Did you keep the large brown envelope in your possession until Hughes' death on April 5th, 1976?"

"Yes."

"Mr. Forsythe, you testified that you left the McKay envelope at Melvin Dummar's gas station. Who told you to do that?"

"I got telephone instructions."

"When?"

"I believe on January 7th, 1976." Forsythe repeated what he had told me about the note he wrote on the back of the invitation to the Christmas party on December 24, 1975. I had the card with the note on the back marked as an exhibit.

"What does *Vent* stand for?"

"Whenever Mr. Hughes had someone call me an' that person said 'Ventura,' I knew it was from Mr. Hughes."

"When did Howard Hughes first use this code name in communicating with you?"

Again Bradley Marcus objected. "Fifth Amendment!"

"Did you ever open that large envelope that you took out of the Bayshore Inn Hotel?"

"Yeah, in my home in Anchorage, the day he passed away."

"When you opened the large envelope, what did you find in it?"

"Three envelopes."

"Please describe them."

"One had written on it, *mail this one*. Inside was a fat envelope addressed to Mr. Chester Davis in New York City."

"Did you mail it?"

"Yeah."

"From where?"

"From Seattle or San Francisco, one airport or the other."

"You just dropped it in a mailbox in the airport?"

"No. I had to add more stamps to it. That stamp that was on it wasn't adequate enough."

"Describe the second envelope."

"It had on it, *deliver this one.*"

I took the envelope from Forsythe, and had it marked as an exhibit. "On this envelope that has the words *deliver this one,* it appears that in two places something has been ripped off the surface. What caused those marks?"

"Instructions was taped to the outside of this envelope an' I ripped 'em off."

"What were those instructions?"

"It said something like, I wasn't to hand it to nobody, but to leave it somewhere conspicuous."

"What did the third envelope have written on it?"

"*Open this one.*"

"What did you do with it?"

"I opened it."

"What did you find in it?"

"Twenny-eight one-hunnerd-dollar bills."

"What did you do with the money?"

"I kept it."

"Did you use any of the money for expenses to carry out the instructions with regard to the envelope that had on it *deliver this one?*"

"Well, yeah, in a way."

"On your monthly calendar, there's an entry for April 26th which reads, *Leave for Utah today.* Did you leave for Utah on the 26th?"

"I'm not sure. It might have been the 27th, but I think it was the 26th."

"The entry on the 27th of April reads 'Delivered will at Dummar's station, Ogden, Utah.' Did you deliver a will at Dummar's station in Ogden, Utah, on the 27th of April?"

"I know it says the 27th, but I think it was the 26th."

When I asked Forsythe if he had an airline ticket stub showing his trip from Anchorage in April 1976, he produced one showing a trip on Western Airlines leaving Anchorage and arriving in Seattle on April 23, 1976. He also produced a hotel bill showing that he had checked into the Washington Plaza Hotel in Seattle on the 23rd and checked out on the 25th. The airline ticket showed that he left Seattle on the 25th and went to San Francisco, arriving there on the 25th.

"At some time on this trip, did you go to Salt Lake City, Utah?"

"Yes."

"From where did you go to Salt Lake City?"

"From San Francisco. Then I went back to San Francisco."

This, I sensed, was the break I had been hoping for. "Mr. Forsythe, when you and I talked in Anchorage last month, didn't you tell me that you flew from Anchorage to Seattle, and from Seattle to Salt Lake City, and then back to Seattle? And then from Seattle down to San Francisco?"

"I think I did tell you that."

"Now, you've changed your story, haven't you?"

"That could be. Look, I ain't no walkin' memory machine. The way I told you was the way I remembered it. Now I remember it different."

"What changed your memory?"

"I knew I was comin' down here for a deposition an' I wanned to be real accurate. So I went back an' dug up my old bills an' I seen this ticket that reminded me how we went. An' I checked with Dick Sears an' a couple of other guys an' they reminded me how we went. So, now I'm tellin' you how we went."

"What name did you use when you bought a ticket from San Francisco to Salt Lake City?"

"I don't remember."

"Why didn't you use your own name?"

"I never used my own name on a trip for Hughes."

"How did you pay for the airline ticket?"

"Cash."

"Was that part of the twenty-eight hundred dollars?"

"Yeah."

"What time did you arrive in Salt Lake City the day you flew there from San Francisco?"

"Some time in the mornin'."

"What did you do when you got to the airport?"

"I talked to an employee there an' ast him if he knew somebody who'd drive me to Ogden for a hunnerd bucks. He made a phone call an' told me he had somebody comin'. I gave him twenny bucks. An' then him an' I went out front an' this car drove up."

"Can you describe the employee?"

"No!"

"What make of car drove up?"

"How would anybody—I don't recall them details."

"What did you say to the man in the car?"

"I ast him if he knew where Ogden was an' he said, 'Sure.' I showed him a piece of paper, an' I says, 'You know where this place is?' And he says, no, but he could find it."

"Could you describe the driver?"

"Over sixty-five. His hair was kinda gray. Oh, I remember one thing— he said he was retired from some company an' the money he was gettin' wasn't enough to live on."

"Did you pay him?"

"Yeah, when I got in the car I gave him a one-hunnerd-dollar bill."

"Did that one-hundred-dollar bill come out of the envelope that had the twenty-eight one-hundred-dollar bills in it?"

"No. It came outa my pocket."

"But before it came out of your pocket, did it come out of that envelope that had the twenty-eight one-hundred-dollar bills in it?"

"No, it din't. I put those twenny-eight one-hunnerd-dollar bills in the bank."

"Did you put all twenty-eight one-hundred-dollar bills in the bank?"

"Yeah."

"Mr. Forsythe, you testified just minutes ago that you used some of that money as expense money on your trip to deliver this envelope to Dummar's gas station. Now you tell us that all of that money went into a bank. Which is it?"

"Like I said, I put the twenny-eight one-hunnerd-dollar bills into my bank. Later, when I went on the trip, I took out money for expenses. So, in a way, the money I put in the bank, I used for expenses, but all of them one-hunnerd-dollar bills went into the bank the day I opened the envelope."

This, I felt, was where I could nail him for sure. It would be easy to prove that he had made no such deposit. "Mr. Forsythe, when did you make that deposit?"

"The day I heard Mr. Hughes died."

"That was April 5th, 1976?"

"Yeah."

"How long after you heard about the death of Mr. Hughes did you make the deposit?"

"Within an hour."

"What did you do when you heard about the death of Howard Hughes?"

"I went home. I went to that big envelope that I had been savin' an' I opened it an' took out the one that said *open this one*. I opened it an' saw the money an' I went to the bank with it."

"Are you positive that you made a deposit of twenty-eight one-hundred-dollar bills on April 5th, 1976?"

"Positive."

"What's the name of the bank?"

"Alaska National Bank."

"Mr. Forsythe, you knew that you were coming here to testify today and that you would be asked about a deposit which you claim you made the day Mr. Hughes died—a deposit of money you say he gave you in 1972. You knew that, didn't you?"

"Sure."

"Do you have a copy of that deposit slip?"

"Yeah."

"Then, Mr. Forsythe, why didn't you bring that deposit slip to this courtroom with you today?"

"I did."

Forsythe opened his briefcase and took out a deposit slip.

The deposit slip showed that Forsythe had made a deposit in the Alaska National Bank of twenty-eight one-hundred-dollar bills. It was stamp-dated 5 April 1976. The initials of the teller who made the deposit were D.E.

I walked back to the counsel table and showed the deposit slip to Eli and Stanley. Eli grabbed for the slip with his mouth open. Stanley stared over Eli's shoulder and couldn't seem to believe what he saw; his look of pain became a glow. After Eli examined it he looked at me and nodded. I walked over to the contestants' table, where Bittle, Yoakum, and Clairbourne were in an angry conference, showed them the deposit slip, left them huddled over it, and turned back to LeVane Forsythe. "Mr. Forsythe, at any time in 1976, did you make another deposit in your bank of one-hundred-dollar bills?"

"Nope. No other one-hunnerd-dollar bills at any time. And if I put any cash in, it was small."

"We'll check your bank records," I said, and from behind me I heard Yoakum mumble, "You bet your sweet life we will!"

It took about fifteen minutes for everyone to finish examining the deposit slip, and when it was returned to me I read it again. Could it be possible? Could it be possible that my witness was actually telling the truth?

A half hour after we had stopped for the lunch break, Eli, Stanley, and I were still at our table examining that deposit slip. Stanley said, "Either he's telling the truth or he made a deposit the day Hughes died to make his story look good."

"To make what story look good?" I said. "Last April 5th, in 1976, how could Forsythe have known that nine months later he would decide to back up a story to be told by Melvin Dummar here in January 1977?"

Eli weighed the possibility that Dummar and Forsythe were in this together. I couldn't see it. "If Forsythe were in this before Hughes died," I argued, "why didn't he plant evidence for the rest of his story? Why not simply fly to Salt Lake City and keep the ticket copy? Why not check into a hotel there and keep the bill?"

"Could it be just a coincidence?" Stanley said.

"Coincidence?" I said. "He decides in January 1977 to say that he received a fee from Hughes for delivery of the will and he looks around to see what evidence there is available to back him up and it just so happens by coincidence that the day Hughes died, Forsythe had made a deposit of twenty-eight hundred bucks. Some coincidence!"

"That'd be the second coincidence," Eli said. "The first would be that the day Dummar claims that some guy dropped off this will at his gas station in Willard, Utah, here's Forsythe not in Alaska, but in San Francisco just a short hop away from Willard. So if Forsythe decided last January to back up Melvin's lie, he ran into two lucky coincidences." Eli looked at me. "I'd have bet my balls that this shmuck was lying. But now, I'm beginning to wonder."

"Mr. Forsythe, please tell us what you did when you got to Melvin Dummar's gas station."

"There was a guy standin' close by an' I ast him where I could find Melvin Dummar an' he said, 'That's him over there.' I walked back to the car an' got the big brown envelope outa my briefcase. An' I took out the one that was left that had on it *deliver this one*. I opened it an' took out what was inside. The envelope I left with Dummar."

"Was the envelope you left with Dummar browned around the edges?"

"I don't remember."

"Did you read the words on the outside of the envelope addressed to Mr. McKay?"

"No. I din't have my reading glasses on."

"Why didn't you put your glasses on to read what was written on the envelope?"

"Because I din't have no reason to read it. I was told to deliver it, not read it."

"What did you say to Melvin Dummar?"

"The exact words I don't recall, but I wanned to satisfy myself that he was Melvin Dummar so I threw a coupla questions out at him like, 'What do you think of Howard Hughes' death?' or somethin'."

"Why did you ask him that?"

"Well, because the whole thing din't make no sense to me. Where I was at, lookin' at this guy, his being a young fellow—it just din't make no sense to me."

"What didn't make any sense to you?"

"Where I was at din't make no sense. Delivering somethin' of this nature to this—this person—din't make no sense to me. Why would Hughes want instructions about his death or a will delivered to this kid in this gas station?"

"Did you say to him anything like, 'I've been lookin' for you'?"

"I might've said that. I could've because I was lookin' for him ever since I left Salt Lake City."

"Did you say anything like this to Melvin Dummar: 'A will of Howard Hughes' was found near the house of Joseph F. Smith in Salt Lake City in 1972'?"

"I could tell you for sure I din't say that to him."

"Have you ever heard of Joseph F. Smith?"

"No, never before you ast me that question in Anchorage. I told you no then an' I tell you no again."

"How was Melvin Dummar dressed that day?"

"Sorta like a hillbilly."

"Was anything sold at Dummar's gas station other than gas?"

"Look, the only reason I went inside was to drop the envelope off in an obvious place. I din't look to see what they had for sale because I wasn't buyin' nothin'. All I wanned was to get my tail outa there."

"Why did you want to get your tail out of there?"

"Because I din't want him to put me together."

"Did you feel that you were doing something illegal?"

"No, but I din't want no exposure."

"Where inside the gas station did you leave the envelope?"

"I propped it up on the back counter where he could see it."

"What did you do after you left?"

"I ast the driver to take me back to the airport an' I got the first flight back to Frisco."

"Did you at some time get a phone call from a man who said his name was Dan Harper?"

"Yeah. That was Sunday, February 6th."

"At any time before February 6th did you read or hear that Melvin testified in court that someone had come into his gas station last April, talked to him for a little while, dropped the will off on a counter and walked out?"

"Not before I heard from Harper."

"At any time before you heard from Harper, did you intend to volunteer your testimony concerning your part in this?"

"Hell, no!"

"Why not?"

"Why not! It wasn't my obligation to shoot my mouth off. How do you think it's gonna look to my family when they read about all this? What are people gonna think? Things are gonna be in their minds—all this stuff about me knowin' Hughes, an' a lot of other things that ain't nobody's business."

"In this phone call from Harper last February 6th, what did he tell you?"

"He said he wanned me to call down to the Lower Forty-eight an' tell 'em I dropped it off at Dummar's station."

"Did you make that call down to the Lower Forty-eight?"

"Yeah."

"Whom did you talk to?"

"The first night I talked to Dutson. Then, the next night, I talked to you."

"You talked to me on the phone before I met you in the Captain Cook Hotel in Anchorage, Alaska?"

"Yeah."

"I suggest to you that you made two telephone calls, both to Dutson. Does that refresh your memory?"

"It seems to me I talked to you on the phone, but I've talked to you on the phone since, an' I may've gotten things a little twisted."

"Did you tell anybody from 1972 to 1976 that you had this will?"

"No."

"Why not?"

"That wasn't the trust that was placed in me."

"Did you tell your wife you had it?"

"No, least of all her."

"Why least of all her?"

"She talks too much."

"Now, Mr. Forsythe, I'm not asking you about what you did for Howard Hughes, I just want to know when you first met him. Give me the year."

"Don't answer!" Bradley Marcus said, "Fifth Amendment!"

"Did Howard Hughes have anything to do with your son's employment at Hughes Aircraft Company?"

"Objection!" Marcus said, "Fifth Amendment!"

Over the shouting objections of Bittle and Yoakum, I adjourned the deposition at 4:00. That night in Bradley Marcus' hotel room at the MGM, I argued with him until after midnight to persuade him to allow me to get answers to those questions about Forsythe's prior association with Hughes so that this association could either be contradicted or corroborated. Marcus was afraid that one answer from his client about a prior association with Hughes would constitute a waiver of the privilege against self-incrimination, but he finally agreed to a set of carefully worded questions where the risk of waiver was at a minimum.

Eli, Stanley, and I arranged to meet Marcus and Forsythe for breakfast at 8:00 the next morning in the coffee shop. At 8:00 the next morning in the coffee shop, Marcus arrived without Forsythe. "I've got some bad news! Right now Forsythe is at the airport getting on a plane—he got another threatening phone call at two o'clock this morning and he's leaving."

I grabbed my briefcase, ran with Eli and Stanley to our rented car, sped to the courthouse, ran up the stairs, and motioned for Yoakum and Bittle to follow us into Judge Hayes' chambers. "Judge Hayes, Forsythe is about to take a plane out of Las Vegas! Since he's in contempt, would you please phone the police and have—" Before I could finish, Hayes was on the phone, calling the police.

"I want this man placed under arrest and brought back to me at once!" Hayes turned to me. "What airline is he likely to take?"

"Since he'll know we're after him, he'll probably take the first plane going north. If he can't get one to Seattle he'll take one to San Francisco or maybe to Salt Lake City."

An hour later, Hayes called us to his chambers. "They tell me that there's no sign of Forsythe at the airport. He got away."

I learned two days later in a phone call from Forsythe that, figuring we would look for him on a plane heading north, he took the first plane out heading south for Phoenix.

I rehashed it and rehashed it with Eli and Stanley, and put the questions to Sam: If Forsythe were a liar, why did he run? Why did he testify in Las Vegas at all, and how do you explain that deposit slip?

28. THE SCRIPT

The day our Anchorage process server slapped a subpoena on LeVane Forsythe, I rescheduled his deposition to be resumed in Anchorage, and three days later Bittle and Yoakum argued their motion that Forsythe's deposition not be resumed anywhere. Their motion was denied.

On March 15, 1977, the Los Angeles Special Administrator for the Hughes Estate filed the result of his unproductive one-year search for a will. Among the fifty-two documents in that report was a typed letter by Howard Hughes to the First National Bank of Houston, Texas, dated March 3, 1938:

Gentlemen:

There are enclosed to you herewith in the envelope containing this letter, two additional envelopes, marked 'not to be opened,' one of which is marked Envelope No. 1 and the other marked Envelope No. 2. Envelope No. 2 contains my Will. Envelope No. 1 contains instructions to you to hold unopened the envelope containing my Will until definite physical proof of my death or until the lapse of the period of time described in Envelope No. 1.

Will you please set aside for me a safety deposit box large enough to contain these envelopes and send the bill each year for the rental of the box to me, in care of Noah Dietrich, 2920 Gulf Building, Houston, Texas.

In the event of my death or disappearance, you are hereby instructed to take possession of these documents and open *first* the envelope containing the letter of instructions, being Envelope No. 1, and to hold unopened the envelope containing the Will, being Envelope No. 2, in accordance with the instructions contained in Envelope No. 1.

Very truly yours,
Howard R. Hughes

Not only did I fail in Las Vegas to obtain from Forsythe evidence of forgery and a connection between him and Dummar, but I stumbled on evidence that corroborated Forsythe: that deposit slip. After that, Stanley Fairfield began dropping into my office every day to ask about recent developments, and while not ready to commit himself to full-time work on this case, he offered, as a loyal old friend, to help. I asked him to find out if Forsythe had taken a plane from San Francisco to Salt Lake City and back on any airline on either April 26th or 27th, 1976.

Marvin Mitchelson said he was convinced that Melvin Dummar and LeVane Forsythe were liars, even though he could not reconcile this with Forsythe's deposit slip, the phone call to Judge Grant, or the Pitney Bowes imprint on the back of the envelope. Nevertheless, Marvin offered to loan me a monthly amount to live on for as long as I felt that further investigation was required. I thanked him and accepted.

I wrote to Nevada Attorney General, Robert List:

Dear Sir:
When the contestants' attorneys asked you to help them determine if there were fingerprints on the Visitors Center envelope, you helped them. I ask the same help. Deposited with the court is an envelope with 'deliver this one' handwritten on it. Would you please have it examined by the FBI for fingerprints of Melvin Dummar. If Melvin Dummar's fingerprints are on that envelope, which was in the possession of LeVane Forsythe in Alaska, this would evidence a conspiracy between the two, leading to a criminal prosecution.

After the aborted Forsythe deposition in Las Vegas, Bittle and Yoakum obtained a release of Judge Hayes' order freezing discovery proceedings. Alex Morenus told me that after many months, his process server finally caught Levar Myler, one of Howard Hughes' personal aides during the Desert Inn period, and asked if I still wanted to take Myler's deposition. I told him to set it up.

Taking the oath in Alex Morenus' office in Las Vegas, Levar Myler looked like a bartender in a place where they served only beer. Myler testified that he went to work for Hughes Productions in 1950 as a driver, and from 1954 to 1956 did the grocery shopping for Jean Peters. In 1956, Myler was ordered to Palm Springs to wait on call, and waited on call without being called for six years. In 1962, as a reward for his faithful service on call in Palm Springs, Myler was promoted to personal aide to Howard Hughes, to attend him in the Bel Air house in Los Angeles, joining Crawford, Holmes, and George Francom. In 1965, Myler became ill and was off duty until October 1968, when he rejoined Mr. Hughes at the Desert Inn in Las Vegas.

Starting in the 1970s, Howard Hughes said many times that he had written a holographic will, and last talked about it two weeks before he died, when he said, "But don't bother to look for it, you're never going to find it. It's safe. I've given it to someone I can trust."

I asked Myler, "Did you know with whom Howard Hughes entrusted his holographic will?"

"No. None of us knew."

"Did Hughes tell you when he had written his will?"

"In the past, is all I know. One time he mentioned that he had written it in the gray house on the tenth tee at the Bel Air Golf Club."

"Are you sure that those were Hughes' exact words? Gray house? Tenth tee? Bel Air Golf Club?"

"I'm sure."

These were the precise words that Holmes had testified that Hughes used. Why would Hughes have explained to his body servants the details of where he had written his holographic will thirty years earlier? It looked as though someone had supplied Myler and Holmes with words they were to attribute to Hughes, so that when they testified that Hughes had said that he had written a holographic will, that evidence could not be used to support the Mormon will dated March 19, 1968. During the deposition, I tried an old one on Myler. I took a sheet of white paper out of my briefcase and let him see me slip it in under the pile of papers on the table in front of me, with the edge sticking out, ready for me to withdraw.

"Mr. Myler, you understand that you are under oath?"

"Yes."

"About these words that you say were spoken by Howard Hughes—" I pulled out that white piece of paper (it was a list of my 1976 interest payments) and pretended to read from it: ". . . that he had written his holographic will 'when he lived at the gray house, near the tenth tee of the Bel Air Golf Course.' Isn't it true that you saw those precise words on a white Xerox copy of a piece of paper that had typing on it, a copy shown to you a few weeks after Howard Hughes had died?"

"Yes."

"Where were you shown this script?"

"In Los Angeles. I think at a meeting at the Century Plaza Hotel."

"What were you told to do with this sheet when it was handed to you?"

"To read it."

"Who told you to read it?"

"I don't remember."

"What did you do with the script after you read it?"

"I gave it back."

"To whom?"

"I don't remember."

Phillip Bittle said, "Mr. Rhoden, may I see the paper which you characterize as a 'script'?"

"No, sir, you may not."

"Then, I'll tell Judge Hayes about this!"

Myler was still on the board of directors of Summa Corporation and was currently being paid by Summa under a consultation contract to last as long as he lived. Under this contract, Myler was to perform consultation services forty-five days a year.

"With whom are you to consult, Mr. Myler?"

"Summa Corporation."

"With what human beings there?"

"With whoever needs my consultation."

"Who there could need your consultation?"

"I don't know."

"On what subject matter are you to consult?"

"On whatever anybody wants me to consult on."

"What kind of consultation services have you performed up to now?"

"I'm testifying today."

"How much are you being paid by Summa for your testimony today?"

Horace Cummings objected and instructed his client not to answer.

"By the way, Mr. Myler, during the years that you were in the Desert Inn with Howard Hughes, you wouldn't remember what kind of pen Hughes wrote with, would you?"

"I remember. He wrote with a ballpoint pen. And it was a Paper Mate."

"Are you sure?"

"At that period he was using only Paper Mates. We would give 'em to him when he needed 'em."

"How did you happen to remember that?"

"Because that was the kind he always used."

"What did you have to do with the Paper Mate pens?"

"I bought 'em. By the dozen."

"How did Howard Hughes dress when he walked around his Desert Inn suite from the time you joined him in October 1968 until he left in 1970?"

"He wore a pajama top."

"What else?"

"Nothing. He was always nude from the waist down."

"Did he have clothes in that suite?"

"He had pants and a white shirt. And he had oxfords, a brown pair and a black pair."

Having rejoined Hughes in October 1968, Myler knew nothing of Hughes' whereabouts at the end of 1967. Nor did he know if Hughes wrote a will in March 1968. I tried another long shot. "Here's a photocopy of the purported will in this case. You see that in places on each page, the ink smeared. Did you ever see Howard Hughes write on lined yellow tablet paper?"

"That's the kind of paper he always wrote on."

"Did you ever see him spill anything on a memo that he was writing, and then pat it off with Kleenex, causing a smear, and then continue writing that memo?"

"I seem to remember that, yes."

"Will you please give us all the details you can remember?"

"He was using a ballpoint pen. And he spilled water on the pad of paper. He just dabbed it off with a Kleenex, and the ink was smeared."

"Did Howard Hughes ever have a glass of any liquids other than water on the table next to him when he was writing one of those memos?"

"He used to have an orange drink that had rum in it, or brandy."

Phillip Bittle asked Myler, "In your opinion, was this so-called will written by Mr. Hughes?"

"Of course not."

"If it were admitted to probate, would you accept any money under the provisions providing for, and I quote '. . . *my personal aides at the time of my death*'?"

"No."

"Why not?"

"Because I wouldn't have nothing to do with a fraud. This is a fraud, and I know it, and all of us who worked for him know it."

29. THE HOTEL BILL

On April 4, 1977, in an unused courtroom of the Anchorage courthouse, LeVane Forsythe's deposition was resumed. Present were Earl Yoakum and Rex Clairbourne, the Chief Deputy Attorney General of Nevada, Phillip Bittle and a junior attorney from his New York law firm, one lawyer from our local Anchorage law firm, two lawyers hired by LeVane Forsythe to advise him, and Eli Blumenfeld and I. I began the questioning. LeVane Forsythe identified several pictures of Howard Hughes taken during the thirties, forties, and early fifties, published in Noah Dietrich's book, *Howard, the Amazing Mr. Hughes,* as the man he saw in that hotel room in the Bayshore Inn in Vancouver, Canada, in the summer of 1972. "That's him. But he looked a lot older when I seen him in Canada than in them pitchers."

"When did you first meet this man?"

Forsythe's two lawyers, one on each side, whispered to him, and Forsythe answered, "I decline to answer on the ground that my answer might tend an' incriminate me, an' I—what?" One of the lawyers finished it for him: "The witness invokes the protection of the Fifth Amendment."

We adjourned for a ruling to the courtroom of the Anchorage judge. I submitted a brief on the unavailability of the Fifth Amendment privilege as to matters for which a criminal prosecution would be barred by a statute of limitations. Forsythe's two attorneys argued that he was entitled to the privilege. Yoakum argued that Forsythe shouldn't be allowed to testify at all. After a one-hour session, the judge ordered Forsythe to answer all questions concerning any contacts with and missions for Howard Hughes prior to 1970, since any such acts, even if criminal, could no longer be the subject of a prosecution.

When we returned to the courtroom, Forsythe testified that he first met Howard Hughes in 1946 or 1947 at the Corrigan Ranch in the Santa Susanna Mountains in Ventura County, California, where Forsythe, in business with his father, was in charge of a crew grading lakes and building bridges for movie sets for Howard Hughes' RKO Studios. One day, Mr. Hughes himself, on an inspection tour, became fascinated with a new tractor and wanted to be shown how to operate it, and after crew boss LeVane Forsythe showed him how, Mr. Hughes had a lot of fun running it around an open field. That day Forsythe demonstrated his loyalty to his employer by informing him that most of the laborers on the construction crew were working only halftime, many were goofing off most of the time, and some were not working at all, whereupon the outraged Mr. Hughes closed down the whole job, except for the work Forsythe was doing, and ordered the location chief to have everybody "Get their asses on the buses!"

Mr. Hughes appreciated Forsythe's snitching and asked Forsythe to keep his "eyes and ears open," and a few days later, Forsythe won more points by reporting that lumber was cut up at night and taken away by some of the workers. Mr. Hughes then rewarded his informer with the first of what, during the next twenty years, were to be about fifty confidential assignments to discreetly deliver to public servants holding local, state, and federal offices in the United States, sealed envelopes and small sealed packages.

Forsythe was not certain of the year he made his first delivery for Mr. Hughes, but it was when RKO was making the movies entitled *Vendetta* and *The Swordsman*. When those deliveries required Forsythe to travel outside Los Angeles, he bought his airline tickets under fictitious names such as Al Cromer, Carl Anderson—Forsythe once went to school with a Carl Anderson and produced a baggage identification slip with that name on it—Don Wilson, and Jack Schwartz, a name he used several times because he thought it was funny. Forsythe showed us two carbon airline tickets. One was for a flight from Los Angeles to Las Vegas, December 1970, in the name of *Mr. R. Smith*. The other, the same month, also purchased by Forsythe traveling from Los Angeles to Las Vegas for the Maheu hearing, was issued to *C. D. Wilson*. Forsythe testified that he did not remember why he used phony names on those two trips to Las Vegas, but he did remember why he used phony names on the trips to make those deliveries. "I din't want nobody to put me together, you know what I mean? This is the way Mr. Hughes wanned it."

From 1947 to 1972 Forsythe talked to Mr. Hughes on the telephone more than a hundred times. Early in 1972, before Forsythe moved to Paulsbo, Washington, he received a phone call at his mother's house in Torrance, California, from someone who worked for InterTel. When the man didn't use the code name Ventura in asking questions about Howard Hughes, Forsythe hung up. A week later, Forsythe received a call from Howard Hughes himself. Mr. Hughes said he was in the Bahamas and wanted Forsythe to fly there. "I told him I couldn't because I was busy."

"With what?"

"I was involved in a trial, an' I couldn't leave the country then."

"What trial?"

"It was a personal matter."

Yoakum chuckled.

The next telephone call Forsythe received from Hughes was in the summer of 1972 when Forsythe was in Paulsbo, Washington. Mr. Hughes asked Forsythe to meet him in the Bayshore Inn in Vancouver.

I asked Forsythe if he had testified in Las Vegas at the end of 1970 concerning Hughes' departure from Las Vegas. Forsythe said that he was asked to testify about what he saw and heard Thanksgiving night in 1970 and that he did. Some time early in 1970, in Torrance, California, Forsythe was contacted by a man who said that his name was Crawford and that he was associated with Howard Hughes. Crawford said that he wanted to talk to Forsythe about Forsythe doing some excavation work on the Las Vegas airport. A few months later, Crawford asked Forsythe to fly to Las Vegas to meet him in the lobby of the Desert Inn. There Crawford gave Forsythe $500 for expenses and asked if Forsythe would be available to return to Las Vegas on short notice to do a favor for Howard Hughes, and Forsythe said he would. On Thanksgiving Day 1970, Forsythe received another call from this Crawford to fly to Las Vegas immediately. In the lobby of the Desert Inn, he met Crawford again, and was told to station himself in the parking lot later that night to reroute cars to another part of the lot. Forsythe didn't know why. That evening Forsythe saw some men carrying another man on a stretcher out of the Desert Inn and into a car. He could not identify the man on the stretcher, but he heard the man say something like, "Get me Bob Maheu!"

A few weeks later in Los Angeles, Forsythe was contacted by Dean Elson, an ex-FBI agent who worked for Robert Maheu. Elson told Forsythe that Forsythe might have been involved in a kidnapping, and ought to go to Las Vegas and give the sheriff a statement to avoid serious trouble. Forsythe phoned Chester Davis, general counsel for Hughes

Tool Company and one of the men running it, and asked Davis for some proof from somebody—anybody—that Forsythe was at the Desert Inn on an assignment, not to stand guard during a kidnapping. Davis said, "Just keep your mouth shut and sit on your ass and do nothing!" But LeVane Forsythe did not want to keep his mouth shut and sit on his ass and do nothing because he was afraid that Mr. Hughes might have been kidnapped. Forsythe returned to Las Vegas, gave a statement to the sheriff, offered to take a lie detector test, and testified at the hearing about what he had done, seen, and heard. He did not ask anybody for any money for this testimony, nor was he offered any.

"When did you ask Howard Hughes to get your son a job at Hughes Aircraft?"

"I don't remember, but it was before I saw Mr. Hughes in Canada, 'cause I thanked him for it there."

"Did your son know that you were influential in getting him this job at Hughes Aircraft?"

"No, he din't. An' he still doesn't."

"When you walked into that hotel room in the Bayshore Inn, what was the very first thing Mr. Hughes said to you?"

"'You're late!'"

"Were you late?"

"Yeah, but only about twenny minutes. I told him it took me longer to drive than I expected. An' I reminded him about a time I was supposed to meet him in the lobby of the Beverly Hills Hotel an' he was a coupla hours late. An' some security people ast me what I was doin' loiterin' in the hotel an' it was embarrassin'."

"When was this time that Hughes was late?"

"Hell, I don't remember the year, but it was some time before they tore down the Marion Davies home across the street of the hotel."

"What else did Mr. Hughes and you talk about?"

"Oh, we sorta reminisced about the Ventura fiasco."

"Was anything said about the Maheu hearing?"

"Oh, yeah. I let him know that I was a little disappointed that he din't put me together, you know what I mean?"

"No, I don't know what you mean."

"I told him I thought that he should've come out an' put in a word for me. He got on television—remember when he said that Maheu had given him a bad time?—an' he could've put in a word for me an' said he knew I was there. All I got from Chester Davis was a rash a shit, an' I told him that."

"What else was said about the Maheu hearing?"

"I remember tellin' him that I heard him say, 'Get me Bob Maheu,' an' then he said, 'That isn't what I said. I said, "Get that son of a bitch Bob Maheu!"' I could see that Hughes was gettin' irritated at the subject so I dropped it."

"When Mr. Hughes told you about the envelope and the instructions regarding his death, what did you say to him?"

"I said, 'What'sa matter, are you sick or somethin'?'"

"Did he answer?"

"I think he said he was okay."

"Did Mr. Hughes hand the large envelope to you?"

"No, it was layin' on a table, an' when I left I picked it up."

"Was anything else said about that envelope other than what you've already testified to here and in Las Vegas?"

"Mr. Hughes said he din't want me to tell no one I had it, an' he said a coupla times that if he wanned it back, he wanned it back sealed like it was then. There was scotch tape along the edges, an' along the seam on the back an' along the seam at the bottom an' along where the lid closed."

"How did the meeting end?"

"Hughes said, 'You better leave now,' an' I figured that this meant the meetin' was over an' I said goodbye an' left."

"You never saw him again?"

"No."

"You never heard his voice on the telephone again?"

"No."

"Anything else you remember about Mr. Hughes in that hotel room?"

"Only that he—it's not important, let's skip it."

"Let's not skip it."

"Well, he—he kinda smelt."

"He what?"

"He smelt. He gave off an odor like."

I had asked Forsythe to bring with him copies of all deposit slips on that checking account at the Alaska National Bank for 1976. In 1976 there were only two cash deposits, other than the $2,800 deposit the day Hughes died. One was on February 2, 1976, when Forsythe deposited $1,200, but not in one hundred dollar bills. The other was March 29, 1976, when he deposited $300, but not in one hundred dollar bills.

"Mr. Forsythe, did you have in your possession any one hundred dollar bills at any other time in 1976?"

"Not that I remember. By the way, them twenny-eight one-hunnerd-dollar bills were old."

"You mean worn?"

"I don't know, but they were old."

"How do you know they were old?"

"'Cause that's what the girl told me. I forgot to tell you that."

"What girl told you what?"

"The teller at the bank. When I deposited the bills, she looked at 'em kinda funny an' left to talk to somebody. Then she came back an' told me they had different colored seals on 'em that meant they were old."

"What different colored seals?"

"I don't know."

"Mr. Forsythe, when you made the trip to Salt Lake City, you had in your pocket some of the one hundred dollar bills that came out of the envelope that you opened the day Hughes died, isn't that true?"

"Rhoden, are you tryin' to trick me? I told you when you ast me that question in Vegas that every one of the twenny-eight one hunnerd dollar bills I got in the envelope I put in my bank account. Later I drew some money out, but if they were the same bills, it sure as hell was a coincidence. The one hunnerd dollar bill I gave that guy in the car on the 27th in Salt Lake City wasn't one of the twenny-eight I got in the envelope."

"Wait a minute! You're not sure that you were in Salt Lake City on the 27th, are you?"

"Yeah, I'm sure."

"In Las Vegas you testified that you weren't sure whether it was the 26th or the 27th."

"That's right. In Vegas I wasn't sure. But now I'm sure."

"What happened between then and now to make you sure?"

"I dug up my hotel bill for the Holiday Inn in San Francisco." He took it out of his briefcase and showed it to me. "It shows we checked in on the 25th. That was a Sunday. I remember we went to the exhibit. The next day was the day we had the big meetin'. We talked about the project an' I had a tape recorder to take down the specs. You see on my hotel bill it shows that I had lunch at the hotel on the 26th. Now, that wasn't the day I was in Salt Lake City. But on the 27th, there ain't no charges for the whole day. Nothin' for breakfast, nothin' for lunch. The first charge is a phone call at ten-fifteen at night when I got back an' called my wife. I was gone the whole day. The next mornin' we checked out. So the day I went to Salt Lake City from San Francisco was the 27th. Also I ast Alex Bertulius—he's an architect I took with me outa Seattle—an' he's got records that we had the meetin' on Monday the 26th an' that I was gone all day the 27th. That was the day I made the delivery to Dummar in that hick town outside Salt Lake City."

30. THE FLIGHT SCHEDULES

At lunch, Eli and I reveled over that Holiday Inn hotel bill the way we had over the April 5th deposit slip. According to the contestants, sometime after Dummar testified in Las Vegas in January 1977,

Forsythe decided to play the stranger who had delivered the will on April 27, 1976. But if Forsythe had not been in Salt Lake City that day, it would be easy to prove he was not. If his hotel bill had shown that on the 27th in San Francisco he had had lunch or breakfast or a drink in the bar, or had made a telephone call, he'd be through. Instead, on that day, there was a gap in the records until 10:15 that evening when he made a phone call from the hotel. If there were no credit-card or other charge records showing that Forsythe was somewhere other than Salt Lake City on April 27, 1976, this gap would support his story.

And if Forsythe were telling the truth, Howard Hughes wrote the will.

After lunch Earl Yoakum cross-examined. "You told Mr. Rhoden when he first met you here in Anchorage that when you went down to the States in April 1976, you went from Anchorage to Seattle. Then to Salt Lake City an' back to Seattle. An' then to San Francisco. Now you say that you really went from Anchorage to Seattle to San Francisco. An' from San Francisco to Salt Lake City an' then back to San Francisco."

"Yeah, I straightened it out."

"An' you told Mr. Rhoden that you weren't sure whether you went to Salt Lake City the 26th or the 27th, an' that's what you testified to in Las Vegas. And now you're sure it was the 27th?"

"That's right, I straightened that out, too."

"Maybe there's somethin' else you'd like to straighten out. Isn't it true that you never in your life met Howard Hughes?"

"No, that ain't true!"

"Isn't it true, Mr. Forsythe, that you've told so many lies in Las Vegas an' here that—"

"I din't lie once an' I don't like your attitude, you know what I mean?"

Yoakum pressed Forsythe for four hours on Forsythe's deliveries of envelopes and packages to politicians. Forsythe testified that his first delivery was of a package to Minneapolis, followed by several deliveries to Senator William F. Knowland in Sacramento, California. After this he made many deliveries in the Los Angeles area. Forsythe said that he also made a delivery to Earl Warren when he was running for Governor of California. The envelope was left with Warren's secretary. Forsythe didn't know what was in the envelope; he didn't ask, he wasn't told, and he didn't look.

In the sixties, Forsythe made a delivery to the Democratic Fund Raising Chairman in Minneapolis and one to Larry Townsend, the 67th District Assemblyman in Long Beach, California. And over the years, Forsythe delivered envelopes to the mayor of Los Angeles, city councilmen, and members of the Los Angeles board of supervisors.

"Do you claim, Mr. Forsythe, that you made any deliveries to anyone in Washington, D.C.?"

"I draw a complete memory blank on that one."

"Is there anythin' wrong with your memory?"

"Well, I got a coupla telephone calls that din't do my memory no good, you know what I mean?"

LeVane Forsythe testified that his uncle Claude Forsythe once gave LeVane a package to deliver in Long Beach sometime in the early 1960s. Uncle Claude also performed delivery services for Mr. Hughes. Uncle Claude, who had passed away, used to be a U.S. deputy marshal, and was on the train that Hughes took from California to Boston whenever it was that Mr. Hughes was on that train.

Only once did someone refuse one of the envelopes or packages—the man in Long Beach. When Mr. Hughes insisted that Forsythe make a second trip to deliver the package, Forsythe said to Hughes, "What do you want me to do, open his mouth an' stick it down his throat? If he don't want it, I can't make him take it."

"Mr. Forsythe, Ah'm interested in your inability to recall any more than a few names of the some fifty recipients to whom you say you delivered envelopes or packages for Mr. Hughes over a twenty-year period."

"I ain't too enthusiastic about this particular topic."

"Ah notice that everyone whose name you've given me is dead."

"You suggestin' that I killed 'em?"

"Ah'm suggestin' that it would be extremely difficult for any of them to come forward an' deny that they received any of these cash contributions. Why don't you give us the name of someone who's alive? Someone who could come forward an' admit he received cash from Howard Hughes delivered by you?"

"Are you kiddin'? Can you pitcher a politician who got cash in an envelope admittin' it?"

"Will you give us the name of anyone whom you claim was a recipient and who is still alive?"

"No."

"Because you don't remember the names?"

"I got a bad memory an' it's gettin' worse every minute, you know what I mean?"

During the recess I asked Forsythe if he could give me the names of some of those political-contribution recipients who were still alive. "Yeah, I could. But I won't."

"Why not? It's to corroborate you."

"Not without their okay. It'd be chickenshit."

After the recess, Yoakum resumed. "Mr. Forsythe, Mr. Rhoden let you gloss over the matter of that trial you were involved in in Torrance, California, in early 1972. But Ah'm not goin' to let you gloss over it quite so easily. It was a criminal trial, wasn't it?"

"Yeah, an' it was a bum rap. Those crooks who had been runnin' the association was robbin' it blind, an' when I came in I caught 'em, an' threw 'em out, an' when I reported those bastards to the police they tried to gang up on me."

"What were you charged with, Mr. Forsythe?"

"After I dumped them crooks outa there, they got together an' accused me of embezzlement. I din't embezzle nothin'. Two of them people who made them phony charges against me was a coupla lunatics. This was the Southwestern Association for Retarded Children, an' some of the people involved in it made them poor little kids look—"

"What were you charged with, Mr. Forsythe?"

"The jury found me not guilty."

"In addition to embezzlement, weren't you accused of somethin' else?"

Not again!

"One of them crazy lunatics said that I wrote his signature on a check an' then he later admitted that it was his signature."

"Mr. Forsythe, what was the second count in the charge against you?"

"Forgery."

The morning of the third day, April 6, 1977, Yoakum went for the kill. "Ah'd like to ask you about what you wrote here on your calendar in the square for the 23rd of April, 1976. Under the word *Western* there are some numbers. And under *Airwest* there are some numbers. What are those numbers?"

"Flight schedules."

"From where to where?"

"I think from Anchorage to Seattle an' Seattle to Salt Lake City."

"Who did the writin'?"

"I did."

"When?"

"Some time around the 23rd of April, 1976."

"Could it have been a month or two later?"

"No."

"Mr. Forsythe, you're lyin', aren't you?"

"I ain't got no reason to lie an' I don't like your question, you know what I mean?"

"You wrote here in this little square that Western Airlines had a flight leaving at seven o'clock and arrivin' in Seattle at nine o'clock. Now, that flight number is 733, isn't it?"

"How would I remember the flight number?"

"An' under *Airwest,* you have the time schedule for a flight that is flight number 19, isn't that true?"

"Could be, I don't remember no flight numbers."

"Well, Ah can tell you that the records show that those two airlines have those two flights, an' that the times that you wrote down here are absolutely accurate. There's only one thing wrong, Mr. Forsythe. These two flight schedules, 733 for Western, and 19 for Airwest are in existence now. An' they were in existence since the middle of January of 1977. But they were not in existence in April 1976 when you say you wrote them down."

A sick something in my gut spread up into my throat and as I looked at Forsythe's face I could see it being smashed with a baseball bat.

Yoakum snickered at Forsythe. "Now, would you like to explain how it is that in April 1976 you were able to write with absolute accuracy the departure an' arrival times of flight schedules which did not come into existence until nine months later?"

Forsythe stopped for a whispering consultation with his two lawyers, and then answered, "That's the way I remember it, an' I have nothin' more to say about it."

"Well, Ah have somethin' to say about it! Ah suggest to you that when you heard that Melvin Dummar testified in Las Vegas that a mystery man had dropped the will off in his gas station, you decided that you were goin' to be that mystery man. Then you called Mr. Dutson an' Mr. Rhoden, an' while they were on their hopeful trip up here to see you in February, you faked some evidence to convince them that you were tellin' the truth. You took an old calendar an' wrote in some flight schedules for the 23rd of April 1976. You got your information by callin' the two airlines. But you forgot to ask if the airline schedules then in existence in February 1977 were also in existence back in April 1976. You faked these two entries on the calendar the same way you faked the entries for the 26th and 27th about Dummar's gas station! The same way you faked the envelope with the words *deliver this one* on it! Now, what've you got to say about that suggestion?"

"I can't tell you what I got to say about it."

"Why not?"

"Because there's a lady here writin' everythin' we say an' if I tell you what I got to say about your suggestion, no lady is gonna wanna write it, you know what I mean?"

That night at dinner at the Captain Cook, I asked Eli what he thought I could get for what I had in mind.

"Any court would reduce it to manslaughter. You'd never get more than one to five."

Despite a couple of still-unexplained surprises—that April 5, 1976 deposit slip and the Holiday Inn Hotel bill—everything worked according to plan. Bittle's and Yoakum's investigators did dig up evidence that made a liar out of the liar. "But all that does," Eli said, "is eliminate Forsythe as a witness. Aren't we right back where we were after Dummar testified in Vegas and before this lying asshole showed up? We still don't have evidence connecting Forsythe with Dummar. We don't have any more evidence of forgery than we had before."

Three days later, when it was my turn for re-direct examination, I asked Forsythe, "You wrote those airline schedules in the square for the 23rd of April, 1976, last February 1977, didn't you?"

"I must've. I don't remember doin' it, but last night I went over it with Dick Sears an' we kept talkin' it over an' I think I must've. Here's what happened. After I called Dutson in Utah a coupla months ago, I tried to remember how I went down from here to 'Frisco. An' I couldn't remember. So I ast Dick Sears. An' he couldn't remember. So we tried to figure it out together. We figured we musta gone to Seattle an' from there I went to Salt Lake City, an' from there back to Seattle, an' then down to San Francisco. But I din't remember what airlines I took or what the times were. So I musta called a coupla airlines, an' got the information from them an' wrote it down. Instead of writin' it down on a piece of paper, I wrote it down on the square there in the calendar. An' I figured I musta taken one a them flights. But I din't. I went to Salt Lake City from San Francisco instead. That's all there is to it."

"Then, Mr. Forsythe, why did you testify that you wrote down those airline schedules on or about the 23rd of April, 1976?"

"Because I thought I did. I don't really remember writin' 'em down last February. I don't remember when I wrote 'em down. At first, I took it for granned that I wrote 'em down last April. But I checked with Dick an' we figure I musta wrote 'em down right before you an' Dummar's lawyer came up here to see me."

At the next recess, I asked Forsythe, "Do you and Dick Sears sometimes drink together?"

"Sometimes."

"Do you ever drink together before noon?"

"We've been known to belt a few, yeah."

"Belt a few quarts or a few fifths?"

"What is this, Rhoden, you with the AA or somethin'?"

"Dick Sears has a drinking problem, hasn't he?"

"Yeah."

"And what about you, Lee? Do you have a similar problem?"

"Me? No, not me! Not me! I can handle booze like it was water, you know what I mean?"

In the cold cab ride to the Anchorage airport, Eli said, "I can't make up my mind about this guy. One minute I'm sure he's the worst liar I've ever heard and the next minute I believe him. I just can't imagine someone making up fifty deliveries for Howard Hughes and a story that covers thirty years and expecting to get away with it. And yet if he's telling the truth, why did he plug in that phony flight schedule for the 23rd of April? Unless he was drunk at the time."

"Those numbers don't look as though they were written by a drunk. But what sense would it make for him to write in those schedules as evidence that he went from Anchorage to Seattle to Salt Lake City when he testifies that he didn't go that way? Those flight schedules don't back him up, they contradict him! What liar fakes an entry in his calendar to make himself look like a liar? Now, if he's lying, why?"

"Because he's in it with Dummar," Eli said.

"If he went in with Dummar before the will was written, would he have let Dummar put his own name in it and not Forsythe's? If Forsythe had anything to do with the forgery, wouldn't he have written something like 'And I leave one sixteenth to my beloved bagman, LeVane Forsythe'? Forsythe's claimed relationship with Hughes makes Forsythe's name in Hughes' will far more acceptable than Dummar's. And do you think that Forsythe would have allowed Dummar, with his name in the will, to deliver it to the Mormon Church? In broad daylight?"

"Hal, suppose that Forsythe went in with Dummar after the will was delivered by Dummar—no, how could you explain that deposit slip the day Hughes died? How could you explain the missing day of the 27th when Forsythe just happened to be down in San Francisco? Christ!"

"Would a sane liar try anything like this?"

"Where is it written how far a sane liar will go?"

"Eli, you think he might be crazy?"

"Do you?"

"He doesn't look crazy. He doesn't sound crazy. He doesn't act crazy. Maybe he's crazy."

The day after we returned to Los Angeles, I phoned Dutson and asked him if he would find out if Dr. David Raskin would administer a lie detector test to LeVane Forsythe, and if so, if Dutson could pay for it. The following day, Dr. Raskin agreed to give the test, Dutson agreed to pay for it, and Forsythe agreed to fly to Salt Lake City to take it.

31. THE FBI REPORT

On April 29, 1977, four months after Judge Hayes granted my motion that the will be examined by forensic experts, Eli and Stanley joined me in Las Vegas to hear the FBI report. Department 9 was again packed with the press, with a few seats allocated to the first spectators in line to hear the reading of the report by the Nevada Attorney General himself, Robert A. List. Earl Yoakum chuckled at me as he walked his huge barrel of fat into the courtroom. "Hal, you got your concession speech ready? Ah thank you're gonna get to give it today."

Bittle took his usual seat, apparently pinched somewhere and mumbled, "It'll be about time!"

I was quite prepared, if the FBI report showed that either the paper of our will or the ink on it was not in existence in 1968, to withdraw the petition for probate and get the hell out of the case.

Judge Hayes took the bench and announced that we were about to hear the FBI report, and Attorney General List rose and began reading it. "The first part of the FBI report concerns the findings of the fingerprint expert. He found on the Mormon Church Visitors Center envelope, in the lower left-hand corner under the word *Personal,* a left thumbprint identified as that of Melvin Dummar.

"On the book *Hoax* removed from the Weber State Library, on the lower left corner of page six of the index page was found a left thumbprint of Melvin Dummar.

"The *Life* magazine issue also removed from the Weber State Library was examined. No fingerprints of Melvin Dummar or anyone else involved in this case were found on it.

"After a thorough examination of the three-page purported will and the envelope in which it was contained, no fingerprints were found of Howard Hughes. Nor were any fingerprints found on it of Melvin Dummar, Bonnie Dummar, or LeVane Forsythe. Nor were any fingerprints found of President Kimball of the Mormon Church, nor those of the general counsel of the Church, Wilford Kirton, nor any church employees, persons known to have handled it.

"The second part of the report is by the FBI handwriting expert. He concluded that the will was not written by the hand of Howard Hughes." When cheers came up from Yoakum, Clairbourne, and Bittle and their assistants, Judge Hayes glared at them and rapped for order.

"The third part of the report concerns the attempt to age the paper. The FBI expert could conclude nothing about the age of the paper.

"The fourth part of the report is of the examination of the will's envelope addressed to *Dear Mr. McKay.* The FBI found that it had been steamed open. Someone then added glue from another source to the inside flap in an effort to reseal the envelope. The envelope was then put in some type of container at high temperature causing the resultant discoloration."

The judge winced. So did Eli. So did Stanley. Nobody had believed Dummar last January when he testified about steaming the flap open, adding glue to it, and heating it in a hotdog oven. Nobody! Except that long haired *Playboy* writer.

"The fourth part of the FBI report concerns the ink on the purported will. The examination was by a chemist of the Alcohol, Tobacco and Firearms Division of the Treasury Department, where all such examinations are made for the FBI. The chemist reports that the ink on the offered will came from a ballpoint pen. The ink was manufactured by Paper Mate."

Eli nudged me and whispered, "Jesus Christ! Remember what Levar Myler said in his deposition?"

List went on: "The ink formula is 307. It was first put on the market by Paper Mate in 1963. Formula 307 was discontinued by Paper Mate and no longer used in its ballpoints after February 1974."

I looked at Eli's face to see if he, too, knew what this meant. He knew what it meant. At my left, Stanley whispered, "Hal, I'm with you! All the way!"

How could Melvin Dummar in April 1976—as the contestants insisted—have forged this will using ink which had been off the market for two years? How could Dummar have known in those three weeks following Hughes' death in 1976 that in 1968 Howard Hughes wrote with Paper Mate pens? A lucky guess? A lucky guess for Dummar in April 1976 to have selected not only the brand of pen Howard Hughes had used in 1968, but an old pen that had in it an ink available in 1968?

After the report concluded, Judge Hayes looked at me and waited.

"May it please the Court," I said, "as a result of certain documentation recently uncovered, corroborating the testimony of LeVane Forsythe, but more particularly as a result of the scientific findings of the FBI's forensic experts read to us this morning, the proponent is now irrevocably committed to defend the offered will in a trial by jury."

32. FINN TRUDELL

After the reading of the FBI report, Judge Hayes lifted the order banning the depositions of handwriting experts, and ordered the trial to begin at 9:00 A.M. on July 7, 1977.

I phoned Forsythe in Anchorage and told him about the FBI report. He said, "You sound surprised. Didn't I tell you you had the goods?"

"Lee, that girl at your bank who initialled your deposit slip the day Hughes died. Will you ask her if she remembers why she thought those bills were old?"

The evening we heard the FBI report, the banner for a story on page two of the L.A. *Times* read:

FBI CHARGES "MORMON WILL" FORGERY

And in the Los Angeles *Examiner,* the story was captioned:

"MORMON WILL" FAKE SAYS NEVADA ATTORNEY GENERAL

The following day, Forsythe phoned to tell me that the bank teller's name was Dianne Ebnet, and that she no longer lived in Anchorage.

Late that week I received a phone call from Dr. David Raskin in Salt Lake City. He had given LeVane Forsythe a lie detector test, and then, to verify his conclusion, repeated the test three times. The key questions were:

1. In Vancouver, in 1972, were you given an envelope by Howard Hughes?

2. On or about January 7, 1976, did you receive telephone instructions to deliver to Melvin Dummar one of the smaller envelopes contained in the larger one given to you by Howard Hughes?

3. Did you deliver that envelope to Melvin Dummar in Utah on April 27, 1976?

To each question, Forsythe answered yes.

Dr. Raskin explained his scoring method. A minus meant an awareness of deception. A plus meant an absence of an awareness of deception. Anything lower than a plus 6 meant an inconclusive finding. Anything over a plus 6 meant that the subject was telling the truth. A plus 10 was a thoroughly reliable indication of the subject's truthfulness.

LeVane Forsythe scored a plus 14.

Dr. Raskin was prepared to testify that in his expert opinion, there was no doubt that Forsythe was telling the truth. When I phoned Forsythe to tell him the results of the test, he said, "So?"

Forsythe learned, after talking to several people at the Alaska National Bank, that Dianne Ebnet had moved to Honolulu, where she worked as a teller for American Savings & Loan. He told me he phoned her there, and that she said she had a faint recollection of the $2,800 deposit the year earlier but that she recalled nothing about any old bills, and suggested that Forsythe send her his picture.

Stanley Fairfield finally obtained Xerox copies of all airline tickets for April 26 and 27, 1976, from Western and United, the only two airlines flying between San Francisco and Salt Lake City. When I arrived in my office at 10:00 on a Friday morning, two large boxes containing hundreds of tickets were on my desk. The message from Stanley's secretary was that he had left for Palm Springs with Doreen for the weekend. Eli Blumenfeld and I spent the next several hours going through the tickets, eliminating every one in the name of a woman, every one in which payment was other than by cash, and every one with a third city. We narrowed it down to nine possible tickets. I phoned Forsythe to find out which of the nine was the one he had used. Forsythe was uncertain. A few days later he phoned me back and said that he knew which ticket was his:

From Salt Lake City to San Francisco. One-way. Leaving Salt

Lake City at 6:00 P.M. Payment in cash. The name typed was *Linn Trudell*.

Forsythe said that on his way from Dummar's gas station he phoned to reserve a ticket in the name of *Finn Trudell*. He had chosen Finn for "final" and Trudell for "true delivery." When Forsythe arrived at the ticket window, and the agent asked if the name was Linn, Forsythe said, "Do I look like a Linn?" and told the ticket agent that the name was Finn. When the ticket agent asked, "You mean 'Glenn'?" Forsythe let it go at that. The name *Linn* was scratched out, and under it, written in ink was the name *Glenn*.

"Lee, why didn't you tell me this before?"

"I forgot. You never in your life forgot nothin', Rhoden?"

I phoned Dianne Ebnet in Hawaii. She sounded like a teenager and said that the photograph she had just received from LeVane Forsythe had jarred her memory and she recalled that the man in the picture was the man who had made the deposit of the twenty-eight $100 bills. "Oh, yes, I remember that deposit real well now. I even remember the look on the poor man's face, how real sad he looked."

"When did he look sad?"

"When I came back. You see, when I counted the bills he gave me I saw those red seals. I had never seen any bills with red seals and I thought I had been handed some funny money. So I went to my supervisor and asked her what those red seals were. She told me that those were just old bills. Then I went back to the man and he looked at me real sad and said, 'Is there anything wrong with my money?' And I felt real sorry for him and told him there was nothing wrong with the money. That it was just old."

I asked Eli to find out from the Treasury Department what the red seals meant, to get the names of the FBI agents who wrote that report, and arrange for them to give their depositions either in Washington, D.C., or Los Angeles. I particularly needed the deposition of the expert who did the work on the ink.

Three weeks after I had written to Attorney General Robert A. List, asking that he have the *deliver this one* envelope supplied by LeVane Forsythe examined for fingerprints, the Attorney General replied: "It would be violative of the policy of this office, to give any assistance to private counsel in private litigation."

I hired a Los Angeles fingerprint expert to go to Las Vegas with me to examine the "deliver this one" envelope Forsythe had given us, and I invited Yoakum and Bittle to attend. If a fingerprint of Howard Hughes were found on that envelope, the contest would be over and the will would be admitted to probate. If a fingerprint of Melvin Dummar were found on that envelope, it would mean that he and Forsythe were in a conspiracy, and the contest would be over and the will would be thrown out.

Yoakum and Bittle bent over the table to watch the expert work as he chemically treated both sides of the envelope.

The expert found only one partial fingerprint. It was unidentifiable.

As a test I pressed my left thumb on the envelope and asked the expert to find it. The expert couldn't.

In May, Forsythe phoned and said that he remembered something I might be able to use. In the early 1960s, he and his father had told a CPA in Southern California that they had received some cash payments from Howard Hughes for deliveries the Forsythes had made. He thought that the CPA, Alan Hammond, might remember that.

I met Alan Hammond in Orange County for lunch. "Did LeVane Forsythe tell you what he had done for the money he and his father received from Howard Hughes?"

"All they ever said was that the money came from Howard Hughes for certain special jobs. They didn't want to tell me what the special jobs were, and I never asked them."

"Would you be willing to testify to this?"

"No, I would not. Not unless Mr. Forsythe gave me his permission to disclose this confidential information. And I'd have to advise him not to give it. Can you imagine the trouble he'd be in if this were exposed?"

Three days after I had asked Eli to find out the meaning of those red seals, he phoned and hollered, "I've got it! I just talked to an officer of the U.S. Mint! He'll testify that one-hundred-dollar bills with red seals were last issued by the Treasury Department in—are you ready for this?"

"I'm ready."

"In January 1971! Did you hear me? January 1971! Hal, do I have to explain to you what that means?"

"No, Eli, I know."

"Those one-hundred-dollar bills deposited by Forsythe the day Hughes died were five years old! They were no longer in circulation! Those bills deposited by Forsythe had been sitting around for five years! Say, in an envelope!"

"I know, Eli."

"What are those shmucks going to argue? That Forsythe won those twenty-eight red sealed bills in a poker game and just happened, hours after Hughes died, to deposit those old bills in his account? Bullshit! Forsythe may look like the lousiest liar in the world, but that shmuck's been telling the truth!"

"Eli, haven't I said this all along?"

33. FORMULA 307

Albert Lyter appeared in my office in June 1977 to testify in a deposition about his examination of the Mormon will for the FBI. Albert Lyter, a slight, youthful-looking twenty-eight with a dark Vandyke, had been a forensic chemist with the Alcohol, Tobacco and Firearms Department of the United States Treasury Department for two and a half years. He held a B.S. in Biology and a Master of Science in forensic science; he had testified in federal and state courts in eight trials.

In March 1977 Lyter was assigned by the FBI to determine the type and manufacturer of the ink on the purported will and its envelope. First, Lyter took samples of the ink on the three pages and on the envelope, analyzed them with thin-layer chromatography, and determined that the ink on the McKay envelope and on each page of the three-page document was the same ink.

Lyter limited his search in the department's library of inks—where there were approximately three thousand different samples of inks—to ballpoint inks, and then narrowed his possible choices to those that were blue. That left him with three hundred out of which to find the one that was used to write the purported will. After eliminating all but nine of those blue ballpoint inks, Lyter ran a thin-layer chromatography test on those nine inks, and found that only one matched the ink on the will. The sample that matched was an ink made by Paper Mate, dated and labeled formula 307 with a dye called MBSN.

"In March 1968, how many different ink manufacturers had inks on the market?"

"At least twenty-five."

"Could the ink on the questioned document have been put there in March 1968?"

"Yes."

"Suppose that someone in April 1976 wanted to forge a document and wanted to make it look as though it had been written in March 1968. Suppose he bought a Paper Mate ballpoint pen with blue ink, and used that pen to forge this will. Could he succeed in his forgery?"

"Hardly. The blue ballpoint ink on the market in April 1976—it's still manufactured by Paper Mate—is their formula 316. It's easy for a chemist using thin-layer chromatography to distinguish 316 from 307. According to Paper Mate's records, 316 wasn't formulated until 1974."

"How could someone who was not an employee of Paper Mate, and who did not work in your laboratory in the Treasury Department, know this?"

"He couldn't. This information is a trade secret of Paper Mate. It's not available to the public. Not even to its own employees out of the restricted chemistry section. And, we, of course, would not supply that information to anyone."

"Would it be possible from a photograph of a memo handwritten with a ballpoint pen to determine the kind of ink?"

"Impossible."

"Would it be possible from a photograph to determine the manufacturer of the pen?"

"Impossible."

"Suppose that in April 1976 someone bought a Paper Mate pen and wanted to know whether ink in it was the kind which could have been used in 1968. How could he find that out?"

"There's no way he could find that out unless someone at Paper Mate told him. And they wouldn't. Or unless someone in my department told him. And we wouldn't."

"Is there any way that anyone in 1976, other than you or someone in your lab, could have determined which inks were and which inks were not available in 1968?"

"No."

"Suppose someone in 1976 had an old Paper Mate pen which he suspected might have been around in 1968, and he wanted to know if he were correct. How could he find out?"

"He couldn't."

34. SIEG HEIL!

After the FBI report corroborated Melvin Dummar and gave us ink evidence that made a forgery highly unlikely, Hans Verhaeren of Amsterdam realized that he had been right all along and agreed to testify. Henri Ollivier of Marseilles had never wavered, and I had had no communications with Pierre Faideau of Paris after he examined the will last October. Since Lothar Michel of Mannheim, after news of Melvin Dummar's fingerprint on the outer envelope, had reversed his opinion that Howard Hughes wrote the will, I was left with three Europeans. And with the opinions of Americans Ingersol and Casey dissolved by that news of Dummar's fingerprint on the envelope, I was left with Polly Jean Pfau as my only American expert.

I had to learn what questions to ask each of my four experts, and how each wanted to present his opinion to the jury. By demonstration with blowups? If so, of what words, of what letters in what exemplars compared to what in the will? Or by means of overhead projection? To properly prepare this vital phase of the case I had to go to Paris and Marseilles with a translator, then to Holland, and then to Detroit. But I didn't have the money.

I didn't have the money for my traveling expenses or for a translator, or for the experts' fees or their expenses, or for the photography, or for the special equipment the experts would require. I estimated these costs at $100,000. That is, if I ate only at McDonald's.

In those last sixty days before trial, I set up the mechanics and prepared the questions for depositions in Las Vegas of the Summa Corporation executives and of three more of Hughes' aides, and for depositions in Los Angeles of another aide and the doctor on the plane with Hughes when he died. I asked Stanley Fairfield to schedule the depositions of the contestants' handwriting experts in Chicago, Richmond, Memphis, Los Angeles, and San Francisco, while Eli arranged for depositions in Los Angeles of the FBI's experts. I needed someone to interview and depose the autopsy surgeon in Houston and a specialist in Minnesota familiar with the effects of kidney disease on handwriting. But I had a problem with those depositions. The same problem I had with the trip to Europe. No money.

I had to decide whether to retain a large Los Angeles law firm as co-counsel to supply manpower and money for those trial preparations. The disadvantage to me was probable interference with my running the case. I wanted to present the case my way; with help, but without interference. And without an army of lawyers at the counsel table. But any law firm investing its time and money would be entitled to a voice in overall strategy and trial tactics, and this could cause conflicts. The disadvantage to Mitchelson, Fairfield, Blumenfeld, and Dobbs was that after we won and took over the executorship of the estate, the law firm would push itself in and them out.

Marvin Mitchelson urged me not to bring in a law firm, and offered to pay the cost of the trip to Europe, and, if I couldn't get the money elsewhere, to pay the fees and expenses of the handwriting experts. His offer was sincere; his ability to keep it was doubtful.

Eli and Stanley argued that, together, they could provide all the manpower I would need. They would go anywhere at their own expense to take whatever depositions I could not take. They would move to Las Vegas, and Stanley would be available seven days and nights a week, and Eli would be available except on weekends, no matter how long the trial. Stanley said, "I'll back you with deposition breakdowns—you can count on me all the way! We don't need some outside law firm grabbing up all the plum jobs after we win!"

I knew it was a mistake. But I did not want to bring in a big Los Angeles law firm. So I agreed not to.

A week after the FBI report compelled a commitment to trial, Wilbur Dobbs flew to Los Angeles for what he said was a definition of his role.

Over a double Chivas in the Century City Playboy Club, Wilbur said, "Ah know now that Hughes wrote it, an' that you're gonna win. An' durin' the trial, Ah'll examine whatever witness you assign to me. Which ones?"

"Wil, before you can impeach a witness with extrinsic evidence of a prior inconsistent statement, do you have to lay a foundation?"

"Well, Ah may not know every little rule that—"

"Wil, did you understand what I just asked you?"

"No."

"Do you know when a lay witness may give an opinion and when he may not? Do you know the scope of the cross-examination of a character witness? Do you know when you can lead and when you can't?"

"Not even one witness?"

"Not in this case, Wil. I've been through the same thing with Stanley and Marvin."

"All right, no witnesses. But Ah'm still with you. Ah'll move to Las Vegas when you do an' stay there for the whole trial."

"What about your family in Houston? Your law practice there? Your living expenses in Las Vegas for maybe a year?"

"Ah've arranged to borrow money to live on, an' mah family approves. Is there anythin' Ah can do for the case right now?"

Wilbur Dobbs' inexperience in heavy litigation made him less than ideally suited for depositions in this heavy litigation, but if I could spell out exactly what he was to do, his exuberance might make up for his inexperience. When I assigned Wilbur the entire medical phase of the case, beginning with a study of the autopsy report to be followed by depositions in Houston and Detroit, I was afraid he was going to kiss me.

On May 21, 1976, at Marvin Mitchelson's expense, he and I flew to Paris for our first European stop, to spend three days with Pierre Faideau. At the Bristol Hotel we met Honoré Comet, the translator Marvin had hired in Los Angeles, and for two days the three of us studied the English translation of Faideau's twenty-four-page report, comparing thirty-two exemplars with the will. We studied the similarities in pen lifts, in linking lines between letters, in peculiar attaching strokes in the will and in the exemplars. In a small conference room off the main lobby at 3:00 A.M. the morning of our first appointment with Faideau, after five tiring hours of finding the places in the exemplars while I found the corresponding places in the will, Marvin shrieked, "My God! Hughes really did write this! He really did!"

Two productive days later we returned to Monsieur Faideau's third-floor apartment for our last visit. Marvin asked me what we ought to offer Faideau as a fee. I suggested $7,500. He had expected to pay a $10,000 fee and agreed. As we reached the top of the third flight of stairs, Marvin said, "Let's make it seven thousand." As I raised my hand to knock on the door, Marvin said, "Offer him six thousand five hundred." It was Marvin's money. I knocked, and before the door opened, Marvin whispered, "Make it an even six thousand. We can always go up."

"Marvin, for chrissakes, why don't we just ask him to pay us for the experience?"

When our last session with Faideau ended and I asked what his fee would be in addition to his expenses, and he said he would leave it to us, I offered him $6,000. Madam Faideau gasped with pleasure, and pale Pierre smiled, and from his sweeping gesture and the tone of his French to Comet, I knew he was saying that we were extremely generous. That is what he said.

As soon as we left the building, Marvin mumbled, "Son of a bitch! We should have made it five thousand!"

Faideau was dedicated and knowledgeable, but what about his effect on a Las Vegas jury? His calm, relaxed manner might be taken as a lack of self-confidence; his pallor and slow movements might be taken as mental weakness; his delicate gestures might be taken as effeminacy. Still, I felt that Faideau would be more effective than bombastic Ollivier of Marseilles. By far, the best of our three Europeans would be Hans Verhaeren. Our Parisian born translator left us in Paris to meet us in Marseilles in four days, and Marvin and I flew to Amsterdam for our appointment with Verhaeren. The evening Marvin and I checked into the Amsterdam Hilton, where the desk clerk and the bellhop spoke better English than we did, I phoned Verhaeren. He had made a restaurant reservation and insisted on picking us up at the hotel in his little red Volvo. That first evening I sensed an uneasiness in Mr. Verhaeren and in his wife.

I needed Verhaeren. Of the three Europeans, he was our only English-speaking expert, and I was uncomfortable about the competence of our one American, Polly Jean Pfau. Hans Verhaeren's 108-page report was brilliant, and I counted on him to supply the major thrust of our handwriting testimony. I planned to call him as our first expert and to use him on the stand for at least three days, Faideau for three hours, and Ollivier thirty minutes. I needed Verhaeren, and something was wrong.

We spent two days at the Verhaerens' small suburban home. The plumbing must have been installed in the early thirties, the television set had long since passed obsolescence, and the furniture had been somewhere for generations. Their home was charming and they were charming, and those two sunny late-Spring days in Amsterdam at the Verhaerens' home were pleasant and instructive. Verhaeren had a patient way of explaining why the will was written by Howard Hughes, and when Marvin and I were having breakfast in our hotel, or a brandy in the bar at night, we relished the impression Verhaeren would make on that Las Vegas jury.

Marvin also saw an uneasiness in the Verhaerens, and we decided that it was their uncertainty about the fee and their reluctance to bring it up. As soon as we arrived at the Verhaerens' house the morning of our last day with him, we offered him the $6,000 fee we had offered Faideau. Mr. and Mrs. Verhaeren exclaimed shock at so enormous a fee and refused it, but when we told them that that was the fee Faideau had accepted and the fee we were going to offer Ollivier, Mr. Verhaeren graciously thanked us and accepted.

During a delicious raw-herring lunch that day, Marvin and I learned that it wasn't the fee that had been bothering the Verhaerens. Mrs. Verhaeren suddenly stopped eating and nodded at her husband as though to say, Do it now! He looked at her and nodded and sat erect. "There is something I must tell you. It may influence you in your decision to present me as a witness in your case."

Mrs. Verhaeren said, "We should have told you the night you arrived. But it was so very pleasant to see you both. And it was so difficult to tell you."

"Yes, we should have told you sooner. I should have told you when I met you in the United States last year."

Mrs. Verhaeren said, "We considered not telling you, but we knew that it would be wrong not to tell you. If it came out in the trial—and we don't know if it could or not—you might be badly hurt. We could not allow this to happen to you."

Mr. Verhaeren took a long breath. "After World War Two, I was tried as a war criminal by the Dutch government. I was charged with being a Nazi collaborator, which I was. I was sentenced to fifteen years. In 1952, I was released after serving seven years in prison."

By the time Hans Verhaeren had forced out those last words, his eyes were teared. He paused and remained stiff and waited. Marvin sat back to let me decide what our position would be. Mrs. Verhaeren looked at me and she, too, had tears, and she, too, waited.

"Mr. Verhaeren," I said, "I know that this must be a painful thing for you to remember. But what you two are concerned about is of no concern to us in the trial of the Howard Hughes will."

Mr. Verhaeren said, "But, what if the lawyers for the other side learn of this and—"

"Mr. Verhaeren, we want you—we need you as a handwriting expert. What matters is your competence as a handwriting expert. This in your past has nothing to do with your competence as a handwriting expert. It could not—it will not be brought out in the trial. Now, could I please have another piece of this herring?"

"Of course, of course! All you want, all you want!" Mr. Verhaeren said, and I looked down at the food to let him and his wife wipe their eyes without being looked at.

Mrs. Verhaeren said, "Oh, you can't know how good it is to hear you say this! We were so worried, Hans and I. We talked about this over and over again—should we tell you? And how do we tell you? And when do we tell you—so many, many times."

"May I please explain something to you?" Mr. Verhaeren said. "The crime I committed was speaking on the radio to the people of Holland during the occupation. It is true that I urged them to support the Germans, but I did this because of a hatred I had for Communists. And I still feel the same way. The Germans were opposing Communism, and to my thinking, that made them worth supporting."

I changed the subject back to the handwriting work. At the end of our last session, when Verhaeren was ready to drive us back to our hotel, Marvin extended to the Verhaerens for the third time that afternoon his cordial invitation to come to Los Angeles to be his guests at his son's bar mitzvah.

After Verhaeren drove us to our hotel, Marvin and I made straight for the bar, Marvin mumbling, "Our chief expert! What does he turn out to be? A Nazi! How can we still use him?"

"We can use him and we will. We need him."

"What if they ask him on cross-examination what he did during the War to help the cause?"

"They can't. No matter what his crime was, it can't be used to impeach him in Nevada if he got out of prison more than ten years before he testifies."

"But, what if they find out about it and leak it to the press? I can see the headlines the day Verhaeren testifies: MORMON WILL GENUINE SAYS PROPONENT'S NAZI EXPERT. What if that little bastard is on the witness stand and the clerk asks him to raise his hand for the oath and he forgets where he is and gives the Nazi salute and a Heil Hitler!?"

"Cool it, Marvin, we need him."

"How badly are we going to need him if we wind up with a Jew on that jury in Las Vegas and he hears that we're proving our case with a Nazi?"

"That's a risk we've got to take. We need him."

The brandies arrived and we toasted. "Sieg Heil!"

The night we heard the bad news from Verhaeren, Marvin and I left Holland to fly to meet Comet at the Sofietel in Marseilles. Since Professeur Docteur Henri Ollivier held the Légion d' Honneur for his world-renowned expertise in the detection of forgery, I had pictured his office at the end of a long, mirrored corridor in a place like the Palace at Versailles. At 9:00 A.M. the next morning we met the Professeur in his small, dingy office on the second floor of the Marseilles police station.

Henri Ollivier was wearing the same gray flannel slacks and dark blue double-breasted blazer he had worn seven months earlier in Los Angeles. Ollivier didn't speak, he orated. In loud, forceful tones and with proud flourishes, he showed us an example of one phase of his work in this case. His laboratory assistants had photographed and posted in rows on blue paper every fifth small *a* in the questioned document. They did the same on pink paper, with every fifth small *a* in the exemplars. Comet translated, "This way, we use a random selection. We use an objective method. The method of the scientist!" He paused and looked at us, as though waiting for applause. "And when we are through, our work speaks for itself!"

"Doctor," I asked, "in the questioned will are there per page more pen lifts with blunt endings than in the exemplars?"

Comet translated, "A pen lift is common in everyone's writing."

"Mr. Comet, did you understand both of us?"

"Oh, yes. I gave him your question, and I gave you his answer."

"Let's try another one. Doctor, is the shaky line in the will at the bottom of the *b* on line eighteen the same as or different from the shaky line at the bottom of the *b* in exemplar 3 at line twenty-one?"

Comet translated, "Yes."

"Yes, what?" I said.

"Yes, sometimes the pen shakes. The will is genuine. That is all there is to say. It is as simple as that!" Ollivier smiled to reassure me.

Marvin said to me, "Let me try. I have more rapport with him than you have. Doctor Ollivier, see this shaky line in the will at the bottom of the *b* at line eighteen? *Regardez, s'il vous plait.* You see it, *oui? Bien!* Now, *regardez* a shaky line in the *b* in exemplar *vingt-et-un.* Now, do we have *la même chose?* Or do we have *la différence?*"

Comet translated, "Please, kind sir, confine yourself to English, which I cannot understand. Your French is pathetic. Now, the answer to your question is a definite, absolute, and final yes!"

Marvin mumbled to me, "We've got a little problem here."

"Doctor Ollivier," I said, "in your expert opinion, did the man who wrote the exemplars write the questioned will?"

"That you are here means that that is my opinion, yes?"

Marvin asked, "Doctor, how certain are you?"

"Absolutely certain. Without dispute, it is the same hand!"

"Do you have any doubt?"

"I told you, I am absolutely certain. If I had a doubt, I would not be absolutely certain. Now you ask me if I have a doubt!"

"Doctor, could you be wrong?"

"Any man could be wrong. If I were God, I could not be wrong. But the last time I noticed, which was this morning, I was still a man, not God. So I could be wrong. But I am not wrong."

"Have you ever been wrong in a handwriting opinion?"

"Wrong? I? I, wrong?"

"Doctor Ollivier, did you ever testify that a defendant wrote something like, say, a ransom note, and then later, learn that someone else confessed that he was the one who wrote it, not the defendant?"

Ollivier asked that the translation be repeated and then glared at Marvin. "You travel all the way from America to ask me if I am a charlatan?"

"No, no, Doctor, I didn't mean—"

"Young man, your questions are beginning to annoy me. When I say that someone wrote a questioned document, he wrote it! Gentlemen, why are you here? This case is so simple. It is so clear. Why do you need a handwriting expert to testify before a jury? Are your American juries blind? Cannot anyone see by looking at the questioned will and comparing it to a sample of the writing of Howard Hughes, that the same man wrote both?"

Ollivier took us to lunch in a restaurant which he said was world famous for bouillabaisse. In the men's room, Marvin said, "Let's offer the big ass three thousand."

"What if he compares fees with Faideau and gets pissed off?"

"We can tell him we offered him less because we don't plan to keep him on the stand as long. If he bitches we can always go up a grand."

During lunch, I asked Professeur Ollivier if he would mind discussing what, in addition to his expenses, would be his fee for his expert testimony. Ollivier gently patted his mouth with the napkin stuck under his fat chin and said something, and Comet seemed reluctant to translate it.

"My fee will be twenty-five thousand American dollars. And I will pay my own expenses."

Marvin moaned.

35. WHO WAS THE CLOWN?

The day after Marvin and I returned from Marseilles to Los Angeles, I hired a commercial photographer to prepare four-foot-tall blowups of colored photographs of the pages of the will, and of eighteen memos handwritten by Howard Hughes between 1966 and 1971; and twenty-three blowups of lines of writing, eight of groups of words, and seven of enlargements of capital and small letters. And I wanted kits, one for each juror, two for opposing counsel, one for the judge and one for me, each containing colored true-size reproductions of the will and its envelope, and fifty-three pages of memos written by Howard Hughes. The estimated cost was $22,000.

One of these exemplars was an eight-page memo handwritten by Howard Hughes to his personal aide Howard Eckersley in Nassau in 1971. The handwriting on this memo, the shapes of letters, the patched links between letters, the abnormally wide spaces between letters and between words, the high spaces between lines, and the compulsive overwriting of many letters bore a striking similarity to the handwriting of the 1968 will. After the memo was read by Eckersley, he kept it locked in a filing cabinet until it was sent with other papers to the Summa office in Hollywood in 1972, where Kay Glenn kept it locked in a safe until it was turned over to the Special Administrator in March 1977. The memo was written on yellow, lined, legal-sized paper:

Howard I want to see if I can be comfortable on board Aleta.

I don't know how many more summers I have left, Howard, but I don't expect to spend all of them holed up in a hotel room on a Barcalounger.

You may not think about these things. You are young and smart and I have left you and the others in my staff, who have been loyal to me, well-protected. . . .

. . .

I have had in existence for some time a holographic will covering the principle features of the points of substance set forth herein.

It was carefully written seated at a desk, and complying to all the rules governing such wills (such as no other typed or printed material on any of the pages). . . .

. . .

. . . you as well as other members of my staff were identified by description rather than by name. . . .

. . .

There are a few honorable men left in the world, and although you may not share my confidence with respect to every last member of the Howard Hughes Tool Company board of directors, I have full faith and trust in my Hughes Tool Company board of directors and officers, acting in that capacity as a group or combined body or entity.

The evening I ordered the blowups, I left for depositions of the contestants' handwriting experts in Washington, D.C., and Chicago and then Las Vegas for the depositions of Hughes' other personal aides and his top executives. In the meantime Wilbur Dobbs took the depositions of doctors in Minneapolis and Houston, and Eli attended the depositions taken by the contestants of handwriting experts who had examined the will for our side and found it to be a forgery.

I asked Alex Morenus in Las Vegas to find at least one local doctor familiar with the effect of kidney disease on a patient's handwriting.

Alex said he would. He didn't. I asked Alex to interview two Desert Inn employees in Las Vegas who claimed to know that Howard Hughes was out of that hotel during his four-year stay there. Alex said he would. He didn't. I interviewed the two and they turned out to be daydreaming derelicts.

Alex Morenus knew someone who knew Gordon Margulis and arranged for me to interview him in Alex's office. Gordon Margulis, a strong, stocky cockney, had come to the United States from London's East Side in 1967 and worked first as a full-time busboy and then as a cook for Howard Hughes. When the Hughes party left the Desert Inn on Thanksgiving 1970, Margulis was one of the crew who stayed behind as a decoy on the ninth floor to make noise and order dinner to fool the hotel guards into thinking that Hughes was still there. A few days later, Margulis joined the Hughes group in Nassau and remained with him until a few hours before his death.

Margulis said that Hughes had slipped and broken his hip in London in 1973 and, although after surgery he was able to walk, he never did again. "Not even to the bathroom." Because of Margulis' weightlifter's physique, he was the one who most often lifted Hughes from a bed to a chair or to a stretcher, and on and off airplanes, during the next three years. In answer to my question, Margulis explained, "The boss'd crap the bed."

"Who cleaned up?"

"Whoever was on duty at the time."

"During those last three years, did he ever sit on a chair?"

"Sometimes."

"And when—"

"He'd crap the chair."

"And whoever was on duty had to—"

"That's right. And to lift the boss wasn't easy, because it was like liftin' a bloody baby. You're afraid you're gonna break somethin'."

"What did Hughes call you?"

"Gordon."

"What did you call him?"

"I sure as hell didn't call him Howard. I'd call him Mr. Hughes or just boss."

"Did you ever have a conversation with him?"

"Oh, sure. Him an' me got real friendly-like. I usually sat next to him in the airplane, an' he'd talk to me about flyin' an' the weather. Those things interested him. They didn't interest me, but I didn't tell him that."

"Did Mr. Hughes ever ask you any questions about your family or your wife or children?"

"No, never."

"Did the other aides—"

"Hey, hold it! What do you mean, other aides? I wasn't no aide! I worked for the boss, but I bloody well wasn't one of those aides! Just last year, when some smart son of a bitch in a bar kept sayin' I was one of Hughes' aides I rammed my fist into his bloody mouth. Look, I've been around an' I can take a little shit without blowin' up, but bein' called one of Hughes' aides is one thing I don't stand for, I don't!"

"Why don't you like his aides?"

"Why? In Acapulco the boss was dyin', he was! We all knew it. We could see it. He was just a bag a bones—an' I begged 'em to get the boss to a hospital in Acapulco. But, no, they says, we got orders, they says. Fuck the bloody orders, I says, the boss is dyin'!"

One month before trial I didn't have money for the European experts. McIntosh had reactivated the trust fund for certain expenses, but not for handwriting experts. Then three weeks before trial, Dummar's lawyers agreed to put up $75,000 for the handwriting experts, and for the interpreter for the two Frenchmen. Twelve days before trial, three of the universities, Rice, Texas, and California, and the Boy Scouts agreed to pay the jury fees and the cost of the daily transcripts. The estimate for these two minor items was $40,000. The University of Nevada and the Mormon Church declined to contribute.

After Melvin Dummar's lawyers told me that they had exhausted their borrowing ability in order to provide the fund for experts, Marvin Mitchelson assured me that I could count on him to continue his monthly loans to enable me to support my family in Los Angeles and myself in Las Vegas for as long as the trial lasted. I had no other source of money, and without Marvin's I could not live in Las Vegas to try the case. I thanked him and assured him that the loans would be repaid win or lose. Marvin wanted my promise that after we won I would give him an opportunity to prove himself on the executor's staff as supervisor of the bequest of the hundreds of millions to scholarships. I gave him my promise.

In the Las Palmas Apartments in Las Vegas, I rented a one-bedroom apartment large enough to double as an office, and arranged to move in on July 1, six days before trial. In the same complex, Wilbur Dobbs rented a bachelor apartment, Eli took a bachelor, and Stanley rented a large one-bedroom and had a second lock with an inside deadbolt installed on the front door to protect Doreen from rape.

Back in my Los Angeles office, I reviewed the law on the admissibility in evidence of lie detector test results, and on the Nevada hearsay exceptions to allow the testimony of Judge Paul Grant; and on Friday, July 1, 1977, I was in the law library of our suite reading cases on the burden of proof when a phone call from Judge Keith Hayes in Las Vegas reined everything to a stop.

"Mr. Rhoden!" Judge Hayes' voice strained to keep his rage from breaking loose. "In a phone call to LeVane Forsythe did you say that I was friendly to your side in this case?"

"Sir, if I did, I couldn't have said that you ever said any such thing—"

"Did you or didn't you?"

"Judge, I'm not sure. This was months ago. When I was trying to con Forsythe into coming to Las Vegas I may have given him my opinion that—"

"Did you ever tell that man that as a Mormon I wanted this will admitted to probate?"

"Judge, I have a vague recollection that I speculated that you would welcome him—but it was only to—"

"How could you have done anything so stupid? Mr. Bittle has just filed a challenge for cause against me! I'm charged with being biased and prejudiced in your favor! And the accusation of judicial misconduct is based on what you said about me in a taped phone conversation with Forsythe!"

"Judge Hayes, please let me explain—I had been trying to persuade—" I shut up because he hung up.

I phoned Forsythe in Anchorage. "Why in hell did you give Bittle that tape?"

"Why in hell not? He ast me if I had any tapes of phone conversations with you, an' could he borrow 'em. I ain't got nothin' to hide. I'm tellin' everybody the truth, Rhoden, an' I'm givin' everybody everythin', you know what I mean?"

On July 6, 1977, Judge Hayes vacated the trial date and transferred the case to the Chief Judge to assign another judge to rule on the challenge. Earl Yoakum rose to address Judge Hayes. "Your Honor, this challenge made by Mr. Bittle is one in which Ah did not participate, an' Ah shall remain completely neutral."

After the hearing, Wilbur Dobbs said, "Neutral! In Houston, I heard Yoakum say that with the Mormon Church as one of the big beneficiaries, there was no way he was going to allow this case to be tried by a Mormon Judge. Neutral, mah ass!"

Eli and Stanley drove from the courtroom to the Las Palmas Apartments to indefinitely delay their rentals.

In Los Angeles I prepared a sixteen-page affidavit in opposition to Bittle's motion, and I was researching the cases for a brief on the law in his defense when Eli and Stanley stormed into the library to urge me to allow Hayes to be disqualified. Stanley argued, "Let them knock him off! The man is sick. The trial might take months. What if he dies during the trial? That'd mean a mistrial, and we'd have to try the whole damned thing over again!"

"No."

Eli fought hard. "Look what's going to happen if he stays on the case.

He'll take those remarks you made to Forsythe and shove them up your ass every chance he gets—your remarks are what Bittle's using to bump him, and Hayes isn't going to forget that. And if he stays on, he'll bend over backward to show everybody—Bittle and Yoakum and the press and all the other judges in Vegas—that he isn't friendly toward you. Hal, you've got to let them dump him!"

"No."

"Why do you want him, for chrissakes?"

"It just isn't fair that he be booted out! He didn't do anything wrong. He didn't say anything wrong. I did. I hurt him and I've got to defend him. Now, do I get your help, or don't I?"

The chief judge in Las Vegas assigned Judge William Foreman of Reno to try the charge against Judge Hayes in a hearing in Las Vegas on July 29, 1977.

During the three-week delay, I continued my preparation of questions I would ask the forty witnesses I expected to call, and in reviewing my file on ATF chemist Albert Lyter, I saw a note that I had made during his deposition and had forgotten about: *Find on original handwritten memo by Hughes in March 1968 same ink used to write will in March 1968. Same ink out of 3,000?*

If Hughes wrote the will dated March 19, 1968, wouldn't it be likely that he had used the same pen—or a similar pen out of the same box with the same ink—to write other things in March 1968? We could get samples of the 307 ink formula with the MBSN dye from Paper Mate, but where could we get original memos handwritten by Howard Hughes in March 1968? I remembered that last summer in Las Vegas, a used-car dealer, Sidney Crowley, had shown me two of what he said were ten handwritten memos by Hughes in the Desert Inn in 1968 to his Las Vegas lawyer, Bob Edison. Edison died in 1972, and those memos were held by his widow, the remarried Vanessa Edison Welles. When I had asked Crowley to lend me those two memos for examination by hand-writing experts, he had said that Mrs. Welles and her new husband, an unemployed saxophone player, were unable to make their mortgage payments. After I had told Crowley that suppression of evidence was a crime, he filed those two memos with the court for examination by handwriting experts. Why couldn't I borrow the remaining eight Edison memos and have a chemist compare the ink on them with a sample of Paper Mate's 307 MBSN?

I gave the assignment to Wilbur Dobbs. "First, get a sample of the 307 MBSN ink from Paper Mate. Next, borrow the eight original memos from Edison's widow. Then have a forensic chemist make a comparison the way Lyter did." Dobbs made the arrangements with Paper Mate in Boston and hired one of the top chemists in the United States, a Dr. Michael Camp, also of Boston. Camp said that his first open time to run the tests would be the last week of September. But Dobbs couldn't get the original Edison memos. Crowley told Dobbs that Mrs. Welles was still unable to make her mortgage payments.

In Las Vegas I went with Crowley to meet Vanessa Edison Welles at her home. She was a short, busty, and still-pretty woman with a mop of bright orange hair and perfect teeth. I told her why I had to borrow her eight memos. She said she needed cash. I said I didn't have any. She said she intended to hold on to those Hughes memos because her late husband had been proud of his association with Howard Hughes, and she was proud of having been married to her late husband, and she owed it to his memory to safeguard the memos Howard Hughes had written to him, memos which might be worth a fortune to a collector of Hughes memorabilia. She was afraid that if I borrowed them and they became court exhibits she wouldn't get them back, and would be disloyal to her late husband's memory and lose the opportunity to peddle the memos to a collector.

When I told her that if she would not lend us the memos, I would subpoena them, she smiled and displayed all those perfect teeth and, sitting like a beauty queen about to be crowned, purred that her doctor had told her that she was emotionally distraught because of her financial problems, and she feared that in her emotionally distraught condition, if her treasured memos were subpoenaed, she might not realize what she was doing when she burned them. I explained that if she burned the memos, she would be burning money because if her memos in this celebrated trial were used to prove the validity of Howard Hughes' will, their value to a collector would be enhanced; and I assured her that I would obtain a court order releasing her memos after the trial.

Mrs. Welles left the room with Crowley for a private conference, and when they returned, she told me that to do her bit for medical research, the other charitable beneficiaries, and our judicial system, she would allow me to have a chemist examine the eight memos. But only on the condition that the memos would remain in the physical custody of her husband, who had to be provided with a round-trip ticket, first class, and all expenses as he accompanied the memos wherever they went for chemical tests.

At the hearing on Bittle's motion to disqualify Judge Hayes, Bittle called me to the stand as his first witness. "You say that when you told LeVane Forsythe that Judge Hayes was friendly toward your side and that as a Mormon he wanted the will admitted to probate you were stating your opinion. Wasn't your opinion based on something?"

"It was based on nothing but my imagination and speculation. Judge Hayes never said that he was friendly toward my side. And he never said he wanted that will admitted."

"Then why did you say that to Forsythe?"

"To persuade him to testify in Las Vegas. He was afraid that a Nevada judge might be hostile to him. I wanted to reassure him that he'd be welcome."

Bittle then called Judge Hayes as his next witness.

"Judge Hayes, in your hospital room in Houston, did you and Mr. Rhoden discuss this case without opposing counsel?"

"Yes, we did. We discussed a matter of procedure. This was a few days before Mr. Yoakum came to see me in the same hospital room, also without opposing counsel. Mr. Yoakum tried to persuade me to rescind an order allowing the deposition of Judge Grant. And the day that Mr. Rhoden came to see me was a couple of days before I received a two-page mailgram from you, denouncing Mr. Rhoden's attempt to take Judge Grant's deposition and urging that I disallow it."

"Judge Hayes, in that hospital room outside the presence of opposing counsel, what did Mr. Rhoden say about this case?"

"That he wanted to get out of it. Now, would you like me to tell what you said to me, outside the presence of opposing counsel, in my chambers on July 1st to persuade me to disqualify myself instead of facing this?"

"Judge Hayes, I'm doing what I must do to protect the interests of my clients."

"If the interests of your clients were hurt by my meeting with Mr. Rhoden last January, why did you wait seven months to charge judicial misconduct? Excuse me—I forgot that I am here as a witness. Please continue your exercise in hypocrisy."

"I have no further questions."

Judge Foreman said, "Judge Hayes, is there anything you would like to say in your own defense?"

"Yes, if I may." There were tears in his eyes. "I am not ashamed of anything I have done. I have no bias. I have no prejudice. I have a sacred respect for the law and my oath as a judge, and I would never violate that oath." His voice cracked and he paused to take a deep breath. "As a Mormon, I have very clearly defined obligations to my Father in Heaven. And they do not include my assisting in any illegal attempt to provide money to my Church. If I did any such thing, I would suffer eternal damnation."

The second day of the hearing, in an hour-long argument, Phillip Bittle urged that in addition to my comments to Forsythe, the bias and prejudice of Judge Hayes was evidenced by his having given an opportunity to Melvin Dummar last January to "publicly proclaim his innocence in a three-day circus. Your Honor, I made this challenge not only to ensure a fair trial for my clients, but to protect the Nevada judiciary from the public distrust which has been raised in this matter."

Earl Yoakum argued, "Judge Hayes' bias is shown by the way he allowed himself to be so flagrantly abused by this Los Angeles lawyer for the proponent. But, Your Honor, Judge Hayes ought to be disqualified from trying this will contest whether he is biased or not. He ought to be disqualified because a charge has been made that he is biased. This charge has cast a cloud on his integrity. To clear the air, to remove that cloud, Judge Hayes ought to be disqualified."

I argued, "Mr. Bittle calls the three-day examination of Dummar a circus. I examined Dummar for three hours, while Mr. Bittle examined him for a day and a half, including in his questions long statements about his client's intimate physical afflictions, and about his own poverty-stricken childhood. If the Dummar hearing was a circus, who was the clown?

"Mr. Bittle argues that because Judge Hayes is a Mormon, he would tend to rule in favor of the admissibility of testimony by a Salt Lake City judge who is also a Mormon. Does Mr. Bittle mean that no Mormon judge ought to hear a case in which a witness is a Mormon? Does it then follow that no Protestant judge ought to hear a case in which a witness is Protestant? Or does Mr. Bittle single out Mormon judges as having this inability to make honest rulings?

"Mr. Bittle argues that he made his motion to avoid public distrust of the Nevada judiciary in this matter. But if there is any public distrust of the Nevada judiciary in this matter, it was caused by Mr. Bittle's own motion!

"And Mr. Yoakum argues, 'Let's remove the cloud cast on Judge Hayes' integrity by removing Judge Hayes. He argues, 'Let's clear the air!' Who polluted the air?

"Is a respected judge to be disgraced by being disqualified from trying a case merely because a lawyer in that case, in persuading a witness to testify, shoots off his big mouth? I am the one who made those stupid statements to Forsythe, not Judge Hayes. Those statements are evidence of my bad judgment, not evidence of the attitude of Judge Hayes."

On August 9, 1977, in Reno, Nevada, Judge William Foreman signed his decision:

As a result of these proceedings, Rhoden's statements to a witness in Alaska have been widely publicized, and if Judge Hayes continues to preside in this case, a cloud of unwarranted suspicion will hang over it. Therefore, Judge Hayes is hereby disqualified from acting further in this case.

36. THE EDISON MEMOS

On August 15, 1977, Judge Hayes instructed his clerk to draw out of a box the name of another judge to try the case if Hayes failed in his petition for a writ to the Nevada Supreme Court for an order reversing Judge Foreman. The name drawn was Judge Monroe Cassidy. Two days later Alex Morenus phoned me in Los Angeles to tell me that at a Las Vegas bar dinner attended by several judges the night before, he heard Judge Cassidy say, "When the Mormon will case is turned over to me, my first judicial act will be to revoke the privilege given to Rhoden to practice in Nevada, and my second judicial act will be to walk down from my bench and personally kick that Los Angeles bastard's ass out of my courtroom." Alexander Morenus enjoyed telling me that.

The court in Texas had set November 14, 1977, as the date for jury trial in Houston of the same will contest. If the Nevada trial began before November 14, I would have an acceptable excuse for not being ready to present the same case in Houston. But if trial did not begin in Las Vegas before November 14, I would have no excuse for not being ready in Houston, and if I were not ready in Houston when the case was called, the Mormon will could be destroyed by default. And there was no way I could have tried the case in Texas because I needed the deposition testimony of LeVane Forsythe and of several of Hughes' aides, and since those depositions were taken only in the Nevada proceeding, they couldn't be used for a trial in Texas. It was imperative that the trial of the Mormon will begin in Las Vegas before November 14.

Alexander Morenus advised me that under Nevada judicial procedures there was no way that the Supreme Court could rule on Hayes' petition within six months. I felt that the Nevada Supreme Court, knowing that the case would never be tried in Nevada if it were not tried promptly, would rule promptly. Eli and Stanley concluded that the Supreme Court would not rule before January 1978, and went to the Las Palmas Apartments to get back their deposits.

As to the chances of Hayes' winning a reversal, it was the general consensus that he had a better chance of tossing ten consecutive sevens at a crap table.

On August 25, 1977, the Nevada Supreme Court rendered a unanimous decision:

We order Respondent Court to vacate his opinion and order of August 8, 1977, and to restore the Hon. Keith Hayes as trial judge in case No. 7276 in the Eighth Judicial District Court.

The day after Hayes was reinstated, I moved into my Las Vegas apartment. Two days later, Wilbur Dobbs moved in from Houston. When Marvin Mitchelson wanted to know how else he could help me, I told him that I wanted to borrow his secretary for the trial. For the past several years Marvin had relied heavily in his practice on his efficient and devoted secretary, petite Linda Acaldo. Marvin said he would continue to pay Linda's salary and all her expenses, and had Linda move into an apartment in the Las Palmas, rent a typewriter and supplies, and arrange for the installation of a Xerox machine.

On August 30, 1977, Judge Hayes made his expected malice-toward-none speech assuring us that while he personally disapproved of the conduct of all counsel, particularly of mine, he would never allow his resentment to influence his rulings. "Now, gentlemen, under Nevada Rule 8, each side is required to file a Pre-trial Statement designating every witness it intends to call, and summarizing what each witness will testify to. Any witness not so designated cannot be called. This rule is to prevent one side from unfairly surprising the other during a trial. And, gentlemen, I will not tolerate trial by ambush. This trial was set to start on July 7th, but neither side complied with Rule 8, a rule which has been on our books for thirty years. Trial is reset to begin October 3rd. Two weeks before October 3rd, I expect compliance with Rule 8!"

Outside Judge Hayes' courtroom I asked Alex Morenus to join me in the corridor around the corner for a private conference. "Did you know about Rule 8 and forget, or did you learn about it the first time a few minutes ago?"

"This sounds to me like criticism."

"It sounds like that to me, too. You made a mistake, but we can correct it. Please get me a copy of that damned rule, and I'll start preparing the thing tomorrow morning."

Without answering Alex swung around and walked quickly to the stairs.

That evening in my Las Vegas apartment I received a phone call from Alex. His speech was slurred by a few drinks. "I want an apology for your criticism this morning."

We were about to start the trial and this was no time for me to hunt for new local counsel. "You have it. I'm sorry, Alex."

"You're a fine one to criticize anybody after what you did! What you said to Forsythe was a breach of ethics! You almost ruined one of the sweetest little guys who ever took the bench!"

"I've apologized publicly to Judge Hayes, I shouldn't have said what I said to Forsythe, and I'm sorry. And that's the last I want to hear about it from you!"

"It was a breach of ethics! When I learned what you had said to Forsythe, my first impulse was to not have anything more to do with you. And I still have that same impulse."

"That does it! I'll help you with your impulse. Tomorrow I'll look for new local counsel to replace you. It may take me a few—"

He hung up.

The following day I replaced Alex Morenus with the Las Vegas firm of Beckley, Singleton, DeLanoy & Jemison. Stanley Fairfield phoned me from Los Angeles and said that he had been called by Alex Morenus. "Alex is sorry he lost his temper. He'd like to stay in."

"He's staying out."

In the September pre-trial motions, Judge Hayes' demeanor toward me was, at the warmest, hostile. The first motion by contestants was for an order, not only that I not be allowed to present evidence of the results of the polygraph test given by Dr. David Raskin to LeVane Forsythe, but that I not be allowed to call David Raskin to the witness stand to testify to the reliability of the polygraph. I submitted a fifty-page brief on the law that, while a judge has discretion to exclude the results of a lie-detector test, he must first allow the side offering that evidence an opportunity to show that the test was reliable. Judge Hayes granted contestants' motion. After the ruling, Eli fumed in the hallway. "I knew this'd happen! I warned you!"

Contestants' next motion was for an order that in opening statement I not refer to, or in the trial attempt to present, the testimony of Judge Paul Grant concerning the phone call he had received in July 1972. I argued that while Judge Grant could not testify that the will was genuine and could not corroborate Melvin Dummar's story about how he got the will in April 1976, Grant could furnish some evidence that the will—which contestants contended was written by Dummar after April 5, 1976—was in existence in 1972. I argued three exceptions to the hearsay rule, and after Judge Hayes patiently heard everything I had to say in opposition to contestants' motion, he granted it. As we left the courtroom, Eli whispered, "Twice in one day!"

The following morning, Judge Hayes heard my motion on the burden of proof. The party who carried the burden of proof would have the right to make his opening statement first, present his evidence first, and make the opening and closing summations: an enormous tactical advantage. Under Nevada law, the contestant of a will is the plaintiff. The proponent is the defendant. The plaintiff always carries the burden of proof and always gets the right to put on his case first. Therefore, Yoakum argued, the contestants as plaintiffs carried the burden of proof and had a right to go first. I felt it vital that I put on my case first, and in an eighty-two-page brief, I cited cases in twenty-seven states in support of my argument that because of the suspicious circumstances surrounding the delivery of the offered will, the presumption was that it was invalid, and that therefore the burden rested on the proponent to prove that it was valid. With this burden came the right to go first.

After a heated three-hour argument, Judge Hayes ruled that as proponent, I carried the burden of proof, and consequently would go first.

Wilbur Dobbs invited James Spiller, a big, young private detective from Houston, to come to Las Vegas to offer his services. Spiller said he would consider it a once-in-a-lifetime opportunity to be allowed to work on this case, without a fee and at his own expense, and wanted to know what I needed.

"Evidence that puts Forsythe in Salt Lake City on the 27th of April, 1976. I'd like the ticket agent who wrote the name Glenn Trudell in ink on Forsythe's airplane ticket when he left Salt Lake City that day. And I'd like reliable evidence that at any time during Hughes' four-year stay in the Desert Inn, he was out of it. Particularly out of it in the end of December 1967."

"When do y'all want this evidence?"

"By noon yesterday."

Spiller looked at his watch. "That isn't gonna give me much time."

"I don't want you rushed. Take until noon tomorrow."

He offered his hand. "If what y'all need is out there, Ah'll find it."

I received several phone calls from people volunteering to testify that they saw Howard Hughes somewhere other than on the ninth floor of the Desert Inn between 1966 and 1970. I gave those names and phone numbers to Wilbur Dobbs to check them out for us. Wilbur reported that they were all cranks or kooks until: "This one's for real! He saw Howard Hughes at a mine in Nevada in 1967! Hal, I believe him!"

During the last week of September 1977, I sweated out a phone call from Wilbur Dobbs in Boston with Vanessa Edison's new husband and the eight original memos. Each day for three days Wilbur phoned me to tell me that Dr. Camp would have an answer the next day. A failure by Camp to find that Hughes wrote a memo in 1968 with Paper Mate's 307 MBSN ink would not mean that Hughes did not write the will. But if, out of three thousand possible inks, Hughes wrote some March 1968 memos with the same ink as that used to write the March 1968 will, we would have compelling circumstantial evidence of the will's authenticity.

In early September, Bittle and Yoakum obtained permission from Judge Hayes to take another deposition of Melvin and Bonnie Dummar in Ogden. From their questions it was obvious that Bittle contended that while Melvin did the research, Bonnie was the forger, and that Yoakum contended that while Bonnie did the research, Melvin was the forger. During a recess in Bonnie's deposition, I received another phone call from Wilber Dobbs in Boston. "Hal, the case is over! Camp ran it three times and he's positive! He used only two of the Edison memos, and on each one he found that ink used by Hughes to write those memos to Edison in March 1968 was made by Paper Mate! Formula 307 with MBSN dye! The same as the ink on the will! We've got it made!"

37. THE EASTERN DIVISION

I filed a supplement to my list of witnesses to add the name of Dr. Michael Camp and a summary of what he would testify to. A week later, Phillip Bittle scheduled the deposition of Dr. Camp in Boston, and added to his list of witnesses a chemist to testify on the same subject, Peter Fitzrandolph of Chemlabs, Inc., in San Francisco, and I scheduled the deposition of Fitzrandolph.

The week after I met Spiller, he phoned me from Willard, Utah. He had just found someone who said that in Willard, on April 27, 1976, near Dummar's gas station he had spoken to a man he identified from photographs as LeVane Forsythe.

I sent Wilbur, who knew more about the technical aspects of the ink than Eli did, with Eli, who knew more about the rules of evidence than Wilbur did, to take the deposition of Bittle's chemist, Peter Fitzrandolph. Eli called me from San Francisco. "Hal, you won't believe this! After Bittle heard what Dr. Michael Camp had found, Bittle had Fitzrandolph analyze the ink used on a dozen memos written by Hughes between February and May in 1968. Guess what Fitzrandolph found! Fitzrandolph found that ink on those memos written by Hughes was exactly what Camp had found on the ones he examined! Paper Mate's 307 with the MBSN dye! But Bittle was unhappy about this, so he gave a second batch of memos to Fitzrandolph. On a few of those memos in the second batch, a couple in March 1968, Fitzrandolph found that the ink was Paper Mate's 307 with a PAGO dye, and this, Bittle thinks, is a score for his side! Don't you love him?"

I knew from the deposition testimony of Hughes' personal aides and of his top executives at Summa, and from memos written by Hughes, that other than his aides, the closest person to Hughes in his last twenty years, a man he liked and trusted, was Tim O'Neil. I subpoenaed O'Neil for a deposition in Las Vegas in the office of our new local counsel. Tim O'Neil, lean and, like Hughes, a few inches over six feet, testified that as a vice-president of sales at Lockheed Aircraft, he had sold several planes to the Hughes Tool Company, and that his being a pilot had led to his friendship with Howard Hughes. In 1971 O'Neil left Lockheed to work for Mr. Hughes.

"Mr. Hughes put me in control of his Eastern Division."

"What did the Eastern Division do?"

"Whatever Mr. Hughes wanted it to do."

"What did Mr. Hughes want it to do?"

"Mr. Hughes never decided."

"Where were the headquarters of the Eastern Division located?"

"Wherever I was."

"No, I mean, where were the offices of the Eastern Division?"

"Wherever I was."

"You mean, there were no offices of the Eastern Division?"

"That's right."

"How many people were you in control of in the Eastern Division?"

"I was the only one."

"You mean, that when Howard Hughes put you in control of the Eastern Division, he put you in control of yourself?"

"If you want to put it that way."

O'Neil was in Acapulco when Hughes was carried on the Lear Jet on the morning of April 5, 1976. Months earlier, Hughes had given O'Neil a key to Hughes' bedroom, so that O'Neil could see Hughes without having to obtain permission of the aides. When the aides learned of this, they changed the lock on the door.

"And then, you couldn't get in to see Hughes?"

"That's right."

"Did John Holmes ever stop you?"

"Yes, he did."

"John Holmes is about five feet six. He's frail and gentle. Now, exactly what is it that kept you from seeing Hughes when Hughes wanted to see you and you wanted to see him?"

"You didn't do things that way. You don't seem to understand. If the aides said you didn't get in, you didn't get in. The aides was in charge."

"Not Hughes? His aides?"

"His aides. They was in charge."

"In the few days before Hughes died, did his doctors know what was wrong with him?"

"No."

"Why not?"

"They weren't allowed in to examine him."

"Who kept them out?"

"The aides."

I looked at the autopsy report for accuracy. "You mean, that Hughes lay there dying of uremic poisoning, weighing about ninety pounds, emaciated and dehydrated, and with his left arm separated from his shoulder, and that though he had four doctors in attendance, his personal aides kept the doctors from seeing him?"

"That's your conclusion."

"What's yours?"

"I don't have one."

Before O'Neil signed his deposition transcript, he scratched out his testimony that he had been a pilot.

In Salt Lake City, Spiller found the United Airlines ticket agent who identified his handwriting on the Trudell ticket. But the agent could not remember the purchaser of the ticket. Nor why he had changed the name from Linn to Glenn.

Three days later, Spiller obtained a sworn statement from a dentist that in 1970 in the Desert Inn, Kay Glenn, the Hughes Tool Company executive to whom Hughes' aides reported, had said that Howard Hughes frequently left the Desert Inn without his aides knowing about it, and that once when Hughes was out in the desert something happened to him, and he was picked up by someone in a car and dropped off in Las Vegas.

One week before the trial was to begin, Bittle and Yoakum filed another pre-trial statement under Rule 8 designating twenty-eight new witnesses. I had to ask Judge Hayes for time to take depositions of those twenty-eight, and Judge Hayes angrily granted me a delay of trial to November 7, 1977, one week before the trial was to begin in Texas.

By November, I owed Marvin Mitchelson over $80,000, Herman Falitz $45,000, and another lawyer $25,000. The bank took title to my airplane, but the loan officer generously promised to wait until the end of the trial before foreclosing. I borrowed another $50,000 secured by a second mortgage on my house, and then another $20,000 secured by a third. If I lost, I would be wiped out.

Ever since the December 1976 news of Dummar's fingerprints on the Mormon Church envelope, the press had been contemptuously against the will. But I knew that Howard Hughes wrote it. And I knew that there was no way we could lose.

PART TWO

THE TRIAL

38. THE DESERT INN RECORDS

The voir dire examination of prospective jurors took two weeks, with each side allowed only four peremptory challenges. Because I needed jurors who could reason logically, I knocked off two morons, and because the Mormon Church was a named beneficiary known to be bigoted against blacks, I used my last two challenges to bounce two blacks. Bittle and Yoakum removed three Mormons and a witty, well educated Jewish woman who obviously could reason logically. Our jury was composed of three women and five men.

I carefully planned my opening statement. I would tell the jurors that after witnesses Noah Dietrich and Levar Myler, Treasury Department chemist Alfred Lyter would testify that the ink on the March 1968 will was Paper Mate's 307 MBSN. Our fourth witness would be chemist Michael Camp to testify that on two March 1968 memos written by Hughes, the ink was Paper Mate's 307 MBSN. The same ink out of three thousand possible inks. At 8:15 the morning we were to make opening statements, Eli burst into my apartment. "Our ink evidence just blew up! Albert Lyter phoned me from Washington to warn me! There was a mistake! The ink on the will is Paper Mate's 307, but not with the MBSN dye! The dye in the 307 ink on the will is PAGO!"

"Oh, no!"

"Paper Mate goofed when they labeled their sample in the ATF library. What Camp found on the 1968 memos by Hughes was 307 with the MBSN dye. Shit! We no longer have a chemist to testify that the ink on the will is the same as the ink on memos written by Hughes! Can you believe it? On the morning of our opening statement we lose our ink evidence!"

"I'll revise the opening. I'll—wait a minute! This news doesn't hurt our case. It helps it!"

"Helps it?"

"Helps it! 307 PAGO went off the market in 1972. That's four years before Dummar supposedly used it to forge the will. But 307 MBSN, that we thought was on the will, was on the market until 1974."

"But, for chrissakes, what really matters is that Camp was going to testify that the same kind of ink that's on the 1968 will was on memos written by Hughes the same month in 1968! And now we can't use him!

He didn't find any 307 PAGO on those Edison memos! After he found 307 MBSN on two of them we didn't bother with any more tests!"

"So what? We don't call Camp."

"Then we lose our point that the ink on the will is the same as the ink on memos written by Hughes around the date of the will!"

"No, we don't lose our point. We lose Camp. But we make our point! We make it with evidence Bittle and Yoakum can't dispute! We borrow Bittle's chemist Peter Fitzrandolph!"

"We what?"

"Didn't Fitzrandolph find on some memos written by Hughes in March 1968 that the ink was Paper Mate's 307 with PAGO? The same ink that Lyter now says is on the will?"

"He did! Son of a bitch, that's right!"

The idea of proving a vital point in our case by using our opponent's chemist was scintillating.

In my opening statement to the jury I previewed the evidence. First, the ink phase. Then the medical phase. The ink and medical evidence, I hoped, would make the jurors more receptive to the hard-to-follow testimony of our handwriting experts, and more receptive to the hard-to-believe testimony of LeVane Forsythe and Melvin Dummar.

"Members of the jury, you'll find that LeVane Forsythe is a crude bagman, sophisticated in the ways of the gutter. A believable witness? No! He'll testify that he received the will from Howard Hughes and was later instructed to deliver it to Melvin Dummar. A believable story? No! No, not until you hear the testimony of witnesses whose credibility you can't question, and see evidence on paper that will compel you to believe Forsythe.

"You'll find that Melvin Dummar is a gentle dunce. He committed perjury when he denied that it was he who had delivered the will to the Mormon Church Headquarters in Salt Lake City. Dummar will tell you that on April 27th, 1976, a stranger dropped the will off at Dummar's gas station. An unbelievable story told by an unbelievable witness. Unbelievable until you hear and see evidence that proves he's telling the truth—evidence such as the testimony of agents in the scientific labs of the FBI.

"The will itself is bizarre. Bizarre in what it says, in the way it was written and in the way it was kept for eight years. And bizarre in the way it was delivered to the Mormon Church. But this was the bizarre way of the man who wrote it."

". . . and then, after Dietrich left him in 1957, Howard Hughes slid into a deep pit of seclusion, surrounded by worms who were his personal aides. From the testimony of these aides, and of others from whom he bought obedience, and from his handwritten memos, you'll piece together a true picture of Howard Hughes. Not the brave pilot. Not the inventive aeronautical genius. Not the decisive industrialist. That's the legend, but not the truth. Instead, by 1957, Howard Hughes had deteriorated into a petty, Jell-o brained, self-centered tyrant, indifferent to the feelings of the body slaves who served him. A spoiled boy who had grown old but not up. Howard Hughes spent most of his last twenty years as a self-condemned prisoner, cringing in hotel rooms behind closed curtains, sitting in his excrement, drenched in his urine, watching movies and television, and playing monopoly with hundreds of millions of real dollars.

"One contributing factor to his behavior was the physical illness I mentioned before. During those last twenty years, Howard Hughes' brain was poisoned by a flushing back of the waste his diseased kidneys couldn't excrete. This disease causes abnormalities in handwriting and spelling, and those abnormalities will be seen by you in his will.

"In November 1966, Howard Hughes moved with his attendants onto the entire ninth floor of the Desert Inn Hotel here in Las Vegas. Mr. Hughes didn't gamble, and since the management wanted the suites on that ninth floor for high rollers, they asked Mr. Hughes, after six months, to please check out. But Mr. Hughes didn't want to check out. When the management insisted, Mr. Hughes had no choice. He bought the hotel. When he found that this was a lot of fun, he bought other hotels along the strip. Then he began buying Las Vegas.

"Mr. Hughes enjoyed watching movies on television between midnight and dawn, and to see the movies he wanted rerun, he bought a local television station. Since Mr. Hughes had much money and much free time between his favorite television programs, he attempted to buy the government of Nevada. He even tried to buy the right to select the man to fill a vacancy on the United States Supreme Court. . . .

"Members of the jury, from your own examination of the will in comparison with hundreds of samples of Hughes' handwriting, you will see that the offered will was written by Howard Hughes."

In his opening statement, Phillip Bittle said that he would prove that the actual forgery was by Bonnie Dummar after Melvin did the research. Bittle's contention of conspiracy between Dummar and Forsythe, as written in one of Bittle's Answers to Interrogatories, was that in Alaska in February 1977:

. . . LeVane Forsythe knowingly chose to assist Melvin Dummar in his false version of the events about having received the will in his gas station from a stranger. Witnesses who have more precise knowledge of the collaboration between Dummar and Forsythe are Dummar's lawyer Roger Dutson and Noah Dietrich's lawyer Harold Rhoden.

Mountainous Earl Yoakum moved his massive frame front and center for his turn. "Ladies an' gentlemen of the jury, Ah know y'all are gettin' tired of hearin' lawyers talk at you, so Ah'll be brief. Ah'd jest like to kinda visit with y'all for a few minutes to simplify this case. Ah know you're not gonna let your minds be poisoned by Mr. Rhoden's openin' remarks, like callin' Mr. Hughes' executive staff assistants—those fine, God-fearin' men— callin' them worms. Ah'm not gonna sink to that level. Where Ah come from, we don't engage in name-callin'. Instead Ah'm gonna point out some facts. For example, here's one fact. In Salt Lake City, Utah, last December, when we took the deposition of Melvin Dummar, we let him know that we found his fingerprints on the Mormon Church Visitors Center envelope. That's the envelope he put his forged will into when he delivered it. An' at lunch that same day, Mr. Rhoden told Melvin Dummar that if we did have his fingerprints on that envelope, Dummar could safely lie an' state that someone had planted them there."

I jumped to my feet and hollered, "Your Honor, I never said that! And Mr. Yoakum knows that there's not the slightest hint of evidence from any source that I did! I cite him for contempt for deliberately—"

"All right, all right, all right! Ah'll withdraw mah remark an' the jurors can disregard it. Now, ladies an' gentlemen, let me show you how simple all this really is. This so-called will names Melvin Dummar as a beneficiary. Melvin claims that Mr. Hughes knew him because one fine night in late December 1967, Melvin Dummar, the good samaritan, picked up Howard Hughes in the Nevada desert an' gave him a lift to Las Vegas. An' a quarter. But we're gonna show you that Howard Hughes didn't leave the Desert Inn at any time in December 1967. In fact, he didn't leave it once in the four years he was there! Therefore, Howard Hughes could not have met Melvin Dummar in the desert. An' therefore, Howard Hughes could not have written a will namin' Melvin Dummar. An' therefore, this will is a forgery!

"Now, how're we gonna prove that Howard Hughes never left the Desert Inn at the time Melvin Dummar says he picked him up? One of Mr. Hughes' personal aides was with him every minute durin' that entire four-year period, but how can they remember when they were on duty, an' what they did an' saw ten years ago? They cain't. Nobody could. At first, it looked like we were gonna have a real problem. We couldn't find any calendars or diaries or airplane tickets to show who was on duty that night. We just didn't know how we were gonna be able to show you the truth. For many months now, Ah've had a search made of all of Summa's records, but we couldn't find anythin'. Then, just a few days ago, we got lucky. Somebody found the records we needed. Records that showed when each man was on duty. His expense records an' hotel charges. An' these records have now refreshed the memories of Mr. Hughes' personal aides. An' they will testify from these records an' tell you that when Melvin Dummar says he picked up Howard Hughes in the desert, Howard Hughes was on the ninth floor of the Desert Inn in Las Vegas!"

That night in my apartment, I faced three worried-sick colleagues. Stanley Fairfield paced back and forth across my living room. "I don't see how you can be so calm about it! If Yoakum has those records, we're through!"

Eli was tense. "And he wouldn't have said he had them if he didn't."

Wilbur poured himself another brandy. "Looks like they got us!"

"One word from Yoakum," I said, "and the three of you are ready to throw in the towel. What the hell's the matter with you guys? This is a fight and we're bound to get hit a few times."

"This isn't getting hit," Stanley hollered. "This is having our balls cut off!"

"How do we treat those records?" Eli asked.

"First, we examine them. I don't think they'll show what Yoakum said they will."

"But, Jesus Christ," Stanley shouted, "what if they do? What if they do?"

39. WHERE ARE THE LIONS?

Noah Dietrich was approaching his eighty-ninth year, and this was likely to be his last appearance fencing from a witness stand with belligerent cross-examiners. In the courthouse, Noah Dietrich, wearing white slacks, a dark blue blazer, and a maroon striped tie, puffed as he reached the top stair of the second floor, his left hand pressing on his silver handled cane, his right arm braced by big Mary. Noah spotted me and raised his cane and asked, "Where are the lions?" and then smiled at the news reporters and cameramen circled around him.

"Mr. Dietrich, do you believe Melvin Dummar and LeVane Forsythe?"

"All I know is, Howard Hughes wrote that will."

"What about the handwriting experts who say it's a fake?"

"What about those who say it isn't?"

"Would you care to comment on the experts who are going to testify that it's a forgery?"

"Only that they might do well to consider another line of work."

"Mr. Dietrich, it's been said that you not only built but ran the Howard Hughes empire for the thirty-two years you were with him."

"Whoever said that is well informed."

The courtroom was packed, and then Judge Hayes said, "Counsel, call your first witness," and I announced, "Mr. Noah Dietrich," everyone, except sneering Earl Yoakum and tight-lipped Phillip Bittle, watched the stooped little giant slowly walk without his cane to the witness stand: a tired old fighter entering the ring for the last time.

Noah Dietrich testified that in 1925 in the Ambassador Hotel in Los Angeles, when he was a thirty-six-year-old CPA, he was hired by nineteen-year-old Howard Hughes. The boy from Houston had inherited the controlling shares of stock in his father's Hughes Tool Company and had acquired the remaining shares from his relatives, and after an election in which he was the only candidate and the only voter he made President. Noah's first assignment was to prepare Howard's income tax return and to explain to him the Company balance sheets and financial statements. "Howard couldn't understand them. And he didn't want to learn how. So he never learned how."

"Did Mr. Hughes graduate from high school?"

"In a way. Thatcher gave him a diploma in recognition of his scholastic achievement in writing and donating to the school a check for five thousand dollars."

For the next three years at the Ambassador, Noah worked and Howard played. One day, practicing his putting stroke in the living room of his suite, Howard gave Noah another assignment. "I'm going to be the world's best golfer. And the world's best aviator. And the world's best movie producer. I'll take care of the first one myself, but, for the other two, Noah, I'll need a little financial help, and that's where you come in. I want you to make me the richest man in the world."

"Of course, he was joking."

"Howard never joked."

"How did you carry out your assignment?"

"I made him one of the richest men in the world."

"How?"

"I took charge and reorganized the company. In 1925 the Hughes Tool Company was worth six hundred thousand dollars. By 1935, the profits were over six million before taxes."

"What did Mr. Hughes do with those profits?"

"Howard asked me to use some of it to buy him the controlling stock in RKO so that he could make movies. Then he wanted the controlling stock in TWA. He liked airplanes."

"Did the movie venture make money?"

"It lost about ten million for Hughes. RKO itself lost about five million while Hughes owned it."

"Did Mr. Hughes take an active part in running the Hughes Tool Company?"

"Never. Howard's only interest in the Tool Company was the profit figure. He didn't talk to anybody in the company and nobody in the company talked to him. I established plants in Ireland and Germany and it wasn't until two years after those plants had made millions in profits that Howard found out that he even owned plants over there."

"From 1926 to 1940, did Mr. Hughes make policy decisions for the Tool Company?"

"No. Howard had a problem with decisions."

"What problem?"

"He couldn't make them."

"What was he doing during that first half of your relationship with him?"

"Making movies and starlets. And enjoying his other hobbies. Like flying."

"What was your top salary with Hughes?"

"Five hundred thousand a year. But the government was getting ninety-two percent of it in income taxes!"

Noah Dietrich took Howard Hughes to several clinics to satisfy him that his fear of imminent heart failure was medically unfounded. In the late 40s, Howard's attention switched from heart attacks to germ attacks. Once, when Noah walked into Hughes' room and dropped his briefcase on a chair, Hughes covered his face and ran to an open window to inhale air uncontaminated by the germs stirred up in the room when the briefcase hit the chair. One day in 1950, Noah saw Howard on the lawn of his estate burning all his germ-ridden clothes, and the following year Howard said that to keep his social disease from spreading, he wanted his entire wardrobe burned. Noah packed all of Howard's clothes, and after solemnly promising to burn them, delivered them to the Salvation Army. By the early fifties Howard required that white gloves be worn by everyone in his presence.

"You, too?"

"Hell, no! I told him no white gloves, and he made me his one exception."

After a conversation in which Hughes repeated the same phrase—"Noah, here's what I want you to do"—about twenty times in five minutes, Noah persuaded Hughes to see a doctor. After the doctor recommended a rest, Hughes landed an airplane in Shreveport, Louisiana, where he was arrested on a charge of vagrancy.

Because of his fear that he would be a target for robbers, Howard Hughes refused to carry money. To pay taxi drivers and to bribe policemen not to give him tickets, he used IOUs. By the mid-fifties, Hughes kept fourteen Chevrolets on twenty-four-hour call as an obstacle to anyone wanting to install a listening device in a car to be used by him. One day in an automobile in the Nevada desert with the president of Lockheed, Hughes requested that Noah and the president stop talking whenever a car passed in either direction, and when they pulled to the side of the road, Hughes got out, cased the sagebrush to make sure that no one was loitering or planted to overhear his secret conversation, and then returned to the car and talked to the waiting president about nothing secret.

By the time for the lunch recess, I was afraid that a half day of testimony was all that Noah Dietrich could handle. "If the Court please, could we adjourn until tomorrow morning? Mr. Dietrich is feeling tired."

Noah Dietrich looked up at Judge Hayes and said, "Who's tired? I'm not tired."

Judge Hayes said, "Mr. Dietrich, I'd be willing to adjourn until tomorrow morning if you'd like a rest."

"Judge, I don't need a rest. Let's get on with the questions. That is, if my lawyer isn't too pooped."

"Was Howard Hughes really an inventor?"

"Well, I'm not sure it was an invention, but he did draw extensive blueprints and spend days writing a detailed technical description of the construction of a device to be used in *The Outlaw*. An uplift brassiere for Jane Russell."

"Did Howard Hughes ever make any political contributions?"

"The mayor and almost every councilman, every supervisor in Los Angeles was on Howard's payroll. Congressmen, senators, governors — you name it."

"How do you know this?"

"I set it up for him. You see, Howard wanted political influence, but he didn't want to be in politics because that meant talking to people. So he decided to get political influence by buying it. Here's the way he did it. I established a company in Canada and saw to it that in dealing with the Tool Company it made a profit of about four hundred thousand a year. That money then went down to the South Hollywood Branch of the Bank of America in an account in the name of Lee Murrin. Murrin would draw out the cash, put it into an envelope, and do what we told him to do with it. Sometimes I'd take the envelope for a delivery, sometimes it would go to whomever we had making the deliveries for us."

"Were those deliveries always in cash?"

"Always. And always in one-hundred-dollar bills."

"Why a Canadian company?"

"If Howard drew the money out of his own company, he'd have to pay an income tax on that money. Howard didn't want to pay any income tax on that money. Or on any other money. Next to germs and communists, Howard's bitterest hatred was for the income-tax law."

"Did you personally ever deliver cash to politicians?"

"Oh, sure! I delivered several of those envelopes to the Republican House leader to spread among members of Congress as he saw fit."

"How much money was in the envelopes?"

"The average was twenty thousand."

"Any other recipients?"

"Once, in the late forties, we had somebody buy some government-surplus airplanes for the Tool Company and the Tool Company was indicted. So I went to see the chairman of the National Democratic Committee and said that Mr. Hughes wanted to make a cash contribution of one hundred thousand dollars, and I gave him a little package containing a thousand one-hundred-dollar bills. Then, when he thanked me, he said, 'Is there anything I can do for you?' And I said, 'Well now, it just so happens that there is one little favor I might ask of you.' I asked him to quash that indictment and he phoned someone in the Justice Department."

"What happened to the indictment?"

"It was quashed."

"Were you personally involved in any other payments by Hughes to politicians?"

"Yep. Another one I remember is the one to Dick Nixon. The money was going to Nixon's family in the form of a two-hundred-thousand-dollar loan, and the Tool Company was going to take as security a run-down gas station in Whittier. I was against it and I told Nixon that. And I told Howard that. I warned him that it might be bad for his public image if it ever came out that he was making this so-called business loan to the Vice-President of the United States. But Howard said, 'See to it he gets the money,' and I did."

"Where did you live from 1935 to 1949?"

"I ran the operation from Houston."

"Before this case began, had you ever heard the name LeVane Forsythe?"

"No."

"Did Mr. Hughes ever say anything to you about the disposition of his estate after his death?"

"He said he wanted to leave his money to medical research. That was odd, but that's what he said he wanted."

"Why was that odd?"

"Howard Hughes hated doctors. Not as much as he hated lawyers, but he always said that every doctor he ever knew was a quack. And he didn't like people—the suffering of humanity, physical or otherwise, was of no interest to him. He made charitable contributions only because he was told that if he didn't, the press would call him a miser."

"What terminated your relationship with Mr. Hughes in 1957?"

"For several years, he had promised me a one-million-dollar bonus in the form of a capital gain. Every time I'd bring it up, he'd say that he'd get around to it when I had completed a current project for him. In the spring of 1957, he wanted me to go back to Houston to do something, and I told him I would, but that I wanted him to keep his promise to me first. He said he'd think about it after I came back from Houston. I told him I wanted him to think about it before I went to Houston. He told me he didn't like being pressured. I told him that I didn't like his repeated failures to keep his promise, and that if he didn't keep it, I'd quit, and when he said he wouldn't talk about it until I returned from Houston, I quit."

As I looked at my notes to see if I had forgotten anything, Noah added, "I shouldn't have. If I had stayed with him, what happened to him would never have happened to him."

When I finished my direct examination, Bittle glared at Noah Dietrich as though he were on trial for having dynamited a crowded grammar school. "Mr. Dietrich, in the thirty-two years you were with him, when Mr. Hughes wrote a memo to you, his writing was always neat, wasn't it?"

"I'd say so."

"Not sloppy like the writing on this so-called will, was it?"

"No. But his last memos to me were eleven years before he wrote his will in 1968. There were severe changes in the man, and I'd expect severe changes in his writing, wouldn't you?"

"You said he wrote his will in 1968, but you don't know that he wrote a will in 1968, do you?"

"Yes, I do. I recognize his handwriting."

"Are you a handwriting expert?"

"My lawyer tells me I'm not, but since you ask me, I'll admit that I am a handwriting expert when it comes to Howard Hughes' handwriting. He wrote it."

"I have no more questions."

Earl Yoakum was next. "Mr. Dietrich, Ah cain't believe mah ears! Ah must've misunderstood you, sir. It is your testimony that, with a criminal intent, you gave someone a bribe to have the Attorney General of the United States of America quash an indictment?"

"I'd say that's an accurate characterization of my testimony."

"Then you confess to the commission of a crime?"

"Sure! And there are more I could confess to, if you're interested in hearing about my criminal background."

"All right, what other crimes have you committed?"

"Well, in 1929, Mr. Hughes wanted his huge liquor supply in Houston brought to Los Angeles. At that time it was illegal to transport liquor across state lines. I arranged to have it shipped in a boxcar, and to dissuade a railroad guard from examining the contents, I gave him ten dollars. That time, I was guilty not only of bribery, but of smuggling."

"Mr. Dietrich, you know that Howard Hughes would never have written a will namin' you as his executor, now don't you?"

"I know the opposite."

"Wasn't Howard Hughes angry at you in 1957 when you quit?"

"Yes. He had good reason to be."

"What reason?"

"I quit."

"He never got over it, did he?"

"Since I never spoke to him again, I'm not competent to answer your question, but if you want me to speculate, I'll speculate. Howard wouldn't have held a grudge against me for eleven years. By the time he wrote his will in 1968, he had nothing but good memories of my thirty-two years with him."

"Mr. Dietrich, after you and Mr. Hughes separated, did you sue him for your promised bonus?"

"I did and I won."

"When you settled that lawsuit with Mr. Hughes in 1959, did you agree not to write a book about him?"

"I did."

"But, you did write a book about him, didn't you?"

"I did."

"Didn't your writin' this book make Howard Hughes angry?"

"You mean, did my writing this book make him so angry that he would not have named me as executor in a will written by him in 1968?"

"That, Mr. Dietrich, is precisely the point Ah'm makin'!"

"No, my book about him could not possibly have influenced him against naming me his executor in 1968."

"Why not?"

"Because I didn't write that book until 1972."

"Ah have no further questions."

I concluded my examination of Noah Dietrich. "Mr. Dietrich, when you quit, in that last telephone conversation you had with Howard Hughes, what were his final words to you?"

"He said, 'Noah, I can't exist without you.'"

40. THE INK PHASE

On December 5, 1977, I called Levar Myler as a hostile witness to testify that when he worked as a personal aide for Howard Hughes during the Desert Inn period, Hughes wrote only with Paper Mate pens.

As Myler testified that he had seen Howard Hughes spill something on a memo causing the ink to smear, then pat it down with a Kleenex and continue writing, the jurors looked at the three blowups of the pages of the will facing them on two easels next to the witness box. The ink had been smeared in several places on the three pages.

After 1970, Howard Hughes had said more than once that he had written a holographic will which he had given to someone he could trust.

"Did Mr. Hughes tell you where he had written his holographic will?"

"He said he wrote it at the gray house when he lived there. Near the tenth tee of the Bel Air Country Club golf course."

"When did Mr. Hughes live in the gray house?"

"In the forties."

"Did Mr. Hughes tell you he provided for you in his will?"

"Yes."

"When did you first meet Howard Hughes?"

"In 1950."

"You mean, Mr. Hughes said that years before he met you, he provided for you in his will?"

"Your questions are confusing me."

"Mr. Myler, isn't it true that you were given a script of what you were to testify to when asked what Howard Hughes had said about when and where he wrote his holographic will? A script containing the words supposedly spoken by Hughes—'At the gray house near the tenth tee of the Bel Air Country Club golf course'?"

"Well, I got a paper, yes."

"Did you say to whoever gave you that paper something like this? 'How do you know what Mr. Hughes told me? I was there, you weren't.'?"

"No."

"Did you ask why you were given that paper?"

"No."

Myler testified that during the Desert Inn years, Mr. Hughes did not wear the Vandyke that Holmes had said Hughes wore. And that all of Mr. Hughes' fingernails were very long.

"Don't you mean that nine of his fingernails were of medium length and that only one was very long?"

"No."

"In your deposition, didn't you testify as follows: *He had only one that was very long. The others were medium?*"

"I remember it better now."

"Did the aides keep logs at the Desert Inn?"

"I didn't see any logs in the Desert Inn."

"Didn't you testify in your deposition that you did see logs in the Desert Inn?" I showed him the transcript.

"Yes. Maybe my memory isn't as good now."

"The logs that you saw in the Desert Inn were typewritten, weren't they?"

"Yes."

"Is your memory improving as we go along?"

"Yes."

"Did Mr. Hughes ever mention Rice University?"

"He said he went to Rice Institute."

"The name of that institution is Rice University, isn't it?"

"Mr. Hughes called it Rice Institute."

I walked to the blowup of page one of the will facing the jurors and looked at it.

second: one eight of assets to be devided among the University of Texas—Rice Institute of Technology of Houston—the University of Nevada—and the University of Calif.

"What, if anything, did Mr. Hughes say about the University of Nevada?"

"He said he donated millions to it."

I used a pointer to call the jurors' attention to the third provision in the second page:

third: one sixteenth to Church of Jesus Christ of Latterday Saints— David O. Makay-Pre

"What, if anything, did Mr. Hughes ever say about the Mormon Church?"

"He was always complimentary."

Rex Clairbourne examined Myler for the contestants. "Between 1962 and 1966, while Mr. Hughes lived in the Bel Air house in Los Angeles, before the day he moved out, did Mr. Hughes leave that house for even one second?"

"Not while I was on duty. As a matter of fact, he never once left the bedroom."

"Do you intend, in the future, to pursue any interest as a personal aide of Mr. Hughes under this so-called will?"

I objected. "Immaterial! The question calls for speculation, conjecture, and opinion!"

Judge Hayes said, "Objection overruled!"

Myler answered, "No."

"Is that because of your opinion concerning the validity of this so-called will?"

"Yes."

"What is that opinion?"

I tried again. "Objection! Calls for an opinion, no foundation as to this witness' competence as a handwriting expert or as—"

Judge Hayes stopped me. "Objection overruled!"

Myler answered, "Because it's a forgery."

"Mr. Myler, about this piece of paper that Mr. Rhoden calls a script. His suggestion is that that piece of paper was given to you at a meeting at the Century Plaza to tailor your testimony. Now, when did that meeting take place?"

"Within ten days after Mr. Hughes' death."

"Since this will turned up on April 29th, the meeting at the Century Plaza was before this will ever turned up, wasn't it?"

"Oh, yes."

"How are you able to place that sequence of events?"

"Because my mother-in-law died on April 15th, and the meeting at the Century Plaza was between the death of Mr. Hughes and her death."

"And certainly, I guess you'll have to agree with me, Mr. Myler, that before the Dummar will ever surfaced, you read this Xerox paper, and certainly it could not have been for the purpose of tailoring your testimony about the writing of the Dummar will."

"Argumentative!" I said. "Leading, calls for an opinion and speculation, no first-hand knowledge, and no foundation!"

Judge Hayes asked, "Any other grounds, Mr. Rhoden?"

"Also, immaterial!"

"Objection overruled on all grounds!"

Myler answered Clairbourne's question. "I agree with you."

During the lunch recess, Eli, Stanley, and Wilbur urged me to question Myler about Hughes' death in Acapulco.

"No! The issue is, who wrote the will, not who killed Hughes."

"But it might lead somewhere," Eli said.

"Like up the creek. In those depositions I didn't question the aides about Hughes' death, and I don't know what their answers will be."

"Let's find out," Wilbur said.

"The lawyer who cross-examines to find out something is likely to find out that he's stuck his stupid head up his ass. No!"

Albert Lyter testified about his experience as a forensic chemist in the Alcohol, Tobacco and Firearms Division of the Treasury Department, and his participation in the FBI report of its examination of the Mormon will. He admitted an error in his report and explained that the ink standard in the ATF library that matched the ink on the will—one standard out of three thousand—was Paper Mate's formula 307 with the dye named PAGO. Not with the dye named MBSN.

Lyter explained that he had made his comparison with thin-layer chromatography, a process which gives a chemical fingerprint. No two different inks—just as no two different fingerprints—will ever match. When two inks match—such as the ink on a questioned document and the ink on a known sample—it means that the questioned ink is the same as the ink on the sample.

"What is the purpose of making these ink comparisons?"

"It's one way to date the age of a questioned document. For example, suppose we have a document dated 1970 and we want to know if it was really written in 1970. If we find that the ink is identical to a standard ink in our library, and we know from the manufacturer that that standard wasn't formulated until 1975, we know that the questioned document wasn't written before 1975."

I interrupted Lyter's direct to read a stipulation to the jury:

"'Paper Mate's 307 with PAGO dye was first formulated, manufactured and sold in Paper Mate's pens in 1967. 307 with PAGO was on the market until February 1972, when the PAGO dye was discontinued, and replaced in 307 with MBSN dye.

"'In 1974, formula 307 was discontinued and replaced with formula 316.'"

Lyter explained that the information contained in the stipulation was a trade secret not available to anyone outside Paper Mate other than the ATF. And even with an original of a document, such as a memo written by Howard Hughes, no forensic chemist who did not have access to the ATF ink library could have identified or duplicated the ink on that document.

And it would not have been possible in 1976 for anyone—other than a chemist in the ATF lab—to know what inks were on the market in 1968.

Lyter compared the ink on the will with Paper Mate's current ink, formula 316, and was easily able to eliminate 316 as matching the ink on the questioned will.

Lyter testified that the red ink used in making the Pitney Bowes imprint was made by Sanford, and was sold to the public in bulk form, and could be used in Pitney Bowes machines. This red Sanford ink was on the market in 1968.

Phillip Bittle had Lyter explain again the intricacies of thin-layer chromatography and what he could see in the colored imprints left on the photographic plate he used in making his comparison, a plate Bittle marked Exhibit C-15. As Bittle cross-examined Lyter for two days, Wilbur kept bouncing out of the courtroom every twenty minutes for a phone call, and by the second day, Eli, Stanley, the jurors, and the court clerk seemed to be losing their battle to fight off sleep.

Present in the courtroom behind Phillip Bittle was Peter Fitzrandolph, there to advise Bittle in his cross-examination of Lyter. From his name, I had expected Peter Fitzrandolph to look like an aged member of the House of Lords, but instead, in his late twenties, tall and lithe, he was a high school girl's daydream of a disco partner. A minute before Lyter finished, I handed Fitzrandolph a subpoena to testify as my witness.

Fitzrandolph testified that he was hired by Phillip Bittle to identify the ink on some memos written by Hughes, dated March 1968, and to compare that ink with the ink in three samples containing Paper Mate's 307 MBSN, 307 PAGO, and 316.

"Were you able to find a match between the ink on the Hughes memos and the ink on any of the Paper Mate samples?"

"Well, I'd like to explain—"

"Didn't you testify in your deposition that the ink on the Hughes memos matched one of the samples?"

"Yes, I gave that testimony."

"Which sample did you testify matched the ink on the Hughes memos?"

"Paper Mate's 307 with the PAGO dye."

I turned from Fitzrandolph and walked back to my seat, about to say, No further questions, when Fitzrandolph added, "However, further investigation invalidated my opinion that the ink on those Hughes memos was the 307 PAGO."

"Did you or did you not find that the ink on the Hughes memos matched the ink in the Paper Mate sample which contained 307 PAGO dye?"

"Yes, I did."

"Didn't you find that it was an identical match?"

"I'd say a very good match. Not an identical match."

"In your deposition, didn't you testify as follows: *The ink on the will was an identical match with Paper Mate's 307 ink containing PAGO dye?*"

"Yes. But I'd like to correct it. That opinion was invalidated by further investigation."

"What further investigation?"

"I used thin-layer chromatography to compare Paper Mate's 307 PAGO and the ink Paper Mate has been using since 1974, formula 316. And I could not tell the difference."

Eli whispered, "He told me that he didn't do any more work after his deposition."

"Mr. Fitzrandolph, you made this comparison of 307 PAGO and 316 before you gave your deposition, didn't you?"

"Yes."

"And despite this, you testified in your deposition that the ink on the memo was 307 PAGO, didn't you?"

"Well—yes, I did."

"But, as you sit here now, you say that your conclusion that the ink on the memos was 307 PAGO is invalidated because you're not sure whether the ink on those March 1968 memos written by Hughes is Paper Mate's 307 PAGO or the current 316, is that it?"

"Yes, that's it!"

"In forming your opinion, you determined, did you not, that 316 was first formulated in 1974?"

"Yes."

"And you knew that the memos you were examining were dated in 1968?"

"Yes."

"Then you know that the ink on the 1968 Hughes memos could not possibly contain Paper Mate's 316, because 316 wasn't formulated until six years after the memos were written! Isn't that correct?"

"Well, I guess so."

"Therefore, Mr. Fitzrandolph, since the ink on the 1968 Hughes memos could not possibly be Paper Mate's 316, what kind of ink is on the 1968 Hughes memos?"

"Paper Mate's 307 PAGO."

Bittle had marked as an exhibit the thin-layer chromatographic plate made by Fitzrandolph and had him explain why he could not distinguish the vividly colored specks of 316 and 307 PAGO.

"Did you examine Exhibit C-15, the plate made by Lyter?"

"I did."

"On Lyter's plate he has a sample of the questioned ink, and then over there, nine different inks including 307 PAGO and Paper Mate's 316. Mr. Lyter testified that he could see that 316 did not match the questioned ink, but that 307 PAGO did. He said that he could distinguish 307 PAGO and 316. Do you agree with him?"

"I do not. Mr. Lyter's plate is totally inadequate."

"Your witness, Mr. Rhoden."

"Prior to your work in this case for Mr. Bittle, had you ever taken ink from a paper and examined it with chromatography?"

"No."

"Have you ever testified in court before?"

"Well, I—no."

"Have you ever taken a class in chromatography?"

"No."

"Do you have a college degree in chemistry?"

"No, but I did go to two junior colleges."

"You know, don't you, that Albert Lyter is a trained and experienced forensic chemist employed by the Treasury Department?"

"Yes."

"Do you know more about inks than he does?"

"Yes, I do."

"Where do you work?"

"I work for Chemlabs, Inc., of San Francisco."

"What do you do there?"

"I manage the personnel, and I'm involved in the sales work, and I run the laboratories."

"Chemlabs is an ink factory, isn't it?"

"So?"

"Have you ever studied forensic chemistry?"

"I—what do you mean by forensic?"

"I have no further questions."

After the session ended, I asked Wilbur Dobbs to fly to Boston, get another sample of Paper Mate's 307 PAGO, and this time also a sample of their formula 316, and give both samples to Michael Camp to see if he could distinguish the two under thin-layer chromatography as Lyter did.

41. NOSSECK'S

After the first two weeks of trial, Wilbur Dobbs stopped shaving, and by the end of the first month a thick black beard covered much of his face, and nobody could look at him without thinking of a cough drop. Wilbur, always broke, bummed meals from all of us, with our sympathy; and bummed drinks at lunch, drinks after court, and drinks at dinner, with no one's sympathy. He bummed cigarettes and, for those constant phone calls, coins from everyone, including Rex Clairbourne, the bailiff, spectators, and members of the press who couldn't get out of the way in time. When Wilbur wasn't on one of his frequent two-hour phone calls with his wife in Houston or out borrowing money for rent, he was in one of the casinos at a blackjack table losing the money he had borrowed.

In preparation for the medical phase, I presented the deposition testimony of Ron Kistler. Kistler started work at Hughes Productions the summer of 1957, shortly after Noah Dietrich left Hughes.

"Was Hughes Productions involved in making movies?"

"It was involved only in the care and comfort of Howard Hughes and his protégés."

"What were your duties?"

"I ran errands, picked up mail, bought food, delivered envelopes containing cash, and drove the young starlets around."

"You drove them from where to where?"

"From where they lived to where they would go for acting or singing lessons."

"Your instructions were to just drive the girls back and forth?"

"Oh no, we had all kinds of instructions concerning the girls. For example, a girl was allowed only one ice cream cone a day. If she put up a hassle, sometimes we'd bend the rule a little bit, but generally it was one a day. When we drove and approached a dip in the road we were to slow down to two miles an hour because Mr. Hughes didn't want any sudden pull of gravity straining the muscles of the girls' breasts."

"Did the girls go out on dates without one of you men as chaperones?"

"A Howard Hughes starlet go out on a date? Are you serious? They didn't date even with a chaperone. The very contemplation of such an offense would have meant instant excommunication—the end of future stardom and the end of the monthly allowance. Howard Hughes owned those girls."

"How often did Howard Hughes exercise his ownership privileges?"

"That's the craziest part of all. He didn't. You'd think he'd drop in sometimes to check their chastity belts or to take one off now and then, or ask for some other demonstration of their appreciation and admiration. But he never did. He never once saw one of the girls while I worked there."

"Tell us about those envelopes containing cash."

"We would get our instructions by driving up to the building on Romaine Street and honking the horn. Then we'd step out to the curb while somebody upstairs would open a window and lower the envelope or a little package on a string. This was called the fishline technique."

"Were there instructions with the envelopes?"

"Always. Sometimes the instructions on where to make the delivery were quite detailed, like what streets we were to drive on, where to turn and double back two and go forward six, and like that."

"What was in the envelopes you delivered?"

"I wasn't supposed to look. There was money inside. A few times, I accidentally peeked."

"Did you ever get any of these envelopes other than on the fishline?"

"When the amounts were over two thousand, we'd be directed to the L.M. Company for the pickup. That was a code word for Lee Murrin."

"Did you ever get a receipt from anyone to whom you made one of those deliveries?"

"A receipt? Are you kiddin'?"

"While you worked for Hughes Productions as a driver, did you ever see Howard Hughes?"

"Oh yeah. Mr. Hughes lived at the Beverly Hills Hotel in one of the bungalows. Sometimes I delivered paychecks to the aides or a new supply of Kleenex boxes, and I saw him there once or twice."

"Did you speak to him?"

"Hell, no! We had instructions never to speak to him unless he spoke first. Never even to look at him."

"Who gave you those instructions?"

"Kay Glenn. Before Glenn, our boss was Bill Gay, but he was on detached service. His wife had some disease, and so Hughes sent Gay home and told him not to come near any of the other employees until Mrs. Gay got better."

"Did Mr. Hughes ever show concern for any other person's health?"

"Well, his concern was for his own health, not any other person's. Carlyle, a guy who worked for Hughes, once visited a woman who had mononucleosis, and when Hughes heard of it, he sent Carlyle home. Carlyle stayed home with full pay for seventeen years."

"Did Mr. Hughes ever complain about his own health?"

"Only that he was always constipated."

"Were you ever given an assignment that brought you in direct contact with Mr. Hughes?"

"Yeah. Hughes used to go to Goldwyn Studios to watch movies, but one day he heard that the all-black cast of *Porgy and Bess* was using the screening room to look at their dailies, and that was the last time Howard Hughes used the Goldwyn Studios. He began using a screening room at Nosseck's Studios. The first few days there, Mrs. Hughes accompanied Mr. Hughes. They would watch one or two movies, then Mr. Hughes would drive Mrs. Hughes back to the hotel and then return to Nosseck's to watch more movies. But after that, Mr. Hughes was always at Nosseck's without her. Sometimes he stayed there for two or three days straight. It was about this time that Mr. Hughes asked that I be there for twenty-four hours a day to split a shift with two other guys. The projectionist was to be there around the clock. Then Mr. Hughes stayed for four straight months without once leaving the studio."

"Did you stay there for twenty-four hours a day for four months?"

"Mr. Hughes thought I did, but I didn't. Every now and then, I succumbed to the compulsion to go home and take a shower. I'd sneak out when Hughes was asleep and then sneak back in before he woke up."

"At Nosseck's, where did Hughes get his food?"

"The food was brought in by Johnny Holmes. Hughes'd eat fresh whole milk, Hershey bars with almonds, pecan nuts, and Poland water."

"Did Mr. Hughes bring some clothes with him?"

"He arrived wearing a white shirt, tan gabardine slacks, and brown shoes. Those were the clothes he wore all the time he was at Nosseck's until finally the clothes got so filthy and foul-smelling that he took them off. With reluctance, I might add. Then he became a nudist. He asked me to have his clothes cleaned and I told him I'd quit first. So he told me to throw his clothes away. In a back pocket I found a crumpled wad of paper—a five-dollar-bill—mildewed. He did put on clothes for his drive back to the hotel, though."

"Did you ever again see Howard Hughes wearing clothes?"

"Yeah, on December 24th, 1958, when he was entertaining some people on his birthday at the hotel."

"During those four months at Nosseck's what did Howard Hughes look like?"

"Very thin. He didn't have any physical activities. He took up residence in that white leather chair, and the only walking he did was from the projection room to the small bathroom."

"You mean Howard Hughes just sat around all day watching movies?"

"That's all. Watch movies and talk on the telephone. He had a lot of telephone talks with Jean Peters. He told her he was in a hospital undergoing treatment for a disease that the doctors couldn't diagnose."

"During those four months at Nosseck's Studios, where did Mr. Hughes bathe?"

"He didn't. And as to what he did to the bathroom—well, all I can say is, his aim left ample room for improvement."

"Didn't janitors clean the place up?"

"Janitors weren't allowed in during those four months. It was rather unpleasant. Hughes once spent twenty-six straight hours on that john!"

"Did the aides use the same restroom?"

"What? Use the same restroom Mr. Hughes used? He told us to use the wax buckets that had been brought from the Beverly Hills Hotel— the ones that contained the bottled Poland water and the milk, and he selected a room off the lobby that was used for storage of those buckets, and told us that that's where we had to go. Two of the other guys were willing to put up with this, but I kept sneaking upstairs to use the other bathroom."

"Wasn't this insubordinate?"

"Definitely."

"During those four months nothing got cleaned in that studio?"

"Nothing except the telephone. Once I saw Mr. Hughes spend about four hours straight cleaning the telephone with a Kleenex. Cleaning it over and over again."

"What else did Mr. Hughes do at Nosseck's Studios?"

"Well, there was a little table next to his big white chair, with six Kleenex boxes on it. They remained unopened, and sometimes for hour after hour Hughes would manipulate those boxes into various geometric configurations. That really gave him a charge."

"After Mr. Hughes finally left Nosseck's, what happened to you?"

"Mr. Hughes went back to his bungalow in the Beverly Hills Hotel, and I did the same thing I did at Nosseck's. I sat in the room with him while he watched movies."

"Did you have any special orders?"

"Oh, we had a lot of orders. We couldn't touch any doorknobs. We couldn't touch Hughes' telephone or his Kleenex boxes. We couldn't touch his writing pads or his pencils. We had orders to stay off beaches and stay out of Nevada. Hughes felt that beaches were germ ridden, and that Nevada was loused up because of the Atomic Energy tests. And Hughes didn't want any of us coming back to him with radioactivity up our—on our bodies."

"Were you given any other special orders?"

"We weren't allowed to eat any pork products. No gravy. Nothing cooked in sauce. No salad dressings that might contain garlic."

"Why no garlic?"

"I don't know. He sure as hell didn't kiss us."

"What was Mr. Hughes' physical condition in the Beverly Hills Hotel?"

"Much better. He put on some weight."

"What was the purpose of your sitting in the bungalow while Hughes watched movies?"

"Damned if I know. Just sitting in attendance."

"How long did you have to sit at a time?"

"The longest time without a relief that I remember was seventy-four hours. Many times I was there for two days straight. Hughes'd watch movies for two days and then sleep for a day."

"Where did you sleep?"

"I had a hotel room at the Beverly Hills Hotel."

"Were you allowed to see your wife?"

"Yeah, my wife had visitation rights to the hotel."

"Now, surely, the bungalow occupied by Mr. Hughes at the Beverly Hills Hotel was occasionally cleaned?"

"The hell it was! That bungalow wasn't cleaned once in the eighteen months I worked there."

"Did Mr. Hughes, during his stay at the Beverly Hills Hotel, ever see his wife, Jean Peters?"

"Only once. That was on Thanksgiving Day for ten minutes."

"Did Mr. Hughes read newspapers at the hotel?"

"I don't know whether he read 'em or not, but magazines and newspapers were delivered to him. Always in threes. They'd be handed to him so that he could grab the center one with a Kleenex."

"Did you ever hear Hughes talk on the telephone to any of his executives at the Hughes Tool Company?"

"Once I remember he was talking to Nadine Henley and really got mad. He said, 'Miss Henley, I seldom bother you with things to do for me. But on the one occasion that I look for you because I need you, I find that you're traveling at my expense on an unauthorized trip, and to find you in Mexico is very distressing to me. Miss Henley, I want you to get to the airport, and if there isn't a plane in the next half hour, you get your fat ass to the train depot. If there isn't a train in the next half hour, you paddle your fat ass to the bus station. And if there isn't a bus in the next half hour, you run all the fucking way back to Los Angeles and be here tomorrow morning.' That was the end of the conversation. Miss Henley was in Los Angeles the following morning."

"Who brought food to Hughes during his eighteen-month stay in the Beverly Hills Hotel?"

"Food was always delivered by Johnny Holmes in a brown paper bag. Holmes'd wait out in the lobby or in another room for a signal from Hughes, and when Hughes was ready, Holmes'd walk into Hughes' room to the right-hand side of Hughes' chair, and stand there at attention until Hughes recognized him. Then Holmes'd roll back the outer edge of the bag, and stand bent over, holding his bag at a forty-five-degree angle from his body, and Hughes'd take a Kleenex, reach into the bag, and pull out the contents one by one, while Holmes stood there holding the bag."

"What did the bungalow look like in general?"

"Used Kleenexes were piled in hills behind his chair. Does that describe it for you?"

"Did you ever hear Hughes mention Noah Dietrich?"

"Only once. In December 1958, there was a big brush fire moving up Benedict Canyon in Los Angeles, and it looked as though the fire was going to burn down Dietrich's new home, and Hughes was elated at the prospect and kept cheering the fire on."

"Did you ever hear Hughes say anything about medical research?"

"He always said how much he hated the medical profession. But, he said many times that the Medical Institute was going to get his estate, that he wanted to be to the medical industry what Carnegie was to the library industry."

"Did you ever hear Hughes refer to the University of Texas?"

"Yeah, he thought that the University of Texas was a splendid academic institution because of its accomplishments on the gridiron."

"When did you quit?"

"In September 1959. But they kept me on the payroll for fourteen months. That was to keep my mouth shut about Hughes."

"What took you off the payroll?"

"Nadine Henley heard that I wasn't keeping my mouth shut about Hughes."

"Were you ever allowed to speak to Hughes?"

"Nope, never! But every now and then when I'd leave, I'd turn around and say, 'Bye-bye,' and Hughes'd get mad at this. But by the next time I came on duty, he had always forgiven me for the affront. He didn't hold a grudge."

42. THE MEDICAL PHASE

The writing on the three pages of the will was abnormal in the overwriting of some letters and in the patching of some strokes, evidencing a meticulous attention to trivial details. In some pen strokes there were tremors, and in others, erratic scratches, evidencing the writer's lack of motor control. And the inconsistent elimination of articles was abnormal. Some memos written by Hughes in 1968 showed none of those abnormalities found in the will. Others written by him in the same year showed the identical abnormalities.

On December 7, 1977, I read from the deposition transcript the questions Wilbur Dobbs had put to Dr. Jack L. Titus, and Wilbur Dobbs on the witness stand read the doctor's answers.

Dr. Titus was the chairman of the Department of Pathology at Baylor College of Medicine, chief of Pathology Services at Methodist Hospital in Houston, and pathologist in charge of the Harris County Medical District. He conducted the autopsy and signed the certificate of death. The certificate stated that death was caused by:

Chronic renal failure due to interstetial nephritis with papillary necrosis.

"Doctor, in layman's language, what was the cause of death?"
"Kidney failure."

"What did you observe when you first examined the body on April 5th, 1976?"

"The eyes were still open. The pupils were thick and dilated. Time of death was around twelve noon that day. The body was of an elderly white male, about six feet three inches tall and weighed ninety-two pounds. Emaciated—that is, thin with an implication of undernourishment. And the body was dehydrated, which means inadequate fluid."

"Were you given any medical history?"

"I was told by Drs. Chaffin and Thain and by Mr. John Holmes that Mr. Hughes had used phenacetin from 1946 to 1974."

"Did this information prompt you to do anything?"

"It prompted me to check the kidneys. Phenacetin damages the renal papillae and other parts of the kidneys. And, sure enough, my diagnosis was uremic pancreathopathy. Dr. Suzuki examined the brain and found a change consistent with uremia, and nothing to cause this disorder in the brain other than Mr. Hughes' kidney dysfunction."

"How long had Mr. Hughes suffered from this dysfunction?"
"Ten years or longer."

"How did you know how long?"

"For one thing, the size and weight of the kidneys. Their shrunken condition, which was a result of kidney disease, indicated the length of time the individual suffered from it."

"Did you find anything on the scalp?"
"There was a nodule."

"How long had he had it?"

"From five to ten years. It was slow-growing and would not have hurt him. It takes very little to traumatize because it sticks up and bleeds very easily. Combing his hair could have made it bleed. It was located in the left perietal scalp. That's over the left ear."

"Any other abnormalities?"

"Mr. Hughes had a separated left shoulder. The top of the upper arm was separated from the shoulder socket. There was bruising and swelling. This separation occurred prior to death and was there for two or three days and less than two weeks before death."

"What did you learn from the deceased's medical records?" Dobbs asked.

"There were no medical records."

"Did you ask his doctors why they had no records?"

"I certainly did."

"Were you told why?"

"No."

"What did the two doctors tell you was wrong with their patient?"

"They didn't know. They suggested the possibility of diabetes."

"What did the two doctors tell you about how their patient was feeling the last days of his life?"

"They said that for the last few days the patient was confused. On Sunday evening, April 4th, he developed a shocklike state and became comatose. Unconscious."

"Did you ask these doctors what they did when they attended their patient?"

"I got the impression that attending this patient meant being in the vicinity in case the patient wanted to see a doctor. And no more."

"Dr. Titus, if you had been a doctor for Howard Hughes, would you have had more information about his death than those two doctors who attended him?"

"Yes, indeed! If I had been one of Mr. Hughes' doctors, and I knew as little as they knew about their deceased patient, I would have retained a lawyer."

I read Rex Clairbourne's cross-examination in the deposition. "Doctor, you can't tell how long Mr. Hughes had that kidney disorder, can you?"

"Not precisely."

"Thank you, doctor, I have no further questions."

Dr. Titus added, "But I would say that from five to twenty years would be compatible with what we found."

I next read Dobbs' deposition questions put to Dr. William Hill, and Bruce Beckley of our local law firm read the doctor's answers. Dr. Hill, a pathologist, had performed thousands of autopsies. He explained that the kidney is a filter to rid the body of waste products; it separates chemicals in the blood and excretes waste into the urine. Renal failure is the failure of the kidneys to perform their filtering function. Uremia is a state in which, because of the kidneys' failure, there is a flushing back of poisonous waste into the blood system. The brain is adversely affected by uremia because it depends on the blood supply both for its nutrition and for getting rid of its own wastes. When uremia occurs, the blood to the brain is poisoned. Consequently, the nerve impulses sent out by the brain to the motor system are impaired.

One cause of renal failure is overusage of phenacetin, an analgesic painkiller similar to aspirin. After Dr. Hill studied the autopsy report, he explained that the part of the kidneys that was diseased was the lower section and that a longterm use of phenacetin affects that section of the kidney. That section was hard and scarred, and in the absence of evidence of an infection, those scarred tissues indicated a disease of long duration.

"Doctor, from your examination of the autopsy report, and based on reasonable medical probability, how long did the deceased have the kidney disease that took his life?"

"Eight or ten years. It could have been more, but it is not likely to have been less."

The effects of uremic poisoning include jerking of the muscles, and problems in cognition. A uremic patient may, on a drive to work, suddenly find himself twenty miles from where he was going and without knowing how he got there. Uremic poisoning affects a person's ability to write and to spell words he would ordinarily spell correctly; sometimes a patient cannot correctly spell his own name.

"Doctor, take a word such as 'children' in the questioned will. Would a person suffering from this disorder write that word leaving out the *h*?"

"That is precisely the type of abnormality I would expect from a person suffering from uremic poisoning."

Attorney William Singleton of our local Las Vegas law firm read the answers in the deposition testimony of Dr. Alan Rubens. For seven years, Dr. Rubens had been a neurologist at Hennipen County Medical Center in Minnesota, with a specialty in diseases that affect the nervous system. He was the assistant chief of the Department of Neurology and an associate professor of neurology at the University of Minnesota, where he supervised the neurology residents.

"This dysfunction, the failure of the brain to receive the proper cleansing action of the blood, diminishes the brain's efficiency. In untreated cases, it causes lethargy, stupor, coma, and death. One characteristic of uremia is that it's intermittent. A person may suffer from the effects of uremia poisoning one hour, and not the next. One day and not the next. One week and not the next, and this can go on for years. Memory is adversely affected, and memory ability may change from day to day. Personality quirks or neuroses are likely to be aggravated by uremic poisoning. As the disease progresses, the patient may show a variety of bizarre behaviors. He may develop paranoia. He may become less attentive to others, and even to himself. He may have trouble concentrating. But this is a day-to-day problem, and he can be surprisingly lucid for an hour, and then show problems of orientation. And then an hour later, again be lucid."

"Does it affect appetite?"

"Yes. Appetite is reduced and there may be dramatic changes in food preference. Sexual appetite is very commonly markedly depressed. There is often a derangement of the sleep-wake rhythm—that is, patients frequently sleep during the day and stay up at night. As the disease progresses, there is a general tendency to be sleepy, groggy, and this leads to severe depression. And there may be either constipation or diarrhea."

"Doctor, do kidney patients ever need blood transfusions?"

"Yes, of course, transfusions are often required."

"Are the bones of kidney patients affected by the disease?"

"The bones of uremics become more brittle and apt to fracture, and the healing process is slow."

"What about hearing?"

"Some patients will develop varying degrees of deafness."

As the official neurological consultant to the kidney unit in Hennipen, Dr. Rubens had obtained handwriting specimens of patients suffering from kidney disease. "Writing performance by uremics," he explained, "will be decreased. Sentences will be unusually simple. Expression becomes abnormal. Handwriting will be slow, and labored. There may be sloppiness as well as misspellings, and problems with punctuation. The inability to control their hands may be reflected in handwriting tremors."

I then read the illuminating deposition cross-examination of Dr. Rubens by Rex Clairbourne. "Dr. Rubens, you never saw a copy of the so-called will in this case, did you?"

"Yes, I did. I studied it carefully."

"Now, Doctor, surely you cannot say by looking at the will that there are any indications that the writer of it had a kidney disorder?"

"Oh yes. I can! I detected things in the will—such as deletion of letters, faulty punctuation, oversimplification of thoughts, simple sentences—all consistent with the effect on the brain of renal failure. One example is leaving the *h* out of the word *children*. It's the type of attentional error committed by someone suffering from a kidney disorder. Not a spelling error. Capitalization mistakes—for example in the word *My* in the middle of a sentence indicates poor attention and poor concentration. I have seen similar errors in the handwriting of patients with uremic poisoning. The kinds of mistakes in this will were similar to the mistakes made by brain-damaged people."

"Of course, Doctor, that's just your opinion?"

"No, it is not just my opinion. I asked several other neurologists who have uremic poisoning patients to see if their experiences agreed with mine, if they also felt that those errors were indicative of kidney failure. And I received universal agreement that that was the case. You will notice that parts of the will are very carefully—painstakingly—done. Other parts are sloppy. I've seen writing samples from patients who are suffering from brain dysfunctions that looked very much like this. And the irregularity and shakiness in the writing of this will are exactly what I would expect from neurological patients. Note the spelling of *Las Vegas* on the envelope and the correct spelling of it in the will. Some of the misspellings in the will were blatant, and that's what happens when kidney patients affected by uremic poisoning try to write."

"What about the overtracings of some of these letters? Certainly, anybody can do that?"

"Yes, anybody can. I can. And you can. But I don't and you don't. However, some patients suffering from uremic poisoning retrace their letters in exactly the same manner. It is an abnormal attention to details. If you or I write a letter such as *e* legibly, there's no need to keep going over and over it thickening the strokes, and you and I don't do that. That's because we're thinking of what we're writing and want to get on with it. But in uremic patients, when their thinking is abnormal, they center in on one brief moment of activity and are unable to go on."

"Doctor, you don't consider yourself a handwriting expert, do you?"

"In my work, I've made a special study of the examination of handwriting samples written both before and after the patient underwent dialysis treatment. I've found that an examination of handwriting of kidney patients is a good diagnostic tool in determining how the patients were progressing. The quality of handwriting may get worse as the diagnosis progresses and may be a relatively good index of the progression."

"But, surely, no one with that kind of kidney disorder could live with it for ten years."

"Oh, yes he could! He could live with it for twenty years."

43. STILL LOYAL TO HIM

On December 10, 1977, Wilbur Dobbs phoned me from Boston. "Camp just ran the same ink test Lyter ran, and it was easy for him to distinguish 307 PAGO from 316! The ink on the will is what Lyter said it is, 307 PAGO! And Camp said that anyone who can't see the difference can't see."

"Get Camp here, Wil, and the guy at Paper Mate who knows what's in the samples Camp examined!"

"The Paper Mate people won't let their man come to Las Vegas."

"Then phone the Beckley-Singleton office, set up his deposition in Boston, take it, and establish the ink in each sample and—"

"I'm like a whore on her wedding night. I know exactly what to do."

After the first two weeks of trial, the indications were there, but by the end of the first month, there was no doubt about it. Wilbur Dobbs was the victim of a passion that dominated his every waking hour, interfered with his work, and drained him of his energies, which were not many. Wilbur Dobbs was in love. Not with a woman. Not with a man. With the telephone. Any telephone. He had to be near one, hold it, talk to it, listen to it, or suffer. In my apartment when the phone rang, no matter how close I was to it, Wilbur would spring to race me to it. For Wilbur, to be near a telephone was contentment, and to see one was joy, but to press one against his ear was ecstasy. Wilbur could not sit in the courtroom or at dinner for longer than a half hour without leaving to use a phone, and he could not stay in the pool longer than forty minutes because of this affliction. It was worse than a bladder problem.

On December 8, 1976, John Holmes testified that in the Desert Inn, Howard Hughes looked the same for the entire four-year period, and, "During that time, Mr. Hughes wore a Vandyke." I was about to ask my next question when Holmes added, "Because Mr. Hughes called it a Vandyke."

"Was it a Vandyke?"

"No."

"In your deposition, didn't you describe Hughes' beard as covering his chin down to a point with the sides of his face and jawline clean-shaven?"

"Yes, that's a Vandyke."

"Was your description accurate?"

"No."

"Then why did you give it?"

"Mr. Hughes called it a Vandyke. So that's what I called it."

"When you were asked in your deposition to describe what his beard looked like, did you describe what it looked like or what Mr. Hughes called it?"

"I must have been confused by your questions."

"Describe Mr. Hughes' fingernails during the Desert Inn period."

"Quite long."

"In your description, when you were asked if his fingernails during the Desert Inn period were quite long, you answered, 'No.' Why the change?"

"Well, they weren't quite as long as far as Mr. Hughes was concerned."

"Mr. Holmes, does your recollection of what you saw depend upon what you saw, or upon what Howard Hughes thought of what you saw?"

"Objection!" Earl Yoakum barked. "He's arguin' with the witness!"

Judge Hayes ruled, "Sustained!"

"What did Mr. Hughes say to you about providing for you in his handwritten will?"

"Nothing."

"Didn't he say something like this to you? 'Don't worry, Johnny, if anything ever happens to me, I've provided for you and the others in my will. Not by name, but by job description.' Something like that?"

"No."

"In your deposition, did you testify as follows? *'Mr. Hughes said, "Johnny, you don't have anything to worry about if anything happens to me because I've provided for you in my will along with my other aides by job description"?'* And in answer to another question, did you testify, *'Yes, I clearly remember Mr. Hughes saying that.'*"

"When I gave my deposition, I must have remembered it that way, but today it's fuzzy."

I questioned Holmes about the memo shown to me by that *Playboy* writer during Dummar's Las Vegas testimony. Holmes said that he typed the memo and wrote Hughes' reply at the bottom.

"Mr. Holmes, I want to ask you about the lines you typed here. *If the handwritten will is the real will, it could be that you had it updated later to the one Nadine has . . . and you might want to have whoever holds the handwritten one sent to you. . . .* First, when did you show this memo to Mr. Hughes?"

"In 1975."

"What did Mr. Hughes say, if anything, after reading your memo?"

"He said, 'I don't have time to work on this, the way I had time when I wrote my holographic will in the gray house near the tenth tee of the Bel Air Country Club golf course.'"

"Had Mr. Hughes ever before said that he had written his will near that tenth tee?"

"Several times."

"And in 1975, when you showed him this memo, he repeated the same thing again?"

"Yes."

"And you recall his precise words?"

"Yes."

"When did Mr. Hughes live at the gray house?"

"In the 1940s. But I can't tell you exactly when because it was before I began working for him."

"Did you ever see a copy of that same sheet that Mr. Myler had been shown concerning those words supposedly uttered by Mr. Hughes describing when and where he wrote his holographic will?"

"I don't remember."

"By the way, were you at that meeting in the Century Plaza Hotel when Levar Myler and the other aides and Hughes' doctors and some of his lawyers were there, sometime after Mr. Hughes died?"

"Yes."

"When was it?"

"It was before the so-called will surfaced."

"You're absolutely sure of that?"

"I'm absolutely sure of that. It was before the Mormon will was heard of."

"Was there one such meeting there with Mr. Myler present or more than one?"

"Only one."

"Mr. Holmes, at that meeting, as you testified under oath in your deposition that you and Mr. Myler and the other—I'll quote you— *'we looked at this so-called Mormon will, the Dummar will, and were asked questions about what we thought of it.'* Now, was that meeting at the Century Plaza Hotel, attended by Mr. Myler, before or after the Mormon will surfaced?"

"I guess it had to be after."

"During the Desert Inn period, did you hear Mr. Hughes mention his will?"

"Yes, he talked about a will during that period."

Holmes testified that in London, Howard Hughes saw Bill Gay. Then, no, in London Mr. Hughes did not see Bill Gay. At the Britannia Beach Hotel in the Bahamas, Mr. Hughes never once left his apartment until he checked out on February 16, 1971. Then, yes, a log entry reminded Holmes that for five hours and ten minutes on February 15, Mr. Hughes was out of that apartment.

Holmes had recently checked his expense records and saw that on the evenings of December 29, 30, and 31, 1967, he was not on duty in the Desert Inn.

There was no Pitney Bowes stamp meter machine on the ninth floor of the Desert Inn. But Mr. Hughes did have a lawyer named Bob Edison whose office was in Las Vegas, Nevada. Holmes did not know if a Pitney Bowes machine was in Edison's office in 1968.

Holmes testified that his lawyer, Horace Cummings, was the lawyer for each of Mr. Hughes' personal aides and for each of Mr. Hughes' doctors, and that Mr. Cummings' fees and expenses were being paid by Summa.

At the end of his employment contract in a few years, Holmes was to start collecting a salary under his consultation contract, which was to run for as long as he lived. The contract did not specify the subject on which he would consult. Levar Myler was on the board of directors when the board approved Holmes' consultation contract and Holmes was on the board of directors when the board approved Myler's consultation contract.

Eli slid a note in front of me: *Go into Hughes' death in Acapulco!* And

Stanley handed me a note from the other side: *Ask him what he was doing while Hughes was dying in Acapulco.* I looked at each of them and shook my head.

"Your witness."

Earl Yoakum examined John Holmes. "When were you in Vancouver?"

"In March 1972 we flew from Managua, Nicaragua, to Vancouver and checked into the Bayshore Inn. We stayed there until November 1972."

"During that stay at the Bayshore Inn, did Mr. Hughes ever once leave his bedroom?"

"Never once."

"After Mr. Hughes left Canada, where did he go?"

"Directly back to Managua, Nicaragua. Then we left for London the day after the earthquake."

"Why?"

"Mr. Hughes thought there might be another one."

Holmes testified that in London in 1973 on four occasions, Mr. Hughes piloted a twin-engine airplane with an experienced co-pilot in the right seat. In London, Mr. Hughes fell and broke his hip, and after that never again left his bed unassisted.

From London they went to the Xanadu Hotel in Freeport, Grand Bahamas. Since Mr. Hughes liked the hotel, he bought it and stayed in it for two years.

In February 1976, Hughes left the Xanadu for Acapulco, checked into the Princess Hotel and never left it until the day he died, April 5, 1976.

"Mr. Holmes, there's a provision in this so-called will for a lot of money to go to Mr. Hughes' personal aides at the time of his death. Since you were a personal aide at the time of his death, are you gonna try to get some of this money from Mr. Hughes' estate under this here provision, if this thing is admitted to probate?"

"No."

"Mr. Holmes, Ah want you to turn an' look this jury in the eye! An' Ah want you to tell them why it is that you wouldn't accept any money under this so-called will."

"Because I worked for Mr. Hughes for nineteen years and I admired him greatly. I was always loyal to him and I am still loyal to him. And if anyone gets any money under this forged will, it'd be stolen money and I wouldn't take a penny of it."

"Why do you call this forged will a forged will?"

"I can recognize Mr. Hughes' handwriting, and this was not written by Mr. Hughes."

"What's the basis for your opinion that it's a forgery?"

I objected, "No foundation! He's not a handwriting expert!"

Bittle jumped up. "This witness is as qualified as any of the handwriting experts Mr. Rhoden is going to call!"

Judge Hayes said, "Objection overruled!"

Holmes got the nod from Yoakum and answered, "There are many reasons. The will is sloppy. Mr. Hughes was meticulous. A perfectionist. In grammar and punctuation and spelling. He would never have written anything that looked like that, or that had errors in it like that. If Mr. Hughes forgot how to spell a word, he would find out how to spell it. He would never write anything that had misspellings in it."

"Did Mr. Hughes ever discuss with you a desire of his to establish a home for orphans?"

"He never mentioned anything about orphans. He would never have written a provision like that in his will."

"Did Mr. Hughes ever refer to his wife as Jean Peters during the Desert Inn period?"

"Never. He called her Jean or Mrs. Hughes. Never Jean Peters."

"Before he left the Desert Inn, did Mr. Hughes ever refer to his executive staff assistants as 'aides'?"

"Never. That word was coined by the news media in 1971 after the Maheu trial in Las Vegas."

"Did Mr. Hughes ever mention Noah Dietrich with regard to his will?"

"Yes. He once said, 'Can you imagine me leaving Dietrich, that son of a bitch, a nickel?'"

"Now, this here so-called will mentions William Lummis. And the Boy Scouts. And Melvin Dummar. Did you ever hear Mr. Hughes say that he wanted to leave somethin' to William Lummis? Or to the Boy Scouts? Or to someone named Melvin Dummar?"

"Never."

"During the four years at the Desert Inn, did Mr. Hughes write a will?"

"No."

"How do you know?"

"Because if he had, I would have known about it. I knew about everything of any consequence concerning Mr. Hughes. Since I never heard that he had written a will in the Desert Inn, he did not write a will in the Desert Inn."

"You can have the witness back, Mr. Rhoden."

44. ACAPULCO

I took Holmes on re-cross. "Mr. Holmes, in your deposition, you were asked if Mr. Hughes had ever said anything to you about Noah Dietrich,

and you answered, *Yes, but I don't remember what he said about him.*
But now, you remember that Mr. Hughes had made an insulting remark
about Noah Dietrich. What refreshed your memory?"

"Nothing but my effort to be honest."

"In 1968, in a memo to anybody did Mr. Hughes write that, though he
did not want Dietrich to be called back on something pending at the
time and related to television, he contemplated using Noah Dietrich on
some project in the future?"

"I don't know anything about Mr. Hughes ever writing anything like
that in any memo to anybody at any time. And I don't think he would
have."

"I'm going to show you a memo, which it is stipulated was written by
Mr. Hughes in the summer of 1968. Please look at this sentence Mr.
Hughes wrote to Bob Maheu. *Also, I want no dealings with Dietrich on
this matter. Maybe, in the future on some deal not related to TV.* You
never saw this before?"

"No."

"The fact that you didn't know that in 1968, Mr. Hughes contemplated using Dietrich in the future, doesn't mean that in 1968 Mr.
Hughes didn't contemplate using Dietrich in the future, does it?"

"No."

"You say that Mr. Hughes didn't write a will in 1968 in the Desert Inn
because if he had, you would have known about it, and since you didn't
know about it, he didn't. You knew about everything Mr. Hughes was
doing while you worked for him?"

"I'd say so."

"Every eight days, you had how many days off?"

"Four."

"Did you know what Mr. Hughes wrote when you had those four days
off?"

"Well, I—no."

"You told Mr. Yoakum that Mr. Hughes never told you he was going
to leave anything in his will to the Boy Scouts. Did Mr. Hughes ever tell
you he wasn't going to leave anything to the Boy Scouts?"

"No."

"Did he ever make any charitable contributions to the Boy Scouts?"

"None that I know of."

"Since you didn't know of any, does that mean that Hughes didn't
make any?"

"It means he didn't make any."

"I show you a 1967 income-tax return for Howard Hughes individu-
ally. Note a deduction here for a contribution of five hundred dollars to
the Boy Scouts. Now, did Mr. Hughes make a charitable contribution to
the Boy Scouts?"

"Apparently he did."

"The fact that you didn't know about it doesn't mean that he didn't, does it?"

"No."

"Was Mr. Hughes a Boy Scout?"

"No."

"How do you know?"

"Because I never heard of it."

I showed him a letter dated December 29, 1916, stipulated to have been written by Howard Hughes to the founder of the Boy Scouts:

Dear Chief,

I was glad to get your letter and I hope that I can come to your camp next year.

Enclosed please find my Buckskin Badge. I have returned it on account of eating some candy.

With love, from Howard.

"The fact that you didn't know that Mr. Hughes was a Boy Scout doesn't mean that he wasn't one, does it?"

"I guess not."

"You testified that one reason for your opinion that Mr. Hughes did not write the offered will was that it's sloppy, and since Mr. Hughes never would have written anything sloppy, the will must be a forgery. Mr. Holmes, please look at this memo in evidence as an exemplar written by Howard Hughes in 1968. Would you call this memo with its scratched words, and lines written along the margin, and words and letters written over and over again, sloppy?"

"Maybe it could have been a little neater."

"Is it sloppy?"

"All right, it's sloppy."

"Here's another 1968 memo written by Hughes. Sloppy?"

"Yes, sloppy."

We went on like that for nine more sloppy memos written by Howard Hughes in 1968.

"Next, Mr. Holmes, let's take spelling. You say it's your opinion that the will is a forgery because of the bad spelling in it. Now, are some of those misspelled words in the will spelled correctly in other places in the will and on its envelope?"

"Precisely, and Mr. Hughes would never have done that—never have misspelled a word that he knew how to spell. Mr. Hughes did not do absurd things like that, which you're trying to make these jurors believe."

"Mr. Holmes, you mean that in the same document, Mr. Hughes would never have spelled the same word both correctly and incorrectly?"

"Of course not!"

"Mr. Holmes, in the will, the word *Las Vegas* is spelled correctly. But on the will's envelope, it's spelled L-a-s V-a-g-a-s. Is that what you mean by the type of absurd mistake that Mr. Hughes would never have made?"

"Exactly!"

"And the name *McKay* is spelled on the envelope with a *c*, but spelled M-a-k-a-y in the will. That's another?"

"That is indeed another absurd mistake that Mr. Hughes would not have made and did not make. The forger made it!"

"And 'among' is spelled correctly on page two of the will but on page three, it's spelled a-m-o-u-n-g. Mr. Holmes, in your opinion, is that more evidence of forgery because Mr. Hughes would never have misspelled a word which he knew how to spell?"

"You are beginning to understand."

"Now, Mr. Holmes, please take a look at an exemplar numbered E-324 written by Mr. Hughes during the Desert Inn period. Did he spell the word *assets* correctly here?"

"Yes."

"How did he spell the same word down here on the same page?"

"A-s-s-e-t-t-s."

"On E-259, another Hughes memo written around the time the will was dated, did he spell the word *no* correctly?"

"Yes."

"On E-24, written a year after Mr. Hughes left the Desert Inn, how did he first spell that word in the phrase, 'I want no detail overlooked'?"

"He spelled it k-n-o-w."

"On E-277, he spelled the word *paid* correctly?"

"Yes."

"But in this memo dated May 7, 1968, twelve days before the dating of the will, how did Mr. Hughes spell that word?"

"P-a-y-e-d."

"Look at E-39 where Mr. Hughes spelled *Desert Inn* correctly. But read for the jurors how Mr. Hughes spelled the same word on E-422."

"D-e-s-s-e-r-t Inn."

"Mr. Holmes, have you ever known Mr. Hughes to incorrectly spell the name of someone whose name he had spelled correctly in memos for years?"

"No."

"Is Mr. Maheu's name spelled correctly by Mr. Hughes in E-278?"

"Yes."

"How did Mr. Hughes spell Mr. Maheu's name in E-14?"

"M-a-y-h-u."

"Did Mr. Hughes usually spell his own name correctly?"

"That's ridiculous! He always spelled his own name correctly!"

"Mr. Holmes, surely you'll concede that Mr. Hughes did not always spell his name correctly."

"I'll never concede any such nonsense!"

"Spell how Mr. Hughes wrote his last name in exemplar 433 written during the Desert Inn period."

"H-u-g-h-e-s-t."

"Now, Mr. Holmes, let's take a look at a few other misspellings in the will—the kind that supports your opinion that it's a forgery because Mr. Hughes never misspelled any words. In the will, is *companies*—the plural—spelled correctly or incorrectly?"

"It's spelled c-o-m-p-a-n-y-s and that is incorrect."

"Look at E-323 written by Howard Hughes. How is *companies*—the plural—spelled?"

"C-o-m-p-a-n-y-s."

"In the will is the word *divided* spelled correctly?"

"No, it's spelled d-e-v-i-d-e-d."

"You'd think that Mr. Hughes, familiar with corporate dividends, would know how to spell *divided*, wouldn't you?"

"I would. And he could."

"But, did he always? Look at E-326. How did Mr. Hughes spell the word *undivided*?"

"U-n-d-e-v-i-d-e-d. But look at the word *children* in your will—the *h* is left out. Mr. Hughes would never have left the *h* out."

"In E-439, is the word *which* spelled correctly?"

"Yes. Mr. Hughes did not leave the *h* out, you see?"

"I see. Now, on the bottom of the page, how is that same word spelled?"

"W-i-c-h."

"Mr. Hughes left out what letter?"

"The *h*."

"You see? Now, this habit of leaving out various letters was a habit of Mr. Hughes, wasn't it?"

"No."

We reviewed Hughes' spelling of:

Aircraf, truthly, mak (for "make"), *forwith, practi* (for "practical"), *Louisana, stiches, regardles,* and mathmatics.

I reviewed with Mr. Holmes other misspellings in the will: *revolk, forth, eight* (for "eighth"), *aids* (for "aides"), and *executer,* and a blowup of lists of words misspelled by Howard Hughes during the Desert Inn period:

Hubert Humphries, their (for "there"), *Holliday Inn, Puerta Rico, get dunner* (for "done"), *rainey, opointees, waisted, ass-whole, non-chalantly, treatury,* and *montarily* (for "momentarily").

"The misspelled words by Mr. Hughes during the Desert Inn period were in confidential memos that weren't available to the public, isn't that true?"

"Yes."

"How do you suppose that a forger got a peek at those confidential memos to know to repeat Mr. Hughes' habit—not only of misspelling simple words—but his habit of misspelling a word or a name that he could spell correctly?"

"The letter by Mr. Hughes to *Dear Chester and Bill* was the one the forger copied! And it was published in *Life* magazine and in a book."

"But, Mr. Holmes, are there any misspellings in that *Dear Chester and Bill* letter?"

"I haven't looked."

"Here's a copy of it. Do you see any?"

He read it. "No. But it isn't just the misspellings. There are mistakes in using capitals where Mr. Hughes would never have used them. That capital in *My* in your will on the third page up there where it says *of My estate*. Mr. Hughes would never have done that."

"Mr. Holmes, look at 355, page five, there at the bottom. Read what is bracketed in red."

"It says, *Let Me know.*"

"Is the *M* a small letter or a capital?"

"A capital."

"Was this memo, E-355, available to a forger?"

"No."

"Then how do you suppose a forger knew how to insert in his forgery the identical error that Mr. Hughes would make?"

"I don't know."

I reviewed some of the forty-seven instances in Howard Hughes' Desert Inn memos where he incorrectly capitalized a letter.

. . . *be Made, it must* . . .
. . . *it, Believe me* . . .
. . . *able to Reach Moe* . . .
. . . *Meanwhile, Please find* . . .
. . . *exchange, Said opportunities* . . .
. . . *few hours, But please* . . .

Then Holmes and I reviewed the places in the will where the words *Fourth* and *Fifth* were capitalized, but *first, second,* and *sixth* were not, and I had Holmes note the same inconsistency in Hughes' memos:

E-325: . . . *moving West* . . . *to the South* . . . *for the northern boundary* . . . *on the new north-south artery* . . .
E-348: . . . *the Carnival, Freaks, and Animal side of it* . . . *I repeat, the freaks and animals* . . .
E-421: . . . *black and White re-run* . . . *black and white re-run* . . .
E-46: . . . *the Referee must* . . . *the referee has* . . .

"Is your opinion of the forgery, Mr. Holmes, based in part on the choppy, telegraphic style with articles left out?"

"Yes."

"Are you ready to admit that was a characteristic of the writing style of Mr. Hughes in the late sixties?"

"No."

The will had these phrases:

> *second:*   *one eight of assets . . .*
> *third:*   *one sixteenth to Church of . . .*
> *Fifth:*   *one sixteenth of assets to go to Boy Scouts . . .*
> *seventh:*   *one sixteenth of assets . . .*
> *tenth:*   *one sixteenth to be used as school scholarship fund*
>   *for entire Country—*

In exemplar E-14, Howard Hughes had written:

Sorry for delay.

Impossible to reach intelligent decision sooner.

Ready now definitely leave very earliest departure possible by train consistent with maximum security. Want Hooper and same crew we used coming east. Will leave present local men here but in a room. Not visible to public or hotel employees. Expect to bring them west and make a part of permanent group, but not until I give signal.

New location will be last planned west coast (near west coast) location. (High Risers) Want all previous reservations reestablished immediately. This location will be permanent for foreseeable future . . .

Re southern space, will tell you what to do in few hours, but please get started on west coast trip & hotel space at once.

Must be thru. Chi. Must be 20th Cent. and U.P. Streamliner 'City of L.A.' Max. security should be possible. We have had no contact rail people for long time.

And in exemplar E-15 Hughes had written:

It will be broad daylight landing at destination and at hotel. So, what are we going to do about arrival at hotel?

"Mr. Holmes, these two memos, E-14 and E-15, were written by Mr. Hughes and handed by him to you when?"

"In the late sixties."

"Did you keep the originals in your possession from the time he gave them to you until you were served with a subpoena last year?"

"Yes."

"Were either of these memos shown to anyone while they were in your possession?"

"No."

"How do you suppose that a forger happened to select a choppy writing style for his forgery, so similar to Mr. Hughes' choppy writing style? A good guess?"

"I don't know. Ask Melvin Dummar!"

"Is the grammar in the will good?"

"No."

"Is that one indication to you that it's a forgery, since Mr. Hughes always used good grammar?"

"Yes."

I showed the jurors and had Holmes examine Xerox copies of memos written by Howard Hughes during the Desert Inn period:

> E-3: *If this is not true, I better get right thru to the White House* . . .
>
> E-13: *I am sorry you feel badly* . . .
>
> E-59: *. . . have to be awful stupid* . . .
>
> E-58: *. . . but leave the D.I, notes remain a part of the assets* . . .
>
> E-139: *. . . in violation with my desires* . . .
>
> E-292: *. . . has just waked me up.*
>
> E-307: *. . . it is sort like buying* . . .
>
> E-359: *Please reply very, very soonest about Show-Boat* . . .
>
> E-403: *. . . . Denny's stock would represent partly ownership in Denny's restaurants and partly ownership in the newly acquired hotel.*

"There are dashes in place of periods or commas or semicolons in the questioned will. Mr. Hughes used dashes in place of periods and commas and semicolons many times in his memos, didn't he?"

"Where?"

I showed him fifty-eight examples.

"Mr. Holmes, do you still consider yourself competent to form the opinion that the will could not have been written by Howard Hughes for the reason you gave Mr. Yoakum?"

"Yes."

"Were you with Mr. Hughes every day he was in the Bayshore Inn Hotel in Canada?"

"No, I was off for three or four days at intervals."

"During your three or four days off, did you see what Mr. Hughes did do or did not do in that hotel?"

"No."

On the evening of December 13, 1977, I vacillated over my adamant decision to not question the aides on Hughes' death in Acapulco. Holmes' renunciation of any interest in the will was damaging, and it was obvious that each aide would renounce and give as his reason his refusal to take stolen money from his beloved employer under a forged will, and each would profess a loyalty to Hughes even after his death. Evidence that these aides didn't give a damn about Hughes would not only discredit them as hypocrites, but would raise the inference that there was another motive for their renunciation under the will. But to explore an area I had not explored in depositions would leave me open to answers that could splatter egg on my face. I was tempted to take the risk, even though it would mean violating the first rule of cross-examination: Never, never ask a question on cross unless you know what answer you can force out of the witness. Never!

I continued my cross-examination of Holmes on December 14, 1977. "Did Mr. Hughes have a nodule over his left ear at the time of his death?"

"No."

"How do you know?"

"Because I never saw one. If there had been one there, I would have noticed it."

"The autopsy report shows that Hughes had an easy-to-bleed nodule over his left ear. Did you examine the body after death to see if the autopsy surgeon saw what he reported he saw?"

"No."

"When you first began working for Mr. Hughes, in 1957, what were your hours?"

"Twelve to fourteen hours, through the night."

"You didn't have a day off for four years, did you?"

"Nine years."

"You weren't allowed to speak to Mr. Hughes unless he spoke first, were you?"

"That was our procedure."

"Did he ever give you a Christmas or birthday present or send your family a Christmas card?"

"That wasn't the way he was."

"Did he ever once ask you anything about your family?"

"No."

"Did he ever once say anything like, 'Johnny, how do you feel?'"

"No."

"And this was a man you loved, to whom you felt loyalty and affection?"

"Yes."

To hell with it, I decided, let's take a chance on Acapulco!

"Mr. Holmes, during the month before Mr. Hughes died, where were you?"

"After two weeks off, I returned to Acapulco. And I was on duty for the last two weeks of Mr. Hughes' life."

"Did your duties include taking care of Mr. Hughes' physical well-being?"

"Of course."

"What was your salary in 1976?"

"One hundred and twelve thousand. That included my bonus of thirteen thousand."

"Did you get your bonus for 1976 before or after Mr. Hughes died?"

"Half before, half after."

"Was your loyalty to Howard Hughes personally, or to the people at Summa who were paying you the one hundred and twelve thousand?"

"To Mr. Hughes personally."

"Two weeks before Mr. Hughes died, when you returned to duty in Acapulco, did he appear to you to look about the same as he looked the day he died?"

"About the same."

"Then, two weeks before Mr. Hughes died, you saw him when he weighed around ninety pounds, and looked emaciated and dehydrated—a wrinkled bag of bones, isn't that true?"

"No. I thought he weighed a bit more."

"Two weeks before Mr. Hughes died, didn't he look to you like a man who was dying?"

"No. That wasn't discussed."

"During those last two weeks, weren't Mr. Hughes' cheeks so wrinkled and drawn into his facebones as to make him look like he was about a hundred years old?"

"I don't think he looked that badly."

"More than a week before Mr. Hughes died, did you hear one of the aides say, 'We've got to do something because it's going to look bad for us if the world finds out that he died looking like this'?"

"I don't recall any such discussion."

"Exactly what did you fellows discuss during those last couple of weeks of Mr. Hughes' life? Your bonuses?"

"Objection!" Yoakum shouted.

"Sustained!"

"At any time before Mr. Hughes died, did any of his doctors tell you what was wrong with him?"

"No."

"Did you ask any of them?"

"When it became apparent that he was quite ill, the day before he died, we asked them."

"What did they say?"

"That they didn't know what was wrong with him."

"When they said that, did it occur to you that it might be a good idea to call another doctor?"

"That would not have been appropriate."

"Not one of Hughes' doctors told you that their patient had a kidney disorder that was killing him?"

"No. I didn't know that Mr. Hughes had a kidney disorder until after the autopsy."

"Isn't it true that three days before Mr. Hughes' death, one of you aides phoned Kay Glenn from Acapulco and told Glenn that Hughes was in a critical condition with a kidney disorder?"

"That is untrue and impossible!"

"Mr. Holmes, in Mr. Glenn's deposition, he testified that that is precisely what he was told by you people the Friday before Mr. Hughes died."

"I don't know anything about that."

"You were the senior aide in Acapulco, weren't you?"

"Yes."

"How did Mr. Hughes get a separated left shoulder during that two-week period?"

"There was nothing the matter with his shoulder."

"When did Mr. Hughes last eat before he died?"

"He had an entree on Saturday, a dessert on Sunday, and he died on Monday."

"Who brought him his food?"

"Gordon Margulis."

"Gordon Margulis swore in his affidavit that Mr. Hughes didn't eat anything for several days before he died."

"It's like I said. Not like Mr. Margulis says."

"Mr. Holmes, since even to you Mr. Hughes was obviously ill at least a day before he died and since his doctors didn't know what was wrong with him, what were you going to do as part of your duties? Just sit around and wait until he died?"

"Of course not! But I'm not a doctor. We had four doctors in attendance, two on duty at all times."

"You never said to those doctors, 'Since you don't know what's wrong with him, either you get him to a hospital for someone to find out and save his life, or I will'?"

"No."

"Did you have a telephone available to you in your suite in the Princess Hotel in Acapulco?"

"Of course."

"During those last two weeks of his life, did anything prevent you from phoning a local hospital and saying, 'Get an ambulance over here!'?"

"Mr. Hughes would not have wanted to go to a hospital."

"Did anybody ask him?"

"No."

"Why not?"

"He wasn't feeling well."

45. THE LIAISON

The evening of the day John Holmes left the stand, Eli, Wilbur, Linda, and I joined Stanley and Doreen for dinner in the Egyptian Room at the

Hilton. Over her martini, Doreen said to me, "In the article in the *Sun* about your cross-examination of Johnny Holmes, they mentioned your name at least fifty times. But in the deposition that you used to discredit Holmes, didn't Stanley help you select the questions you asked?"

"He did."

"But there wasn't one word about Stanley in that article!"

"I didn't write it."

"Why can't Stanley examine some of those witnesses in the court-room?"

"Because I'm an egocentric, glory-hogging son of a bitch."

"Really, Hal! It's a matter of fairness to your colleagues!"

"If it's fair that my colleague Stanley examine a witness, then it'd be fair that my colleague Eli do the same. And my colleagues Wilbur and Marvin. I'll tell you what. Here's how I can make everybody happy. Instead of one lawyer asking questions, why don't we all do it together? Like a Greek chorus?"

Eli had nothing to say and looked at his soup, and Wilbur had nothing to say and looked at his double Chivas; and glancing at Stanley, I knew how Captain Bligh felt the morning Fletcher Christian gave him that dirty look.

I called Roy Crawford as a hostile witness to force him to contradict Holmes about Hughes' appearance and about logs during the Desert Inn period, and to set Crawford up for contradiction by two witnesses whom I knew would be called by Yoakum: Jean Peters, and Gilbert Boswell.

Crawford testified under questioning by Earl Yoakum that his examination of some recently found Desert Inn records reminded him that in 1967 on December 29, 30, and 31, he was on duty on the shift from 3:00 A.M. to 11:00 A.M. And Crawford recalled that whenever he was on duty, Mr. Hughes was in his bedroom. This testimony was not crucial because it was Dummar's story that he had dropped that old man off in Las Vegas sometime around 2:00 in the morning, and Hughes could easily have been back in his Desert Inn hotel room before Crawford came on duty. The aide I had to worry about was the one whose memory would be refreshed from records that he was on duty on the shift at midnight on the 29th or 30th.

Unlike tiny Roy Crawford in his sixties and slight John Holmes in his late fifties, Clarence Waldron was chunky and pudgy-faced and not yet forty. But like Crawford and Holmes, Waldron spoke softly and slowly and wore well-tailored clothes. Waldron had worked for Hughes Produc-tions starting in 1957 as a driver of starlets. In 1971 when Kay Glenn pulled Roy Crawford out of the Britannia Beach Hotel, he sent Waldron to Nassau as Crawford's replacement.

The aides kept typewritten logs in Nassau, and until Mr. Hughes died.

Waldron destroyed the Acapulco logs by feeding them into the shredder in Mr. Hughes' bedroom in the Princess Hotel.

"Why?"

"Kay Glenn's orders."

"When?"

"A few days before Mr. Hughes died."

"When you made entries in the logs, did you ever deliberately refrain from making an entry that Mr. Hughes was injecting something into his arm with a hypodermic needle?"

"No."

"In your deposition, you were asked, *Why did you deliberately refrain from writing that Mr. Hughes was injecting himself with a hypodermic needle?* And you answered, *Because I wasn't interested in that.* Now, did you deliberately refrain from making that kind of entry?"

"I'd like to change the answer I just gave from no to yes."

"Why did you refrain from making those entries?"

"I wasn't interested in matters like that."

"Pages and pages of these log entries show the minute Mr. Hughes began eating his dessert and the minute he finished. Now, those matters did interest you enough to make those entries, didn't they?"

"Yes."

"In Nassau, did Mr. Hughes walk around his room?"

"Yes, from his bed or a chair to the bathroom and back."

"How was he usually dressed?"

"Usually naked."

"During the time that you served Mr. Hughes, did he brush his teeth regularly?"

"Yes. About once every two years."

Waldron testified that he had the original of a typed letter signed by Howard Hughes, given to Waldron after his daughter was accidentally drowned in Nassau. The letter contained the sentence: "I lost my own mother and father at a very early age." Waldron explained that Mr. Hughes had sent him a condolence message in a telegram, and that when Waldron said he would like to have the same message with Mr. Hughes' signature, Mr. Hughes had Levar Myler, John Holmes, and Waldron type several copies of the condolence message and Mr. Hughes finally selected the one he liked, signed it, and awarded it to Waldron.

"What, if anything, was said by the aides in 1975 in Freeport concerning the memo that Holmes wrote to Mr. Hughes about retrieving his holographic will?"

"Well, we knew that somebody was holding a holographic will for Mr. Hughes. But we didn't know who. And we had to find out."

"Mr. Waldron, is it possible that Hughes could have written a will and gotten it out of his quarters without the aides knowing about it? Say, through a doctor acting as a courier?"

"Yes, that could have happened."

"At any time did Mr. Hughes leave his quarters in the Bayshore Inn in Canada to go to a different floor?"

"Never."

"How do you know?"

"Because I was there with him."

"From the 19th of August to the end of that month, were you with Mr. Hughes at the Bayshore Inn?"

"No, I was on vacation."

"What was your base salary in April 1976 when Mr. Hughes died?"

"Around seventy-nine thousand dollars. And an eight-thousand-a-year bonus."

"After Mr. Hughes died, what was your base salary?"

"Eighty-nine thousand dollars."

"Who gave you the ten-thousand-dollar raise after Mr. Hughes died?"

"Summa."

"What have you done for Summa during the year and a half since Mr. Hughes died?"

"I have an office there."

"What do you do in that office there?"

"What any executive in a corporation does."

"Do you supervise anyone?"

"No."

"Do you receive reports from anyone?"

"No."

"Do you have a title?"

"I'm still an executive assistant."

"What is the name of the executive you assist?"

"They haven't told me yet."

"Exactly what do you do as an assistant?"

"I'm available to consult."

"With whom?"

"With anybody."

"About what?"

"Whatever he wants."

"Has anyone, in the last year and a half, asked you to consult on anything?"

"Well, I'm on the Public Affairs Committee."

"Who's chairman?"

"Kay Glenn."

"What are you on the committee?"

"Vice-chairman."

"How many are there on the committee?"

"We two."

"How many meetings have you had in the past year and a half?"

"One."

"When you finish your employment contract with Summa, do you have a consultation contract?"

"Yes, a ten-year contract."

"That contract provides, does it not, for medical care for you and your family, as well as compensation?"

"Yes."

"How many days a year do you have to do this grueling work as a consultant?"

"Forty-five days."

"If you disclose confidential information about Mr. Hughes without Summa's consent, you lose everything, don't you?"

"Yes."

"During the last two years of his life, did Mr. Hughes take care of his personal needs?"

"No, he depended mainly on myself when I was there, and also on Mr. Eckersley. After he broke his hip in London, he got up on his feet only once, and that was when I held him up. But his legs were too weak after laying in bed a couple of years and he couldn't walk."

"How did Mr. Hughes get to and from the bathroom?"

"I carried him. He always called for me to carry him."

"When, before Mr. Hughes died, did you start your shift in Acapulco?"

"On the 28th of March."

"What caused Mr. Hughes' left arm to be separated from his shoulder socket?"

"I don't know anything about that."

"Did Mr. Hughes look the same on March 28th as he did on April 5th when he died?"

"I'd say so."

"Then, on March 28th, you saw Mr. Hughes weighing around ninety pounds and—"

"I would have guessed that he weighed more than that. I lifted him from the bed and carried him onto the stretcher."

"On March 28th Mr. Hughes appeared to you to be in need of medical attention, didn't he?"

"Not necessarily. Anyway, he had doctors there treating him."

"What kind of treatment did those doctors give him?"

"They took blood samples for tests."

"Were you told anything about the test results?"

"Nobody told me anything."

"In your deposition, you testified: *'They told me that the test reports showed that there was no blood problem, and Dr. Chaffin told me that everything turned out just fine.'* Now, were your deposition answers true?"

"They must be, because I am a truthful man."

"Did anyone administer anything to Mr. Hughes a day or two before he died?"

"Early on the morning of April 5th, Dr. Chaffin gave Mr. Hughes an i.v. It was a mess."

"What do you mean?"

"Chaffin missed the vein and shot the intravenous fluid right into Mr. Hughes' arm. It collected at the bottom of the arm."

"When you saw Mr. Hughes during that last week, looking as he did, and his doctors told you that everything was just fine, did it occur to you that maybe his doctors didn't know what they were talking about, and that it might be advisable to phone for an ambulance to take Mr. Hughes to a hospital?"

"I didn't know he was that sick."

"Isn't it true that several days before Mr. Hughes died, you and the other aides had discussions in the presence of Gordon Margulis in which you expressed your concern that it would look bad for all of you when the outside world found out how Mr. Hughes looked when he died?"

"No such conversation ever took place."

"Mr. Waldron, are you a personal friend of Kay Glenn's?"

"Yes."

"One week before the death of Mr. Hughes, did you try to get him to sign a paper authorizing Kay Glenn to enter Mr. Hughes' safety deposit box, and giving Glenn a power of attorney to sign checks on Mr. Hughes' account?"

"That was so that Mr. Hughes' business could properly be carried out. Mr. Hughes wanted to do this, but he always procrastinated. And that exasperated me. I got so mad I threatened to leave many times because he wouldn't take care of his business matters."

"What difference did it make to you whether or not Howard Hughes took care of his business matters?"

"Well, it was part of my duty to help Mr. Hughes in his business matters, and he wasn't doing what he should have done."

"Mr. Waldron, you were one of Mr. Hughes' messengers, weren't you?"

"I was an executive staff assistant! A liaison."

"You were a messenger, weren't you?"

"No, I was not a messenger. I was a liaison!"

Earl Yoakum examined Waldron.

"Mr. Waldron, tell us how you felt about Mr. Hughes."

"I loved my family, my God, and Howard Hughes in that order."

"Ah want you to tell this jury, Mr. Waldron, from your own heart an' soul an' mind, did you do everythin' you could in Acapulco to help Mr. Hughes?"

"I know in my heart and soul and mind that I did everything I could to help him in every way in his executive decisions and medically."

"An' you were loyal to the man you loved an' admired, isn't that right?"

"That's right, sir. We had a father-and-son relationship. I was loyal to him, and I shall remain loyal to his memory."

"An' as a decent man, would you take as much as one penny that came from a rip-off of the estate of the man you loved as a son loves his father?"

"No, sir, I would not take one penny under this forged will."

"He's your witness, Mr. Rhoden."

I took Waldron back on re-cross: "You call this a forged will. Are you familiar with the written opinions of handwriting experts such as Hans Verhaeren and Pierre Faideau and Henri Ollivier?"

"I've never heard of them."

"Did you compare any of the four hundred exemplars in this case with the handwriting on the offered will?"

"No, I don't have to do that to know it's a forgery."

"Have you heard about the testimony of Albert Lyter, the Treasury Department forensic chemist? Or about the medical testimony of Drs. Hill and Rubens and Titus?"

"No, I don't know anything about that and I don't have to."

"With regard to this strong affection that you had for Mr. Hughes, isn't it true that in the ambulance with Mr. Hughes on the way to the airport on the morning of April the 5th, in the presence of Mr. Margulis, you joked with the Mexican attendants?"

"No."

"Isn't it true that in that ambulance, you were singing?"

"I was what?"

"Singing! To be more precise, in a high falsetto, for the amusement of the Mexican attendants?"

"No!"

"You testified that in Acapulco, you helped Mr. Hughes medically. What did you do to help him medically?"

"One of the doctors said that if your eyes are open, they can become dry and irritable."

"I didn't ask you what the doctor said. What did you do, Mr. Waldron, to help Mr. Hughes medically?"

"I put Murine in his eyes."

"He's your witness, Mr. Yoakum."

46. THE COOK

In my apartment the morning I was to call Gordon Margulis, I was reviewing my notes when Eli walked in, worried as usual. "Hal, you've got a personnel problem. Wilbur's upset."

"He ought to be! Three days and a thousand bucks for airline tickets and hotels and transcripts, and now he's got to go back to Boston and take the deposition over again! And I've got to send you with him to be sure he does it right this time!"

"Hal, he needs your approval."

"He doesn't have it! He said he knew exactly what to do and off he flies for a simple deposition to ask a guy to identify some ink samples and state what was in them. And what does Wilbur forget? He forgets to ask the guy to state what was in them!"

"I know, but look what it's doing to his morale! Hal, you're his father figure."

"You look older than I do, you be his father."

"He respects you—he needs a pat on the head from you."

"What he deserves is a kick in the ass from me for fucking up that deposition. If he doesn't know how to take a deposition, he ought to read a book on how. But he can't read a book. That's because he can't turn the pages. And he can't turn the pages because he's always got a glass in one hand and a telephone in the other."

"Hal, you need him!"

"Yes, I need him. But I refuse to adopt him."

"All you have to do is give him a cookie every now and then. He's the kind of guy who's got to have that cookie!"

"Here's a dollar. Go buy a bag of cookies and you toss one to him every night."

Gordon Margulis testified that after arriving in Las Vegas from London in 1967, he applied for a job at the Desert Inn as a busboy. He thought that meant driving a bus. The day he reported for work he learned that the job was picking up dirty plates and delivering food on room service. After a month, he was ordered to deliver food to the ninth floor. That meant to the ninth floor, not on it. Margulis wasn't to set foot off the elevator.

"After a couple of weeks, they didn't want nobody deliverin' food to the ninth floor but me. Even when I had my day off, one of the aides'd call me back to the hotel to bring the food up. Finally, they moved me into the hotel."

"What was there about your ability to deliver food that was special?"

"It was my ability to keep my mouth shut that was special."

"What did you keep your mouth shut about?"

"About what I was bringin' up to the ninth floor. An' for who. Like it was a big military secret."

"Did you ever get to set foot on the ninth floor?"

"Oh, yeah. When Harvey left—Harvey was the cook—they asked me to take his job. I did, an' I became the cook. But I wasn't fully qualified for the job because I never cooked nothin' in my life."

"Then how were you able to cook?"

"It was easy. The cook didn't cook. All I had to do was warm up Mr. Hughes' food. He'd eat some canned soup an' when he'd stop for a while, it'd get cold an' he'd want it warmed up, so I'd warm it up, an' they'd take it back in to 'im. Then later, when he still didn't finish it, he'd want the same soup warmed up again. So I'd warm it up again. This'd go on for hours with the same bowl a soup. My title was cook, but I was really a warmer."

"What were your hours?"

"Twenty-four bloody hours a day, seven bloody days a week, on call at all times! Wherever I was, I hadda let 'em know 'cause if Mr. Hughes wanted some food, I had to run back to the hotel an' take care of it."

"What about holidays?"

"Every holiday—Christmas Eve, Christmas Day, New Year's Eve, New Year's Day, Easter, always on duty. For some reason Mr. Hughes wanted everybody around on holidays, an' he'd double the aides on duty—two instead a one. He was especially fond of havin' everybody work on Thanksgivin'. Of course, things were quiet on Passover."

"Who selected the soup Mr. Hughes ate?"

"Mr. Hughes. An' real strict about what he ate, he was. But he didn't select a different soup for each meal. For months he ate nothin' but canned chicken soup. Then he ate nothin' but the hotel's vegetable soup—but he didn't want the vegetable soup they prepared for everybody else. For Mr. Hughes, the soup had to be cooked in a special stainless-steel pot, an' the water had to be that Poland water that came in a bottle, not the kind that came out of a faucet. Once I prepared three different bowls a soup for 'im, labeled Batch One, Batch Two, an' Batch Three, for a taste test he wanted,to make. Mr. Hughes sampled each batch, an' told the aide which batch I was to make from then on exactly the same way. Actually, all three batches had the same vegetable soup outa the same can heated the same way."

"Was canned soup your only specialty?"

"I was also involved in the ice-cream project. Of Baskin-Robbins' thirty-one flavors, Mr. Hughes liked banana nut, an' he had two scoops with every meal. So we hadda have a lotta banana nut on hand. Then one day we faced a crisis! We were runnin' low on banana nut, an' Baskin-Robbins stopped makin' that flavor. The aides flew into a fit— each guy refused to be the one to tell Mr. Hughes that banana nut had to be a thing of the past. The way they fussed, you'd think that Mr. Hughes had a fatal disease an' they just found out that the supply a penicillin was runnin' out an' they couldn't get no more. So, Mel Stewart—he was Mr. Hughes' barber—phones Baskin-Robbins in California an' asks 'em if they'll make a special order a banana nut an' ship it fast to Las Vegas. To get the special order, we had to buy three hundred and fifty gallons of it. When the ice cream arrived at the Desert Inn, they put a special cover over it so that nobody'd know it was Baskin-Robbins ice cream."

"Why?"

"So nobody else'd eat any of Mr. Hughes' ice cream. With the security precautions, an' the special guards, an' the lies, an' the whispers, you'd think Baskin-Robbins was deliverin' a new hydrogen bomb."

"Mr. Hughes continued eating banana nut for how long?"

"The day the three hundred and fifty gallons arrived, we gave Mr. Hughes the last a the old banana nut, an' Mr. Hughes decides he was ready for a change, an' says from then on he wanted French vanilla."

"Did you see Mr. Hughes every day after you became the soup warmer?"

"Oh, no. For the years I worked at the Desert Inn, I saw Mr. Hughes maybe four times. Never close."

"How did he look when you saw him there?"

"A long beard an' long hair."

"When was that?"

"Maybe seventy. I don't remember."

"Did Mr. Hughes have a scar on his face?"

"Yeah, he did, but I didn't see it until I was sittin' on a plane next to 'im, an' that was after we left the Desert Inn. He had a small scar under his left eye."

"Was it possible for Mr. Hughes in the Desert Inn to have left the ninth floor without the guard posted at the elevator knowing about it?"

"Oh sure. Why not? It was possible for anybody to've gotten out without bein' noticed. All he had to do was go to the back door an' open it an' go down the stairs."

"During the last years of Mr. Hughes' life, who helped him to the bathroom?"

"Nobody. He didn't go to the bathroom in those last years. After he broke his hip in 1973, he used a urinal, but he wouldn't use a bedpan. He'd just do it in bed."

"Who cleaned up?"

"Usually Chuck Waldron. Or whoever was on duty."

"Did Mr. Hughes have anything wrong with his left shoulder?"

"Oh yeah. He complained about pain in his left shoulder startin' back in Freeport. He always told me to be careful about it every time I lifted 'im. It used to hurt 'im real bad, it did."

"Did Mr. Hughes' eating habits stay the same?"

"Well, his eatin' habits were peculiar, an' they stayed peculiar, but there was a time in Freeport when he began eatin' more, an' for a while it looked like he might get better. But then his eatin' habits went bad again, an' that's when we all knew he was dyin'."

"When did you first know Hughes was dying?"

"In 1975 in Freeport. We talked about it all the time. Johnny Holmes an' Rickard used to say, 'If he dies lookin' like that, what are people gonna think about us?' They were all sayin' that back in Freeport."

"How did Mr. Hughes look in Freeport?"

"Like a witch's brother. A skeleton with real tight, wrinkled skin, sorta whitish, stuck to the bone. An' his hair was gray an' real long an' straggly like dirty weeds—an' his beard—well, he didn't wash, so food'd get matted into his beard, an' the aides'd have to wipe it with a paper towel every now an' then. He was a grim sight, he was. Looked bad an' smelled bad. Then in Acapulco, he really went downhill. Compared to the way he looked in Acapulco, in Freeport he was Robert Redford."

"In Acapulco, did the aides discuss Mr. Hughes' physical condition?"

"Did they! I'll say they did! The Thursday before the Monday he died, we were all in Johnny Holmes' room. Tim O'Neil was there, Dr. Crane an' Dr. Chaffin an' Waldron an' Rickard an' everybody, an' they were all concerned about how the press'd treat 'em when they saw what Hughes looked like after he died, an' would they get into trouble when the authorities saw the body. An' Holmes kept sayin', 'I wanna get outa here!'"

"Then, four days before April 5th, the aides and the doctors all knew that Mr. Hughes was sick?"

"Knew he was sick! They knew he was dyin'! The man was starvin' to death! Those doctors didn't know what was wrong with 'im, an' I don't think they would've known what to do for 'im if they did know what was wrong with 'im. There was only one thing to do—get the boss to a hospital where somebody could find out what was wrong with 'im an' do somethin' for 'im. But everybody said, no, we can't do that, we've got orders! I told 'em where to shove their bloody orders! They said if Mr. Hughes heard that we called the outside, he'd fire us. I said let 'im fire us, but at least he'll be alive to do it. We can't just let 'im lay there an' go like this! But they kept sayin' they didn't have no authority to call a hospital. I says we don't need no bloody authority! I says, for God's sake, let's spoonfeed 'im at least! But Holmes says no, once we start spoonfeedin' 'im, we'll have to keep doin' it for the rest of 'is life. An' I says, If we don't spoon feed 'im, there ain't gonna be no rest of 'is life! But Holmes says no!"

"What was your reply?"

"I said somethin'."

"What?"

"I can't say it here."

"You mean you uttered an obscene expletive?"

"Yeah. I uttered a lotta those in Acapulco."

"Mr. Holmes testified that Mr. Hughes had an entree on a Saturday, his dessert on Sunday, and died on a Monday. Is that true?"

"That's a bloody lie! Mr. Hughes died on Monday, but he didn't have nothin' to eat on Saturday or Sunday. I oughtta know. I'm the one who took care of 'is food, an' I was up around the bloody clock for almost the last three days. Hughes didn't eat for four days before he died. Most a the time from Friday on he was unconscious."

"Did anyone report to Las Vegas about Mr. Hughes' physical condition?"

"Sure. They got orders back from Kay Glenn to start destroyin' the logs, an' Waldron was in Mr. Hughes' room shreddin' like crazy, an' this started three, maybe four days before Mr. Hughes died."

"Did Mr. Hughes say anything the last three days of his life?"

"Hell no! From Thursday on, Mr. Hughes didn't say nothin'—it was too hard for him to talk, an' he didn't for about four days. Except once or twice he'd make a squeaking noise, but you couldn't understand 'im. But Waldron was tryin' to talk to Mr. Hughes those last couple a days, an' he tried real hard, he did."

"What was Waldron trying to talk to Hughes about?"

"Waldron was tryin' to get Mr. Hughes to sign some insurance papers to benefit Waldron, an' Waldron kept naggin' the boss to sign those papers, but the boss was too weak. An' that's not all that bloody Waldron did! He put a picture of 'imself an' 'is family on the stand right next to Hughes' Kleenex box so that if Hughes turned his head over for a Kleenex, he'd see a picture a Waldron's family to remind 'im before he died to sign somethin' to leave some money to Waldron."

"Was Mr. Waldron a personal friend of Kay Glenn's?"

"I don't know, but I remember once seein' a check with the names Kay Glenn an' Clarence Waldron both printed on it."

"Mr. Waldron testified that he lifted Hughes out of the bed and onto a stretcher for the ambulance ride to the airport."

"That's another bloody lie! I lifted Mr. Hughes. Waldron never touched 'im."

"Did anything unusual happen in the ambulance on the ride to the airport?"

"Well, I'd sure call it unusual. There was Mr. Hughes layin' there, dyin', an' here's Waldron, jokin' with the Mexican attendants, an' makin' 'em laugh, an' singin' in that real high-pitched soprano voice of 'is for their entertainment."

"Did Mr. Hughes ever discuss with you any fatherly affection he had for Waldron?"

"Fatherly! Hughes used to say, 'That Waldron is absolutely useless!' I said, 'Then why do you have 'im around?' And he said, 'The only reason I keep 'im is because he's the only one who'll give me an enema.'"

"What, if anything, did Mr. Hughes say about Bill Gay, the president of his company?"

"The boss always said that Gay was a real pain."

"What, if anything, did Mr. Hughes say about James Rickard?"

"Mr. Hughes could never remember Rickard's name. He always referred to him as the 'other guy.'"

"What did Mr. Hughes say about Francom?"

"He liked George Francom an' he never said nothin' bad about Francom."

"In Acapulco, did you hear any comments from Dr. Crane concerning Mr. Hughes' physical condition?"

"Dr. Crane said, 'These guys won't let me in to see 'im.' He kept sayin' that over an' over again. Then he'd just take another drink. It was kinda sad, it was. He'd say, 'I gave up a practice for one patient, an' now I never get a chance to see my one patient.'"

"Did Dr. Crane drink often in Acapulco?"

"I'd rather not answer that question."

"Answer the question, Mr. Margulis," Judge Hayes said.

"Well, he was—he drank a little, yeah."

"A little in the morning?"

"Yeah."

"A little in the afternoon? A little in the evening?"

"Yeah."

"Mr. Margulis, did you ever once in Acapulco see Dr. Crane sober?"

"Well, I'm not a—do I hafta—all right, no."

"In Acapulco, did Dr. Chaffin say anything about Mr. Hughes' physical condition?"

"He said about the same thing that Dr. Crane kept sayin'. Chaffin used to say, 'Gay don't like me, he don't want me around here, an' I'll never get in there, an' that's the end of it.'"

"Did Dr. Chaffin say why Gay didn't want him there?"

"Oh, yeah. Chaffin was always tryin' to nudge Hughes to get off his lazy butt, to get outa that bed, an' start movin' around an' livin'."

Phillip Bittle cross-examined Margulis. "After this will showed up, did you tell anyone that in your opinion it was a forgery?"

"Sure."

"Isn't that because you know that Mr. Hughes never left the Desert Inn to have been picked up by Melvin Dummar?"

"How do I know if he left the Desert Inn? I wasn't up there every night. How do I know what he did or didn't do when I wasn't there?"

"On what did you base your opinion that the will was a forgery?"

"Oh, the fact that the name Spruce Goose was in it. I always had the impression that Mr. Hughes didn't like that name. An' I read in the newspapers that everyone said it was a forgery."

"Your opinion hasn't changed, has it?"

"Well, I'm not so sure anymore."

"What has made you not so sure anymore?"

"What I keep readin' in the newspapers. All of a sudden we have one guy sayin' he never kept a log in the Desert Inn, an' I know they kept logs there. An' one guy says Mr. Hughes had short hair, an' another guy says it was long. One guy says his toenails were too long for him to wear shoes, an' another guy says he wore shoes all the time walkin' to the bathroom. An' I know what we talked about in Acapulco, an' now they say they didn't even know Mr. Hughes was sick until they got him on the airplane, like it was a big surprise. All I know is, there's a lotta lyin' goin' on here, an' I ask myself, why? Why are these guys changin' their stories all the time? I know that Holmes used to tell me that the boss had a handwritten will an' that he gave it to somebody to hold for 'im in secret, an' that the aides didn't know who had it, an' that they wanted to know. Then up pops this handwritten will, an' some guy says that Hughes gave it to him to hold in secret, an' now everybody's tryin' to say that this ain't his will. Well, I ain't so sure it ain't his will. Look, I know that those guys had a problem with tellin' the truth, but that don't—"

"What do you mean by that?"

"For example, take this time with Levar Myler. We're in Florida and the *Miami Herald* published a story where they described what Hughes looked like—his long hair an' his long beard. Myler reads it an' says, 'How can they write lies like this about Mr. Hughes?—We ought to sue 'em for writin' this!' An' I says, 'Hey, come on, they described him exactly like he is!'"

"Mr. Margulis, isn't it true that you've decided that the will might be genuine because if it's admitted to probate you intend to claim that you were one of the personal aides of Mr. Hughes at the time of his death and to come in under the will?"

"You gotta be kiddin'!" Margulis glared at Bittle. "Hughes' personal aides were Holmes, Waldron, Francom, Eckersley, an' Rickard, an' I wasn't one of 'em! Mel Stewart an' I were there an' we worked for Mr. Hughes, but we weren't in the group of his personal aides! His aides've all got big contracts with Summa. Mel an' I don't. I wasn't one of his aides an' I'm not claimin' I was. If this will turns out to be the real thing, it don't make no difference to me, 'cause I don't get a dime out of it."

"You testified that you kept urging Mr. Hughes' aides to phone for an ambulance to get Mr. Hughes to a hospital to save his life. Mr. Margulis, what prevented you from picking up a telephone and doing it on your own?"

Margulis sat frozen by the question and stared at Bittle. Then he sat back in the chair and for the first time in his testimony looked away from the attorney questioning him. The crowded courtroom was quiet as we waited for Margulis' answer, and when it came his voice was weak.

"I should 'ave. I should 'ave. I've asked myself that every day since the boss died. I guess I'll go on askin' myself that. I don't know why I didn't. I should 'ave."

47. THE DOCTOR

I looked forward to calling Dr. Norman Crane and cross-examining him as a hostile witness; scoring on him would be like firing a shotgun where your target was the air. I looked forward to it until I saw him stagger to the witness stand. Dr. Norman Crane looked his seventy-three years. Hesitant in his walk, he seemed unsure of where he was going and what he was doing, and his hand trembled when he took the oath. Dr. Crane slowly sat down on the witness chair and looked at me and smiled as though to say, You're not going to be too hard on me, are you?

"Doctor, when you signed your twelve-year consultation service contract with Summa in January 1977, how old were you?"

"Seventy-two."

"Under that contract, what consultation services are you to perform for Summa?"

"A continuation of the services I performed before."

"What services had you performed before?"

"Medical services for Mr. Hughes."

"Dr. Crane, you entered into this contract with Summa nine months after Howard Hughes had died. You mean that you contracted to continue to perform medical services for a patient who had been dead for nine months?"

"I guess my consultation services were to be something else."

"When was the last time you treated a patient other than Mr. Hughes?"

"I gave up active medical practice, except for Mr. Hughes, more than ten years ago."

"Are the consultation services that you as a doctor are going to render for Summa medical services?"

"Of course."

"What kind of medical consultation services can a doctor render for a corporation?"

"I don't understand."

"If Summa Corporation develops a stomachache, are you going to prescribe a pill for it?"

"I don't like your question."

"Doctor, what is Summa getting for the money they're paying you?"

"They must have thought I would be of value, or they wouldn't have made that contract with me."

"Dr. Crane, isn't it true that you are being paid by Summa to keep quiet?"

"Your question is insulting!"

"Answer it anyway!"

"I don't—I'm not—I don't know what anyone else has in his mind.

"In the spring of 1962, did Howard Hughes say anything to you about his will?"

"Yes, he made many promises to me that he would put me in his will."

"At some time in the late sixties, did Mr. Hughes say anything to you about your being in his will?"

"Yes, he said, 'You are in my will—I've written it and you are in it.'"

"Then Howard Hughes told you that some time between 1962 and the late sixties, he had written a will?"

"I suppose so."

"The Sunday, Saturday, and Friday before his death on Monday, April the 5th, what condition was Mr. Hughes in?"

"He was in a coma since that Friday night."

"Then he didn't eat an entree on Saturday and a dessert on Sunday before his death on Monday, as Mr. Holmes testified, did he?"

"No."

"When your patient went into a coma on that Friday night, did you know what was wrong with him?"

"No."

"Why not?"

"There was no way I could know."

"Did you treat Howard Hughes?"

"I don't know what you mean by 'treat.'"

"It's what doctors do for their patients."

"I gave him an i.v. of glucose the night before he left Acapulco."

"Any other treatment?"

"No."

"Did he appear to you to need any?"

"I couldn't get in to see him."

"What stopped you?"

"Mr. Hughes didn't want to be bothered by any of us doctors."

"How do you know that?"

"I was—I sensed this."

"Why didn't you get your patient to a hospital in Acapulco, doctor?"

"Mr. Hughes didn't want to go to a hospital."

"Did you ask him?"

"No."

"Why not?"

"He was in a coma."

"Then how do you know he didn't want to go to a hospital?"

"I—I—"

"You sensed this?"

"Yes."

"Doctor, several days before Hughes died, somebody sent out a sample of Hughes' urine to an Acapulco laboratory and got word back that Hughes had a kidney problem. Isn't that true?"

"Well, the indications were that there was a possibility—that is, that perhaps that possibility ought to be given some consideration—but, I couldn't make a diagnosis of kidney disorder from the limited information available."

"Who called Kay Glenn in Los Angeles the Thursday before the Monday Hughes died and told Glenn that Hughes had a kidney disorder that was critical?"

"I don't know."

"Why did you give Mr. Hughes the i.v.?"

"I felt that he might be dehydrated. This was the Saturday or the Sunday before he died."

"Clarence Waldron testified that the i.v. was administered by Dr. Chaffin."

"Mr. Waldron was mistaken."

"Where are your medical records of this injection of intravenous fluids?"

"I didn't make any."

"Is it not proper medical practice for a doctor to keep a record of every injection he administers?"

"Yes, but years ago Mr. Hughes requested that I not keep any records."

"And the request of your patient that you not follow a proper medical practice was a sufficient reason to not follow a proper medical practice?"

"It was a sufficient reason in this case. Besides, I was too busy at the time."

"Too busy doing what?"

"I'm not sure at the moment."

"Did you or Dr. Chaffin tell Clarence Waldron that Mr. Hughes' tests showed that he was just fine and that there was no blood problem?"

"I don't know what Dr. Chaffin told Mr. Waldron, but I didn't tell him that."

"Who was Dr. Montemayor?"

"Dr. Chaffin was concerned because, as American doctors, we couldn't practice medicine in Mexico. He called a local doctor who was a specialist in internal medicine. Dr. Montemayor saw Mr. Hughes late Sunday night or early Monday morning, the day he died."

"What did Dr. Montemayor say when he saw your patient?"

"I can't remember."

"Didn't Dr. Montemayor express his shock and disgust at what he saw? Didn't he say that he couldn't understand why your patient was not removed to a hospital days ago?"

"I don't remember those exact words."

"Didn't Dr. Montemayor tell you that Howard Hughes was obviously dying?"

"Not that way."

"Didn't Dr. Montemayor tell you that they had doctors in Acapulco who could have saved the life of Howard Hughes if he had been brought to a local hospital?"

"I don't recall that."

"Didn't Dr. Montemayor say that it was apparent to him that the people around your patient were just waiting for him to die?"

"I don't recall his saying it in that way."

"What did Dr. Montemayor tell you he found as a result of his examination of Mr. Hughes?"

"He found a zero pulse rate and zero blood pressure. I found the same thing."

"The Friday before Mr. Hughes died—when there would have been plenty of time to have taken him to a hospital—did you attempt to take Mr. Hughes' blood pressure or pulse?"

"No."

"If you had taken his blood pressure or pulse a few days before he died, wouldn't you have found some reason to have had Mr. Hughes rushed to a hospital in Acapulco?"

"No, I wouldn't have. We saw no need to get Mr. Hughes to a hospital. And he would not have permitted it if we did."

"Doctor, if you have a patient who's dying of a kidney disease, and who needs a dialysis-machine treatment to save his life—"

"I didn't know he had a kidney disease."

"Doctor, isn't it true that three weeks before Howard Hughes died, you knew that there was something seriously wrong with him that required immediate blood and urine tests?"

"Oh, yes, certainly."

"When was a blood test made?"

"Dr. Clark was going to take the blood to Utah, but Mr. Hughes refused to have a blood sample taken."

"Did you try to take a blood sample?"

"No."

"Did you try to exercise your persuasive ability on Mr. Hughes during that three-week period when you knew that tests were indicated?"

"No, but I did take a urine sample when Mr. Hughes was asleep."

Phillip Bittle examined Dr. Crane. "When you saw Mr. Hughes during the Desert Inn period, was he suffering from a kidney disease?"

"No."

"I have nothing further."

I took the witness for re-cross. "During the Desert Inn period, did you examine Mr. Hughes?"

"Mr. Hughes would not allow the type of physical examination usually performed on patients."

"Then how do you know that in the Desert Inn he did not have a kidney disease?"

"I saw no indication of a kidney malfunction."

"Did you give Howard Hughes blood transfusions during his stay at the Desert Inn?"

"Yes."

"When did you first consider the possibility of kidney disease?"

"When I learned that Mr. Hughes had taken phenacetin in excessive amounts. That was the last weekend or perhaps the very day Mr. Hughes left Acapulco."

"Doctor, isn't it true that in the Desert Inn you knew that Mr. Hughes was taking excessive amounts of phenacetin?"

"I don't remember that."

"Didn't you tell some people during the Desert Inn period, that you were concerned about damage to Mr. Hughes' kidneys?"

"Well, yes, I think I did tell Jean Peters and Mr. Hughes himself that his use of phenacetin could damage his kidneys."

"Doctor, you told Mr. Bittle that during the Desert Inn period, Howard Hughes did not have a kidney disease. If today, you saw a person dying of kidney disease, would you know what he was dying of?"

"Of course."

"But on the day Mr. Hughes died of a kidney disease, you didn't know he had it, did you?"

"No."

"In what branch of medicine did you specialize when you practiced?"

"I was a specialist in internal medicine."

"Nothing further."

Judge Hayes said, "I want to ask this witness a few questions. What was the purpose of flying Mr. Hughes to Houston?"

"Mr. Hughes had said on previous occasions that he didn't want to go to a hospital."

"And so, because on previous occasions, Mr. Hughes had said he didn't want to go to a hospital, you did not send your dying patient to a local hospital for immediate emergency treatment. But instead, you put him on a plane to a hospital hours away in Houston, is that it?"

"Yes."

"What facilities were available, if any, in Acapulco, for a dialysis treatment the morning of April 5th?"

"I have no idea."

"Between five A.M. and the time the plane left that morning, what were his vital signs?"

"Horrible."

"Dr. Crane, did you have any reasonable expectation that Howard Hughes would live to arrive in Houston?"

"None."

In chambers, Phillip Bittle was so upset he could hardly stammer. "Your Honor, this has got to stop! Dr. Crane and Mr. Hughes' aides are all fine, moral men—decent men, men with families! Mr. Rhoden's questions are designed to ridicule these witnesses! Why, he's actually trying to make it look as though they committed murder!"

"First or second degree?" I asked.

"You see, you see? Judge Hayes, Mr. Rhoden is deliberately distorting the facts! I move that he be ordered to stop this line of questioning."

"Motion denied."

At 11:30 the night of Dr. Crane's testimony, after I finished preparing for the first day of Verhaeren's examination, I sat at the pool with Wilbur Dobbs to review the points we had made and the points we had missed with Crane. After a long stare into his brandy snifter, Wilbur said, "Hal, I don't want to be a snitch, but Ah've got to warn you. We've been havin' meetin's in Stan's apartment. Eli, Stan, an' Doreen an' me. They think that the three of us ought to join together to—Ah' don't know how to put it exactly."

"You mean, to form a union to collectively bargain with management?"

"Somethin' like that. Doreen keeps sayin' that you're not bein' democratic, that you're a—a—"

"An egocentric, glory-hogging son of a bitch."

"Well, you've got the flavor. She said that Stan's devoted over a year an' a half of his life to this case, an' that he isn't bein' treated fairly. An' that none of us are. It's a matter of recognition."

"By recognition, you mean your names in the newspapers?"

"Also, self-recognition. We want to feel that we're a part of it. Not just sittin' there writin' notes. Hal, you're goin' to face a real crisis any day now."

"I've seen it coming. Are you with them, Wil?"

"Well, in a way, Ah agree with 'em. Ah think Ah could do a good job, Hal, if you'd give me a chance at a witness. Just one?"

"Wil, I'd like you to stay. I need you. But have you ever tried a case before a jury?"

"No, but—"

"Do you think this is the one in which to learn? We all talked this out a year ago and everybody agreed."

"Then, Hal, you're goin' to have a real mutiny on your hands!"

"Who's bailing out? Only Stan? Stan and Eli? Or all three of you?"

"Ah'm stayin'. But Ah think you're going to get an ultimatum from Stan an' Eli any day."

48. THE HANDWRITING PHASE

I began boring the jury on the morning of December 14, 1977 by having Hans Verhaeren begin his lecture on handwriting movements. As he pointed out similarities between the attack strokes and linking strokes in the will and in exemplars of Hughes' writings, Verhaeren made drawings on transparencies projected on a screen in the darkened courtroom; and the silence in the jury box, I suspected, meant not rapt attention, but restful slumber. At the start of the afternoon session, to get those lights back on and wake the jurors up, I steered the examination to a subject that required my Dutch expert to draw on sheets of paper tacked to the large board next to the witness stand. But the next three hours were equally boring as Verhaeren wrote pages of letters and numbers, and drew graphs and charts showing how he had measured the height of letters in the will—such as the small *e* and the small *l*—and found from the shortest and tallest an unusually wide range of extremes. He did the same thing with the same letters in the exemplars and found the same unusually wide range of extremes.

He also measured the widths—the narrowest and the widest— of letters such as the *m* and again found the same wide range of extremes in the will and in the exemplars, and I had the feeling that the only ones in the courtroom listening to Verhaeren were Verhaeren, the reporter, and I.

"You will notice these letters in the questioned will—the *t* in *Houston,* the *G* in *Gabbs,* and so on—are obviously overwritten. That is, after the letter was written and the pen was lifted from the paper, it was returned to overwrite, several times, the letter already written legibly. We see the identical overwritings here in Hughes' exemplars 2 and 4, and in dozens of others.

"For example, in the word *signed* at the bottom of the third page of the questioned will, the *e* and the *d* were obviously overwritten several times. But they were legible when first written. And you see that the *e* was overwritten more on the left side than on the right. Then see in this exemplar 95—borrowed from Mr. Greenspun's safe—the word *guide.* The *d* and *e* have been overwritten. And again, the *e* is overwritten more on the left side than on the right—exactly what was done with the same two letters at the end of the word *signed* in the questioned will."

"At the bottom of the small *b* on page one, line eighteen in the will, notice that the curved part of the bowl looks as though the writer was trembling. Possibly because he kept glancing at another letter from which he was copying, he wrote it slowly, causing a trembling line instead of a smooth, fast-flowing one. An indication of forgery. But we find in the same letter *b* at line thirteen in the will that the bowl is written in a smooth, fast-flowing line. What are we to conclude? That a forger was able to write a smooth *b* on line thirteen, but that he forgot how to write it a few lines later and had to slow down as he studied his copy?

"Then, we see in the exemplars of Mr. Hughes' writing that same phenomenon. He would write letters smoothly, and then suddenly here is a letter that has a tremor in it. Therefore, this tremorous stroke in various places in the will becomes an indication of genuineness."

After dinner, Mr. and Mrs. Verhaeren were in my apartment for him to brief me on his next subject. But Verhaeren wanted to lecture to the jurors without being guided by questions. After the fourth evening of this, Verhaeren was tired, and in my apartment, Linda and Wilbur and Mrs. Verhaeren watched television, waiting for the session to end, when Verhaeren exploded. Verhaeren was explaining: "There are four different loops in his *l* in the will, and this inconsistency appears in his other writings."

"Now, what about the small *m*'s?"

"Also, he made it four different ways, as I have already explained to you several times."

"I've got it—four different *l*'s and four different *m*'s."

Verhaeren pulled one of the cards out of his small metal index box and said, "I told you that there were three different *l*'s, not four. I suggest that you pay closer attention."

"But I just made a note here that you said you found four different *l*'s and—"

"I've had enough of this!" Verhaeren pounded his fist on the table and shouted, "I said three *l*'s and you say I said four! I will not be contradicted like this!" He put his card back in the box and slammed the lid. "I'm going back to Holland!"

"Please, Mr. Verhaeren, I'm sorry! I thought you said four different *l*'s—I made a mistake in my notes. I didn't mean to contradict you."

The next morning, Hans Verhaeren apologized for his short temper and resumed the stand.

"In the questioned will, in the *F* in *Forth*, you see that a small stroke was added to the lower, curved tail after the tail was finished and the pen left the page. This was a superfluous addition, not necessary for legibility. It looks as though the writer was trying to make his ending stroke look like something he was copying. An indication of inept forgery.

"But look at exemplar 93. This, we know, is the original of a memo written by Mr. Hughes in 1968, and which has always been in the safe of your Las Vegas newspaper publisher Mr. Greenspun, not available to a forger. And we find in the *F* in *Finney*, at the bottom, a superfluous addition added to the lower curved tail after the tail was finished— exactly as in the *F* in the will in *Forth*.

"And in the *F* in *Fifth* in the will, there is another superfluous addition, but this time at the start of the top horizontal stroke. It was obviously tacked on after the horizontal stroke was made. Here again, an indication of a bad forgery.

"But, see the *F* in *Frontier* in a memo known to have been written by Howard Hughes to his lawyer in 1968. This memo also was not available to a forger. When we examine it, we see at the start of the top horizontal stroke, a superfluous addition obviously tacked on after the horizontal stroke was made— exactly as we see in *Fifth* in the will."

"Mr. Verhaeren, were the *i* dots a factor in your opinion?"

"Oh, yes. Look at the word *influence* at line three of the will, and the *i* dot over the first letter. The dot looks like an elongated 2. And it appears only once in the three page will. Now look at this memo by Mr. Hughes written around the time of the dating of the will. We see that he dotted the small letter *i* with the identical elongated 2."

"Mr. Verhaeren, did you examine the handwriting on the envelope containing the words *deliver this one* in comparison with the exemplars of Mr. Hughes' writing?"

"Yes, I did, and I can say that the words *deliver this one* on this envelope were probably written by Howard Hughes. However, since there are only three words, I cannot be certain."

Marvin Mitchelson handed me a note—*I've got an idea. Back soon*— and left the courtroom. Marvin prevailed upon Hank Greenspun to let him examine the Hughes memos in Greenspun's safe. After a three-hour search, Marvin found what he looked for. The next morning, Hans Verhaeren testified, "In the word *this* on the envelope containing the words *deliver this one*, there is an odd ending stroke added to the letter *s*. That letter was first written with an ending downstroke. Entirely legible as an *s*. After the letter was completed something made the writer add a horizontal stroke to the *s*. Another superfluous addition. It was, I would say, an abnormally meticulous attention to a trivial detail. Last night I was shown a memo written by Howard Hughes in April 1968, and I see, in three instances on the same page, the small *s* written with the identical superfluous addition."

"Mr. Verhaeren, you stated yesterday that in your opinion, the words *deliver this one* were probably written by Howard Hughes. Does this finding of the small letter *s* in these memos affect your opinion?"

"I would now have to revise my opinion by saying that it is very probable that Howard Hughes wrote the words *deliver this one* on this envelope."

"Back to the will. Was it written with good control?"

"In various places in the questioned will, it appears as though the hand of the writer went out of control. This indicates some disturbance of motor coordination. When we look at exemplars 1 to 16, we see indications of the same disturbance, but not nearly as strong a disturbance as we see in the questioned will. However, when we look at exemplars 91 and 95, written by Mr. Hughes in early 1968, we see a motor disturbance which is even stronger than that which we find in the questioned will."

"From your examination of the questioned will and these hundreds of exemplars of the writing of Howard Hughes, do you have an opinion as to who wrote the questioned will?"

"I have. I am convinced that the man who wrote the exemplars, whom I am told was Howard Hughes, is the man who wrote the questioned will."

"Do you have any doubt about that?"

"I'm certain of that beyond any reasonable doubt."

"Is it possible for it to have been a forgery?"

"No, of course not."

On December 19, 1977, Judge Hayes declared a recess for the holidays and ordered us to resume on January 4, 1978. Verhaeren and his wife had intended to take a tour of the United States after his testimony was completed; they agreed, instead, to take their tour during this two-week holiday. I explained to Mr. Verhaeren that his return on January 4, 1978 was essential. Since he had given testimony damaging to the contestants, they had a right to cross-examine him, and if he did not return, and deprived them of that right, they would move for a mistrial and get one, and we'd have to start the trial over again with a new jury. Since we couldn't afford this, the will would fall. "Please sir, it's essential you return here to be cross-examined starting on January 4th."

"I give you my word that I will come back here for cross-examination."

I asked Eli to fly to Seattle to get a signed statement from Alex Bertulius, and then to fly to Anchorage to get one from Wil Painter, two witnesses in support of Forsythe. Then he was to go to Ogden, Utah, to take the deposition of the dentist found by Jim Spiller, then to attend the depositions that Bittle was going to take of the other Utah witnesses Spiller had found to support Forsythe.

A second deposition was to be taken of Gilbert Boswell in Houston on December 29, 1977, and since Wilbur was going to be home at the time, he was the most likely choice, but when Yoakum told Judge Hayes that Boswell had records which could refresh his memory concerning his daily contact on tax matters with the ninth floor of the Desert Inn during the last few days of December 1967, Boswell's deposition became crucial. Since I couldn't trust Wilbur to take it alone, I asked Stanley if he would go to Houston after Christmas to take Boswell's deposition, and Stanley said he would be happy to fly there with Doreen.

Linda and I stayed in Las Vegas to prepare for Faideau's direct and for the first week of witnesses after the vacation. On Sunday, January 2, 1978, I received a phone call from Stanley Fairfield in Los Angeles. "Gilbert Boswell killed us! There's no way you can argue that on the night Dummar's talking about, Howard Hughes was out in the desert on his knees with a flashlight looking at one of his mines!"

"Who said anything about a flashlight or Hughes on his knees looking at any mine? What the hell happened?"

"I've given it a lot of thought—it's got to be a forgery! I just don't believe that Hughes was out in that desert!"

"We always faced a problem proving Hughes was out in the desert, but what about all the evidence that proves he had to be out there? Evidence that he wrote the will? The ink evidence? The medical? Our handwriting experts and the—all right, what's the bottom line?"

"I don't think the case ought to be continued. You can't stay there in good faith."

"The hell I can't! You don't know what this case is all about—you didn't attend half the depositions, you didn't read the transcripts, you don't have an overall picture of the case—you focus on one detail and jump—"

"I'll get Eli and we'll fly in and talk it out."

"Trial resumes on the 4th, and after that I'm not going to have time for this. I'll expect the two of you here tomorrow."

"We'll be there."

I phoned Wilbur Dobbs in Houston and asked him to take the first plane back to Vegas, and I met him at the airport. "Wilbur, what happened at Boswell's deposition?"

"Ah'm not sure Ah know what happened. When it ended, Stan was happy about it. Boswell's a problem, but a minor one—an' he can be impeached—he's all fucked up! Stan did a good job on him, an' was really gung ho for the case, an' my wife an' Ah were goin' to meet him an' Doreen for dinner. Then by dinnertime, everything changed. Doreen kept sayin' that Stan was riskin' his future an' his reputation an' that the case was no good, an' by then Stan's whole attitude about it switched. He even had me in the dumps. He was bitchin' about everything—about the case, about you, an' he said he wanted out."

"He's got what he wants."

"We're not goin' to lose Eli, too, are we?"

"I hope not."

Stanley and Eli didn't show up on January 3, 1978, and there was no call from either of them. Trial resumed on January 4, 1978, with Hans Verhaeren back on the stand.

After nine days of direct, Phillip Bittle cross-examined Hans Verhaeren for two days.

"In the so-called will, where the small *v* follows an *a*, *e*, or an *i*, there's always a rounded shoulder on the *v*, isn't there?"

"Yes, sir."

"Now, I show you a group of memos written by Mr. Hughes, and I ask you if you can find one instance—even one—in which Howard Hughes wrote a small *v* that had a rounded shoulder when the previous letter was an *a*, an *e*, or an *i*."

"May I study these and answer your question after lunch?"

After lunch, Verhaeren was ready to answer. "In the exemplars written by Mr. Hughes that you have shown me, what you say is true. There are no rounded shoulders on the small *v* when the previous letter is an *a*, an *e*, or an *i*. But may I be permitted to call your attention to certain exemplars you did not show me? In exemplar 139, in the name *David*, you see that following the *a*, there is a rounded shoulder as the line makes the *v*. This is identical to the writing of the word *David* on line fifteen of the questioned will. The same is true in the word *give* in exemplar 153, and in *divided* in exemplar 154, and you will find the same in exemplars 325 and 329. Striking similarities, would you not agree?"

"Mr. Verhaeren, the margins in the offered will are not like the margins in exemplars 2 or 3 or 9, are they?"

"No, sir, they are not. But why do you skip exemplars 5 and 6 and 8 and 11 and 13? The left margin observed in the will is quite similar to the left margin observed by Mr. Hughes in the memos I have mentioned."

"How much are you being paid for your testimony as a handwriting expert?"

"I received a thousand dollars when I came to the United States last year, and six thousand dollars for my services on this occasion and for the fifteen months of work I did in Holland in the interval."

Phillip Bittle had Verhaeren agree that most of the *d*'s in the offered will had looped towers. Bittle then showed Verhaeren numerous exemplars of Hughes' writing in 1968, in which the towers of the *d*'s were written without loops, but instead, with an overlapping up and down stroke. Bittle said, "I'm going to call these looped *d*'s the male *d*. The unlooped *d*'s, the female *d*. Now isn't it true that in 1968, Mr.

Hughes wrote female *d*'s? But that in the so-called 1968 will, the *d*'s are male *d*'s?"

"What you say is true, sir. But you have not shown me all of the exemplars of Mr. Hughes' writing during that same period. If you will look at exemplars 2, 4, 5, and about thirty others in the same year, 1968, you will find scores of *d*'s written with looped towers, exactly as Howard Hughes wrote them in his will—the *d* which you refer to as the male *d*. And also, if you will note, there are some *d*'s in the will which are written as what you call a female *d*. In other words, Howard Hughes was inconsistent in the manner in which he wrote the *d*. Sometimes he wrote it with a loop, and sometimes he overlapped the upper and downstrokes so as to leave no loop. The same inconsistency that we find in the will, we find in his exemplars. And this sameness, sir, is an indication of genuineness."

On redirect examination, I stood before the drawing made by Bittle of the looped male *d* to the left, and the *d* with the overlapping up-and-down stroke, Bittle's female *d*, to the right. "Mr. Verhaeren, in addition to what Mr. Bittle calls the male *d* and the female *d*, isn't there in the will and in these exemplars a third kind of *d*?"

"Yes, there is. Mr. Hughes sometimes wrote the *d* in which the tower was looped, but the loop was so narrow as to hardly be noticeable. It would look like a downstroke overlapping the upstroke unless you looked at it carefully and then you could see a faint lightness between the two."

In the middle, between Bittle's male *d* and his female *d*, I drew a *d* with the up and down stroke as Verhaeren had described it. "Then, Mr. Verhaeren, this third kind of a *d*, which I have drawn here, is not exactly a male *d* or a female *d*. But rather, something in between. Now, using Mr. Bittle's labels, wouldn't we have to call this kind of *d* a gay *d*?"

"Hermaphroditic."

Monsieur and Madame Faideau checked into the Las Vegas Hilton a few days before Verhaeren finished his testimony, and working with him was easy; but working with our UN interpreter, André Visco, a pudgy young man who needed a haircut, wasn't. The conditions Visco imposed on us the day before I was to call Faideau had us scurrying the way Hughes' aides must have scurried the day they learned they were running low on banana-nut ice cream.

"I cannot do my best unless I can have a hand-held microphone with a long cord to allow me to move freely in the courtroom from the witness stand to a blackboard."

"But we don't have a hand-held microphone."

"If I can't have one, I can't do my best, and if I can't do my best, sir, I do nothing. Also, I must be given a rest every ten minutes, and allowed to keep my bottle of Perrier water nearby so that I may freshen my mouth whenever I wish. This is for me to be in perfect voice and give you my best. Otherwise, I shall not be able to go on."

André Visco did go on, and, with a hand-held microphone Marvin Mitchelson rented, Visco's simultaneous UN-style translation worked smoothly. Faideau pointed out the way in which Howard Hughes, in the exemplars, would frequently pinch the top of a letter such as an *h* or an *l* or the bottom of a *y* or a *g* to a point instead of rounding it. In other writings of those same letters in the exemplars, the top or the bottom, normally rounded, would be flattened. These pinches and flats were also found in letters in the questioned will.

"*Deliver this one* was probably written by Howard Hughes," Faideau said, "but the text is too short for me to go further than that."

After a day of direct examination, I asked Monsieur Faideau for his opinion of the offered will.

"The questioned document was written by Howard Hughes."

"How sure are you, Monsieur Faideau?"

"I know in my soul and conscience that this is so."

Phillip Bittle cross-examined first. "You refer to your soul and conscience, sir. But, you know, do you not, from the history of Europe, that for many centuries, men of soul and conscience believed that the sun rotated around the earth—"

I interrupted. "Your Honor, I obj—"

"Sustained!"

"Mr. Faideau, I want to show you a capital *E* written by someone named Melvin Dummar, and a capital *E* in *Ella* in the will. Will you not concede that there is a great similarity between the two?"

"Sir, to you there may be a similarity. To me the dissimilarities are numerous and obvious. The two capital *E*'s were not written by the same man. Would you like me to point out to you the various reasons why this is so?"

"No."

Rex Clairbourne cross-examined. "Mr. Faideau, look at the way in which these two letters in the so-called will, the *a* and the *s*, are joined. The line after the *a* comes to a blunt stop, and the pen is lifted from the paper, and then put back down on the paper in almost the exact spot where it had been lifted up. And then a blunt line continues to the *s*. Isn't that an indication of forgery?"

"Yes, it is. It is an indication, I might add, of a very bad forgery. But sir, you will notice in the writings of Mr. Hughes the exact same characteristic. Look over here at this blowup of an exemplar and you will see the same thing. Therefore, that which you call an indication of forgery is really an indication of genuineness, do you not see this?"

"Mr. Faideau, have you ever before examined a will to determine whether it was genuine or not?"

"Oh, yes, I have had many cases involving wills. Perhaps one or two hundred on an official basis. You see, in France, for a will to be valid it must be entirely handwritten, signed, and dated."

"What is your fee for coming here?"

"Six thousand dollars, and my expenses."

"Paris is a long distance to go to obtain a document examiner, isn't it, Mr. Faideau?"

"The distance between Las Vegas, Nevada, and Paris, France, is, I agree, long."

"Mr. Faideau, isn't it true that you came all the way here to testify in defense of the proponent's cause for money?"

"It is true that my expenses have been paid, and that I have been paid a fee for my work in preparation and study and for my time in coming here to testify. And I will add that I received another kind of compensation. I have thoroughly enjoyed my two stays here in Las Vegas. But, sir, I came here to testify, not to defend a cause."

"Have you considered the possibility that any one of the five signatures in the will has been traced?"

"There are no indications of a tracing of the signatures or of any word or letter. Sir, I am waiting for you to show it to me."

"Sir, you will have to wait until we present our side of the case. I have no further questions."

Pierre Faideau rose and faced Judge Hayes. "Your Honor, may I please thank you for the courtesy you have shown me. And for your patience in listening to me. And for the privilege of being allowed to contribute what I could to what I have been told you have called a search for the truth." Then Faideau faced Clairbourne and Bittle. "Gentlemen, may I please thank you for the kind manner in which you put questions to me. Although it is your function as advocates to attack my opinion, I appreciate your goodness in not attacking my personal integrity."

On Sunday evening, January 15, 1978, after no word from Stanley or Eli for two weeks, Stanley phoned and asked if he and Eli could fly to Las Vegas to have a drink with me. I told him I'd be waiting. That evening in my apartment, Wilbur, Linda, and I greeted Stanley and Eli. To spare them more embarrassment than they were suffering, I suggested that Stanley and I each take a snifter of brandy and go to the rec room on the other side of the building for a private talk. In the rec room, sitting opposite me at the chess table, Stanley said, "The financial strain is just too much—I didn't know the trial would take this long. I can't borrow any more money, and I've got to get back to L.A. to try to put my practice back together again."

"Stan, I'm well able to understand the financial strain this case has put on you. What time does your plane leave for L.A.?"

"In about an hour."

"Have a good flight."

Stanley was relieved. I walked Stanley back to my apartment, and Eli and I took our brandy snifters and our short walk to the rec room, and, sitting in the same chair at the chess table that Stanley had just used, Eli told me that for financial reasons and because of his obligations to his tax-troubled clients, he could no longer stay in Las Vegas to help with the case. "But if you need me for anything specific—a deposition, or someplace you want me to go to see a witness—I'll help you. But living here, going to court every day, working every night and then trying to run back to L.A. on weekends to see my other clients—"

"I understand your problem, Eli. Thanks for all your help. I don't know how I could have got this far without you. I mean that. Have a good flight back with Stanley."

"Hal, I'm sorry. I really am."

After Eli and Stanley rushed out of my apartment, I turned and faced my sad secretary and my sad and sole surviving assistant in the preparation of my next thirty-eight witnesses and in the preparation for cross-examination of contestants' expected forty-two witnesses: Wilbur Dobbs, sitting dejected with a brandy snifter in one hand and a cigarette in the other, staring at the telephone.

49. THE OVERLOADED PLATES

When trial resumed after the holiday recess, I worried about how the absence of Eli Blumenfeld and Stanley Fairfield from the counsel table would look to the jurors. Would they suspect that two of the four attorneys for the proponent had deserted? And what if a new problem popped up and I couldn't work on it because I was working on a witness?

On Monday morning, January 16, 1978, I called Dr. Michael Camp of Boston. A forensic chemist with a Ph.D. in chemistry, Camp was an assistant professor of forensic chemistry at the University of Boston, the administrator of the doctoral programs of forensic chemistry at Northeastern University, a forensic consultant for the Massachusetts State Police, the head trace analyst for the Crime Lab in the Wisconsin State

Laboratory, and a post-doctoral fellow at the Atomic Energy Commission Laboratory at Iowa State doing pure research, and his works had been widely published in forensic literature.

"Dr. Camp, Albert Lyter testified that the ink on the questioned will matched only one ink of the three thousand in the ink library in the Treasury Department. Paper Mate's 307 with PAGO. In making this comparison, Mr. Lyter compared Paper Mate's current 316 with the questioned ink and found that they did not match. And Mr. Lyter's plate, C-15, shows Mr. Lyter's chromatograms. What did you find from your examination of C-15?"

"It's obvious that the ink that came from the questioned will matched only one of the samples on the plate. And that was Paper Mate's 307 PAGO. Another sample on the plate was Paper Mate's 316, and the questioned ink did not match 316. Mr. Lyter was right."

"A young man who works in an ink factory, Peter Fitzrandolph, retained by Mr. Bittle, testified that he looked at C-15 as you did, but that he couldn't see what you did. He couldn't see any difference between the questioned ink, 307 PAGO, and 316. Why is it that you and Albert Lyter could see a difference, while Mr. Fitzrandolph couldn't?"

"The difference between the questioned ink, 307 PAGO, and 316 is quite obvious. There's an extra band in the 316 that's not in the 307. I can easily see the difference and I don't know why anyone else can't."

"Mr. Fitzrandolph also testified that the chromatograms on Lyter's plate, C-15, were inadequate. Are they?"

"Mr. Lyter's chromatograms on C-15 are not inadequate. They are quite adequate and most professional."

"Did you make your own test?"

"Yes, I compared a sample of Paper Mate's 307 PAGO ink with Paper Mate's 316, using thin-layer chromatography. And I was able to tell the difference between the two, as Mr. Lyter was."

"Dr. Camp, if someone wanted to conclude from a test comparing two different inks that he could not distinguish one from the other, could he rig a test to get this result?"

"Yes. He simply overloads the plate."

"What does that mean?"

"He uses too much ink in the samples. When he does, the bands will merge—that is, two bands will blend into one, and he won't be able to see that there are two at the top, near the solvent front. It will then be indistinguishable from a chromatogram with only one band at the top."

"Dr. Camp, please look at another chromatogram plate, the one made by Mr. Fitzrandolph. He testified that from his plate he could not tell the difference between Paper Mate's 307 PAGO and Paper Mate's 316. Looking at Fitzrandolph's plate, can you tell the difference between the two inks?"

"No, I cannot."

"Why can you tell the difference on Lyter's plate, but not on Fitzrandolph's?"

"Because the Lyter plate, C-15, is properly loaded. But this plate prepared by Mr. Fitzrandolph is overloaded."

"Is it possible that the ink on the questioned will could conceivably be Paper Mate's 316 ink, its current ink?"

"It could not possibly be."

"Cross-examine."

After the twenty-minute direct examination, Phillip Bittle cross-examined and argued with the witness for two full days. The ink on the offered will remained Paper Mate's 307 with the PAGO dye, and the ink on memos written by Howard Hughes in March 1968 remained Paper Mate's 307 with PAGO dye.

"Dr. Camp, do you have any basis to believe that Mr. Fitzrandolph rigged his test?"

"Fitzrandolph's plates are overloaded. I don't know why."

"Doctor, are there times when your plates are overloaded?"

"I did it deliberately, about a month ago."

"Oh? Now, there wasn't anything fraudulent in your doing that, was there?"

"Not at all. You see, when plates are properly loaded, the chromatograms are faded—washed out. When plates are overloaded, they have much richer, brighter, more vivid colors, and my daughter at school wanted to show her class what her father did for a living, and so I made some overloaded chromatography plates for her to bring to class. The plates were very pretty."

I congratulated Wilbur Dobbs for an excellent job. Wilbur was proud of his work in gathering the ink evidence, and, despite a foulup or two, and an assist from Eli Blumenfeld, he had a right to be. But he had been so nervous about Camp's testimony he was unable to stay in the courtroom for more than ten minutes each session. Wilbur spent most of those two days in the Golden Nugget either over a blackjack table, at the bar, or in a telephone booth.

I knew that I owed it to the case to get the judgment of someone I could rely on, someone to argue with me, someone else to look at all there was to look at in this trial. I could miss a detail. I could forget a rule. I could make a wrong choice in a crucial tactical decision.

On the morning of January 20, 1978, the testimony of George Francom of St. George, Utah, was read from his deposition. He testified that in 1954, after years as a manual laborer in heavy construction, he became a driver for Hughes Productions, and after six years he was finally promoted to guard duty. In 1963 he became one of Mr. Howard

Hughes' executive staff assistants and held that job until Mr. Hughes' death in April 1976. In December 1976 Francom was given a lucrative contract with Summa that required him to serve forty-five days a year as a consultant. He did not know with whom he was to consult, nor on what, nor where, nor when. Francom did not recall whether he was on or off duty the last few days of December 1967.

In 1975 in Freeport, Mr. Hughes told him that he had written a holographic will.

"Did you ever ask him where it was?"

"Oh, yes. He said it was his business and nobody else's. He said, 'Do you think I'm going to tell you where it is?' We tried to assist him by getting him to tell us. But he just said, 'Don't bother looking for it, you're not going to find it.' We told him we didn't know when he had written it."

"What difference did it make to you when he had written it?"

"Well, we weren't sure if he wrote his will prior to his knowing us. If he wrote one earlier than the time we began working for him, a will that old wouldn't have carried out his latest intent as to the disposal of his estate. And we wanted to be sure that his intent was carried out."

James Rickard reluctantly flew from Provo, Utah, to Las Vegas to testify in the afternoon session on January 20, 1978, after Judge Hayes ordered Earl Yoakum, as attorney for the temporary administrator of the estate and for Summa, to produce him for me.

In his late fifties, unimposing with a bony, weathered face, James Rickard testified that in 1953 he went to work for Hughes Productions as a driver. After five years he was moved into public-relations work, which had nothing to do with public relations, and because of his success in public relations, he was assigned in 1972 to be a personal aide to Howard Hughes in Vancouver, Canada.

Rickard testified that at no time in Vancouver did Mr. Hughes leave the penthouse of the Bayshore Inn for a meeting with anybody in any room on any floor. In Vancouver, Rickard worked an eight-hour shift for a six-week tour, with fourteen days off between tours.

At the time of his court appearance, Rickard was an executive staff assistant under contract to Summa. When asked whom at Summa he had assisted during the year and nine months since the death of Howard Hughes, he testified that he was still awaiting his assignment. He, too, had a contract to serve Summa as a forty-five-day-a-year consultant-at-large.

"Did Mr. Hughes have scar tissue a little bit below and to the left side of his left eye?"

"Yes. Close to the cheekbone."

"Did you personally destroy any of the logs that were kept of Mr. Hughes' minute-by-minute activity?"

"No."

"In your deposition, you made this statement. *'Many of the Canadian logs in Vancouver were destroyed.'* And when you were asked, *'Who destroyed them?'* you answered, *'Myself.'*" I showed him a page in his deposition transcript and he read it.

"My answers there must have been a mistake."

"When you testified on this next page, *'We had a shredding machine, a very good one and I used it myself,'* was that another mistake?"

"Well, I remember now that we did destroy some of the Vancouver logs, yes."

"Mr. Rickard, we have as an exhibit in this courtroom copies of the Vancouver logs for each day Mr. Hughes was there. The logs that were destroyed were not the Vancouver logs, were they?"

"I guess not."

"The logs that were destroyed were the logs for what period?"

"I don't remember."

"Did Mr. Hughes ever tell you anything about his will?"

"He said he had written a will."

"Did he say that once or more than once?"

"Oh, more than once. Many times. Constantly."

"When was the first time that Mr. Hughes said that he had written a will?"

"Well, actually he said that only once."

"You just testified that Mr. Hughes had said that more than once, many times, constantly. Now you say only once. Which is it?"

"I'd say several times."

"Did Nadine Henley ever tell you that Howard Hughes had written a holographic will?"

"No."

"In your deposition, when you were asked if Nadine Henley had ever told you that Howard Hughes had written a holographic will, you answered, *Yes, she did.* Was that answer the truth?"

"Yes. The correct answer is the one I gave in the deposition. She did tell me. Yes."

"Did Mr. Hughes ever tell you that the place where he had written his will was Los Angeles?"

"No, he did not tell me he had written it in Los Angeles."

"In your deposition, you testified as follows. *'Mr. Hughes told me he took a month off in Los Angeles and wrote his holographic will, and he indicated that he wrote it when he was in the Los Angeles area.'* Was that deposition answer of yours the truth?"

"Well, when I said that in my deposition, I just assumed that Mr. Hughes had written it in Los Angeles. He didn't actually tell me that."

"When did you last see Mr. Hughes alive?"

"Around April the 1st, the week before he died. It was my turn to go home."

The last of Howard Hughes' personal aides to testify as a hostile witness called by the proponent was Howard Eckersley. In his late forties, tall and bulky, Eckersley was puffy and pale; and like his fellow executive staff assistants, carefully choosing and speaking his words was something he was used to. Smiling wasn't. As soon as Eckersley sat down, Earl Yoakum made enough noise to be sure that I saw him take from Rex Clairbourne a packet of papers, and I knew from Yoakum's gleeful grin at me that he was going to use Eckersley's Desert Inn records to prove that Howard Hughes could not have been picked up by Melvin Dummar.

50. THE ECKERSLEY CALENDARS

Howard Eckersley testified that in 1976 his salary was $75,000 or $95,000 a year; he said he didn't pay much attention to it. Plus a bonus of $10,000 or $20,000; he didn't pay much attention to that either.

"What have you done for Summa for this money the year and nine months since Mr. Hughes' death?"

Eckersley thought a minute. "Testify." Eckersley saw Yoakum wince, and added, "And whatever else they asked me to do."

"What else did they ask you to do?"

"Nothing."

Howard Eckersley was the best-educated of the aides with a year short of a degree in industrial psychology, which meant advising management on how to keep the help happy. He had become an executive staff assistant to Mr. Hughes in 1962 in the Bel Air house.

"Did Mr. Hughes leave the Bel Air house between the time he moved in and the time he moved out?"

"Never once."

"I suggest to you that on one occasion when Mr. Hughes lived in the Bel Air house he was out driving with his Houston tax lawyer, Gilbert Boswell. Is your memory refreshed?"

"No."

"Was Mr. Hughes sick in Boston in 1966?"

"No."

"Can you tell us what this means in exemplar 410? After a reference to landing at Logan Field in Boston, these words are in Mr. Hughes' handwriting: *Let's face it, I am sick.* Is your memory now refreshed that Mr. Hughes was sick in Boston in 1966?"

"No."

"Look at E-409. These first words were written by somebody else. *'His appointment tomorrow morning and tests involved require his taking an enema tonight, an enema in the morning, and no food or water from midnight on, etc., therefore, nothing to be accomplished on day of his arrival because of the preparations, so he felt it was better tonight.'* Doesn't that remind you that Mr. Hughes went to Boston because he was sick?"

"Well, I wouldn't say he was seriously sick."

"But maybe a little bit sick?"

"Maybe."

"And Howard Hughes took a train from Los Angeles to Boston because maybe he was a little bit sick? A slight cold, perhaps?"

"I don't know why he went to Boston."

Eckersley testified that during the Desert Inn period, Howard Hughes took Empirin with phenacetin in it. Later, Mr. Hughes began injecting himself with a hypodermic needle, taking pure codeine.

"What did Dr. Crane say during the Desert Inn period about Mr. Hughes' physical condition?"

"Dr. Crane told me that he was concerned that there might be damage to Mr. Hughes' kidneys."

"Around 1968, did Mr. Hughes have any blood transfusions?"

"Yes. He was quite sick at that time."

According to Eckersley, Howard Hughes never sat at a desk in the Desert Inn; he wrote either sitting in a lounge chair or sitting in bed with his back against pillows. The aides gave Mr. Hughes a clipboard, but he rarely used it.

Logs were kept during the Desert Inn period, recording everything Mr. Hughes did.

"Were those Desert Inn logs destroyed?"

"Not all of them. I saw some last year."

"Where?"

"I can't remember right now."

"Did you see some of those Desert Inn logs in Mr. Yoakum's office?"

"It could have been."

Bittle and Yoakum jumped to their feet, objecting in duet. Yoakum hollered, "This is Mr. Rhoden's normal propensity for distortion!" Bittle hollered, "Mr. Rhoden is still trying to structure an artificial impression by tricking the witness!"

"Mr. Eckersley, let me read from the deposition you gave in Texas when I wasn't there to trick you. You testified, *'I think most of the Desert*

Inn logs were destroyed. I know all of them should have been, but I also know that some weren't.' Was that answer true?"

"Yes. But I can't remember whether I saw those Desert Inn logs in Mr. Bittle's office or Mr. Andropolis' office or where."

"But you did see some undestroyed Desert Inn logs somewhere sometime last year?"

"Yes—well, I want to back off of that."

"You testify that you saw some undestroyed Desert Inn logs last year, and then after an objection by your side, you want to back off of that!"

"Mr. Rhoden's arguin' with the witness!" Yoakum snarled.

"He's right," I said, "the objection is well taken. At the Desert Inn, did Mr. Hughes cut his hair?"

"Yes. He cut it fairly short a couple of times. He had a barber on duty and used him."

"Describe his beard."

"Mr. Hughes did not have a thick beard. The hairs were very sparse."

"During the Desert Inn period, did Mr. Hughes have a scar on his face?"

"Yes, a small scar under his eye. Under the right eye."

"Your fellow executive staff assistant, James Rickard, and Gordon Margulis testified that that scar was on the left side."

"Yes, and so did Melvin Dummar, and all three of them were wrong. The scar was under his right eye."

"Mr. Crawford testified that during the Desert Inn period, Mr. Hughes never wore any shoes because his toenails were too long. But Mr. Holmes testified that in the Desert Inn, walking to and from the bathroom Mr. Hughes constantly wore a pair of brown shoes. Mr. Holmes also swore that in the Desert Inn Mr. Hughes never wore a shirt and pants, while Mr. Francom testified that walking to and from the bathroom in the Desert Inn Mr. Hughes sometimes did wear a shirt and pants. But never any shoes. Now, three of the aides agree that in the Desert Inn Mr. Hughes walked around naked most of the time. Did he?"

"No. He was rarely uncovered."

"Is it true that he walked mainly from the bed to the bathroom and back?"

"Yes."

"How was he dressed during those walks?"

"Pajamas or a towel or something."

"Did he put on street clothes for those walks?"

"Of course not. Why would he put clothes on to—that's ridiculous!"

"Isn't it true that at various times in the Desert Inn you saw Howard Hughes wearing a long-sleeved white shirt, trousers, and footwear?"

"No, that is not true."

"Did you ever say it was true?"

"Never."

"Listen to these questions asked of you and your answers when you testified under oath in your deposition:

Q: *You never saw him with clothes on at all during the Desert Inn period?*

A: *Sure I did. Normal clothes, trousers, and shirts and shoes, sandals. Long-sleeved shirts. White.*

Q: *And you saw him dressed in the Desert Inn with a white shirt, pants, and sandals?*

A: *Yes, I did, at various times.*

"Were those answers true, Mr. Eckersley?"

"Well—I—yes, those answers were true. When I said *various* times in my deposition, I meant that he wore clothes the day we arrived and the day we left."

"When you said *various* times, you meant two?"

"That is what I meant. Various can mean two."

"Did Howard Hughes ever refer to you executive staff assistants as his aides?"

"Never."

"Did you testify in your deposition as follows? '"*I said, "Well what good is it to us if nobody knows where your will is?" And Mr. Hughes said, "None of the aides know where it is."'* Weren't you quoting Mr. Hughes correctly when you said that he referred to you men as aides?"

"No, that's a mistake by the shorthand reporter."

"Did you ever see Mr. Hughes write a memo, spill something on it, pat it down with a Kleenex, and go on writing the same memo?"

"Yes."

"When was the last time Mr. Hughes told you he had prepared a handwritten will?"

"About a month before he died."

"Tell us what he said."

"Mr. Hughes said it was in a safe place. He said that nobody had seen his will except himself. He said something like, 'I gave it to someone I can trust to hold it for me.' He told us not to worry about it, that when the time comes it'll be there. He said it would probably take ten years before anybody would get anything under it. He also said that he provided not only for us but for a few other people."

"What did he tell you about providing for you?"

"He said he provided for us not by describing us by our names, but by general category or position."

"Did Mr. Hughes say anything about Maheu in regard to his will?"

"He said that whoever was holding it was not a guy who would betray a trust, and he said, 'We're not dealing with Maheus this time.'"

"Did he give you the name of the man with whom he had entrusted his handwritten will?"

"No."

"Did you ask him?"

"Yes. He said that it was none of my business. But in a nice way."

"In Mr. Hughes' memo to you written in Nassau sometime in 1971, there's a reference to a provision in his will for his personal aides by general category rather than by specific names. Have you seen the clause in the offered will in which he leaves a portion of his estate to his personal aides at the time of his death?"

"Yes. I thought it extraordinary that the memo and the will said basically the same thing."

Phillip Bittle examined Eckersley. "What was your relationship with Mr. Hughes?"

"A very strong family relationship."

"May I ask how deep? That is, was he father, mother, or baby, or what?"

"He would fit into all three at one time or another. Like we all do."

"And sir, you loved him very much, didn't you?"

"Yes, I loved him as a member of his family."

The next day, Earl Yoakum examined Eckersley. "Now, Mr. Eckersley, you don't really remember last year seein' any undestroyed logs that were written durin' the Desert Inn period, do you?"

"No."

"And your statement that you did was the result of a bad memory for the moment, isn't that true?"

"Yes."

"During the Desert Inn period, how did Mr. Hughes refer to his wife, Mrs. Hughes? Did he call her Mrs. Hughes or Jean or Jean Hughes?"

"I heard him refer to her as Jean Peters. Never Mrs. Hughes."

"Mr. Eckersley, you must have misunderstood me. Ah say, durin' the Desert Inn, how did Mr. Hughes refer to his wife—who was then Mrs. Hughes?"

"Jean Peters."

"Do you renounce any interest under this so-called will?"

"I most certainly do."

"When Mr. Hughes was in Vancouver, Canada, at the Bayshore Inn, in 1972, did he once leave before the day he checked out?"

"He did not."

"Now, let's come to this so-called pickup in the desert by Melvin Dummar of Howard Hughes sometime between December 28th and the 31st of 1967. When Mr. Rhoden took your deposition last year and asked you if you were on duty durin' any of those days, you told him you couldn't remember, didn't you?"

"Yes."

"Of course you couldn't remember. That was ten years ago. But your memory was refreshed recently from lookin' at your work schedule entered into your 1967 calendar, isn't that right?"

"That's right."

Earl Yoakum made a slow production of walking to my table and handing me a courtesy copy of the pages of a Month-at-a-Glance calendar for December 1967 and January 1968, and copies of expense records, Desert Inn charges, and of several airline tickets. "Mr. Eckersley, take a look at your calendar for December 1967, an' tell us what you see about your work schedule."

"On December 27th, I was on the shift from seven P.M. until three in the morning. The same is true of the 28th and 29th and 30th. I finished at three A.M. on the 31st."

"Mr. Eckersley, what was the purpose of your makin' these entries in your calendar in 1967 an' early 1968?"

"It was to remind me of what schedule I was on."

"Were these calendar entries of your schedule accurate?"

"Of course they were accurate. I would have no reason to make inaccurate entries."

"At any time while you were on a shift assistin' Mr. Hughes, did he leave the Desert Inn?"

"Never."

"Was there ever a time when you were on a shift when Mr. Hughes wasn't there?"

"Never."

"What are these airline tickets for?"

"Whenever I went back home to Salt Lake City, my travel expenses were paid. These are copies of some of the tickets that I submitted to the company for reimbursement in December 1967 and January 1968."

"Then, is it true that your memory is now refreshed, an' that you now clearly recall that on every night from December 28th to the 31st, from seven P.M. to three A.M. Mr. Howard Hughes was in the Desert Inn, an' not out in the desert somewhere gettin' a ride back to Las Vegas?"

"That is correct."

As Earl Yoakum triumphantly turned to walk from the witness stand to his table, he lifted his hands above shoulders as though to say, We've just proven our case, and grinned his way back to his seat. "You can have the witness back, Mr. Rhoden. An' thank you, sir, for callin' him."

I handed my copy of the Eckersley records to Wilbur Dobbs and asked him to take them to the Las Palmas to study them with Linda. "We'll work on them tonight." Wilbur was thankful for an excuse to leave the courtroom.

I took Eckersley on re-cross. "Mr. Eckersley, you stated that you loved Mr. Hughes as would a member of his family. What was the longest shift you ever worked as one of Mr. Hughes' family members?"

"Eighty hours."

"When Mr. Hughes defecated in his bed, who cleaned it up?"

"Whoever was on duty."

"I object!" Bittle shouted. "And I move that the Court caution Mr. Rhoden not to cause embarrassment and needless concern among a lot of fine people!"

"Objection overruled! Motion denied!"

"In the Desert Inn," I asked, "who stored bottles of Mr. Hughes' urine?"

"We did."

"Why?"

"Mr. Hughes' orders."

"When did you leave Acapulco?"

"I went home to Salt Lake City ten days before he passed away."

"Try again! You went to New York, didn't you?"

"No, I went home."

"Didn't you testify a year ago in your deposition that you went to New York?"

"Where did I say that?"

I showed him.

"Yes, I remember now that I did go to New York."

"Where were you when Mr. Hughes died?"

"On my way to or from or in New York."

"You don't remember where you were when you heard the news that Mr. Hughes had died?"

"No."

"Why did you go to New York?"

"A business trip."

"Business for Summa or for yourself?"

"I don't remember."

"Did you see somebody on that business trip in New York?"

"Probably, but I don't remember."

"When you heard the news of Mr. Hughes' death, was your business interrupted?"

"No."

"Then you can recall that news of Mr. Hughes' death did not interrupt your business, but you can't recall what business it was that was not interrupted?"

"That's correct."

"Did you have any reason to want to get out of Acapulco?"

"No."

"When you heard that Mr. Hughes had died in Houston, what kept you from flying there?"

"I coordinated my activities with the company."

"Does that mean you called Summa to get permission to go to the funeral?"

"It was a family matter and I respected their wishes."

"Did any member of Mr. Hughes' family express a wish that you not attend?"

"No, but they may have. I didn't go to his funeral out of respect both for Mr. Hughes and his family."

"By family, you mean his aunt whom Mr. Hughes had not seen since 1938?"

"Yes, I was very concerned about the lady's wishes."

"Did you call her to ask her what her wishes were?"

"No."

"If you were so concerned about her wishes, why didn't you call her to ask what they were?"

"I didn't even know her."

"I still don't understand why you didn't go to the funeral of the man you loved as a man loves his father, his mother, and his baby."

"Because I wasn't invited."

"You weren't invited by whom?"

"The funeral was all over before I even heard about it."

"You heard on April the 5th that Mr. Hughes died, and he wasn't buried that day. Now, it wasn't all over before you heard about it, was it?"

"I guess not."

"What, if anything, did Mr. Hughes tell you about providing for Jean Peters in his will?"

"He told me that he loved his wife and was concerned about her welfare, and wanted to make sure she had everything she needed."

"While Mr. Hughes stayed at the Bayshore Inn in Vancouver, from March 1972 until the time he left about six months later, was a log kept recording everything Mr. Hughes did, every minute of every day?"

"It was, and you have a copy of the logs."

"I do, and I want you to take a look at this entry for March 17th, 1972. *No records kept for this day.* Why was no record kept for that day?"

"I don't know. Possibly we might have been busy doing something and just didn't keep it."

"You mean something kept each aide on each shift so busy as to prevent any of them from making even one entry in a log that day?"

"Perhaps."

"Isn't it true that every time Mr. Hughes went to the bathroom an entry was made of the time in and the time out?"

"Yes."

"Explain this entry on March 16th, 1972. It shows as the time that Mr. Hughes went to the bathroom, six-thirty A.M. Then the next entry at eleven-twenty-five A.M. is that Mr. Hughes again went to the bathroom. No entry showing that he had come out after his six-thirty trip, or what he did for five hours. Where was he during the five-hour gap?"

"I don't know."

"On July 14th, 1972, there's an entry that Mr. Hughes finished his dessert. Then there's an entry three hours later that he went to bed. What was he doing during the three hour gap?"

"We didn't record all our activities in the logs. Only the significant ones."

"You mean significant like what time Mr. Hughes finished his dessert?"

"That could be of significance."

Eckersley was unable to explain gaps in the records of two hours and ten minutes on July18, a five-hour gap on August 17, a seven-hour gap on the 18th, or a four-hour gap on August 20, 1972.

"At any time during those six months in the Bayshore Inn, did Mr. Hughes bathe?"

"He may have. I'm not certain."

"Here's a memo written by Mr. Hughes during the Desert Inn period, number 436. In it, he wrote, *I feel better doing something highly secret like this when Howard was on and it is at night.* When you were on and it was night, what was the highly secret thing that Mr. Hughes did in the Desert Inn?"

"I don't remember."

Judge Hayes granted my motion for an early adjournment to complete my cross-examination of Eckersley the following morning. I sped back to my apartment and went straight to the phone to hear what Linda and Wilbur had found in Eckersley's records. Linda said that after looking at them for five minutes, Wilbur became depressed and at 3:00 left for the nearest bar. She was still trying to reconcile certain entries in the calendar with Eckersley's expense records, hotel charges, and airline tickets, and she would let me know the bad news as soon as she finished. An hour later, Wilbur staggered in, grunted a "Howdy," and poured himself a brandy. "Did Linda find anythin'?"

"She's still working on it."

Wilbur lit a cigarette, plopped down in the large armchair, and stared at his snifter. "Aren't you goin' to ask me how Ah feel?"

"I can see how you feel. All right, how do you feel?"

"Scared shitless." He waited. "Aren't you goin' to ask me why?"

"I know why."

"Did you see that look on Yoakum's face when he handed you those calendars? Jesus, if Hughes couldn't have been picked up by Dummar, the case is over! Everythin' we've put into it goes down the drain."

"Wil, you want to go back to Houston? If you do, I'll understand."

"'Not me! Not me! Ah said Ah'd stay an' he'p all the way to a verdict no matter what, an' Ah will. Nobody'll ever say that Ah left a sinkin' ship."

"You think this ship is sinking, Wil?"

"No, no, no, Ah didn't mean it that way, but—well, it might be. Look at Eli and Stanley. They're no dummies, an' they sure as hell think it's sinkin' or they wouldn't have pulled out on you. Maybe Gilbert Boswell hurt us more than Ah thought. He's got records, too. But those Eckersley calendars—Ah tell you, they scared the shit outa me! What are you goin' to do about 'em?"

"I'll know when I look at them. And I'll look at them when Linda gets through with them. The three of us'll look at them together and we'll find where Eckersley is wrong. Wil, he's got to be wrong because Hughes was out of the Desert Inn and was picked up by Melvin Dummar one of those nights at the end of December."

Wilbur gulped down his drink, lit a cigarette, and said he needed a walk around the block, which meant a drive to the crap tables at the Landmark, and staggered out. A half hour after Wilbur left, Linda came in. "Have I got records for you!"

The next morning I began the last subject of my cross-examination of Howard Eckersley. "You don't really remember those last four nights of December 1967, do you?"

"No."

"And when Mr. Yoakum said that your memory has been refreshed, and that you now clearly recall that time—that wasn't true, was it?"

"No, but I know that my calendar entries were accurate."

"And you're relying on the accuracy of those entries, not on your memory, isn't that right?"

"That's right, and my entries were accurate. If my calendar shows that I was on duty, I was on duty."

I walked to the witness stand and looked at his calendar with him. "Mr. Eckersley, in the square marked January 8th, 1968, is the number *eleven*. What does that *eleven* mean?"

"It means that I was on the eleven A.M. shift. That's eleven A.M. to seven P.M."

"On January 9th, there's a *three*. What does that *three* mean?"

"That means that I was on duty on the three A.M. shift. That was from three A.M. to eleven A.M."

"And we have the same number *three* written for January 10th, 11th, and 12th. Does that mean that you were on the same three A.M. to eleven A.M. shift those three nights?"

"It does."

"You don't really remember those shifts, do you?"

"Of course not. That was ten years ago. But I know I was on those shifts because those numbers are entered in my calendar, and my calendar entries were accurate. If I wasn't on duty, my calendar wouldn't show that I was on duty."

"You're sure you made all of these entries on these two calendars back in 1967 and 1968?"

"I'm absolutely sure."

I walked from the witness back to my table and saw a grin of delight on Yoakum's face. I turned back to face Eckersley. "Sir, won't you please concede that your calendar entries could be in error?"

"I will not! Those entries are absolutely accurate!"

I took my copy of one of Eckersley's airline tickets and placed it on the table in front of him. "Mr. Eckersley, let's look at this together. It's a Western Airlines ticket for a roundtrip from Las Vegas to Salt Lake City and then back to Las Vegas. It's in the name of an H. Eckersley. Is that you?"

"Yes, that's one of my tickets. So?"

"Now, according to this airline ticket, when did you leave Las Vegas, Nevada, on flight 24 to go to Salt Lake City?"

"January 7th, 1968."

"Can you tell us from this ticket when you left Salt Lake City and took a flight back to Las Vegas, Nevada?"

"On January 12th."

"Doesn't that mean, Mr. Eckersley, that from January 7th to January 12th you were in Salt Lake City?"

I left Eckersley studying the ticket, and as I walked back to the counsel table, I saw Yoakum, Clairbourne, and Bittle scowling in a tense huddle examining their copy of the same ticket.

"What about it, Mr. Eckersley? From the 7th of January, 1968 to the 12th, were you in Salt Lake City as shown on your Western Airlines ticket? Or were you on duty in the Desert Inn as shown on your calendar?"

"There must be some mistake."

"You think that Western Airlines made a mistake in dating their ticket?"

"No, but there must—I can't understand this."

I turned and walked back to my seat, ready to pass the witness, when I heard him say, "Wait a minute! I've got the answer now! I can explain it."

"Explain it."

"It was undoubtedly my son, John. You see, he lived in Salt Lake City then, and he often came to visit me in Las Vegas, and I could have ordered a ticket for him and it could be that someone made a mistake and wrote my name on the ticket. Yes, I'm sure that's what happened here."

"Mr. Eckersley, if your son came from Salt Lake City to Las Vegas to visit you on a round-trip ticket, he would have started in Salt Lake City and his return would be to Salt Lake City, isn't that correct?"

"Yes."

"This is a ticket from Las Vegas to Salt Lake City and then back again to Las Vegas. That couldn't possibly be your son John, could it?"

"No, it couldn't."

"Mr. Eckersley, isn't it true that this ticket took you out of Las Vegas on the 7th of January, 1968 to Salt Lake City, where you remained until January the 12th and then returned you to Las Vegas?"

"Yes, I guess it is."

"And your calendar for the month of January 1968, with those entries showing that you were on duty in Las Vegas at the Desert Inn during those same five days, is not accurate, is it?"

"No."

51. THE MOST TRUSTED ENVOY

The evening Eckersley left the stand, I flew my 310 back to Los Angeles to talk to Sam Mayerson. Sam guessed why I was in his den and not working in Las Vegas; he knew that two of my three fellow mountain climbers had left me stranded halfway up, and that my remaining climber had some difficulty finding the mountain.

I told Sam I could promise him nothing. If he took an early retirement from the DA's office to help me in Las Vegas, and if we won, there might be no fee for him for years. And he would have to pay his own expenses.

Sam said, "I wouldn't sit at your counsel table in Vegas no matter what the fee—I just couldn't—if I weren't convinced that your will was genuine. I'll give notice in the office tomorrow morning and I'll be with you in Vegas by the end of February. Rent an apartment for me."

To convince the jurors that the deliveries LeVane Forsythe made for Howard Hughes were deliveries that Howard Hughes wanted made, I had had Noah Dietrich testify to his part in similar deliveries; and this point was made again in the testimony of Ron Kistler. To drive it home, before presenting the testimony of Forsythe I called two other witnesses, hoping to lay for Forsythe a carpet of credibility.

Nadine Henley arrived at the courthourse, protected from the masses by an entourage of two meek college boys, a burly, bald bruiser, and a frail, middle-aged pipe smoker. Miss Henley, as she said she liked to be called, was a squat lady in her early seventies with silver hair worn in a beehive popular in the 1950s. Seated in the corridor waiting to be called, surrounded by her escorts, Miss Henley chain-smoked long cigarettes at the end of a long gold cigarette holder, and as she courteously refused to answer the reporters' questions, she glared at them out of the corners of her cat-green eyes trying to smile like a grandmother proud of her strawberry pie, but her smile failed to disguise her disgust at the reporters' audacity in addressing her directly, and what she seemed to wish she could tell them had nothing to do with strawberry pie. This was the lady who had been Howard Hughes' secretary in the 1940s and who, after Noah Dietrich quit in 1957, promoted one of her drivers, Bill Gay, into the presidency of the Hughes Tool Company, and who, with Gay and attorney Chester Davis, formed the triumvirate which controlled the mighty conglomerate for the next twenty years.

On the stand, Miss Henley, rigid and regal, smiled patiently at the jurors like Queen Victoria reviewing the troops. Her Majesty testified that she went to work for Mr. Hughes in the early 1940s, last saw him in the early 1950s, and last spoke to him by phone in the early 1960s.

Yes, Mr. Hughes did contribute cash to politicians. The cash came from the South Hollywood Branch of the Bank of America out of an account in the name of Lee Murrin.

On occasion, Miss Henley communicated with Mr. Hughes using a double envelope. She would seal her memo in an envelope, and then put that envelope into a larger envelope and seal the larger one.

In the late 1940s, she typed a will for Howard Hughes. In it, the first-named executor was Noah Dietrich.

"Did Mr. Hughes sign that typed will?"

"No. But he must have signed some will. He was such a careful man, I cannot believe that he would have died intestate."

Earl Yoakum examined Miss Henley.

"This here so-called Mormon will provides that some of Mr. Hughes' fortune is to go to key people in his company. You certainly were one of the key people in his company, ma'am. Would you take anythin' under this will if a miscarriage of justice took place an' it was admitted to probate?"

"I would not!"

"Why not, ma'am?"

"Because I know that this Mormon will is a forgery."

"Please tell these jurors how you know that, Miss Henley."

"Mr. Hughes was very well versed in the English language and its proper usage. He was very knowledgeable about punctuation and sentence structure. He would pick up mistakes on me, and I was an English major. He was a perfect speller and it would bother him if he found that a secretary had misspelled a word. He could always catch me. He was meticulous. A perfectionist. He would argue with me over whether a word had a hyphen in it or not. He could not possibly have written those three pages."

"Did you ever once in your many years of close service to Mr. Hughes hear of LeVane Forsythe?"

"Never."

I took the witness back. "In 1976, when Mr. Hughes died, what was your salary?"

"One hundred and seven thousand a year."

"Six months after Mr. Hughes died, did you give yourself a raise?"

"Well, I—yes."

"How much?"

"Eighteen thousand."

The process server phoned to tell me that when he served Guido Carlucci with a subpoena, the big-nosed big man in Las Vegas politics barked obscenities about the process server's sexuality, about mine, about Noah Dietrich's, and about the case's. Short, muscular, with close-cut gray hair at the sides of his big head, Guido Carlucci still walked as he did as a World War II Marine captain, and sat down like one. Carlucci was granted permission to state that he was testifying under subpoena and under protest.

Carlucci owned a mortgage brokerage company and a string of pawnshops. During the Desert Inn period, he had worked for Howard Hughes on a yearly retainer as a representative in "the political arena." He never saw nor spoke to Howard Hughes; the two communicated by memos hand-delivered by the aides.

"Why did Mr. Hughes need a representative in the political arena?"

"As a good citizen of Nevada, Mr. Hughes wanted to be involved in the political process. He loved the people of Las Vegas and the people of Nevada."

"Did Mr. Hughes ever go out in Las Vegas and walk among the people he loved?"

"I don't think so."

"What were your duties?"

"I consider them private. They have nothing to do with the writing of any will. I decline to answer."

"The question could lead to relevant evidence," Judge Hayes said, "I must ask you to answer."

"I was supposed to persuade the legislators of Nevada to keep in mind Mr. Hughes' wishes on certain bills."

"What certain bills?"

"On every bill."

"Did Mr. Hughes wish certain bills defeated?"

"Yes."

"What bills did he wish defeated?"

"He didn't want any sales tax. He didn't want dog racing. He didn't want any censorship or any anti-pornography laws."

"Did Mr. Hughes ask you to request that the Atomic Energy Commission refrain from doing anything?"

"Judge, do I have to answer that?"

"Yes."

"I was to ask them to stop conducting the tests in Nevada."

"Where in Nevada?"

"Near Tonopah."

"Did Mr. Hughes tell you to ask the Governor of Nevada to persuade the federal authorities not to interfere with a purchase Hughes wanted to make?"

"Yes. The Stardust."

"Did you ever try to prevent the calling of a special session of the Nevada Legislature?"

"Yes. Mr. Hughes felt that legislatures were unnecessary, and the fewer the sessions and the shorter each session, the better."

"Did Mr. Hughes want you to do anything about the Clark County school integration plan?"

"He didn't want it to go through."

"On what else did Mr. Hughes want his wishes considered by the Nevada Legislature?"

"He wanted a say before they realigned any streets in Clark County. He didn't want McCarran Airport expanded because he had another airport in mind. And he didn't want rock festivals in Clark County. Mr. Hughes didn't want Jay Sarno to get a license. And he didn't want any communist entertainers in Las Vegas."

"Mr. Carlucci, did you ever deliver anything to any politicians in Nevada?"

"I don't know what you mean by 'deliver.'"

"Would you like a dictionary?"

"No, I know what the word means, but I don't know what you mean by it."

"I mean what a mailman does when he hands someone a letter. Now answer the question."

"All right, I participated in contributions to political candidates, which is a proper part of the American political process!"

"Cash or by check?"

"Cash."

"In what denominations?"

"One-hundred-dollar bills."

"What was the most in any one envelope?"

"Fifty thousand."

"Were the deliveries made in manila envelopes?"

"Yes."

"Did you get receipts?"

"Well, there wasn't any—we didn't see—all right, no!"

"Did you once deliver ten thousand dollars in cash in a manila envelope for the governor of an eastern state?"

"No. Well—yes."

"About how many times did you deliver one-hundred-dollar bills in envelopes?"

"About a hundred. Let me make this perfectly clear! This was Mr. Hughes' way of being involved in the American political process. There was nothing wrong in it! It wasn't a crime to make political contributions. Mr. Hughes contributed to many politicians—on the city level, the county, and the state. Why, he was so fair he frequently contributed to opposing candidates running for the same office. All this was public knowledge."

"Mr. Carlucci, weren't you admonished to keep these deliveries absolutely secret?"

"Yes."

"The amounts were secret and the names of the recipients were secret, isn't that true?"

"Yes."

"Weren't you told by Hughes himself never under any circumstances to divulge any of his financial affairs to anyone?"

"All right, yes."

"Did you keep any records of these deliveries?"

"No."

"Did you ever make the statement that the quickest way to get fired was to keep a record of a political contribution made by Howard Hughes?"

"Well, I—I may have—all right, I said it."

"Do you still say that Mr. Hughes' cash contributions to politicians were public knowledge?"

"Well, all the politicians knew about it."

"Did you ever make an accounting of the cash that went to these politicians?"

"Yes, I did."

"I am going to read your answer in your deposition when you were asked the identical question. *'No, there was never any accounting made to anyone with respect to the cash I was responsible for.'* Now, Mr. Carlucci, do you want to change your answer from 'Yes, I did' to 'No, I did not'?"

"All right, there was no accounting!"

"Mr. Carlucci, pursuant to a subpoena duces tecum, did you bring with you a list of politicians to whom you delivered cash from Howard Hughes?"

"Yes, I did. If you want to expose these people and hurt them, it's your doing, not mine. Here's your list."

I took the several-page list back to the counsel table and studied it. On the second page was Judge Monroe Cassidy, who had threatened to kick me out of the case if Hayes was disqualified.

Another was Attorney General Robert List.

And there was Senator Paul Laxalt, the ex-Governor of Nevada.

And, what do you know—there was Theodore Andropolis, Yoakum's local counsel, who had been a Las Vegas judge before becoming a lawyer for Summa.

I did not examine Carlucci further about any of the names on the list. "Mr. Carlucci, perhaps you can explain something in this memo written to Mr. Hughes in the late 1960s. It states that in one year, nine hundred ninety-eight thousand and twenty dollars was distributed to politicians, and that you distributed three hundred and eighty-five thousand dollars of that sum. Who distributed the other six hundred thousand dollars?"

"I wouldn't know."

A week before Carlucci testified, I received from one of the deputies in the Texas Attorney General's office copies of eighty-three more memos handwritten by Hughes, and I had them admitted into evidence by stipulation. I gave my copies to Linda to examine for possible use during the trial, and when I returned to my apartment after the first day of Carlucci's testimony, I phoned Linda and asked her to finish reading those memos and to look for anything about Carlucci. At 11:30 that night, Linda phoned me. "You've got to see this memo right now!" Two minutes later Linda bounced into my apartment. "Number 438! Is it not beautiful?"

The next morning before recalling Mr. Carlucci, I asked for permission to read to the jurors parts of a few memos in evidence, handwritten by Howard Hughes during the Desert Inn period:

> *Next, the new Supreme Court Justice to replace Fortas could be the most urgent item before us with the TWA suit coming up.*
>
> *You remember I told you the sky was the limit in campaign contributions and I really expected as a result to have some small chance to propose a few people for consideration for these positions in government, all of which were re-elected as a part of the new incoming administration. So please, please Bob, let us have some small voice in the selection of the new Justice.*
>
> *Now, while you're carrying this on I want you to contact Laxalt*

*again at once and pick up the intra-state deal with him but real
solid and real firm. Surely he should be happy to have both Airwest
and my new company competing for the privilege of serving Nevada
and I expect his full support.*

*Please tell him I consider this a firm commitment and I want to be
sure he does likewise. Please tell him, also, I hope he will tell Mr.
Nixon that as always, he has my complete support and I will
communicate with him regarding the details.*

The next excerpt was from a memo written by Mr. Hughes to Robert
Maheu:

*Bob: Is Carlucci or are you making any progress with the
governor toward persuading him not to go to Washington at this
time?*

The last one was dated October 1969 and addressed to Robert Maheu:

*Will you please ask Guido Carlucci to contact the governor at
once and after making sure there is no one else present in the room
with him, please to tell the governor for me that I listened to his
statement as it was broadcast this morning and I am very happy
with his decision and further, I want him to know I am confident he
will not regret this choice.*

I recalled Guido Carlucci to the stand to conclude his direct examination. "Mr. Carlucci, did you have a counterpart in Los Angeles who did
the same thing there that you did in Nevada?"

"I don't know what you're talking about."

"We have in evidence a statement by Mr. Hughes while he was in the
Desert Inn that he had a most trusted envoy in Los Angeles—a man
with whom he felt he could trust his life—to deliver a sealed envelope
unopened and—"

Bittle and Yoakum sprung to their feet and Bittle shouted, "That's a
deliberate misrepresentation, and I cite Mr. Rhoden for contempt!"

Yoakum roared, "Your Honor, there is no such evidence in this case!
Mr. Rhoden is tryin' to brainwash this witness by suggestin' the
existence of someone whom Mr. Rhoden knows never existed. A trusted
envoy in Los Angeles! Mr. Rhoden has LeVane Forsythe in mind, an'
LeVane Forsythe's workin' for Mr. Hughes is pure perjury!"

Judge Hayes leaned forward. "Mr. Rhoden, I don't remember any
such evidence in this case."

"Your Honor, I stated that there was such evidence, and if I didn't
believe that, I would not have made the statement. Of course, I could be
mistaken, and so I'll drop it for now and—"

"He'll drop nothin'!" Yoakum growled. "This lawyer lies to the jury
about what's in evidence an' when he gets caught, he thinks he can just
drop it! Ah challenge him, Your Honor, to show us where in the

evidence we can find this so-called statement by Howard Hughes about a trusted envoy in Los Angeles! An' if he cain't do it, Ah move that he be ordered to stand before this jury an' admit that he deliberately lied!" Volcanic Mount Yoakum was about to erupt with indignation.

I looked up at Judge Hayes and whispered meekly, "Your Honor, I'm willing to come back to this subject at a more appropriate time."

Judge Hayes said, "You've been challenged, Mr. Rhoden. It's up to you to either back up what you said or admit that what you said is in evidence isn't."

"All right," I said, "if it please the Court, I'll interrupt the cross-examination of Mr. Carlucci to read to the jurors a part of exemplar 438." I walked back to the first row behind our counsel table where Linda was ready to hand me my copy of E-438.

"It is stipulated that this memo was handwritten by Howard Hughes during his stay at the Desert Inn. I'll quote from the bottom of page six:

I will send a most trusted envoy to him from Los Angeles—a man with whom I would trust my life and this envoy will bring the message to me unopened.

"And then at the bottom of page seven, Mr. Hughes wrote:

I offer to send a special trusted envoy from Los Angeles to pick up a sealed message and bring it to me.

"Mr. Carlucci, as I was saying before the storm, there is in evidence a statement by Howard Hughes in which he referred to a most trusted envoy in Los Angeles, a man with whom Mr. Hughes would trust his life. This man Mr. Hughes would trust to not open a sealed envelope, and to deliver it as instructed. Now, do you know the name of this most trusted envoy in Los Angeles?"

"No."

52. THE FORSYTHE PHASE

A subpoena issued by a court of one state has no effect served in another, and LeVane Forsythe was intractable. "Rhoden, I ain't goin' back there! I'm too busy up here, an' I don't like answerin' questions, an' my lawyer charges too fuckin' much, an' if that Vegas judge ever sees me I'm in Hurt City, an' I ain't goin' back there, an' that's it!"

Judge Hayes ordered me to assure Forsythe that he would be forgiven for skipping Las Vegas during his courtroom deposition, if he would voluntarily return to testify at the trial. Judge Hayes said that instead of Forsythe's deposition testimony being read aloud, he wanted the jurors to have the benefit of observing Mr. Forsythe's demeanor. But I did not want the jurors to have the benefit of observing Mr. Forsythe's demeanor. A courtroom reading of Forsythe's deposition answers would be bad enough; but LeVane Forsythe in person, with his twisted memory, brusque mannerisms, and irreverence for the proceedings would be far worse. I told Judge Hayes that I would relay his offer to Forsythe, and I did, confident that Forsythe would still refuse to leave his legal sanctuary in Anchorage, and I reported to Judge Hayes that LeVane Forsythe still refused to leave his legal sanctuary in Anchorage.

On Friday morning, January 24, 1978, Eli Blumenfeld returned to Las Vegas, and from then until Sunday midnight, we marked for reading portions of Forsythe's six-volume deposition, including every section in which Forsythe contradicted himself so that there would be nothing left for Bittle or Yoakum to read in cross-examination. In court, for the next three days, I read most of my deposition questions and some of Yoakum's and Bittle's to Forsythe, and from the witness stand, with commendable courage, Eli read Forsythe's answers.

For their cross-examination, Yoakum and Bittle had cleverly prepared an elaborate surprise. Their chief investigator moved two large speakers, a tape deck, and an amplifier into the courtroom and replayed much of the testimony Eli and I had read, but this time, from the tape made by the deposition reporter in Anchorage, the jurors heard the gravel voice of LeVane Forsythe. Forsythe sounded awful.

Plump twenty-one-year-old Diane Ebnet of Honolulu had ventured from her North Wisconsin farm in January 1976 to seek her fortune as a bank teller in the Alaska National Bank in North Anchorage. Smiling and nervous, with a faint Swedish accent, she identified a picture of LeVane Forsythe as a bank customer in Anchorage. From her April 5, 1976, deposit slip she knew that Mr. Forsythe had come into her bank that day around noon, not later than 2:30. She took the deposit of twenty-eight $100 bills from Mr. Forsythe, and when she saw that, unlike the green seals on current $100 bills, the seals on Forsythe's bills were red, she suspected counterfeit. She showed the twenty-eight bills to her superior, and was told that the bills were out of an old issue. She then explained to her worried customer that the bills were good; just old.

Diane Ebnet's testimony was followed by a reading of a stipulation that, if called as a witness, Herbert Krisak, a representative of the Bureau of Engraving and Printing in Washington, D.C., would testify that the only paper currency printed by the United States in $100 denominations with red seals were those last printed and delivered to the United States Treasury in January 1971.

James Braegger, closer to seven than six feet tall, was, like Earl Yoakum, mountainous, but Yoakum's mass was fat; Braegger's was rock. A rancher in Willard, Utah, in 1976, he traded at the Maverick gas station, not at Dummar's down the road a quarter of a mile. The incident that James Braegger related occurred on April 27, 1976; Braegger knew the date because of a canceled check showing his purchase at Maverick's. At Maverick's he saw a man walking from a car toward him. At first, he thought that the man was a friend from Salt Lake City, but as the man got closer, Braegger saw that the man was a stranger. When the man asked if this were Dummar's gas station, Braegger pointed to the Maverick sign, then down the road toward Dummar's station. The man said that he had something important to give to Melvin Dummar, and asked if Braegger knew if Dummar would be there. Braegger said he didn't.

Braegger was shown a photograph of LeVane Forsythe as Forsythe looked in 1976 without his mustache, and Braegger identified the man he spoke to in Willard, Utah, on April 27, 1976, as the man in the photograph. And he was positive.

"When you knew that you had information that might back up Melvin Dummar's story, did you volunteer this information to anyone in this case?"

"No."

"Why not?"

"I mind my own business."

Phillip Bittle strained to move Braegger into conceding that the date on his check could have been a mistake. Braegger didn't move. This attack on Braegger's credibility enabled me to invoke the rule that a prior statement of a witness, although hearsay, is admissible, if consistent with his attacked testimony. Under this rule, I called Emma Wood.

Emma Wood, a feisty little lady who looked as though she might have chewed tobacco in the old days with Wild Bill, managed the Shack, the only saloon in Willard, Utah. In late January 1977 when there was much publicity about Melvin Dummar's admission that he had delivered the will to the Mormon Church, and about his claim that he had received it from a stranger at his gas station on April 27, 1976, Big Jim Braegger was in the Shack talking to Emma and some of her customers. When the customers concluded that Melvin was lying, Big Jim said that he believed that Dummar was telling the truth.

"Jim said that he was in the Maverick station that day and that a man asked for directions to Melvin Dummar's station and said to Jim, 'I have something important to give to Dummar,' the very day Dummar said he got the will."

When Bittle tried kindly to coax Emma into admitting that her memory of the incident a year ago could possibly be impaired by her age, she snickered at the weary lawyer.

I phoned Forsythe and asked him if, before he had stopped at Dummar's station, he got out of his car to ask someone for directions.

"No, I didn't do nothin' like that, I just drove—hey, wait a minute! I remember now, I made a U-turn in the road. Yeah, I ast some hick where Dummar's gas station was, an' he showed me."

"Lee, why in hell didn't you testify to that in your deposition?"

"I forgot."

"You forgot! Jesus Christ! You testified that you didn't get out of the car before you got to Dummar's station, and today a guy testified that you were out of the car asking for directions! If you had only testified to this—"

"Where does it say I gotta remember every fuckin' detail? So I forgot somethin'! So what?"

Alan Hammond testified through a reading of his deposition that he had been a certified public accountant since 1955. He first knew LeRoy Forsythe, LeVane's father; he met LeVane in the early sixties. "Then one day, LeRoy came in carrying boxes. A tool box, old suitcases, packing boxes, all kinds of trashy-looking boxes, and asked me to open them up and start counting."

"Tell us what you saw."

"I couldn't believe what I saw! Twenties, fifties, and a few hundreds! Old money in odd amounts! And then in came LeVane with more boxes! Now, they didn't want it check-counted, they wanted it measured. They had between four hundred thousand and six hundred thousand in cash! In cash! Unbelievable!"

"Did LeVane Forsythe tell you where he got the money?"

"Hearsay!" Bittle banged his fist on the table and bounced to his feet ready to wage a righteous war to stop the reading of Hammond's answer.

"Sustained."

I continued reading other questions and answers from Hammond's deposition. He testified that one day at a coffee shop, LeRoy Forsythe brought him a box that contained about $50,000. Another time LeRoy brought $250,000 to Hammond's office. At other times $10,000 or $20,000. Many of these times, LeVane was with his father.

"They had some one-hundred-dollar bills, and a few one-thousand-dollar bills, but they preferred fifties. They took bills in other denominations and converted them into fifty-dollar bills—more than half the money would be in fifties. It was crazy!"

"Did you ask LeVane Forsythe why they showed you the money?"

"He and his father said that they wanted advice on where they could put the money to grow for them without having to tell anyone how they got it or from whom or when."

"Why did they have to show you the money to get the advice?"

"Ask Forsythe. It never made any sense to me."

"What advice did you give them?"

"I told them that sooner or later, if they invested or deposited it anywhere, they'd have to explain to the IRS where this money came from."

"Did you ever ask LeVane Forsythe where that money came from?"

"Yes, I did."

"When?"

"In 1964, about a year after President Kennedy's death. My curiosity just got the best of me. This was an awful lot of money in cash. So I asked them where they got it. And LeVane said—"

"Objection! Hearsay!" Bittle hollered again.

I turned to Judge Hayes. "Your Honor, as an exception to the hearsay rule, I offer this out-of-court declaration as one against pecuniary interest of the declarant. Further, it is offered as a prior consistent statement of LeVane Forsythe's at a time when there would have been no reason for him to fabricate."

"Objection overruled."

Hammond's answer was read. "LeVane told me that they got the money for doing special jobs for Hughes. I said, 'You mean the famous Howard Hughes?' And LeVane and his father both said, 'That's right.'"

"Was anything more said by the Forsythes concerning their special jobs for Howard Hughes?"

"LeRoy said that LeVane would tell me all about it when it was time for me to know. I had the feeling that LeRoy knew he didn't have long to live. He died shortly after that. LeRoy told me that LeVane would continue doing these jobs for Howard Hughes and that LeVane was doing most of them by himself at that time."

"At any time did LeVane Forsythe say that he was a courier for Howard Hughes?"

"Yes. And from what he said from time to time, I knew that this had been going on for years. No, wait—I can't say I remember his using the word *courier*. I don't remember that particular word."

I wasn't sure how I would argue Hammond's testimony to the jury. Because he was a certified public accountant, he had some credibility— he wasn't a used-car dealer—but his testimony about the cash the Forsythes had shown him was, as he himself observed, unbelievable. How much money could the Forsythes have earned in fees from Howard Hughes? How could they have stolen from him?

But, if Hammond were lying to corroborate Forsythe, why not invent only the lie about the "special jobs" for Howard Hughes? Why louse up the lie with an unbelievable story about all that crazy cash?

On February 8, 1978, Wil Painter testified that he held a degree in engineering from Princeton and that he worked as an engineer for Modern Construction in Anchorage. On February 5, 1977, a Saturday, working at his desk, he answered the telephone around 10:00 A.M. A long-distance operator was putting through a station-to-station call— one where the other party cuts through to talk to the operator to clarify something. The man making the call said that his name was Dan Harper and that he wanted to talk to LeVane Forsythe. Painter wrote down the name Dan Harper and brought that paper to court. Painter told the operator that Forsythe no longer worked for Modern and gave her Forsythe's new number.

A day after the Dan Harper phone call, LeVane Forsythe phoned Painter at his home. "Mr. Forsythe told me that he had received a call from this Dan Harper and wanted to know everything Dan Harper had said to me on the telephone. And I told him. Nothing."

"Did Forsythe tell you what Harper had said to him when Harper reached him?"

"No."

Before that phone call from Dan Harper, Wil Painter had met Forsythe only once. Painter had no reason to lie, and no reason was suggested. And there could be no mistake about the name or the date. Painter's testimony that he had received a call from Dan Harper had to be believed. But who was Dan Harper?

If Dan Harper were not someone planted by LeVane Forsythe to make the call to Painter, it was Harper's phone call to Forsythe that forced Forsythe to phone Roger Dutson in February 1977 to tell him about the delivery of the Mormon will to Melvin Dummar the previous April 27. Harper must have been connected with the Hughes organization, and must have had some reason for wanting the Mormon will admitted to probate. But if so, why didn't Dan Harper volunteer to testify?

That a Dan Harper didn't come forward suggested that he was someone who had been planted by Forsythe to make the phone call to Wil Painter. But if so, why wouldn't Forsythe have recorded the contrived telephone conversation as proof that the threatening call was made, instead of relying on the memory of a casual acquaintance? If the Harper call to Painter were a plant, why wasn't Painter fed more information by Dan Harper about the purpose of his call to Forsythe? And why wasn't Painter fed more information by Forsythe when he told Painter about having been reached by Harper?

Alexander Bertulius, a licensed architect in Seattle, was a graduate of the University of Washington, and in April 1976, he was the managing architect for Forsythe's hospital project in Anchorage. Forsythe was in charge of gathering bids for the construction of the hospital and for its equipment. In Seattle, on April 25, 1976, Bertulius joined architect Dick Sears and Forsythe on the second leg of their trip to San Francisco.

From a small pocket calendar Bertulius carried on that trip, he was able to detail where he went and when, and what he did. The next morning, Monday, April 26, 1976, he and seven men on the project met in the conference room where Forsythe tape-recorded the meeting late into the evening. The next morning, Tuesday, April 27, 1976, Bertulius had breakfast with Dick Sears, Forsythe's close friend. Forsythe was not there.

After breakfast, Bertulius and Sears walked to the Convention Center Hall to inspect the hospital equipment on exhibit. Forsythe was not there.

Bertulius and Sears then walked to Union Square to look at some architecture. At lunch, Bertulius left Sears for an appointment at the Fairmont Hotel, and after his appointment, Bertulius taxied back to the Holiday Inn, and again met Sears. Forsythe was not there.

Bertulius and Sears then taxied to an architectural firm where Sears and his old buddies reminisced. At 4:00 Bertulius taxied to the Embarcadero Center and shopped for a rare California port. At 6:30 he took a cab back to the Holiday Inn for dinner with Sears. Forsythe was not there.

After dinner, in the cocktail lounge, Bertulius found some of their group, and that evening around 9:00, up popped noisy LeVane Forsythe.

"Did you ask Mr. Forsythe where he had been all day?"

"No."

"Why not?"

"Why should I? He wasn't a friend of mine. He was a friend of Sears. I had met him only two or three times before. Where he had been didn't interest me."

"Since April 1976, what has your relationship been with LeVane Forsythe?"

"We've had many business encounters. But nothing of a social relationship. Except that, a few times in a bar, we had some private discussions."

"Private discussions on what subject?"

"Objection!" Bittle yelled. "Hearsay!"

Bittle cross-examined. "You say you're not a social friend of LeVane Forsythe's, and yet in some bars you had some private discussions with him?"

"Yes."

"In these private discussions, did Mr. Forsythe tell you anything to refresh your memory concerning his absence on Tuesday, the 27th of April, 1976, from your group in San Francisco?"

"He did not."

"Did Mr. Forsythe ever tell you where he was on the 27th when you say you didn't see him in San Francisco?"

"I don't think the subject ever came up."

"Then what were those private discussions about that you had with him?"

Before the witness could answer, Earl Yoakum raised his palm in a stopping gesture to the witness not to answer, and leaned forward and whispered something to Bittle, but Bittle shook his head and looked at the witness for an answer.

"He told me about his association with Howard Hughes over a period of years."

Earl Yoakum winced.

Bertulius continued. "Lee didn't like discussing this subject in the presence of other people, but privately, especially after a drink or two, he did discuss it with me a few times."

"Mr. Bertulius, what LeVane Forsythe told you about his having met Howard Hughes he told you after January 1977, when Melvin Dummar took the stand here in Las Vegas, isn't that true?"

"No, that's not true. Mr. Forsythe told me about this several months earlier in the summer of 1976. I remember where we were and what I was doing at the time. We were in a bar in Seattle when he told me how he first met Mr. Hughes on some movie site at a ranch near Los Angeles. Lee told me in early August of 1976 that when he had told Howard Hughes that some movie personnel were robbing him, Lee was given another job closer to Hughes."

Again, Yoakum whispered to Bittle, and again Bittle shook his head and continued his cross-examination. "Mr. Bertulius, haven't you confused something that Mr. Forsythe told you after he told the whole world about his having known Howard Hughes with conversations you had with him back in 1976?"

"No, I have not. Would you like me to tell you how it is that I can be so certain of exactly when he told me?"

"No, never mind. That's all."

"That's not all," I said, and took the witness back for re-direct. "In these private discussions that Mr. Bittle asked you about, did Mr. Forsythe tell you what he did when he was given a job closer to Howard Hughes?"

"Objection!" Bittle barked. "Hearsay!"

"Your Honor, when Mr. Bittle elicited testimony from this witness concerning conversations with LeVane Forsythe, he opened the door to allow me to elicit from the same witness the rest of those same conversations on the same subject."

Judge Hayes thought a moment. "Objection overruled."

Earl Yoakum's hands covered his eyes.

Bertulius answered the question. "It was very strange. Lee said that he had to be on call within reach of a telephone at all times. He always had to leave a number where he could be available, and sometimes long periods of time would go by without his receiving a call from Mr. Hughes. But when a call came, he had to be available to carry out these errands. He was sort of a private messenger for Mr. Hughes, who wanted money delivered to politicians. He mentioned Bebe Rebozo, President Nixon's confidant. One thing that stands out in my mind that

Lee told me was that all the politicians he delivered money to were corrupt because they took it, with only one exception in all the years he did this for Howard Hughes."

If Earl Yoakum's look at Phillip Bittle could have carried out Yoakum's purpose, Phillip Bittle would then and there have taken his place in that happier world with Howard.

53. THE DUMMAR PHASE

For the will to be admitted to probate, the jurors had to believe that at the end of 1967 Melvin Dummar picked up Howard Hughes in the desert. I planned to pave the way for Melvin Dummar with testimony from other witnesses that during the Desert Inn period there were times when Howard Hughes left that ninth floor of the Desert Inn.

Jim Spiller had obtained a signed statement from a Utah dentist, Dr. Joseph Garn Ford, that near the end of Howard Hughes' four-year stay in the Desert Inn, Kay Glenn said that Hughes had been sneaking out of the Desert Inn without his personal aides' knowledge, and that once, after some trouble, Hughes was picked up in the desert and driven back to Las Vegas. Glenn's statement was vital to our case. But, as an out-of-court statement made by someone not subject to cross-examination when he made it, it was hearsay. And inadmissible in evidence.

Kay Glenn would never admit that he had knowledge of Howard Hughes' absence from the Desert Inn and his pickup in the desert, but there was a rule of evidence that allowed me to get this information to the jurors. If I forced Kay Glenn to testify as a hostile witness, and allowed him to deny knowledge of the incident, I would have the right to ask him if he had ever stated that he did have knowledge of it. Kay Glenn's denial that he had made any such statement would supply the foundation I needed to present the testimony of Dr. Ford that Kay Glenn had made the prior statement, inconsistent with Glenn's trial testimony. As a setup for the testimony I really wanted—that of Dr. Ford—and for a few other matters, I subpoenaed Kay Glenn as a hostile witness.

Kay Glenn was medium-sized and the last man, no matter how many others were in a room, to be noticed. He had first worked for Hughes Productions as a male stenographer in the 1950s, and last spoke to Howard Hughes when he brought Jean Peters to see him in Boston in 1966. That time Glenn's conference with Mr. Hughes consisted of mutual hellos. Glenn didn't see Howard Hughes again until February 1976 in Acapulco. There were no hellos.

"What did you do with the logs after Mr. Hughes checked out of the Desert Inn?"

"I ordered them shredded and the remains burned."

"Howard Eckersley testified that sometime last year he saw some of the Desert Inn logs. Do you know anything about any undestroyed Desert Inn logs that might help us in this case?"

"No."

"If Mr. Hughes had left the Desert Inn during his four-year stay there, would that activity have been recorded in those logs?"

"You'd have to ask the men who made out the logs. I wouldn't know."

"These personal aides of Howard Hughes' reported to whom?"

"To me."

"And you reported to whom?"

"Mr. Bill Gay, the president of the company."

"During the Desert Inn period, did Mr. Hughes own a Chrysler?"

"Yes."

"During the Desert Inn period, did Mr. Hughes own a cabin in Tahoe?"

"Yes. A facility he purchased along with Harold's Club."

"You never saw Mr. Hughes again anytime after the day of his arrival in Acapulco?"

"That's correct. The day he arrived was the last time I saw him. I didn't stay in Acapulco after Mr. Hughes arrived."

I touched Glenn's deposition transcript on the counsel table. "Mr. Glenn, did you ever swear that you saw Mr. Hughes in Acapulco several days after the day he arrived?"

"You know, I just happened to think of it—I did see him about a week or two after he arrived in Acapulco."

"On Friday, the 2nd of April, 1976—three days before Mr. Hughes died—did one of his aides phone you and say that there was something wrong with Mr. Hughes?"

"I don't think any of them knew what was wrong with him."

"I'll read to you what you testified to in your deposition, in answer to the same question."

"Well, it's possible one of them called me."

"Did any of the aides tell you that there was something wrong with Mr. Hughes' kidneys?"

"No. They couldn't have told me that. They didn't know. If they had known that, they—my answer is, no."

"This is what you testified to in your deposition. *'The aides told me, three days before he passed away, that there was a kidney concern.'* Well, Mr. Glenn?"

"Yes, I guess they did tell me that there was a kidney concern."

"Who told you?"

"I don't remember."

"In your deposition, did you testify as follows? '*I am sure I heard it from all of them. I'm sure I heard it from Johnny and I undoubtedly heard it from Chuck and from Jim Rickard. I probably heard it from all of them.*'"

"Yes, I guess I did hear it from all of them."

"Mr. Glenn, didn't you know at that time that without proper medical care, if someone's kidneys weren't functioning, he would die? And that to save his life, all you had to do was take him to a hospital where they could put him on a dialysis machine and clear the poison out of his system?"

"I'm not a doctor. All I know is that maybe I might have heard from one of the doctors that there was a kidney problem."

"Mr. Glenn, you're certain that you heard that from the doctors, aren't you?"

"Yes, I'm certain I heard it from Dr. Chaffin, and Dr. Crane probably, and some of the staff. Two days before Mr. Hughes died."

"Oh, just two days? Not enough time to have saved him? Does this refresh your memory, Mr. Glenn? Gilbert Boswell testified in a Texas deposition that the Thursday—four days before Mr. Hughes died—he was told by you that Howard Hughes was critically ill. Now, you knew about this five days before Hughes died, didn't you?"

"I don't remember the number of days."

"Dr. Norman Crane testified that he had no idea of what was wrong with Hughes until after the autopsy. And Mr. Hughes' aides testified that none of them knew anything about a kidney problem. But you now admit that the aides and Dr. Crane told you that there was a kidney problem when there was plenty of time to save Hughes' life. Now—"

"Objection!" Yoakum barked. "Mr. Rhoden isn't askin' a question, he's makin' a summation for the jury!"

"I think he's right, Mr. Rhoden," Judge Hayes said.

"So do I, Your Honor. Mr. Glenn, during the Desert Inn period, did the aides of Mr. Hughes report to you everything of significance?"

"Yes."

"As part of your duties, during the Desert Inn period, did it come to your attention that Howard Hughes had left the Desert Inn without any of his aides knowing about it, and was lost for a couple of days?"

"I never heard anything like that."

"Do you know a Utah dentist named Dr. Joseph Garn Ford?"

"Yes."

"Did you see Dr. Ford and your cousin, Dr. William G. Burdett, in Las Vegas sometime in 1970?"

"Yes."

"Did you ever say anything like this to Dr. Ford? 'Hughes would take off into the desert without his aides having knowledge of his whereabouts, and once when Mr. Hughes was out there, something happened and he was picked up and brought back to Las Vegas.'"

"I never said anything like that either to Dr. Burdett or to Dr. Ford."

I read the excellent deposition questions Eli Blumenfeld had asked in Salt Lake City of Dr. William G. Burdett and Dr. Joseph Garn Ford, with Eli back on the witness stand to read the answers of the two dentists. When Dr. Burdett was asked if any such statement had been made by Kay Glenn concerning Howard Hughes' absence from the Desert Inn, he answered, "He may have, but I don't recall."

"Did you tell Dr. Ford about any such absence of Howard Hughes from the Desert Inn?"

"Whatever may have been told to Dr. Ford along this line, it certainly was not told to him by me."

Dr. Joseph Garn Ford, a thirty-eight-year-old dentist, testified that he and his father-in-law, Dr. Burdett, and their wives attended a dental convention in Las Vegas in November 1970. Kay Glenn, a cousin of Dr. Burdett's, had made reservations for them at the Desert Inn, and the evening they arrived they saw Kay Glenn. "I can't be positive whether it was in Dr. Burdett's room or in the lobby that I met Kay Glenn. Either Mr. Glenn or my father-in-law stated that Howard Hughes would take off in the desert without the aides' having knowledge of his whereabouts. And that Mr. Hughes had gone out in the past to the desert and something happened out there and he was picked up and brought back into Las Vegas by someone passing by in a car."

"In September 1977, in Salt Lake City, did you have a conversation with Melvin Dummar's lawyer, Roger Dutson?"

"Yes, I did."

"When you spoke to Roger Dutson, were you telling him the truth?"

"Of course."

"What did you say to Mr. Dutson at that time?"

"I said that it didn't surprise me that someone had picked up Howard Hughes in the desert because I recalled that I had heard that same statement from Kay Glenn. But I want to retract all that."

"You want to retract all what?"

"Well, the whole thing is unclear in my mind. I can't be positive."

"You can't be positive about what?"

"Whether this was told to me by Dr. Glenn or Dr. Burdett."

"How would Dr. Burdett know about Howard Hughes being out of the Desert Inn and picked up in the desert?"

"Well—I don't know."

Dr. Ford admitted that a few days before his deposition in Salt Lake City, he had received a phone call from Kay Glenn. Kay Glenn was upset.

In early February 1978, Jack Cherry, one of the attorneys in our local law firm, told me that he had heard from a client that Jasper Wilkes, a

Summa engineer who was now in litigation with Summa, had stated that he knew that Howard Hughes was in Tonopah at the Mizpah Hotel and lost for a few days around the time Dummar claimed to have picked up some old man in the desert. I arranged for an interview with Mr. Wilkes in his lawyer's office at 5:30 on February 26, 1978, and asked Cherry to have Wilkes served with a subpoena fifteen minutes before the interview, requiring that Wilkes appear in court the following morning. I interviewed Wilkes for a half hour in the presence of his attorney and made notes of what Wilkes said.

The following morning at 9:00 A.M., Wilkes' attorney told me that Wilkes had decided not to testify.

"Tell your client that I decided he will testify."

"He doesn't want to."

"He's going to."

Jasper Wilkes, around fifty, a sullen, small man, wore a lemon-colored suit with braided lapels and a chartreuse string tie.

"When did you go to work for Summa?"

"In 1967."

"Sometime after the Frontier Hotel was opened, were you in the Mizpah Hotel?"

"Yeah."

"When did the Frontier open?"

"August of 1967."

"Did you know Billy Joe Updike?"

"Yeah."

"Whom did Mr. Updike work for?"

"Hughes."

"In the lobby of the Mizpah Hotel on this occasion, did you see Mr. Updike with a group of other men?"

"Yeah, but I don't remember nothing about it."

"Last night when you spoke to me, didn't you remember enough about the occasion to describe it to me?"

"I didn't tell you nothing last night!" Wilkes' grimace showed a close-to-uncontrollable urge to hit somebody in the mouth.

"Did you and I talk in your lawyer's office for a half hour last night?"

"Yeah!"

"What did we talk about?"

"You asked me if I talked to Jack Cherry in a bar, and I told you I did, and that's all we said."

"What did we do for the rest of the half hour, just sit there and look at each other?"

"I don't know what you were doing, but I didn't answer no questions."

"At the Mizpah Hotel, when you saw Billy Joe Updike in the lobby with a group of men, did you say to Billy Joe, referring to one of the group, 'Is that who I think it is?'"

"No, I didn't say nothing like that to him!"

"Last night in your lawyer's office didn't you tell me that that is exactly what you asked Billy Joe, and that he answered, 'Yes, it is.'?"

"No, I didn't tell you that!"

"Do you know if, when I spoke to you last night, I had a tape recorder in my briefcase?"

Wilkes looked at his lawyer. "No."

"In the Tonopah Hotel when you saw Billy Joe Updike, isn't it true that you said to him, 'Is that who I think it is?'"

"Well, it's true that there was a statement made in the hotel, sir, but I'm not necessarily the one who made it. That is, I mean, I don't recall making it."

"Last night, you told me that you made it, didn't you?"

"Well, I don't deny I told you I made it. Somebody asked that question of Mr. Updike, and maybe it was me. My memory isn't that good."

"When somebody asked that question of Mr. Updike about a man in the group, what did Mr. Updike reply?"

"Objection!" Bittle snapped. "Hearsay!"

"Sustained!"

"The next morning at the Mizpah Hotel, did you notice something unusual in the lobby?"

"Well, there was a certain amount of excitement there in the lobby and four or five gentlemen told me—"

"Objection! Hearsay!" Bittle snapped again.

I turned to Judge Hayes. "Your Honor, I will lay the foundation for the 51.095 excited utterance exception to the hearsay rule. Mr. Wilkes, describe what you saw before the men spoke to you."

"The Summa people were going crazy. There was a lot of commotion. Everybody was running around sort of confused and upset."

"What did these people, who were going crazy, say to you?"

"Objection, hearsay!" Bittle barked.

Judge Hayes said, "Under the excited utterance exception to the hearsay rule, I'm going to allow it."

"What did they say to you, Mr. Wilkes?"

"I can't remember."

"You remembered last night, didn't you?" I opened my briefcase and put my hand inside. My briefcase was empty. "Do I have to play a tape for you, Mr. Wilkes?"

"Well, I—they told me they were trying to locate Mr. Hughes. That's all they told me. And I remember saying, 'Well, when you find him, let me know, and I'll buy him a beer.'"

Phillip Bittle cross-examined Wilkes. "When you talked to Walter Hinson, the investigator for the Attorney General's Office, you didn't tell him that you recognized Howard Hughes in Tonopah at the Mizpah Hotel, did you?"

Yoakum leaned over in front of Rex Clairbourne and whispered to Bittle. But Bittle continued his cross-examination, and said, "Answer the question, please."

"No, I did not tell him that I recognized Howard Hughes there. The guy got it all mixed up, and when I saw that letter written by the Deputy Attorney General, I wrote him that he was all wet."

Bittle then had Wilkes identify a letter he had written to Deputy Attorney General Lyle Rivera stating that everything in Rivera's letter was inaccurate. I made no objection to Wilkes' letter to Rivera and as it was marked by the clerk, Yoakum grimaced, sensing what was coming. And it came as soon as I could take Wilkes back on redirect. I asked, "Mr. Wilkes, this letter of yours was in response to Deputy Lyle Rivera's letter, wasn't it?"

"You bet it was!"

"Your Honor, at this time, I offer into evidence the letter of October 25th, 1977, written by Deputy Attorney General Lyle Rivera, to which Mr. Wilkes' letter is a reply."

Bittle's furious objection was overruled, and I read Rivera's letter to the jury:

Mr. Wilkes stated that Billy Joe Updike informed Wilkes that Howard Hughes was lost in the Tonopah area for two or three days about the time Melvin Dummar claims he picked up Mr. Hughes and drove him back to Las Vegas.

"Mr. Wilkes, did you or did you not make the statement attributed to you in Rivera's letter?"

"No, I did not tell him that they told me Howard Hughes was lost in the Tonopah area. What I said was, they told me they were trying to locate Mr. Hughes, not that Mr. Hughes was lost! They just said, 'We can't find the old man!' and that they were pretty upset."

"Are you a close friend of Kay Glenn?"

"I think so."

"I thought so. That's all."

Bittle wanted the witness again. "When these men told you they were trying to locate Mr. Hughes, couldn't they have meant that they were just trying to reach him by telephone?"

"Well—yeah, I suppose that's possible."

As Wilkes left the witness stand, Yoakum angrily shoved a note in front of Bittle. Bittle read the note and his lips tightened as he crumpled it in his fist and shoved it into his briefcase.

When we adjourned for lunch, I saw Wilbur Dobbs at the door waiting with a look of panic. Judge Gregory in Houston had originally set November 14, 1977 as the trial date for our will contest, but on that date he began hearing the domicile issue first, delaying the start of the trial of the will contest. And now that the domicile issue was about to be resolved, Judge Gregory ordered that the jury trial on the will contest start in three weeks in Houston.

"Does your good judge know that we're trying that same case here in Las Vegas?"

"He knows."

"Does he know that the will is here? That the exemplars are here? That hundreds of exhibits are here? That the witnesses are here or have come and gone? Does he know that it's cost a fortune to bring these experts to this court and—"

"He knows, but like Ah told you, he said months ago in court that he didn't care what was bein' tried in Las Vegas, he was goin' to run his court as he saw fit. It's be there or else."

"Or else what?"

"Or else lose by default in Texas!"

"And if I were to walk out of the trial here—which I sure as hell am not about to do—I'd lose by default here in Nevada! Are you sure that your good judge understands this?"

"He understands it. But as they say in Texas legalese, he doesn't give a shit! He said that you've had plenty of notice of the trial date he set an' he expects you to be ready on that date."

"Please explain to him, very slowly, that I will be happy to obey him and try the case in Houston as I simultaneously try it in Las Vegas as soon as I figure out how I can try the same case in two places at the same time."

"It won't do any good. He's pissed off at you. He thinks you should've held off doin' anything in Las Vegas until after the will contest was tried in Houston. He really feels that you took that trial away from him."

"Go back to Houston and petition your Court of Appeal for a writ of prohibition to keep your good judge from abusing his jurisdiction and ramming a knife up my ass."

"A writ of what?"

"Wil, do you know a lawyer in Houston familiar with appellate writ proceedings?"

"I think so."

"Get him! I'll talk to him directly and explain what we need."

Jake Owens, six feet three, in his late forties, rugged and weathered, looked as though he had just galloped out of Marlboro Country. Owens worked as a Superintendent of Public Works for Clark County. He testified that he used to ride horses in Nevada, and that in 1967 on a riding trip with his wife and son near American Flats, southwest of Virginia City, he saw a man walking alone on a deserted road leading to an abandoned mine, miles from a place of business or a home. Owens didn't see a car or a horse, and thinking that the man might need help, left his wife and son and rode down the hill to the man. Owens knew what happened to people in the desert who didn't have enough water and didn't know how to find any. The man held a walking stick in one hand and a paper sack in the other, and as Owens reached the man and asked him if he needed any help, the man grunted no.

"When he looked up at me, I recognized Howard Hughes."

"Do you have any doubt about that man being Howard Hughes?"

"No doubt at all."

"How close were you to him?"

"I was on my horse right next to him, looking down at him eyeball to eyeball. His face was maybe three feet from mine."

"How long did the encounter last?"

"A minute, maybe a little less."

"Describe the man."

"A mustache. Gray in it. His face was lined. He was around six feet tall. Thin. I'd say in his late fifties. He looked like he had had a fresh shave."

"Describe his clothes."

"He wore an old felt hat and street shoes—not the kind of shoes you wear in the desert. His clothes looked like secondhand clothes. I remember that his jacket didn't match his pants."

"How is it that ten years later you can recall that his jacket didn't match his pants?"

"Color is something I remember. I'm a painter, and a little colorblind, and color to me may not be what it is to you. Details like that stay with me."

Owens testified that after he left the man, he looked back and saw a car, but he couldn't see if anyone was in the car. When Owens rode back to his wife and son, he did not tell them that he had seen Howard Hughes. But Owens did tell Charles Martin, a cabinetmaker in Lake Tahoe, that he had seen Howard Hughes near American Flats, and Owens told the same thing to Bob Stutzman, known in the area as Bearclaw Bob, and to Badwater Bill. Martin's reaction was "Big deal!" Bearclaw Bob and Badwater Bill reacted to the news by ordering another beer. Martin was still living in Lake Tahoe. Bearclaw Bob was around somewhere, but Badwater Bill was dead.

Bittle cross-examined Owens. "You're positive that that man was Howard Hughes?"

"Positive."

"Did you have a camera with you?"

"Yes."

"But you didn't take a picture of Howard Hughes, did you?"

"It never occurred to me."

"Describe the walking stick."

"It was rosewood."

"And you can remember that ten years later?"

"I used to make knife handles out of rosewood, and I know rosewood when I see it."

"Here's a map of Nevada, Exhibit 30, showing some of the mine acquisitions of Mr. Hughes in the late sixties. Point to American Flats."

Owens pointed to American Flats near Virginia City, surrounded by black dots indicating where the Hughes Tool Company bought some mines in the late sixties. Other mines were purchased around Tonopah.

"You say that as you rode away from the man you looked back and somewhere in the area you saw a car. What kind of car?"

"A Chrysler."

Jack Tims was short and stocky, and between his broad shoulders and square head, he had no neck. A pilot with a multi-engine rating, he lived in Reno, Nevada. After he was shown several pictures of Howard Hughes, Tims testified that he first saw Hughes in 1955 and 1956 in the Bonanza Airline hanger at McCarren Airport in Las Vegas where Tims worked as a line mechanic. All the employees at Bonanza knew that the man was Howard Hughes. Bonanza Airline later became Hughes Airwest.

In the spring of 1970, Tims worked as a security guard at the Arlington Towers in Reno, Nevada, where Harold's Club rented an apartment for VIPs. One day a car pulled up and two men got out, one a tall man. When the two men entered the lobby, Tims recognized the tall man as Howard Hughes. As the two men waited for an elevator, the tall man walked back to the door and asked Tims his name, and when Tims said, "Jack Tims," the tall man said, "That's a coincidence, my name is Jack, too."

I asked permission of the Court to interrupt the examination to read to the jurors from records in evidence Desert Inn charges for the ninth floor of the Desert Inn while Howard Hughes was its occupant from 1966 to 1970. The name used by the occupant was Jack Trent.

The morning after Howard Hughes entered the Arlington Towers, a woman tenant stopped to get her mail in the lobby and said to Tims, "I'll bet you can't guess who I saw when I was coming in the back door this morning?"

Tims said, "No, who?"

The woman said, "Howard Hughes."

Phillip Bittle cross-examined Tims. "When did this take place?"

"In May or June of 1970. Shortly after the announcement that the Hughes Tool Company bought Harold's Club."

"How was the tall man dressed?"

"He wore a striped business suit."

"Did any other Hughes Tool Company officials ever walk into that lobby?"

"Yes, I know of one. Robert Maheu."

"When is the first time you ever told anybody about seeing Howard Hughes stroll into the Arlington Towers in 1970?"

"The next day. Millie Florence MacTavish was a tenant, and the next morning I told her that Howard Hughes was her neighbor the night before. I told her that Mr. Hughes—"

"I have no further questions."

I read to the jurors excerpts from memos written by Howard Hughes suggesting that some unusual episode had occurred around the end of December 1967. The first memo was dated January 1, 1968:

Please call O'Neil and ask him if he will arrange to clear his office so he can receive a message from me personally in absolute privacy.

The second memo, undated, had this second paragraph:

I prefer the new place and I have reason to believe there will be no repetition of the Desert Inn episode. Of course, I am not sure. But I have taken steps.

According to the deposition testimony of Roy Crawford and Hughes' Houston tax attorney, Gilbert Boswell, the following was written by Howard Hughes on December 30, 1967:

Make sure please we have Boswell's firm promise of secrecy. From everyone! Tell him again at the end, and tell him I have additional property to acquire in that area and any leakage of these plans— boom—impossible.

In that memo of December 30, 1967, Hughes wanted a promise of secrecy about what? He referred to his contemplated acquisition of additional property in "that area." What area? At the time of the writing of the memo, Hughes was contemplating the acquisition of mining claims in the area of Tonopah, and Hughes would not have wanted it known that he contemplated buying property in the Tonopah area because that would increase the sellers' prices. But Hughes would not have wanted Boswell's promise of secrecy about that acquisition of property near Tonopah, Nevada, because Boswell, a Houston tax lawyer, had nothing to do with Hughes' acquisition of property in Tonopah, Nevada. Since Boswell had made many phone calls to the ninth floor during those last few days of December 1967, it could be argued that Boswell had accidentally learned that some unusual episode had occurred, involving Hughes in "that area," and that it was this that Hughes wanted kept secret.

The last memo by Hughes on this subject was undated. It was probably written to his wife during the Desert Inn period:

> *The crux of the whole deal is that if you come, we have no option or choice—From that point on, we are irrevocably committed to the place where we land. If I go alone—or if you go alone, either of us can look around—describe what he sees—what is available—and where. Then the die is not cast until the other arrives—but not over fifteen days.*

Melvin Dummar took the stand wearing a dark-blue Western sport jacket and light blue sport shirt. At the time of his testimony he was employed by Jackson Distributing Company in Ogden, Utah, delivering Coors Beer at $2.60 an hour.

Melvin Dummar admitted that he had committed perjury in his deposition. He said that he had lied because he knew that if he had told the truth about how he got the will and what he did with it, nobody would have believed him.

Melvin told the same story that he had told me the first day I met him in my office in Los Angeles about picking up an old man in the desert and dropping him off at the Sands. And he testified as he did on the same witness stand for three days in January the year before, about the delivery at his gas station on April 27, 1976, of an envelope by a man he did not know. The direct examination lasted one day.

Earl Yoakum cross-examined first and took one afternoon. "Do you remember my askin' you relatively few questions when you were here in Las Vegas about a year ago, an' do you remember me tellin' you why?"

"I don't remember how many questions you asked me."

"Then let me remind you of what Ah said to you." Earl Yoakum then slowly read three pages of the introductory statement he had made to Melvin Dummar during his cross-examination in the January 1977 hearing, in which he reminded Dummar of the lies he had told in the Utah deposition the month before. After a review of Dummar's lies and Yoakum's exposure of them, Yoakum said, "Now, Ah'll tell you why Ah had very few questions to ask you last January. Ah've spent most of my adult life questionin' witnesses as a trial lawyer in an effort to determine whether a witness is lyin' or tellin' the truth. An' when Ah left Salt Lake City, Utah, after your deposition, Ah knew that you had been lyin'. That's why Ah had very few questions to ask you after that."

I addressed the Court. "Your Honor, Mr. Yoakum's illustrious career and his reasons for not asking this witness questions in a proceeding a year ago may be of great interest to Mr. Yoakum's biographer, but this is cross-examination—the time for questions to the witness, not the time for Mr. Yoakum to evaluate his splendid work in this case."

"Objection overruled!"

"Melvin, can you think of one good, solid, single, solitary reason as to why Ah should now believe anythin' you tell me?"

"I don't know what you should believe."

"Didn't you write it, Melvin?"

"No, I did not."

"You tell us that durin' this ride back from the point where you picked up the old man down to Las Vegas that he asked you your name?"

"Yes, he did."

"Didn't you testify in your deposition in Salt Lake City that the man didn't say anythin' to you on that trip until you got to Las Vegas?"

I said, "Your Honor, if there is any such statement in Melvin Dummar's deposition, let Mr. Yoakum show it to him!"

"Never mind," Yoakum said. "I withdraw the question."

I rose again. "Your Honor, Mr. Yoakum withdraws the question because he has deliberately misstated Mr. Dummar's testimony in that deposition!"

"Ah want to go on to somethin' else," Yoakum said. "You were in the military service from February 25th, 1963, until October of that same year?"

"Yes sir."

"That was right in the height of the Vietnam War, wasn't it?"

"I think it was a coupla years before the war even started."

"Isn't it true that you wanted to get out of the Air Force because of a girl?"

"Well, there was a girl, but also I wanted to go back to school."

"And so you conned the Air Force to get out rather than to go to Vietnam where you had signed up to go?"

"I never signed up to go nowhere. They never planned to send me to Vietnam."

"Where were they goin' to send you? We weren't fightin' anywhere else, were we?"

"We weren't fightin' much in Vietnam, if I remember. All I know is that I was at Beale Air Force Base an' they wasn't plannin' on sendin' me nowhere. The Vietnam War really got goin' a coupla years later." Melvin looked up at Judge Hayes. "Didn't it?"

"Ah have no further questions."

Phillip Bittle cross-examined for two days. "Didn't you go on the game show 'Let's Make a Deal' four times within a period of five years in violation of federal law?"

"Yes."

"Melvin, theatrics and lying are a way of life for you, aren't they?"

"I don't think that what you say is true."

"Didn't you once tell Mr. Stiverson in Willard, Utah, that if you got money under this will you would buy him a Cadillac?"

"He worked for Cadillac Motors for thirty years, an' he's an awful nice old gentleman, an' he never had anythin', an' he always wanned a Cadillac, an' I thought it would be nice to tell him that an' give him somethin' to kinda look forward to."

"You saw LeVane Forsythe in Alaska, thanks to Mr. Rhoden. Was the man you saw in Alaska the man who delivered this so-called will to your gas station, as you say, on the 27th of April, 1976?"

"I'm jest not certain. I know I seen him before, but I jest cain't tell you where."

"You say you steamed open the envelope after the stranger left it there at your gas station. Then, after you read what was inside to get it closed again, you added some glue. Where did you get that glue?"

"From a coupla other envelopes."

"Mr. Dummar, didn't your lawyer or Mr. Rhoden tell you what the FBI report said about where the added glue came from?"

"No."

"Well, I'll tell you! According to the FBI report, glue was added to the lid of the envelope that contained the so-called will, but that glue did not come from other envelopes. It was the type of glue that is not used on envelopes. Do you want to tell the truth about the glue?"

"Yes."

"Good!" Bittle jumped to his feet. "Where did the glue come from?"

"I got it from a coupla other envelopes."

On February 23, 1978, I read the deposition testimony of FBI agent Parker Saeta, an expert in the examination of questioned documents, including paper and glue. On April 18, 1977, three months after Dummar testified in Las Vegas to having steamed the envelope open, added glue, and to having then baked it, agent Saeta examined the envelope and wrote in his report:

> Additional adhesive, different from the original water-soluble adhesive on the glue of the envelope has been added to the flap.
>
> The presence of this additional adhesive, as well as other features are consistent with envelopes which have been steamed open and resealed.
>
> The bleeding of the inks on the envelope, the wrinkled nature of the flap, the discoloration of the paper around the edges, and the presence of this additional adhesive, indicate that at some time the envelope was sealed, steamed opened, and then resealed.

Saeta testified that he saw discoloration in the envelope around the four sides. When he examined it, fragments fell off because of their brittle state. The discoloration and brittleness were more noticeable on the upper flap edge and on the lower edge than on either of the two sides, and the discoloration was more noticeable on the left side than on the right.

Saeta examined the postage-meter mark to determine the date. MAR was readable but the day and year were obliterated. The Pitney Bowes imprint was consistent in configuration and size with a Pitney Bowes postage meter imprint on file with the FBI. Under magnification, he could read the last three digits of the machine number: 4 2 3 or 4 2 5.

The stains in the writing and the running of the ink could have been caused by water in the form of steam, but he was not certain.

Phillip Bittle read his cross-examination of Saeta in the deposition. "How much glue was added?"

"Just a dab such as an amount one would get on the end of a finger. It was put in four different places under the lid."

"In your opinion, was this added glue from another envelope?"

"No, not in my opinion. Because it was not water-soluble, as envelope glues obviously must be."

On February 24, 1978, I read the deposition testimony of Quintus Ferguson, the FBI fingerprint expert. In his examination of the copy of *Life* magazine submitted to the FBI he found 868 prints. None of them was a print of Melvin Dummar's. Nor did he find the prints of anyone else involved in this case. Nor did he ever report to anyone that he had found in *Life* magazine the fingerprints of Melvin Dummar, and he had been surprised to see newspaper accounts of statements by some lawyers that Melvin Dummar's prints had been found in *Life* and wondered where anybody had got that idea.

On November 18, 1976, Ferguson received a copy of *Hoax* from the office of the Nevada Attorney General.

"What condition was the book in?"

"Fair, normal condition."

"Was anything cut out of it?"

"I examined it for fingerprints, and I didn't notice that any pages had been cut out."

"What did you find?"

"The left thumb print of Melvin Dummar on the sixth page of the index of the book. I found five other latent fingerprints that were not Dummar's, and not the prints of anyone involved in this case."

He also examined a copy of *Bashful Billionaire,* and found no fingerprints of Melvin Dummar.

Ferguson examined the will and its envelope and found the prints of a court clerk and of some Las Vegas policemen. But no prints of Howard

Hughes, Melvin Dummar, Bonnie Dummar, or LeVane Forsythe. Ferguson explained that about half the time, someone handling a paper will not leave a fingerprint.

Patty Lou Dummar, Melvin Dummar's sister-in-law, testified that in the late 1960s, at the time Melvin was having trouble with his first wife and after he had taken a trip to Los Angeles, Melvin told Patty that he had picked up a crazy old bum in the desert south of Tonopah and that the bum had said that his name was Howard Hughes.

William John McMaster and his wife Dorothy testified that in 1968 when they lived in Anaheim, California, Melvin was a neighbor, and that he told them of finding a man at the side of a road, picking him up, driving him to Las Vegas, and dropping him off behind some hotel, and that the man had said his name was Howard Hughes.

I read into the record the stipulation that Howard Hughes' attorney, Robert Edison, lived in the Sands Hotel from September 1967 to February 1968.

After Bonnie Dummar completed the ninth grade, she worked in the factory at the Mattel Toy Company in Los Angeles, and then for a manufacturing company making wire harnesses for washing machines. At the time of her testimony, she lived with Melvin in Ogden, Utah, with her three children and with Melvin's daughter, Darcy. In April 1976, they lived over the gas station in Willard, Utah.

I asked, "Did you ever tell Melvin Dummar anything about Uncle Howie leaving something in his will to Melvin?"

"Sometimes when Mel was worried about bills, he'd say to me, 'Why did you marry me?' An' I'd tell him I married him for his money. An' when he was depressed I used to joke an' say that we were gonna inherit money someday. It was just to cheer him up."

"Before the death of Howard Hughes, did you ever refer to Uncle Howie in those cheering-up sessions?"

"No, I din't. Never before. But after Howard Hughes died, I did say that Uncle Howie would leave us somethin' in his will. But it was just a joke."

"Did Melvin ever tell you that he picked up a man in the desert who said that his name was Howard Hughes?"

"I don't think Mel ever told me that until after the will was found."

"When did you first learn that it was your husband who delivered that will to the Mormon Church Headquarters on the 27th of April, 1976?"

"It was in January of 1977, the night Mel admitted it to you."

"What did you say to him when he told you that he had delivered it to the Church?"

"I said, 'You're kiddin'!' An' that was the night he asked me if I had anything to do with it. I couldn't believe he actually suspected me."

"Mrs. Dummar, you've been accused by Mr. Phillip Bittle of being the actual forger while Melvin did the research—"

Bittle jumped up. "I object! That's a flagrant and deliberate misrepresentation!"

"If it please the Court, I would like to read to the jurors this contention made by Mr. Bittle in his sworn answers to interrogatories: 'The quality of Bonnie Dummar's penmanship and her spelling habits, which evidence participation in the forgery, were made plain by her deposition.' Now, Mrs. Dummar, did you commit the crime that Mr. Bittle accused you of committing?"

"Of course not!"

Phillip Bittle cross-examined Bonnie Dummar for four hours. Bittle first marked in evidence samples of Bonnie Dummar's writing given during her deposition the previous September, where she had written *company's, devided,* and *revolk.* When she was asked to write something dictated to her, she wrote *texas, university of California* and *orfaned children.*

"Mrs. Dummar, didn't your husband once write a song which he entitled 'A Dream Becomes Reality'? with this as one of the lines. 'A beggar becomes a king'?"

"Mel wrote a lotta songs, an' I think that was one of the titles but I'm not sure of the lyrics."

"What did you sell in the store part of your gas station?"

"Potato chips an' hotdogs, an' some school supplies an' things of that sort."

"Mrs. Dummar, you understand that I'm not here to try to abuse you or cause you any disgrace."

"I know. You're just doin' your job."

"Thank you for understanding that, Mrs. Dummar. Now weren't you accused by a complaint filed in the Municipal Court in Orange County of knowingly and, with intent to deceive, making a false statement?"

"It wasn't false at the time. Can I explain? I was—"

"Were you or were you not accused of that crime?"

"Well, I still don't know what the crime was, but they charged me with somethin' an' I had to go to court. If you'll let me explain—"

"Mrs. Dummar, weren't you convicted as a criminal, and didn't you serve ninety days in the county jail for fraudulently making false statements with an intent to deceive?"

"Yes, I did go to jail, but I never was sure of exactly what—"

"I have no more questions."

Earl Yoakum cross-examined Bonnie Dummar. "I'm interested in those school supplies that you sold in your little grocery. Did those supplies include glue?"

"I think we sold Elmer's glue, a little white squeeze bottle."

Rex Clairbourne whispered something to Yoakum and Yoakum said, "Ah have no further questions."

Bonnie Dummar's testimony was adjourned until the following Monday. On Monday morning, February 27, 1978, I completed her examination. "Mrs. Dummar, you wanted to explain this matter of your welfare fraud conviction. Explain it."

"Well, my first husband left me several times. He'd leave me every time I was pregnant, an' I had to go on welfare 'cause I couldn't work an' he din't support me. He'd leave an' keep comin' back an' then leave again, an' come back, an' he never gave me any money except for his car payments an' for extra food for him. So one day I called the welfare people an' told 'em about this, an' the next thing I knew they put me in jail."

"What was the false statement that Mr. Bittle asked you about, the one that you allegedly made with intent to deceive?"

"I don't know. I never did know. I tried to explain it to them an' to the judge, an' they wouldn't let me explain any more than Mr. Bittle did. No one at the welfare agency told me that I was doin' anythin' wrong, an' when I asked them, they told me it'd be all right, an' the next thing I knew I was in jail."

"When you were in jail, did you have any contact with Melvin Dummar?"

"I didn't know him very well then, but when they took me to jail, my sister came an' took my little girl, but she couldn't find no place for the boys an' so the welfare people put 'em in an orphanage." She stopped to cry. "Mel came an' got 'em out, an' took 'em to a ranch."

"Mrs. Dummar, before last Friday, did your children know that you had spent time in jail?"

"No, they didn't."

"Did your children read the newspapers about this case?"

"They didn't have to." She sobbed, "Their schoolmates told 'em."

The jurors looked at Phillip Bittle as though they were a lynch mob eager to get on with it.

54. PROPONENT RESTS

Since Polly Jean Pfau had been paid $5,567.88 for her initial work in this case in 1976, I was jarred by her new bill for an additional $14,146.99

for her preparation of the demonstration exhibits to be used in her trial testimony. When she assured me that there would be no further bills except for one more expense of no more than $200 for some additional photography, I told her to go ahead, and I paid the $14,146.99. But on December 16, 1977, for this additional photography, Polly Jean sent me another bill for $12,714.53. I was tempted to tell her to stay in Detroit and frame her photography, but I had told the jurors in my opening statement that I was going to call one American handwriting expert, and I was afraid that if I didn't, the jurors would speculate that it was because my American's opinion was unreliable, or had changed, or that I had lied to them. So I paid off.

On February 28, 1978, matronly Polly Jean Pfau testified that she had been a handwriting expert for twenty years. She had a certificate in police administration, which included handwriting identification, from the University of Detroit, and she was soon to get her Bachelor of Science degree at Empire State University with a major in questioned documents. She had worked on over five hundred cases a year, mostly for sheriffs and county attorneys, sometimes for the Ethics Committee of the Detroit Bar Association, and regularly for the Board of Professional Responsibility and the Michigan Attorney General's Office. She had testified in federal and state court hundreds of times in Michigan, Minnesota, North and South Dakota, Wisconsin, Nebraska, and Iowa.

Polly Jean had had prior experience examining holographic wills, and in 1977 she had two such cases in addition to the Hughes will. She had found each of the other two to be forgeries; in one case the forger confessed, and in the other, criminal charges were pending.

In the Hughes case, she first examined eleven exemplars of the writing of Howard Hughes, copied individualities, and made notations of size, spacing, and slant. Next, she did the same with the writing in the questioned will. Then she made a comparison of her findings.

She saw in the questioned will tremors, overwritings, patchings between letters and within letters—all indications of forgery. But she found the same things in the exemplars.

"It is my opinion that the writer of the exemplars which were presented to me is the same individual who wrote the questioned will."

"In your opinion, who wrote the words *deliver this one* on this envelope?"

"The same person who wrote the exemplars and who wrote the questioned will. Howard Hughes."

Pfau had had her high-priced photographer prepare for each letter of the alphabet a hard-back, fold-open exhibit. On the left side were rows of photographs of that letter, capital and lowercase, in the questioned will; on the right side were samples of the capital and lowercase of that same letter taken from some four hundred exemplars of Howard Hughes' writings. One of the fold-open exhibits was handed to each juror, one to

Judge Hayes, and two to contestants' counsel to examine as Polly Jean Pfau pointed at a screen on which a slide of the foldout was projected.

Polly Jean Pfau's emphasis was on the similarity of the variations. The letter *a* in the questioned will was sometimes a bulbous form rounded at the top, sometimes with a sharp angle at the top, sometimes with an ending stroke stopping at the baseline, sometimes with an ending stroke curving up into a flair. These inconsistencies, she explained, were natural variations, and in the letter *a* as in most other letters written by Howard Hughes, there were six or seven variations, an unusually high number of variations. In the exemplars of Howard Hughes' handwriting of the letter *a*, there were those same six or seven variations. The similarity of these variations, she said, was a strong indication of genuineness.

As Polly Jean finished her lecture on each letter, I gathered up the foldouts from each juror and handed them to Sam Mayerson, who was ready with the foldouts of the next letter. Then Polly Jean had us hand out sets of more foldouts to be used in her comparison of overwritings, patchings, flats, pinches, uncrossed *t*'s, crossed *d*'s, and examples of a wild lack of motor control on the part of the writer of both the questioned will and the exemplars.

I expected to use certain of Pfau's exhibits in discrediting handwriting experts to be called by the contestants. The *G* was particularly impressive. In *Gabbs* in the questioned will, the stem of the *G* was short and pointed, and instead of curving to the left and up and over, made a sharp swing up to the right, giving the stem the appearance of a *V*. In exemplar 101, a memo dated May 14, 1968, handwritten by Howard Hughes to Robert Maheu, there was a *G* in which the stem was short and pointed, and instead of curving to the left and up and over, made a sharp swing up to the right, giving the stem the appearance of a *V*. The two *G*'s were almost identical. And there was no way in which a forger could have had access to exemplar 101, which, from 1968 to the time of trial was locked in a safe in the office of the *Las Vegas Sun*.

"Now, extreme awkwardness," she explained, "is another common feature between the questioned will and the exemplars. The *V* in *Las Vegas* looks like an awkwardly drawn *U*. Most often in the exemplars, Mr. Hughes wrote his capital *V* like a printed *V* with a sharp point at the bottom, quite unlike the capital *V* we see in *Las Vegas* in the questioned will and its envelope. But But in other exemplars written by Mr. Hughes around 1968, he wrote the capital *V* like an awkwardly written *U* exactly as in the questioned will and envelope.

"The same is true of the awkward *J* in *Jean* and in *Jesus*. Usually, Mr. Hughes wrote his *J* in a more conventional manner. But here are samples of the writing of Mr. Hughes' in which he also wrote his capital *J* in the same unconventional, awkward manner as he did in the will.

"I am absolutely convinced that the writer of the exemplar is the writer of the questioned will."

Rex Clairbourne cross-examined Polly Jean Pfau for three days. "Mrs. Pfau, when you made your comparison you were looking for consistencies, weren't you?"

"No. I was looking to see what was there."

"Isn't it true that you looked at the questioned will, picked out a feature, and then began searching through hundreds of exemplars until you found a similar feature?"

"No, that is not true. I examined the exemplars first."

"Mrs. Pfau, an expert from Holland, and one from Paris, France, testified that the words *deliver this one* on the Forsythe envelope were, at best, probably written by Howard Hughes. They could not be certain because they had too few words to work with. But you tell us that you are certain that Mr. Hughes wrote those three words?"

"Yes, I am certain. Those three words were enough for me."

"I'm going to show you some samples of the handwriting of Mrs. Melvin Dummar. In all fairness now, isn't it true, Mrs. Pfau, that there are indications—if not conclusive proof—that Bonnie Dummar participated in the writing of this questioned will?"

"Are you serious? The evidence is overwhelming that Howard Hughes wrote the questioned will. Whoever this Bonnie Dummar is, one thing she is not is the writer of this will."

"You say that in the offered will there are some symptoms of lack of motor control. Are you a doctor?"

"I am not a doctor. I am also not blind. The disruptive motor coordination evidenced in the questioned will in various places is also evidenced in the writings of Mr. Hughes in the spring of 1968, and I consider this to be very important."

"I have no further questions."

Phillip Bittle cross-examined Polly Jean Pfau. "Was there a time, Mrs. Pfau, after your examination of the original will when you considered not testifying for the proponent?"

"Yes."

"Wasn't that because you had reason to believe it was a forgery and you didn't want to be discredited?"

"That is not the reason I hesitated. I hesitated because somebody was trying to intimidate me. I was asked not to testify."

"By whom?"

"By someone in a high official position in my profession."

"You mean to tell us that you were threatened?"

"Not with physical harm, no. But it was an intimidation nevertheless.

I was told that if I testified in the Howard Hughes trial—and these were
the words used—'against one of our own,' that I would never be
accepted by my colleagues in this country. And that it would be very
difficult for me to continue in this profession. But I felt that I had to do
what was right, and I am here."

Phillip Bittle spent three days in an attempt to persuade Polly Jean
Pfau to change her mind. She didn't.

Rex Clairbourne again cross-examined Polly Jean, this time for two
days. "Isn't it true, Mrs. Pfau, that you gave an opinion to the Nevada
Gaming Control Board that certain writings were forgeries only to have
the Board reject your opinion in favor of other handwriting experts?"

"I don't know what the Board did, but the signatures that I said were
forgeries were absolute tracings."

"Mrs. Pfau, you will notice in the questioned will the *R*'s in the name
Howard R. Hughes. On four of these *R*'s there's a hook back to the left,
and on the *R* on the bottom of page one, the hook is so pronounced as it
goes to the left that it almost looks like a capital *B*. In any of these
exemplars, have you ever found Howard Hughes to make a capital *R*
with a hook going back to the left?"

"I certainly have! And if you'd like, I'll give you a list of the Hughes
signatures in those promissory notes in evidence where he wrote his
middle initial exactly the same way. I agree that the capital *R* in the will
that you asked me about resembles a capital *B*. What is your theory,
Counsel? That the forger, who had written the name *Howard R. Hughes*
on line two, and who knew whose will he was supposed to be forging,
suddenly forgot when he reached the bottom of that page what Mr.
Hughes' middle initial was, and thought it was a *B*?"

"Mrs. Pfau, let's consider these numbers appearing in the date. In all
the exemplars you examined, isn't it true that you looked for a similar
number six, and that you didn't find one?"

"It is true that I did look. And it is true that I didn't find one. But I now
have one to show you. Linda, Mr. Rhoden's secretary, found it in an
exemplar I had never seen, and Mr. Rhoden showed it to me three days
ago. It is almost identical. Would you like to see it?"

"I sure would."

"You will find it in exemplar 432."

Clairbourne pulled the exemplar, looked at it and smiled. "Mrs. Pfau!
In exemplar 432, I see a six! And I ask you to look at it in comparison to
the six in the offered will! You will notice that in the offered will the six
has a straight back. And there is something quite unusual about the
bowl. It's flat at the bottom and flat at the top. A six very slowly and
carefully written. But this six in exemplar 432 is a six with a curved
back, and a rounded bottom—nothing flat about it anywhere. A very
fancy, and fast-written six. Don't you see that?"

"You are right, Counsel. The six in the offered will bears no resemblance to the six in exemplar 432 that you are looking at. But would you please look down four lines in 432? There you will find another six. You will notice that that second six has a straight back, and that the bowl is flat at the bottom and flat at the top. Exactly like the six in the will. Don't you see that?"

Henri Ollivier took the witness stand wearing those same gray flannel slacks and double-breasted dark-blue blazer. With André Visco translating simultaneously as he had with Faideau, I asked Dr. Ollivier what it was that had earned him the highest award given by France, the Légion d'Honneur. The answer as translated was, "In order to pay tribute to my merit which is that of being a helper of justice."

I slowly presented Ollivier's impressive credentials as director of the Laboratory of Scientific Police in Marseilles, his experience in handling four hundred to five hundred questioned documents a year, about fifteen or twenty involving wills. Then Dr. Ollivier explained his objective method of examination, and showed the jurors long foldouts to demonstrate that method. He stated his opinion that Howard Hughes wrote the questioned will. "It is a certainty."

"Is it possible for a forger to have written this offered will?"

"It is not possible. It is possible for a forger to write a letter—an *a*, a *b*—but it is impossible for a forger to assemble those letters into words and be able to fool me. If this could possibly be a forgery, I would not be here today addressing this Honorable Court."

"What about the Mormon Church envelope?"

"It has a bad smell of forgery, and I believe that Melvin Dummar wrote it. The disguise is by an amateur. But in this opinion that I give you on that envelope, I am only seventy-five to eighty percent certain. The opinion I give you concerning the will is that I am one hundred percent certain that it was written by Howard Hughes."

"What about the words *deliver this one* on this envelope?"

"If I may use a percentage again, I would say there is an eighty-five percent probability that it was written by Howard Hughes. But I will not say this with certainty because I do not believe that three words are ever enough for a firm opinion that leaves no room for doubt."

"Dr. Ollivier, was it an easy or a difficult task to form your opinion in this case?"

"It was very easy for me."

"What made it easy?"

"Because there is an abundance of similarities for comparison in the exemplars of the writing of Mr. Hughes'."

"Dr. Ollivier, even though you say you are one hundred percent certain that Howard Hughes wrote the questioned will, would you leave room for some small doubt?"

"There is no room, my good sir, for any doubt even the smallest. I am certain, and on this certainty I would stake my life."

"Cross-examine."

"No questions," Phillip Bittle said.

"No questions," Earl Yoakum said.

I said, "We thank Dr. Ollivier for coming to this country to testify."

Henri Ollivier rose and faced Judge Hayes and the translator said, "Your Honor, may I please be permitted to thank the Court for graciously allowing me to present my—"

Earl Yoakum banged his fist on the table and growled, "Your Honor, this flowery gratitude has no place in a courtroom! He's nothin' but a paid witness an' since there's no cross-examination, he can go back to France!"

Dr. Ollivier heard the translation and faced Yoakum and bowed, and then, holding his head high, he stepped down and slowly walked out of the quiet courtroom.

After Ollivier left, the jurors looked at Yoakum, again as a lynch mob, this time ready for the second feature.

On March 15, 1978, after four months and fifty-four witnesses, whose testimony was transcribed on 8,448 pages compiled in sixty-seven volumes, when Judge Hayes looked down and said to me, "Call your next witness," I announced, "Proponent rests."

55. ZOMBIES

The contestants led off with a reading of the Texas deposition of Annette Gano Lummis. Howard Hughes' eighty-seven-year-old aunt had last seen and talked to him in 1938 when he referred to her son as "adorable William."

"Yes, Howard got into Cal Tech by bribing somebody. He also went to Rice Institute here in Houston in 1927."

The will named as a beneficiary Rice Institute of Technology. A forger doing research to learn where Howard Hughes had gone to school, could have found that before 1960, its name was William M. Rice Institute for the Advancement of Literature, Science and Art, commonly called Rice Institute. After 1960, the name was changed to William Marsh Rice University, commonly known as Rice University. A forger might have used the old name that Howard Hughes would have been familiar with, Rice Institute, but why would a forger have used a wrong name, Rice Institute of Technology? A forger wouldn't.

But would Hughes? From the testimony of Aunt Annette and Hughes' aides, we knew that Hughes had called the school Rice Institute, its name when he went there. Hughes could have confused that name with the California Institute of Technology, another college he had attended in the late twenties.

Earl Yoakum then read the Los Angeles deposition Stanley Fairfield had taken of Jean Peters. Jean met Howard Hughes in 1946 and married him in January 1957 in Tonopah, Nevada. Why Tonopah? She didn't know. That's where Howard said he wanted to get married and so that's where they got married. Jean and Howard and his entourage left in a four-engine Constellation from Los Angeles. In Tonopah, they were met at the airport by one of Howard's Los Angeles lawyers, and driven to a motel where they were solemnly married by a waiting justice of the peace. At Howard's insistence—to avoid publicity, he had said—she used the name Marion Evans; he used the name Rick Garrison. Immediately after the ceremony, they flew back to Los Angeles. She never asked Howard why he couldn't have avoided publicity by getting married in his guarded bungalow at the Beverly Hills Hotel, instead of flying to Tonopah.

Jean Peters last saw her husband at the Ritz Carleton in Boston, in 1966. "At that time he had a short beard. A Vandyke. And his hair was short. There was nothing garish about him—no long hair or long beard, or unseemly fingernails! There was nothing shocking or disturbing about his appearance!"

The same Parker Saeta whose deposition I had read to corroborate Melvin Dummar's testimony about the steaming, regluing and heating of the will envelope was also the expert who had made the handwriting comparison for the FBI. He had found the questioned will to be a forgery, and Yoakum had Rex Clairbourne read Saeta's deposition testimony on the handwriting aspect of his work.

Saeta testified that in addition to being an expert in handwriting comparison, and in paper and glue, he was an expert in the examination of Xerox copies, photocopies, photocopying machines, and typewriters, and an expert in the counterfeiting of securities. "It's one of the poorest attempts I've ever seen to simulate someone else's handwriting. Definitely an unskilled forger."

I read portions of Saeta's deposition as cross-examination. "Was the writing on the questioned will made by one forger or more than one?"

"I can't say."

"You mean it could have been written by a committee?"

"You have my answer."

"You examined a sample of Melvin Dummar's handwriting. Is it your opinion that Melvin Dummar is the forger?"

"I can't say. The forger was sufficiently skillful to leave out his personal characteristics so as to prevent an identification."

"Does this skill indicate to you that he was a skillful forger? Or unskilled as you said a minute ago?"

"Take it either way you like."

"What in the questioned will indicates to you that it's a forgery?"

"Blunt endings and blunt beginnings. Tremorous strokes. Retouchings. Pen lifts in illogical places."

"But, Mr. Saeta, when you examined the exemplars of Hughes' writing, didn't you find blunt endings and blunt beginnings of strokes? And tremors and retouchings? And pen lifts in illogical places?"

"Yes, but of a different nature."

"As to the forms of the letters in the questioned will, are they like those in the exemplars?"

"Yes, most are."

"Isn't that evidence of genuineness?"

"No, that's evidence of copying. Certain capital letters do not appear in the *Dear Chester and Bill* letter which the forger used as a model. When it came to those capital letters, the forger had to guess, and he was way off the mark. There's not one letter in the will formed the way it is written in the exemplars."

"But didn't you testify a minute ago that most letter forms in the will are like those in the exemplars?"

"Sir, you can do whatever you wish with my testimony. What I said is in the record, and I do not intend to argue with you."

"What about the capital *B*?"

"In the forged will, the lower bowl was made larger than the upper and stuck out farther to the right. That is not the way Mr. Hughes wrote capital *B*'s."

As Saeta testified, I pointed to an enlargement of Polly Jean Pfau's *B* chart and to the exemplars of *B*'s written by Hughes where the lower bowl was larger than the upper, and stuck out farther to the right.

"And I considered the small *g*. In the questioned will they're all the same form. Mr. Hughes had natural variations when he wrote the small *g*, but obviously the forger didn't know this."

And obviously Mr. Saeta didn't know that in the questioned will the small *g* had exactly the same natural variations as were found in the exemplars of Hughes' writing. In the will, some of the small *g*'s looked like *9*'s, and others looked like *8*'s. Some were closed at the top, and some were open at the top. Some had stems with curved loops, and some had straight lines going down without any return. Each of these variations that appeared in the questioned will was found in Hughes' writing in memos which were not available for study by a forger.

"Mr. Saeta, can handwriting experts form opposite opinions concerning the genuineness of a document and both be honest?"

"Yes, experts many times disagree on a particular document and they can do so honestly."

Four weeks after Stanley Fairfield's farewell, he still had not returned to move his belongings out of his Las Palmas apartment, and because of the extra lock he had installed, the building manager couldn't get into his apartment to clean it out and rerent it, and I couldn't get in to get several deposition transcripts which Stanley had agreed to summarize. I particularly needed the transcript of the deposition of Gilbert Boswell, whom Yoakum had warned would deliver a decisive blow for his side.

Rex Clairbourne next read the deposition of Montgomery Bagby, a handwriting expert hired by the universities named in the will and by the Boy Scouts. It was his opinion that it was a "very poorly concocted, simulated forgery."

I read the cross-examination of Bagby by Eli Blumenfeld. "Before you examined the will on the 23rd of June, 1976, were you aware of the opinion of Spencer Otis?"

"Oh sure, I heard Spence on television say that it was a bum. And a few days after that I talked to him."

"Then, before you left Sacramento to go to Las Vegas to see the original will, you knew it was a bum?"

"Sure, I knew that long before I saw it."

"How long did you examine it in Las Vegas?"

"About an hour."

"Did you give equal weight to all the exemplars?"

"Equal weight to all. The dates ranged from 1936 to 1971 and I considered all of them equally."

"Weren't specimens of Mr. Hughes' writing close to the date of the questioned will of greater value in making your comparison?"

"No, not when Hughes was writing as consistently as he did through his lifetime."

"Between 1936 and 1971, weren't there any differences in the writing of Mr. Hughes?"

"None at all."

In the depositions of the contestants' handwriting experts Spencer Otis, Jeremy Bluedecker, and Edwin Arledge, each had testified that the earlier exemplars—anything before the 1950s—were of no value to them because of the great change in the handwriting of Howard Hughes from his earlier years to the 1960s.

"What were the factors that you considered in forming your opinion of forgery?"

"Spelling was one. I examined many exemplars of Howard Hughes and I didn't find one that contained any misspellings. Hughes was a good speller. This was very important."

"Tell us more."

"The will has all these retracings where the forger retraced a letter many times. This indicates a forgery."

"And in the exemplars of Mr. Hughes did you not find one instance where he retraced the same letter?"

"None."

"Mr. Bagby, please take a look at the Eckersley memo. Have you ever seen this before?"

"No."

"Is the writer of the Eckersley memo the writer of the purported will?"

"Let me examine it. No, it is a different handwriting."

"I've timed you, Mr. Bagby, you examined the eight pages of the Eckersley memo for about four seconds to determine that it had a handwriting different from that on the questioned will. Am I accurate?"

"I'd say so."

"Would you say that handwriting comparison was an exact science?"

"It's as good as latent fingerprint examination."

"In your studies as a handwriting expert, have you ever heard or read about any physical condition that would cause a person to misspell a word or affect his handwriting?"

"No."

"Have you ever heard of renal failure?"

"What's that?"

Next, Rex Clairbourne read the deposition of Grace Kemp, the second handwriting expert hired by the universities and the Boy Scouts, who, like Mr. Bagby, concluded that the will was a forgery. I read another thorough cross-examination by Eli Blumenfeld.

Before Grace Kemp saw the original will, she contacted her friend Spencer Otis, whom she had known since he was a boy; he was an expert for whom she had great respect.

"When you examined the original will here in Las Vegas, did you look at copies of exemplars of Mr. Hughes' writing?"

"Not to a great extent."

"You mean you determined that the original will was a forgery primarily by examining the original will alone?"

"Primarily. The indications of forgery are there for anyone to see. Never from the first moment I saw it did I have any doubt about its being a forgery."

"What were the indications to you of forgery?"

"Unusual places where the pen is lifted, and retracings. Whenever these appear, sir, the work is a forgery."

"Take the letter *a*. Did that tell you anything?"

"The small *a*'s in the forged will are all fatter than those in the exemplars."

From Polly Jean Pfau's first foldout exhibit, it could be seen that there were many *a*'s in the will which were thinner than those in some exemplars.

"The small letter *x* in the will is not formed as that letter was written by Mr. Hughes in the exemplars. I didn't find any instance of the small *x* written by Mr. Hughes the way it appears in your will."

The *x* was significant aside from the fact that Polly Jean Pfau's exhibit picturing that letter could be used in argument to discredit Grace Kemp. In the questioned will, there were four natural variations of the *x*: sometimes the top of the horizontal stroke was round like a hill, other times it was sharply pointed like a mountain. Sometimes the vertical cross stroke was short; other times it was extremely long, extending far below the baseline. Exemplars of Hughes' writing of the *x* had those identical four variations. There was no way that a forger could have learned from the supposed model, the *Dear Chester and Bill* letter, of those four natural variations, because in that document there was only one small *x*.

"Aren't some of the letter forms in the questioned will quite similar to the letter forms in exemplars of Mr. Hughes' writing?"

"I would say that as to many letters, you can find the same characteristics in the will and in the exemplars. It is a very good attempt to copy the formation of the letters."

"Mrs. Kemp, have you ever been wrong?"

"I'm sure I have been."

Judge Hayes called the attorneys into chambers. "Mr. Yoakum, Mr. Bittle, I don't want you to consider this a complaint. You have every right to present your entire case, if you wish, by reading depositions to the jury. But I feel it's my duty to suggest to you that you are boring them. You sure are boring me! Don't you have any witnesses willing to come here and get on that stand and testify in person?"

Next, Rex Clairbourne read the deposition testimony of Rupert Ingersol, who had worked for thirty years for the federal government as an expert in inks, paper, and handwriting. He had been hired by me to examine the original will, and after he gave a favorable opinion, I designated him as one of my experts.

"What is your opinion as to the authenticity of the offered will?"

"Well, after I saw the original in Las Vegas, I gave Mr. Herman Falitz and Mr. Rhoden my opinion, and I'll stand on it."

"Did you conclude that the will was written by Mr. Hughes?"

"I did not."

"Did you conclude that it was written by someone else?"

"I did not."

"What did you conclude?"

"In Las Vegas I gave Mr. Falitz a note, and I kept a copy of it, and I'll read it to you:

> The will and the genuine writings show a marked resemblance in such a sizable number of writing situations as to provide the basis for forceful testimony regarding the will. However, there are several discrepancies which remain irreconcilable and which preclude a positive opinion that the will is authentic, and conceivably due to a highly sophisticated simulation."

I read the well-prepared cross-examination of Ingersol by Wilbur Dobbs. "Was this your first report to Mr. Rhoden after you examined photographs of the original will and compared it to exemplars that he gave you?

> There exists a degree of writing correspondence and significant penmanship elements which collectively favor the opinion of genuineness concerning the will."

"Yes, that was my opinion."

"As to the note that you say you gave Mr. Falitz in Las Vegas, if he or Mr. Rhoden had received any such report indicating that you did not have a positive opinion of authenticity, you would never have been designated as an expert to be called by the proponent, would you?"

"I can't account for the actions of any attorneys."

"In a conversation with Mr. Rhoden after you saw the original in Las Vegas, did you tell him that you were ninety-five percent certain that it was genuine, and that that was as certain as any handwriting expert could ever be?"

"I did not! All I told him was that it was fifty-fifty. And Mr. Rhoden asked me, 'Are you fifty percent certain that Hughes wrote it? Or fifty percent certain that he did not?' And I explained to Mr. Rhoden that I was fifty percent certain that Hughes did not write it."

"In that same phone conversation, did you give Mr. Rhoden your opinion as to who had written the Mormon Church Visitors Center envelope?"

"I told him I believed that Dummar may have written it. I also told him that Dummar did not write the questioned will."

"What are the factors which negated authenticity?"

"In the questioned will there are evidences of a disturbed motor control of the writer. I didn't see that in any exemplars of Mr. Hughes' handwriting."

"What about the letters in the will that were retouched? Did this indicate a forgery to you?"

"Absolutely not. That isn't evidence of forgery or of copying. It's an indication of a person trying to improve the appearance of his writing."

"What about the will's obvious slowness in places?"

"Often a person writes slowly because of an inability to write faster. That's all."

"What about the capital *D* in the questioned will?"

"There was a great resemblance in the capital *D* in the questioned will and in the writings of Mr. Hughes. But not in the capital *B*. In Mr. Hughes' exemplars, the vertical stroke starting the letter was practically straight up and down, perpendicular to the baseline. In the will it was generously slanted down to the left."

But in Polly Jean Pfau's *B* foldouts there were many examples of Hughes' capital *B*'s with the initial vertical stroke generously slanted down to the left.

"Were the dashes a factor?"

"Yes, I questioned the dashes in the will. I didn't find any in the exemplars."

"Mr. Ingersol, would your opinion be changed if we showed you hundreds of dashes used by Mr. Hughes in his memos?"

"No, my opinion isn't going to be changed."

"What about spelling?"

"This was a definite factor. I did not see any misspellings in Mr. Hughes' exemplars."

"Were you ever in a case in which you disagreed with Grace Kemp or with the FBI handwriting experts?"

"I've been opposite Mrs. Kemp and the FBI experts in many, many cases. In a recent case I testified against two ex-FBI handwriting experts and Mrs. Grace Kemp, and the jury was out for only thirty minutes before coming in with a verdict in favor of the side for which I testified."

"Sir, as a result of your examination in Las Vegas, you cannot say that the will was written by Howard Hughes or that it was not written by Howard Hughes, is that correct?"

"Well, during the coffee break, a few minutes ago, I wrote down my revised opinion. If you would like, I will now show you my final opinion."

"Thank you. I'll read it into the record.

"I am more positive that the will in question was not written by Mr. Hughes than that it was."

"Mr. Ingersol, you mean that you are positive that Hughes wrote the will. And you are positive that he did not. But you are more positive that he did not than that he did?"

"I cannot explain my findings any clearer."

"You were subpoenaed to bring to this deposition all the notes you made during your examinations. Did you do so?"

"Yes, you have before you all of my notes in this case."

"Mr. Ingersol, when did you write these notes?"

"Last night."

"Where are the notes that you made at the time you examined the will?"

"I disposed of them."

"How?"

"In an ashcan."

"When?"

"Last night."

"Why, when you were subpoenaed to bring them here, did you dispose of them in an ashcan?"

"I decided to rewrite them, to get them in a better perspective so that this deposition could be more intelligently conducted. Some of my original notes were erratic and made in haste."

During the recess after the reading of Ingersol's deposition, I asked Sam Mayerson, "Why? When they're calling only American handwriting experts, why did they read the deposition of an American handwriting imbecile? And one who contradicts their other experts? Why?"

"If you were more objective about this case, you'd know why."

"Tell me! Sam, tell me why! I've got to know why!"

"Comedy relief."

Frank William Gay, a reserved, thin, soft-spoken man in his late fifties, testified that in 1947, he took a part-time job doing errands for Nadine Henley, and that shortly after that, and for the next ten years, he had daily contact with Howard Hughes. During that decade, Mr. Hughes demanded that Bill Gay be available twenty-four hours a day, seven days a week, and that he have no outside activities or interests. "That meant absolutely none. Mr. Hughes demanded full devotion to himself from those who worked for him."

Gay testified on cross-examination that he first became aware that Mr. Hughes was ill on the Saturday before Hughes died. John Holmes had phoned him and said that Hughes had not taken any food for some period of time. On Sunday, Gay was told that Hughes was unconscious.

"It was John Holmes who told you Mr. Hughes was in a coma?"

"No, not a coma! Mr. Hughes was just unconscious."

Yoakum took Gay on re-direct examination. "Do you believe that there is one chance in the world that Mr. Hughes left the Desert Inn an' went out in the desert, an' that the aides would not have told you about it?"

"Oh, there is a possibility they would not have told me, yes. It depended upon who was with him."

Earl Yoakum's irritation at the unexpected answer was apparent. "Mr. Gay, listen carefully to mah question! If Mr. Hughes had been wanderin' around out in the desert an' had been injured, don't you think it would have been known by the officers of the company?"

"I think it is quite possible he could have left his room at the Desert Inn and they not telling me."

Yoakum glared at his witness and growled, "That's all!"

Robert Maheu, an ex-FBI agent, began his relationship with Howard Hughes in 1957, right after Noah Dietrich had quit. He was the Hughes executive in charge of the Nevada operations until 1970, when he was summarily discharged in the *Dear Chester and Bill* letter published in *Life* magazine. The Las Vegas court hearing, following the departure of Mr. Hughes from the Desert Inn was to determine whether it was really Howard Hughes who had written that letter firing Maheu. The Court determined that it was.

Maheu testified for Earl Yoakum that at the end of 1967, he was deeply involved in Howard Hughes' year-end tax problem, and that from December 26, 1967, to January 1, 1968, he had ten to fifteen phone calls a day with Hughes personally. But, Maheu could not testify that he spoke to Hughes on any evening during that period. The fact that Maheu spoke with Hughes during the day on tax matters was not inconsistent with Hughes being out in the desert on one of those nights on another matter.

In the late 1960s, while the Atomic Energy Commission was preparing another atom bomb test near Tonopah, Nevada, Howard Hughes was passionately concerned about the effects of that test upon the inhabitants of nearby Las Vegas, among whom was Howard Hughes. Hughes instructed Maheu to spend whatever hundreds of millions of dollars were necessary to have that test conducted somewhere else. Anywhere else. Far from the inhabitants of Las Vegas. When Hank Greenspun, publisher of the *Las Vegas Sun,* wrote an editorial objecting to the atomic bomb tests, Hughes instructed Maheu to use whatever hundreds of millions were necessary to arrange for Greenspun to be awarded the Pulitzer Prize. Hughes ordered Maheu to make personal contact with Senator Hubert Humphrey to assure him that money was no object in stopping that goddam test, and Howard wrote that he expected the full cooperation of President Johnson in this emergency matter. Howard's alternatives were equally obnoxious to him: He could stay where he was and suffer radiation contamination, if not disintegration by the blast; or leave Las Vegas for the day; but to leave Las Vegas, Howard would first have to leave the hotel, and what if a waiting process server ran up to him?

My cross-examination took ten seconds. "Were you ever at the Arlington Towers in Reno?"

"Yes, some time around 1970."

"During the Desert Inn period, how did you refer to Howard Hughes' personal attendants?"

"I called them aides."

"Any other name?"

"I also called them zombies."

"I have nothing further."

While Bittle and Yoakum consulted about whether to take Maheu on re-direct, Sam Mayerson whispered, "You got him to admit that the word 'aides' was used in the Desert Inn—why did you want to know if he called them by any other name?"

"Bittle just might take the bait and ask Maheu what he meant by 'zombies.' If he does, Maheu'll clobber him."

"You really think that Bittle would ask a question like that? Never!"

Bittle took Maheu back on re-direct. "Mr. Maheu, you meant, didn't you, when you called Mr. Hughes' aides 'zombies,' that they didn't get enough sleep and always walked around looking as though they needed some?"

"No, Counsel, that is not what I meant. And since you asked me, I'll tell you what I meant. Those aides were well used by Mr. Frank W. Gay and his gang in the theft of the control of an empire from a very sick—psychologically and mentally sick—old man. That theft required the assistance of obedient, mindless men without morals. I call those men zombies! Anyone who would deliver an employer to Houston in that deplorable condition, I call zombies! Howard Hughes slandered me and I had to sue him, and I'm not going to pretend I liked him—I admit I didn't, but I live in a civilized world, and no prisoner in any civilized country in this world would ever be allowed to die like that. And anyone who would follow orders and take part in any such operation, I call a zombie! That is what I meant."

"Thank you for your explanation, Mr. Maheu. I have no further questions."

Not since the day that Earl Yoakum saw his own witness, Howard Eckersley, contradicted with an airline ticket Rex Clairbourne had given us, had Yoakum been in so undisguised a rage at the counsel table.

56. THE GAME PLAN

Gilbert Boswell, in his late sixties, every stocky inch a senior partner of Yoakum's Houston law firm, testified that he first met Howard Hughes in 1959 and last saw him in Los Angeles in an automobile. He said that his relationship with his famous client was somewhat unconventional.

Mr. Hughes would have someone phone Boswell to instruct him to wait on a deserted street corner at 3:00 or 4:00 in the morning, and sooner or later, usually later, Mr. Hughes' chauffeur-driven car, after reconnoitering the area, would pick up the waiting tax lawyer. There were never any banalities such as "How are you?" and Boswell would never speak first; he would sit quietly in the car until Mr. Hughes was ready to start talking about taxes. Sometimes the automobile conferences would go on for hours.

In early 1967, Howard Hughes elected to come under the Subchapter S tax law. Boswell explained that after a corporation pays a tax on profits, those same profits, distributed as dividends to a shareholder, could be taxed again as income to the shareholder. Howard Hughes didn't like that. To avoid the double tax, a shareholder may elect a Subchapter S status in which only he, not the corporation, pays a tax on those profits. This was the problem worked on by Gilbert Boswell during the last days of 1967.

Earl Yoakum asked, "What exactly was it you were doin' on this problem in Texas to help Mr. Hughes in Las Vegas those last few days of 1967?"

"In order to keep his Subchapter S status, Mr. Hughes had to generate about twelve million dollars in active income before the end of the year. Active income is other than passive income such as a stock dividend. Although I kept urging Mr. Hughes to make these arrangements during the last half of 1967, he characteristically waited until the last few days. His first plan was to sell some land he owned in his own name to the Sands Corporation, which he also owned. Since Mr. Hughes controlled both his land and the Sands, he felt confident that he could set a price agreeable to both. The price he wanted to set would give him as seller a twelve million dollar profit. But I explained to him that since he was both seller and buyer, the IRS would probably look upon the transaction with some suspicion.

"Mr. Hughes next came up with the idea to sell that land to an outsider who would pay a price resulting in a twelve million dollar profit to Mr. Hughes. At the same time, Mr. Hughes would make a secret deal with the buyer to later buy back the same land at the same inflated price. I again had to advise Mr. Hughes that he could never get away with this.

"Then Mr. Hughes came up with a final solution. He owned the Silver Slipper in his own name. When the gambling tables sell chips, the money goes into drop boxes. If the drop-box receipts could represent a profit under Subchapter S directly to Mr. Hughes, he could give his employees money to buy twelve million dollars in chips at the tables, then quietly cash in the chips at the cashier's windows and give Hughes his money back, while the records would show the twelve million dollar profit as a result of the tables' drop-box receipts. As you can see, Mr. Hughes' mind was extremely active, and he had a thorough understanding of the tax laws."

"How did you communicate with Mr. Howard Hughes about this matter?"

"One of his aides on duty would phone me and read to me, word for word, a memo Mr. Hughes had written. Sometimes I would answer it on the spot, other times I would call back with an answer and the aide would write it down word for word and take it to Mr. Hughes."

From some of those memos, phone bills, and his calendar, Boswell testified that on December 29, he worked from 10:00 in the morning until 7:00 at night, Houston time.

On December 30, he worked until 7:30 at night Houston time.

On December 31, he worked until one in the morning.

I cross-examined. "When was the last time you saw Mr. Hughes in person?"

"Sometime in the late fifties. I can't pinpoint the date."

"Did you ever say that the last time you saw Mr. Hughes was in 1964 or 1965?"

"No, I don't think I ever said anything like that."

"I show you your deposition given in Texas where you were asked when you last saw Mr. Hughes, and you answered under oath, *1964 or 1965.*"

"That was my answer at that time."

"Sir, until the mid-sixties, isn't it true that you saw Mr. Hughes a half-dozen times a year?"

"No, I do not think I saw Mr. Hughes in the mid-sixties at all, let alone a half-dozen times a year."

"When you gave your testimony in Texas, and were asked how many times between 1948 and 1964 you saw Mr. Hughes, didn't you answer, *Half a dozen times a year until the mid-sixties?*"

"Well, that must have been just a guess on my part. I have no recollection that I ever saw Mr. Hughes in the mid-sixties."

"You have no what?"

"I have no recollection."

"No? In your deposition you were asked this question and you gave this answer:

Q: *So you saw him, probably the last time in '64 or '65?*
A: *That is my recollection.*"

"All right, all right, I did give that answer, and at that time that was my recollection, but it isn't my recollection now."

"Mr. Boswell, you testified on direct that the last time you saw Mr. Hughes was when you and he were in an automobile in Los Angeles. Tell us about that."

"Well, Mr. Hughes was driving the car. He parked the car at a house, got out, then came back, and said his wife and his mother-in-law were both in the house sick. That's all I can remember."

"Since Mr. Hughes referred to his wife, it had to be after 1957, which was when he married Jean Peters, isn't that true?"

"Yes."

"This was a house in Los Angeles? Not the Beverly Hills Hotel?"

"I said it was a house."

"The only house Hughes lived in in Los Angeles after 1957 was the Bel Air house. He lived there between 1961 and 1966. So that the last time you were riding in a car with him had to be sometime between 1961 and 1966, isn't that true?"

"I suppose so."

"Well, all of Mr. Hughes' aides have testified that he never once left the Bel Air house from the day he arrived in 1961 until the day he left for Boston in 1966. They swore that not once in those four years did he even leave his bedroom—the same thing they've all said about his four years in the Desert Inn. But you tell us Mr. Hughes was out driving a car at some time when Mr. Hughes was living in the Bel Air house."

Yoakum and Bittle rose, and Yoakum said, "Ah don't interpret it that way," and Bittle said, "Neither do I!"

"Gentlemen," Judge Hayes said, "This isn't the time for either side to argue its interpretation of the testimony. Continue the cross-examination."

"When, prior to the time of Mr. Hughes' death, were you told something about a problem with his health?"

"I was told that he was quite ill the Thursday before he died."

"Who told you?"

"Kay Glenn."

"And on that Thursday—four days before Mr. Hughes died—what did Mr. Glenn tell you?"

"Well, I can't be sure, but I know that the second call, on Friday, Glenn said that concern was rapidly escalating about Hughes' health. The disorder was becoming increasingly acute. He said that Howard Hughes was deteriorating."

"What did you say to Kay Glenn?"

"Well, I told him that we had to come up with a game plan."

"Game plan?"

"One of the considerations was selecting a hospital in which there could be security arrangements."

"Security against what?"

"It was essential that Mr. Hughes not go where he could be harassed by process servers."

"Was there a time when attorney Ed Strauss in your office gave Howard Hughes advice on how to prepare a holographic will?"

"I don't recall anything about that."

"But in your deposition, didn't you testify that you knew that Ed Strauss had given Mr. Hughes advice on how to prepare a holographic will?"

"Well, that may have been my recollection when I gave my deposition. I don't know what my recollection was based on."

"Are you the one who negotiated a contract for Dr. Thain to be paid by Summa for consultation services?"

"Yes."

"Tell me how Summa Corporation is going to benefit from the money the corporation is going to pay Dr. Thain."

"That's irrelevant! Summa isn't going to get anything for the money it's going to pay the doctor."

"Then why pay him?"

"It's what the board wanted. Ask them!"

"At any time in the month of December 1976, did you speak to Howard Hughes himself on the telephone?"

"No."

"On the 29th of December, after seven o'clock Houston time—five o'clock Las Vegas time—did you have any further contact with anyone on the ninth floor of the Desert Inn?"

"No."

"Is the same true of the 30th?"

"Yes. My last phone contact would be either five or at the latest five-thirty Las Vegas time."

"Now, Mr. Boswell, do you know whether Mr. Hughes watched television those two evenings?"

"No."

"Do you know where Mr. Hughes was, or what he was doing, or whom he was with, or in what he was riding those two evenings?"

"No."

After Boswell left the stand and we adjourned for the day, I turned to Wilbur Dobbs. "This is the witness Fairfield was so goddamned worried about?"

Phillip Bittle next called the man who had donated the book *Hoax* to the Weber State College Library in December 1975. The book was new. A middle section had photographs of Howard Hughes and others, and photographs of Hughes' handwriting on two pages of his letter addressed to *Dear Chester and Bill,* and of two of Hughes' signatures on Answers to Interrogatories in the Clifford Irving forgery case.

Phillip Bittle followed with John Paul Enright, an investigative accountant for InterTel, who had been assigned to check the libraries in Utah. In July 1976 in the Weber State Library, Enright found the book *Hoax* which had been put on the shelves in January 1976. When he first saw that book, he noticed a gap between pages in the middle of the book.

"I know that the pages containing photographs of Hughes and a sample of his handwriting had been removed."

On cross-examination, I asked Enright, "Had you ever seen a copy of that book *Hoax* before the day you saw it in the Weber State Library?"

"No."

"Then how did you know what was missing from it?"

"Well, I've since learned."

Jack Tobin testified that in early August of 1976 at the request of Summa's general counsel, Chester Davis, he examined the Weber State Library's volume of *Hoax* and found that the middle section of the book containing the pictures had been carefully cut out with a sharp knife or razor. He didn't know if the binding threads were cut. Because of an electronic device in the Weber State Library turnstile, no volume could be taken out of the library without being properly checked out.

An investigator for the Nevada Attorney General's office testified that in late August 1976 he had been ordered to go to Weber State Library and pick up its copy of *Hoax* and its January 1971 issue of *Life* magazine. Another investigator in that office testified that he delivered the book *Hoax* and *Life* magazine to the FBI for its examination, and that when the FBI was through he took both volumes back and deposited them with the Court as exhibits in the case. Neither of the two Attorney General's investigators testified that they saw that anything had been cut out of the copy of *Hoax* that was brought to Ferguson at the FBI.

Something odd about the removal of the pages was that the binding threads had not been cut. Whoever removed those pages did so with skill, leaving not even a cut edge of the pages that were removed.

Wilbur Dobbs knocked at my door and caught me in my robe watching the "Tonight Show." "Want company?"

I didn't. "I want company. Come in and find a clean glass."

Wilbur found a clean glass and poured a drink in it, then sat at the edge of the couch and waited for me to shut off the television. I shut it off and waited for him to unload.

"Ah know we've been through this before. Ah know you keep sayin' that for it to be a forgery, Dummar has to be the forger, an' Dummar couldn't be, so it cain't be a forgery. Ah can see that Dummar couldn't, but that nobody else could—well, that keeps bouncin' back into mah mind, an' Ah jest cain't sleep."

"Not the inside job again!"

"Now, don't get pissed off!"

"I won't get pissed off. But I am going to make a tape of this so the next time it bounces back into your mind, you can replay the tape and then get some sleep."

"Will you let me be devil's advocate once more? Jest once more?"

"Sure, go ahead. The forger was one of the aides."

"That's right! In the Desert Inn in March 1968, he steals one of the Paper Mate pens Hughes wrote with."

"Good point! That would explain why the ink on Hughes' memos in March 1968 was the same as the ink on the will."

"An' he steals a couple of memos Hughes wrote in March 1968, an' copies— or he has a pro do it— he copies those crazy overwritins an' the shakes an' the bad spellin' an' all."

"Another good point!"

"An' the aide uses a Pitney Bowes machine somewhere in Las Vegas in March 1968 to stamp the envelope."

"Point three! That's it?"

"That's it."

"Those facts fit your theory. And if we stop here, an inside job forgery would make sense. But, Wil, do we stop here? Do we stop thinking at this point? Or do we test that theory by applying more known facts to it to see if they also fit? In the will is 'Melvin Du Mar of Gabbs, Nevada.' Why does your aide put that name in Howard Hughes' will? Someone unrelated to Hughes. Someone who didn't work for Hughes. If Hughes had never even met Dummar, how and where would this aide—"

"But what if Hughes did meet Dummar? Exactly as Dummar said. Suppose Hughes told his aides about that real nice kid who gave him a lift in the desert. Maybe the aide felt that rememberin' the kid in his will was the kind of nutty thing a nut like Hughes would do. So the aide puts Dummar in the will."

"Then wouldn't your aide, who wants his forgery to pass, want the world to believe that this real nice kid had in fact given Howard Hughes that lift in the desert? If so, tell me why every one of Hughes' aides broke his ass to testify that Hughes could not have been out in the desert to have been given this lift by Dummar. How does this fit your inside-job-by-an-aide theory?"

Wilbur looked at the ceiling. Then at the walls. Then at the floor for a while.

"Wil, did this aide forge the will to get money for himself? Or money for Melvin Dummar and the other beneficiaries he put in to make it look good?"

"Himself."

"But every one of Hughes' aides made sure that he would never get a nickel under this will! In testimony and in writing, each one—in addition to branding the will a forgery—legally renounced any interest under the will in the event that it's admitted to probate as genuine. Now, exactly what is it about that inside-job-by-an-aide theory that interferes with your sleep?"

"What about one of Hughes' doctors?"

"Where in the will is a doctor named as a beneficiary? What's next? Want to explore the premise that the will was forged by a Boy Scout? How about an orphan? Or how about a combination? An orphaned Boy Scout who was a devout Mormon and yearned for a scholarship to Rice University."

"All right, all right, the forger had to be Dummar or nobody." Wilbur lit a cigarette and smiled at me and nodded his satisfaction with my arguments. But there was no way he was going to get a good night's sleep.

Phillip Bittle called Harold McNair, a professor of chemistry at Virginia Polytechnic Institute. Dr. McNair had examined Albert Lyter's chromatograms on plate C-15, from which Lyter had concluded that the questioned ink matched only one of their three thousand samples, Paper Mate's 307 with PAGO dye; not Paper Mate's 316.

"Do you agree with Mr. Lyter that the questioned ink is identical to Paper Mate's 307 with the PAGO dye?"

"I agree with that. Those two are identical. The problem I have is—I find it difficult to eliminate 316 as being the same as the questioned ink. They look similar."

"Your witness."

"Dr. McNair, were you informed that not only Albert Lyter, but Dr. Michael Camp was able to distinguish Paper Mate's 316 from the questioned ink and from Paper Mate's 307 with the PAGO dye?"

"Yes."

"Did you run your own test using thin layer chromatography to see if you could tell the difference between Paper Mate's 307 PAGO and Paper Mate's 316 formula?"

"No, I did not run my own test."

"You knew, didn't you, that it was very important in this case that we know whether the ink on the questioned will can be distinguished from 316?"

"Oh, yes, I knew that that was very important."

"Then, why didn't you run your own test as Albert Lyter did, and as Dr. Michael Camp did to see what your conclusion would be?"

"I wanted to run my own test. But Mr. Bittle told me he wanted nothing more done."

Yoakum read the deposition of Norman Love, who testified that he began working for Hughes Productions in 1957 as a driver and gofer, picking up films and lunches for the people at operations. When, after a week and a half, his loyalty was recognized, he was sent to Palm Springs to guard a parking space for Mr. Hughes in case Mr. Hughes decided to go there. But Mr. Hughes didn't decide to go there, and after three months, Love was assigned to attend Mr. Hughes at Nosseck's Studio where Mr. Hughes watched movies. After several years of service for Mr. Hughes, Love had the audacity to take a one-week vacation. Thereafter, he was always referred to by Mr. Hughes as "that goddam Norman Love," and thereafter, Love obeyed Mr. Hughes' order that he was forever to remain out of Mr. Hughes' sight.

During Mr. Hughes' four-year stay in the Desert Inn, Love saw Mr. Hughes about six times. His Desert Inn job was to buy supplies and run errands, and on one occasion, in order to be able to fix Hughes' toilet, he was assigned to enroll in a plumbing school. During the Desert Inn period, Norman Love bought for Mr. Hughes four pairs of slacks, two blue and two tan, and one pair of slippers.

On cross-examination, Love was asked if he purchased any pens for Mr. Hughes.

"Yes, I purchased ballpoint Paper Mates."

"Why Paper Mates?"

"I was told by Johnny Holmes to purchase Paper Mates, and I purchased Paper Mates. Only Paper Mates. Mr. Hughes wanted a free-flowing ballpoint pen and I suggested that they send Chuck Waldron to Paper Mate to get a pen like the kind Mr. Hughes wanted. We were dealing just in Paper Mates at that time. We were afraid to give him any other pen. He didn't use any other pen except Paper Mate until sometime in 1970."

I was certain that after Phillip Bittle's failure to obtain even a hint of evidence of conspiracy from his depositions of Melvin Dummar's Aunt Erma or her son Willy, Bittle would not read their depositions. I was wrong.

But I knew I couldn't be wrong about what had to be Bittle's decision not to call Inez Stanton as a witness. She testified in her deposition that on April 27, 1976, working at the reception desk on the main floor of the Mormon Church Headquarters Building, the woman whom she saw holding an envelope and asking for directions to President Kimball's office was about five feet eight and had black hair—or something black about her—was around forty years old, and very well dressed and very trim. Her description did not fit short, broad-hipped Bonnie Dummar, nor anyone else connected with Melvin Dummar, and Inez Stanton admitted when she saw Bonnie Dummar in 1977 that she had never seen Bonnie Dummar before. I knew of no reason for Bittle to call Inez Stanton. Bittle called Inez Stanton.

Phillip Bittle then read the deposition of Linda Diego, Melvin's first wife, who testified that she was with Melvin on December 31, 1967, in

Los Angeles. If Linda was right, and if Dummar picked up a man in the desert, it had to have been on either December 29 or 30.

Phillip Bittle's last deposition witness to attack Melvin Dummar was Frances Heil, the woman who held the lease on Melvin's gas station in Willard. She had once threatened to sue Melvin for slander, and when he didn't pay his rent on time in December 1976, she evicted him on three days' notice. Her arguments with Dummar stemmed from his failure to repair his septic tank, his failure to keep his children from playing in the backyard where they sometimes hollered at each other, and his failure to always open the gas station at 6:00 in the morning and keep it open until midnight.

Although the lady could not be sure of the dates—she said "dates escape me"—she had heard Melvin say that someday he would be a millionaire, someday he would be a lawyer, someday he would be a pilot, and someday he would buy a casino in Nevada and buy a lot of property.

On cross-examination, she was asked if she harbored any resentment toward Melvin Dummar.

"Resentment? I hate him with a passion, that fat bastard!"

57. THE BIG GUN

On April 10, 1978, Bittle called his big gun, Spencer Otis, reputed to be the most competent handwriting expert outside New York City. Like Dudley Woodcock of New York, Spencer Otis of San Francisco was stiff and smiled only when custom compelled it. Everything about Spencer Otis was medium-gray: his suit and tie, his few strands of hair, and his complexion. A slight man in his 60s, his walk was agile and his voice was crisp. With the polished manner of a professional witness, Otis recited his impressive qualifications as a handwriting expert. He had worked on the staff at the crime lab of the San Francisco Sheriff's Office and had testified in hundreds of cases for the District Attorney and for the Public Defender in San Francisco and in other counties in California, as well as for private industrial firms. But his principal work had been for private attorneys and insurance companies, testifying in state and federal courts in most of the western states thousands of times.

Otis, along with Edwin Arledge, Yoakum's handwriting expert from Chicago, had sat among the spectators during the testimony of Verhaeren and Faideau, taking pages of notes. Since I felt that Otis and

Arledge would be vulnerable on cross-examination, I served them with subpoenas to testify for me as hostile witnesses. It was my insolent plan to try to ruin them as experts on cross-examination before Yoakum and Bittle could present them favorably on direct, and to enrage Yoakum and Bittle. On a motion to quash the subpoenas, Yoakum and Bittle raged that this was part of my insolent plan to discredit contestants' witnesses before contestants could have a chance to credit them, and Judge Hayes quashed the subpoenas.

Spencer Otis began with the lecture he had given to a thousand juries. "Writing is movement without conscious direction, almost an automatic process. For someone to forge someone else's writing successfully, he has to drop all his own handwriting characteristics, and at the same time pick up all the handwriting characteristics of the person whose writing he is forging. Even with a few words this is difficult, if not impossible. But to successfully forge someone else's handwriting for three pages is absolutely impossible."

"Mr. Otis," Bittle asked, "what is your opinion concerning the writer of the questioned will?"

"The questioned document was not written by Howard Hughes. It is a rank forgery. Rank!"

"Are you able to tell us, after examining Dummar's handwriting, if it was written by Melvin Dummar?"

"I cannot tell you that the forger was Dummar. But I can tell you that this forgery is a slavish copy. The line quality is slow. There is patching. Unnatural pen lifts. There isn't the natural variation in letters which everyone has in his handwriting and that's a dead giveaway. This is a rank forgery!"

At this point, Wilbur Dobbs whispered, "Ah've got some phone calls to make," and walked out of the courtroom.

Otis testified that on May 5, 1976, he examined the original of the questioned document in the courthouse in Las Vegas after having reviewed exemplars in San Francisco, and that day declared the document a forgery. During the following year, Otis studied 453 more exemplars of Hughes' writing.

A letter of particular interest to Otis was the small *p*. "In the 1970 *Dear Chester and Bill* letter—which was used by the forger as a model— all of the *p*'s are two-stroke *p*'s, a printed form which Mr. Hughes clearly did not make in 1968. The will is dated 1968 and has two-stroke *p*'s in it, and that is not the way Mr. Hughes was writing *p*'s in 1968. That's one reason why I say that this is a rank forgery!"

"Give us another reason."

"Another factor is the capital *F* in *Fifth* in the questioned will. See the little initial stroke at the beginning of the letter? It's tacked on. It isn't a part of the initial motion. This is the work of a forger."

Otis showed the jurors a blowup of photographs of the word *of* taken from the questioned will on the left side, and on the right side, the same word taken from exemplars. "You will notice that the word *of* written by Mr. Hughes in his exemplars contains natural variations. But the word *of* taken out of the questioned will is written the same every single time as though stamped out of the same mold. This is a very strong indication of forgery, and is another of the many reasons why I say that this is a rank forgery!"

For the next two days, Spencer Otis demonstrated with several superbly photographed blowups of letters and words, dissimilarities between the writing in the questioned will and the writing in the exemplars.

In Otis' opinion, the words *deliver this one* on the Forsythe envelope were not written by Howard Hughes.

"What did you find from your examination of the Pitney Bowes imprint on the back of the envelope which contained the questioned will?"

"First of all, you are not going to be able to put an envelope into a Pitney Bowes machine and get a meter mark as far down as this one appears on the envelope. The image is about a third of the way down, too far down to have been made by a Pitney Bowes machine.

"Next, the number of the machine is not decipherable. You can read the month, but not the day or the year. And so I came to the conclusion that the thing was never run through a Pitney Bowes machine."

"Can you explain how that mark, which looks something like a Pitney Bowes imprint, got on that envelope?"

"Yes. It isn't a bona fide Pitney Bowes mark at all. It's an artifact. The forger took a Pitney Bowes imprint from another envelope, and then with a pin, punched holes in it along the lines. He then placed this over the envelope on which he wanted an imprint to appear, and patted some red ink down on the real Pitney Bowes imprint so that it would come through the little dots and leave an imprint on the forger's envelope. With this tattooing method, an imprint was made. And this is still another reason why I say that this is a rank forgery!"

In my apartment, the night before I was to begin my cross-examination of Spencer Otis, Wilbur Dobbs came in, poured himself a drink, lit a cigarette, and asked if he could interrupt my work. I told him he could, and he sat down opposite me at my table. "Hal, are you scared?"

"Of what?"

"Of losin'?"

"No."

"Ah am. Ah'm so scared, Ah'm sick half the time. Ah jest cain't sit there in that courtroom an' take it."

"Wil, why don't you go back to Houston for a week and see your family? If you want to, check out and go back to Houston until the trial is over."

"Ah cain't go back. There's nothin' Ah can go back to."

"What about your practice?"

"Ah gave up mah practice. Ah don't even have an office anymore. An' everybody knows that Ah'm on this case with you. Ah cain't go back now. Ah don't know what to do. Ah cain't go back an' Ah cain't stay in that courtroom every day. Ah keep thinkin' about what it'd mean if we lose. Ah owe everybody in Houston. Ah don't have any way to support mah family. Ah've staked everythin' on this case. An' Ah know you have, too. What would it mean to you if we lose?"

"The same thing it'd mean to you. I'm in debt up to my ass. I've given up my practice, too. And clients don't flock to losers. But I don't expect to lose."

"But what if you do? What if you have to go back to your home and you don't have money for the payments? An' you don't have any practice any more? An' you cain't support your family?"

It was like asking me how I'd feel if I were to wake up tomorrow morning and find that I had lost my arms and legs, I was deaf and blind, and with a bad case of hemorrhoids.

When Bittle turned Otis over for cross-examination, Otis smiled at me in gleeful anticipation of the pleasure he was going to savor in punishing me for daring to question his expertise. I faced a tightly compressed iron coil ready to spring at my mouth.

"Mr. Otis, did you say that from what you found, Mr. Hughes clearly did not make two-stroke p's in 1968?"

"Yes, that is what I said, and that is what I found, and that is what is true."

"Mr. Otis, is the two-stroke p, in your opinion, really inconsistent with Howard Hughes' writing of that letter in 1968?"

"Yes, it is absolutely inconsistent!"

"In 1968 Hughes made only one-stroke p's."

"Now you're getting it."

"Let's take a look at Howard Hughes' writing in exemplar 282 dated May 15, 1968—two months after the dating of the questioned will. You see this p? How many strokes?"

"Two."

"Here's another one dated May 1968, and here's a p in it. In this memo did Howard Hughes write a one-stroke or a two-stroke p?"

"Two. But—"

"Here's another one, 346, dated April 27th, 1968—just one month after the dating of the will. How many strokes made the p?"

"Two. Now, if—"

"And here's number 311, dated December 1967. How many strokes in the *p* in this memo?"

"All right, two!"

"In exemplar 414, dated some time between 1967 and '69, there are fourteen *p*'s. How many strokes, one or two, on these fourteen *p*'s?"

"Two!"

"You prepared a beautiful blowup of a lot of *p*'s. On the left are the two-stroke *p*'s from the questioned will. On the right are a lot of one-stroke *p*'s from the exemplar of Mr. Hughes' writings around 1968. Why did you leave out of your blowup his 1968 two-stroke *p*'s that I just showed you?"

"You are attempting to mislead the jurors! Most of the *p*'s written by Mr. Hughes around 1968 were made with one stroke! And when I presented my exhibit to them, I tried to show them an honest picture of the way Mr. Hughes really wrote in 1968. I'm not concerned about a few mavericks."

"How many mavericks before they become a herd? All right, let's look at some more. I have a whole stack here. Dozens! Now, Mr. Otis, are you willing to admit that in 1968 and in 1969, Hughes was writing *p*'s in two forms—sometimes with one stroke and sometimes with two strokes, and that he would interchange them?"

"No."

"Here's your answer to that identical question in your deposition: *'Back in '68 he was making the small* p *in two forms, sometimes with one and sometimes with two strokes, and he would often move from one line to the next and change the form.'* Isn't that your opinion?"

"Yes."

"Seconds ago when I asked you if this were your opinion, you said, *No.* Now, you say, *Yes.* Which is it?"

"I know what you're trying to do!" The coil sprang and he shouted, "You're trying to confuse things! You ignore the fact that Mr. Hughes wrote mainly one-stroke *p*'s in 1968, and ignoring that fact is a form of cheating!"

"When you made this blowup for the jurors and selected from Mr. Hughes' exemplars one-stroke *p*'s made in 1968 and ignored pages and pages of memos where he wrote two-stroke *p*'s in 1968, wasn't that a form of cheating?"

"No! No!"

"A one-stroke *p* is normally written faster than a two-stroke *p*, correct?"

"Correct."

"Were any of those fast one-stroke *p*'s written in 1968 written by Howard Hughes when he was writing something like his last will and testament?"

"No."

"Mr. Otis, when you compare the handwriting on two different documents, don't you have to consider what the two different documents are? That is, isn't a man going to write slower and with more care when he writes his last will than when he writes his grocery list?"

"I suppose so."

"Mr. Otis, let's look at your blowup of photographs of the word *of*. You said that all of the *of*'s in the questioned will were stamped out of the same mold."

"And that's why I say it's a forgery!"

"Mr. Otis, you forgot something. You meant a rank forgery, didn't you?"

"I accept your correction. A rank forgery!"

"Now, the jurors and I can see that some of the *f*'s in the word *of* on your blowup, taken from the will, have a stem. Some have no stem. Do you agree?"

"Yes."

"Some of these *f*'s in *of* in the will shown on your blowup have a fat bowl at the bottom. Some have a narrow bowl. Some of the bowls are big. Some are small. Do you agree?"

"I agree."

"Some of the *f*'s in the will have an overlapping upstroke, and some have a loop. True?"

"True."

"Now, about this one mold that you say was used to stamp out all of the words *of* in the questioned will—does that mold have a stem or no stem? A fat bowl, or a narrow bowl? A big bowl, or a small bowl? An overlapping upstroke or a loop?"

"Naturally, there are some differences."

"Why do you tell the jurors that all of the words *of* in the will are written exactly the same way, when they can see with their own eyes that this is not true?"

"Counsel, in attempting to be picky in this matter, you're trying to mislead the jurors!"

"Mr. Otis, which do you want the jurors to believe? What they hear you say or what they see?"

"There is no difference between the two! I tell you, this is not only a rank forgery, but one of the rankest forgeries I have ever seen! It's pathetic—it's really kind of sick!"

"On May 5th, 1976, how much time did you spend making your comparison?"

"About two and a half hours. But I had the impression that it was a forgery in the first fifteen minutes."

"What exemplars did you use in your comparison?"

"The *Dear Chester and Bill* letter, another memo written by Mr. Hughes, and two signatures."

"Did you use a photograph or a Xerox copy of the *Dear Chester and Bill* letter?"

"Both a photograph and a Xerox."

"In your deposition, you testified that you used only a Xerox copy of *Dear Chester and Bill*, didn't you?"

"Where did I say that?"

"Here."

"Yes, I gave that answer."

"You didn't really compare the will with a photograph of *Dear Chester*, did you?"

"I don't have a specific recollection."

"Then why did you just testify that you did?"

"I can't remember a trivial detail like that."

"In making your comparison, did you look at the originals of any of Mr. Hughes' memos to his attorney Bob Edison on file with the Court?"

"Yes, now I recall that two memos to Edison were in the courtroom for me to use in my examination."

"No, Mr. Otis, the originals of the memos to Bob Edison were not filed with the Court until a month after you made your examination. You want to withdraw that?"

"All right, perhaps I was mistaken! I didn't need them anyway!"

"Exactly what did you look at when you made your comparison?"

"Four Xerox copies of samples of Mr. Hughes' writing. Sufficient for me to see that it was a rank forgery. Here they are!"

"You're handing me the four exemplars you looked at in making your comparison?"

"Didn't I just tell you that, Counsel?"

"Mr. Otis, think back! You were in the jury room. Photographers were there. The sheriff's investigator wearing a holstered gun was there. The judge's clerk was there, and the court reporter was writing down everything everybody said. Remember? Mr. Otis, you looked at the three pages of the questioned will and at the envelope. But you didn't look at any exemplars at all, did you?"

"All right, I may not have looked at any of the exemplars at that time. It would have been a useless exercise."

"You mean you decided that the questioned will was a forgery after comparing it to nothing?"

"I was familiar with Mr. Hughes' handwriting!"

"You mean you compared it only to your memory of Mr. Hughes' writing that you had seen on Xerox copies?"

"I didn't have to look at anything more!"

"Why did you just testify that you looked at these four exemplars in making your comparison?"

"You asked me what exemplars I took along with me."

"No, I didn't! I asked you what exemplars you looked at in making your comparison, not what exemplars you took with you and kept in your briefcase. Are we to understand that you had exemplars with you in your briefcase?"

"Yes."

"But you didn't bother to open your briefcase to take out the exemplars to look at them in making your comparison?"

"I didn't think it was necessary."

"You were certain enough that it was a rank forgery on May 5th, 1976, to announce it on national television, weren't you?"

"I was. The rankest forgery I had ever seen!"

"We're beginning to get that point. But then why, during the next year and a half, did you study the four hundred and fifty-three exemplars in this case?"

"To confirm my opinion. Just to confirm it! Not to change it."

"How much were you paid by Mr. Bittle before you went to Las Vegas?"

"Five thousand dollars."

"Didn't you have an agreement that you were going to get another twenty thousand if you found it to be a forgery?"

"No."

"In your deposition, you were asked this question: *'Did you have an agreement that you were going to get a retainer of twenty-five thousand dollars if you found it to be a forgery?'* 'And you answered, *'Yes.'*"

"But I was to receive that retainer of twenty-five thousand irrespective of what I found."

"You mean you had an agreement with Mr. Bittle that you were to be paid five thousand dollars to go to Las Vegas to inspect the will, and that if you found it to be genuine, Mr. Bittle was going to give you another twenty thousand dollars as a bonus?"

"I was going to receive an additional twenty thousand dollars as a retainer to compensate me for work I would do at one hundred dollars an hour."

"Oh, if you found the will to be genuine, Mr. Bittle was going to pay you twenty thousand dollars more to put in two hundred hours of work to help prove the will to be genuine?"

"That was our understanding."

"What's your fee up to today?"

"I'm going to bill Mr. Bittle at the conclusion of my work."

"Mr. Otis, isn't your bill going to be over one hundred thousand dollars?"

"I don't—it may—all right, around that."

"Did you give a written report to Mr. Bittle of your opinion in this case?"

"No."

"Why not?"

"There was no need for me to spell out details in a written report."

"Didn't you receive a letter from Mr. Bittle telling you not to put your report in writing?"

"You're just trying to—"

"Mr. Otis, yes or no?"

"Yes."

"If a writer is toxic, would this have an effect upon his handwriting?"

"Of course."

"Are you familiar with studies of the effect on handwriting of a kidney disorder?"

"Yes."

"Can kidney failure cause tremors in handwriting?"

"Yes."

"Can that disease cause a person to keep the pen in the same place going over and over a line?"

"Yes."

"Mr. Otis, as an expert in handwriting, can you tell us if renal failure can cause mental confusion and misspelling?"

"It can, but I will tell you that this is a—"

"We know—a rank forgery. Will kidney disease cause someone to write in a telegraphic style, leaving words out?"

"Yes."

"When you were in the jury room examining the original will, did you see any indications in it that the writer might have been sick?"

"I considered the possibility of Mr. Hughes' physical condition causing him to write like that. But I ruled out that possibility."

"When did you rule it out?"

"During my examination of the questioned will in the room back there."

"How did you rule it out?"

"I ruled it out by searching my memory."

"When you searched your memory, what did you find?"

"In 1970, when I testified in the Maheu case, I was told by Morton Galane about Mr. Hughes' physical condition in 1968."

"Morton Galane is a doctor?"

"No, a lawyer."

"Did Mr. Galane ever lay eyes on Howard Hughes?"

"Not as far as I know."

"What did Mr. Galane tell you about Mr. Hughes' health?"

"He said that Mr. Hughes was seriously ill in 1968, but that it was late in 1968."

"That was the extent of your searching your memory?"

"No, I also relied on what I remembered Mr. Maheu had told me."

"What?"

"I don't remember."

"Did Mr. Maheu tell you he had seen Howard Hughes in 1968?"

"He once saw him in an elevator or going in an elevator."

"Mr. Hughes in an elevator? In 1968? That's interesting. Now, you told us that one factor you considered was that of misspellings in the questioned document."

"I meant abnormal misspellings such as *children* with the *h* left out."

I showed him the blowup of lists of words written by Howard Hughes with letters left out, including the *h* in *whichever,* a word which Hughes spelled correctly a few lines down on the same page. "Is the fact that the questioned will has a word with a letter left out still evidence to you that it was not written by Howard Hughes?"

"It still is, and it always will be! And the fact that in the will the writer spelled certain words both correctly and incorrectly is further evidence of forgery."

I showed Mr. Otis the blowup of lists of words in the exemplars spelled both correctly and in other places incorrectly, sometimes on the same page. "Do you still say that the fact that the will has the same words spelled both correctly and incorrectly is evidence that it could not have been written by Howard Hughes, when Howard Hughes had this same habit?"

"I still say it's a rank forgery!"

"And as we continue this cross-examination, that forgery gets more and more rank, doesn't it?"

"You might say that."

"Didn't you find in the memos of Howard Hughes the same tele-graphic style with words left out that appears in the questioned will?"

"I did not. I found that Mr. Hughes' memos were rather eloquent and well written."

I showed Mr. Otis eight blowups of examples taken from memos by Howard Hughes in which he wrote in the same telegraphic style which appears in certain places in the questioned will. "Mr. Otis, I'll bet it's your opinion that there is no similarity between the two telegraphic styles."

"You just won a bet."

"Is it really your opinion that the forger used as a model the *Dear Chester and Bill* letter?"

"That is my opinion and that will remain my opinion."

"Are there any misspellings in the *Dear Chester and Bill* letter?"

"No."

"What about the eight capital letters in the questioned will which do not appear in *Dear Chester and Bill?* First, let's take the capital *E* in the questioned will which is not in what you call the model. How did the forger do in writing the *E* to make it look like Hughes' *E?*"

"The *E* is a close copy. Not too bad."

"You mean it's a close copy of something the forger didn't have from which to copy?"

"It was a good guess."

"How did the forger do on the capital *O* that's not in the model, writing it with the overlapping strokes on the left side and the flatness at the bottom the way Mr. Hughes wrote it?"

"There, he did the best job of all."

"There's no capital *U* in your model, but there are capital *U*'s in the questioned will which are quite similar to the way Mr. Hughes at times wrote that letter. Another good guess?"

"Yes, yes, yes, another good guess!"

"And what about the capital *S* missing from the *Dear Chester?*"

"The *S* isn't too far off."

"Another good guess. We have eight missing capital letters and eight good guesses. That isn't bad—eight out of eight. Tell me, Mr. Otis, have you ever known a rank forger to be such a good guesser?"

"Twist the facts any way you wish, Counsel, it's still a rank forgery!"

"Mr. Otis, was there a time, some years ago, when you testified that a defendant charged with forgery had written the questioned document, and it turned out that he was innocent? You were shown other exemplars after you gave your opinion and you then changed your mind. Did that happen?"

"Yes."

"If you hadn't been shown those other exemplars, an innocent man might have gone to prison on your testimony, isn't that true?"

"That's a possibility."

"And in this case, you formed an opinion in fifteen minutes, comparing the questioned will with your memory of what Hughes' handwriting was like on memos that you didn't bother to take out of your briefcase! You then committed yourself on national television to the opinion that it was a rank forgery. Mr. Otis, if you had waited until you had studied a dozen exemplars of Hughes' writing, spending weeks as our European experts did, might you not have reached a different conclusion? Wait, I'll bet again that I know your answer. It's that you wouldn't have changed your opinion no matter what you were shown."

"That's two bets you've won today."

"Is handwriting examination an exact science?"

"It is."

"Now, about the Pitney Bowes imprint on the back of the envelope. You said that you can't put an envelope into a Pitney Bowes machine and get an imprint at the location where the imprint appears on this envelope. If I showed you a dozen envelopes, each with a genuine Pitney Bowes imprint in exactly the same location on an envelope as the one on the questioned envelope, would you admit that you're wrong?"

"No."

"As an expert in the detection of forgeries, you're familiar with the work of forgers, aren't you?"

"I am."

"Now, in this instance, MAR for March is clearly readable on the imprint on the envelope. But the day of the month and the year aren't. Why would a forger, who wants us to believe that the imprint was made in March on or after the 19th, in 1968, go to the trouble of tattooing a Pitney Bowes imprint, and then leave off the day of the month and the year?"

"I don't know."

"Mr. Saeta of the FBI said that as to the Pitney Bowes machine number, he could decipher the last three digits under magnification. And on your own blowup, we can all see those last three digits, though not the first three digits. But with the naked eye, we can't see any of the digits. How could a tattooer be able to tattoo the last three digits visible under high-powered magnification, but not to his own naked eye?"

"I don't know."

"And why would he?"

"I don't know."

"Now, in order to have done this tattoo job, the forger had to have an actual Pitney Bowes imprint made by a machine issued to someone in Las Vegas, Nevada, correct?"

"Yes."

"Let's say you were in Willard, Utah, between April 5th and April 27th, 1976, and that you wanted to tattoo a Pitney Bowes imprint on the back of an envelope. How would you go about getting an imprint made by a machine used to mail something out of Las Vegas, Nevada?"

"I haven't the slightest idea."

"Are you as certain in your opinion about this will as you are about the Pitney Bowes imprint?"

"I am."

"You know, Mr. Otis, we've gone for about fifteen minutes now without your once reminding the jurors of your opinion about the will. Now just in case they've forgotten, would you like to tell them for the twentieth time?"

"I'll be happy to." He turned to the jurors. "It's a rank forgery!"

To support Spencer Otis' opinion that the Pitney Bowes imprint on the back of the will envelope was a tattooed fake, Phillip Bittle called Thomas Barker, a representative of Pitney Bowes. Barker pointed out features of the imprint on the will which he said were not characteristic of an imprint made by a Pitney Bowes machine. "And as to the location of the imprint on the back of the envelope, it's inconsistent with the location of our imprint when an envelope is put through our machine in a conventional way."

"As an expert, can you tell us if this is a legitimate Pitney Bowes meter mark?"

"The quality is too poor to make a positive identification."

"Your witness."

I had been waiting for this. "Are you telling us that this Pitney Bowes imprint on the back of the will envelope was not made by a Pitney Bowes stamp meter machine?"

"No, sir, I am not saying that. All I am saying is that I can't identify it positively as having been made by one of our Pitney Bowes meters."

"Then it's your expert opinion that you don't have an opinion?"

"That's true."

I had asked Linda to run some envelopes through the Pitney Bowes machine in the office of our local law firm to see if she could get an imprint on the envelope in the same location as that on the will envelope. Linda tried four times and succeeded four times in getting an imprint as far below the top of the test envelope as the imprint on the will envelope. And when an envelope is forced into a Pitney Bowes machine awkwardly, the imprint comes out at an angle pointing down to the left; that is the way the imprint appeared on each of Linda's four test envelopes, and that is the way the imprint appeared on the back of the will envelope.

"Mr. Baker, please take a look at the imprints on these four envelopes dated today. Tell us, is the imprint on each of these envelopes in the same location and at the same angle as the Pitney Bowes imprint on the back of the will envelope?"

"Yes, they are all in the same location. And at the same angle."

"Spencer Otis testified that the imprint on the will envelope was too far down to have been made by a Pitney Bowes machine. He was wrong, wasn't he?"

"He was wrong."

"You testified that the imprint on the back of the will envelope had characteristics which you don't normally find on Pitney Bowes imprints. The eagle's head wasn't distinct. The top line wasn't there. The bottom line was wavy. The numbers didn't come out. The stars didn't look like stars. Did you say that imprints with those defects are not characteristic of imprints made by your machines?"

"Yes, those defects are not characteristic of imprints made by our machines."

"I'm going to show you two more envelopes. These have been marked Proponent's exhibits 138 and 139, and were mailed by two local banks a couple of days ago, each with a Pitney Bowes imprint. In 138, what do you see when you look at the eagle's head?"

"Well, I admit it's not clear."

"The top line over the eagle isn't there at all, is it?"

"No."

"The circle around the amount of the stamp isn't round, is it?"

"No."

"On 139, you can read the Pitney Bowes meter number, but can you read it on 138?"

"No."

"The stars on the Pitney Bowes imprint on the will envelope don't look like stars. And this, you felt, was an indication that maybe a Pitney Bowes machine didn't make the imprint, correct?"

"Correct."

"Take a look at the imprint on 138 that was made by one of your machines a few days ago. Do those dots look to you like stars?"

"No."

"Mr. Spencer Otis testified yesterday that he was positive that the Pitney Bowes imprint on the back of the will envelope was tattooed on there. As an expert on Pitney Bowes meter imprints, do you want to tell us the same thing he did?"

"Oh, no, sir!"

During the afternoon recess following the testimony of the Pitney Bowes expert, Wilbur told me that the Texas Court of Appeal had denied our petition for a writ of prohibition to prevent the Houston court from conducting a trial when we couldn't be there. "Hal, what do we do?"

"What the hell can we do? We allow your Lone Star Chamber proceeding to go on without us."

"But then we'll lose for not bein' there!"

"That's right. We'll lose for not being there at a time when we cannot possibly be there. You have another suggestion?"

He didn't have one.

58. THE DEATH OF UNCLE CLAUDE

On April 4, 1978, Earl Yoakum opened his attack on the credibility of LeVane Forsythe by reading portions of the deposition I had taken of Attorney Chester Davis. Davis had seen Mr. Hughes face to face only four times; first in Nassau in 1971 and last in the Grand Bahamas in 1974. The second time, Davis had only a glimpse of Mr. Hughes in an adjoining room while the two men talked to each other on the telephone.

Davis testified in answer to my question that that first time in 1971, Mr. Hughes did not have hair down to his shoulders.

"There's been testimony that he had a beard down to his waist."

"Good heavens, no!"

"Did Mr. Hughes ever discuss with you the making of a will?"

"Yes, more than once. By telephone and in memos. He said that he was making plans for the future control of the Tool Company and that he had an existing will in which he provided for the control to go to the Howard Hughes Medical Institute. This was in 1969."

"Mr. Davis, about the time that LeVane Forsythe testified about the departure of Howard Hughes in 1970 from Las Vegas, did you give him any money?"

"Not a cent."

"Did anybody?"

"Not to my knowledge."

"Did LeVane Forsythe ask anybody for any money?"

"Not to my knowledge."

"Did LeVane Forsythe testify in that hearing that he had had contact with Roy Crawford, one of Mr. Hughes' executive staff assistants?"

"On the witness stand, Forsythe said that he had been contacted by someone who said his name was Roy Crawford. But when we showed him a picture of the real Roy Crawford, Forsythe said that it was not a picture of the guy who gave him five hundred bucks to go to Las Vegas to be a guard when Mr. Hughes left. Now, it's confusing, because someone purporting to be a Roy Crawford did call my wife in New York, and it wasn't the Roy Crawford who was an aide to Howard Hughes. So there probably was someone using the name Roy Crawford. Then, during a recess at the Las Vegas hearing in 1970, someone who wasn't too dissimilar from the real Roy Crawford did come in to shepherd Mr. Forsythe, and Forsythe testified that the guy who came in was the man he knew to be Roy Crawford."

I read as cross-examination some of the deposition questions put to Chester Davis by Phillip Bittle. "Isn't it true that Mr. Forsythe tried to ingratiate himself with you by suggesting that he was a servant of Mr. Hughes' and could be helpful to you?"

"No."

"Mr. Forsythe lied, didn't he, when he testified that he saw Howard Hughes being carried out of the Desert Inn Hotel to an automobile calling, 'Help'?"

"Well, Mr. Bittle, everything that Forsythe testified to turned out to be spurious in the sense that it did not involve the real Mr. Hughes. Whether or not Forsythe had been subjected to a mockup by some other people, I can't say. One of the reasons I took a long time in questioning Forsythe was that he appeared to be describing something which he had actually seen take place. That's what puzzled me. And as it turned out, in some aspects anyway, he was describing what I refer to as a mockup somebody put him through. But it had nothing to do with the real departure of Mr. Hughes."

The reading of the deposition of Chester Davis concluded with one subject noticeably not covered. Davis was not asked about the letter which Forsythe swore was addressed to Chester Davis, and which Forsythe had mailed from either Seattle or San Francisco in April 1976.

Earl Yoakum next called Dean Elson, a retired FBI agent who had worked for Robert Maheu in Las Vegas from 1969 to 1971. During the 1970 hearing in Las Vegas, Elson received a phone call from someone stating that he had information concerning Hughes' departure from Las Vegas. Elson flew to Los Angeles, and, in a bar in the International Hotel, he met LeVane Forsythe and another man.

"LeVane Forsythe said that he had been contacted by someone named Crawford in Las Vegas and asked to be at the Desert Inn Hotel at nine o'clock on Thanksgiving Eve, 1970. When he arrived, Forsythe was told that he was to be a perimeter guard in the north parking lot of the hotel and to not let anybody come through who didn't wear an identifying button. Around one A.M. two men carried an elderly, feeble man from the hotel to the car. Forsythe said he could not identify the man but heard him say, 'Get me Bob Maheu!'

"Forsythe said that later he read about charges of kidnapping in the departure of Hughes, and that he had received some strange telephone calls from people who refused to identify themselves. Forsythe said that he didn't know the good guys from the bad guys, and that he had done nothing wrong, but that he was afraid he might have been involved in a kidnapping."

Elson convinced Forsythe to return to Las Vegas and tell his story to Bob Maheu's lawyer and to the FBI and the sheriff in Las Vegas; and Forsythe did, and repeatedly offered to take a lie detector test.

In cross-examination, Elson admitted that at no time did LeVane Forsythe, or his friend, or anybody representing Forsythe ask Elson or Bob Maheu or anyone else for any money for Forsythe's cooperation.

"From your investigation of all the facts, did LeVane Forsythe lie about what he had said he had seen?"

"Well, when Forsythe was on the stand, he was badly confused about the chronology of events. It was pathetic. But he gave the same story on the witness stand that he gave to me and to Mr. Maheu. Where Forsythe made himself look bad was in recalling the chronology of what happened. Forsythe would relate incidents happening at one time when they actually happened later, and it became awfully jumbled."

"Did you ever come across any evidence contrary to the evidence given by LeVane Forsythe concerning the departure of Howard Hughes from the Desert Inn?"

"No."

Contestants' next witness against Forsythe was Robert M. Ornstein, a Los Angeles attorney, who testified that in December 1972, while working for InterTel in New York, he was assigned to Los Angeles to interview LeVane Forsythe. Ornstein phoned Forsythe's mother's house and went there in an effort to find Forsythe, but was unsuccessful.

On cross-examination, Ornstein admitted that his memory of having gone to see Forsythe on InterTel's business was refreshed by a memo. With that testimony, I was able to get the memo into evidence:

The investigator said he was unaware of any change in Forsythe's testimony in the Maheu hearing from the first time the investigator had heard it. He knew of no perjury by Forsythe, nor of any attempt by anyone to persuade Forsythe to perjure himself or change his story in any way.

Phillip Bittle next read the deposition testimony of a custodian of the records at Hughes Aircraft to show that LeVane Forsythe, Jr., was hired on March 21, 1972, after making a written application for employment. Bittle followed with a reading of the deposition of LeVane Forsythe, Jr., who testified that he had not been prompted to make his application for a job at Hughes Aircraft by any suggestion from his father. But his father did tell him some time after February 1977 that a Dan Harper had threatened to get Forsythe, Jr. fired if Dad didn't tell that it was he who had delivered that envelope to Melvin Dummar.

I read the cross-examination of LeVane Forsythe, Jr. "Are you certain that at the time you applied for work with Hughes Aircraft, you did not discuss the matter with your father?"

"I could have."

"Were you hired the very day you applied at Hughes Aircraft?"

"That or the following day."

"During the six years of your employment, were there, in your division, layoffs of men who had more seniority than you?"

"Yes."

After the adjournment following the reading of Forsythe, Jr.'s, deposition, Sam and I returned to the Las Palmas Apartments and saw Wilbur Dobbs waiting for us, pained and pacing over a carpet of half-smoked cigarettes. "Hal! Ah just heard from Houston! We lost!"

"I hope they said that we put up a good fight."

"The judge called the case an' asked if you were there."

"What did I say?"

"When nobody answered, he sent his bailiff out into the hall an' the bailiff called your name three times."

"I guess I didn't hear him."

"When the bailiff reported that nobody answered for us, the judge told the contestants to proceed. They read a few pages of the deposition of Grace Kemp that it was a forgery."

"Did they read the good stuff she said about the small x?"

"And then the judge ruled that it was a forgery an' threw out our petition!"

"Wil, you seem sad. Don't be sad, Wil. Come on in and we'll have a drink and then you won't be sad anymore."

Earl Yoakum rose and addressed the Court. "Your Honor, Ah wish to offer into evidence a death certificate of someone named Claude Forsythe." Yoakum faced Judge Hayes and, pretending to address him, reviewed the matter for the benefit of the jurors. "Your Honor may recall that we've heard the testimony of LeVane Forsythe that he had an uncle Claude Forsythe, an ex-federal marshal, who was one of the guards on the train when Mr. Hughes went to Boston from Los Angeles in 1966. May a certified copy of the death certificate of Claude Forsythe be admitted into evidence?"

"It may be admitted," Hayes said.

"With Your Honor's permission, Ah wish to read this here death certificate to the jury." Yoakum slowly walked to the jury holding the death certificate out at arm's length as though it contained the answer everyone had been waiting for. "It says here that the deceased, Claude Forsythe, died in Los Angeles, California, on June the 1st, 1961!"

During the next recess, I phoned LeVane Forsythe in Anchorage. "Lee, they just hit us with evidence that your Uncle Claude died five years before Howard Hughes' 1966 train trip to Boston!"

"Is that when he died? Well, Uncle Claude used to work for Hughes, I know that. An' he made a lot of trips for him. An' it just seems to me he was on that train to Boston, but if he died five years earlier, I guess I must be mistaken."

"Do you know what this mistake makes you look like?"

"Rhoden, why is it that every time you call me, you're bitchin' about some little mistake I made? I told you before, I ain't no fuckin' memory machine! Now if my mistakes give you a problem, I'm sorry, but that's the way it goes, you know what I mean?"

59. INCOMPETENT OR CROOKED

The second of the three handwriting experts the contestants called live was Jeremy Bluedecker. Unlike Spencer Otis, Jeremy Bluedecker enjoyed smiling. A retired special agent for the FBI, he had been hired by Chester Davis of Summa, through InterTel, for $16,000. Bluedecker testified under Rex Clairbourne's questions that handwriting examination is a science. "Yes, if two handwriting experts are diametrically opposed, it follows that one of them is incompetent or crooked."

Bluedecker had made no study of Hughes' writing before he examined the original will in Las Vegas. After two hours he concluded that it was a forgery. He could spot a forgery, he said, without looking at any exemplars. He could tell from the pen lifts in illogical places, retouchings, and tremors.

After a three-hour direct, Clairbourne turned him over to me for cross. During his career with the FBI, Mr. Bluedecker had qualified as an expert in photography, typewritings, inks, glue, shoe prints, and tire treads.

"How many will cases have you handled?"

"Four."

"How many of those did you determine were forgeries?"

"This is my first."

"You didn't make a written report to the attorneys who hired you in this case, did you?"

"No. Mr. Yoakum and Mr. Clairbourne asked me not to."

"Before you made your examination, were you aware of the opinion of the celebrated Spencer Otis that this will was a rank forgery?"

"Yes."

"Are you a very close friend of Spencer Otis?"

"No, I wouldn't say that."

"Yes, you would. You did in your deposition last year. You said, '*I am a very close friend of Spencer Otis.*'"

"Well, let's say, just a friend."

"Are you also just a friend of FBI agent Parker Saeta?"

"Yes."

"Did you speak to him about this case after you had examined the will and while he was examining it?"

"Yes."

"You testified on direct that if two handwriting experts are diametrically opposed, one of them is either incompetent or crooked. Do you really mean that?"

"Yes, sir, I do."

"Did you ever testify in a case against Rupert Ingersol?"

"Yes."

"Since you and he were diametrically opposed, does that mean that Mr. Ingersol, a witness whose testimony was presented by the contestants, is either incompetent or crooked?"

"Yes, that is my opinion."

"And one of the top men in the field of handwriting comparison in the United States is Dudley Woodcock. Do you have the same opinion of him, having been diametrically opposed to him?"

"Yes."

"A handwriting expert from Amsterdam, Holland, Hans Verhaeren, gave an opinion diametrically opposed to yours. He studied the will not for hours, but for weeks before he reached even a tentative opinion. And then for many more weeks, he compared it to numerous exemplars, and supported his opinion in a one-hundred-page report. Do you know all of the factors upon which Mr. Verhaeren based his opinion?"

"Not all of them."

"Without knowing all the factors upon which Mr. Verhaeren based his opinion, you still tell us that he is either incompetent or crooked?"

"I still say it."

"And what about Pierre Faideau of Paris and Henri Ollivier of Marseilles? In your opinion are those two men either incompetent or crooked?"

"I would have to say yes."

"Spencer Otis testified for the contestants that it was a rank forgery by an amateur. But Rupert Ingersol, in his deposition read by the contestants, said that it might be a highly sophisticated simulation. With which do you agree?"

"I don't agree with either."

"FBI expert Saeta testified in his deposition for the contestants that the forger was skillful enough to keep out his own handwriting characteristics. Do you agree?"

"I do not agree that the forger was skillful."

"Mr. Saeta testified that the forms of many letters in the will were very similar to those in the exemplars. But Mr. Saeta also testified that not one letter in the will was similar to those in the exemplars. With which statement of his do you agree?"

"I don't agree with either of them."

"But, didn't you find some letter forms in the exemplars similar to the letter forms in the will?"

"Some are similar. Some are not."

"The FBI expert, Mr. Saeta, testified that the upper portion of the small *g* in the will was always shaped in the same fashion."

"I must say that Mr. Saeta was wrong. There are considerable variations in the upper part and in the bottom part of the small *g* both in the exemplars and in the will. Both have a very wide variation. But the capital *G* is clearly an indication of forgery."

"Is it? Isn't the capital *G* in the offered will in the word *Gabbs* very, very similar to the capital *G* in exemplar 101 written by Mr. Hughes? Please look at this."

"I've never seen this *G* in 101 before. Yes, I see what you're pointing to. The two *G*'s are similar. But my opinion was not based solely on the capital *G*."

"Now, let's turn to some of the other bases for your opinion that the will is a forgery. One was the overwriting in the will?"

"Yes."

"Note in the word *signed* at the end of the will, the *e-d*. Did this indicate to you a forgery?"

"Yes, in the absence of similar overwritings in the exemplars."

"Look at the word *guide* in exemplar 95, written in 1968 by Mr. Hughes. Note the *d-e* in *guide* and compare it to the *e-d* in *signed*. Aren't these overwritings strikingly similar?"

"Yes."

"How do you explain the similarity?"

"Coincidence."

"What about the overwriting of the *r* in *revolk*?"

"The forger was trying to cover up a pen lift when he reworked the *r*."

"Mr. Bluedecker, do you really mean that? Between the *r* and the *e* isn't there an obvious pen lift that wasn't reworked?"

"Yes."

"Then why would the writer have tried to cover up a pen lift in the *r* and not a second pen lift in the linking line after the *r* going into the *e*?"

"I don't know."

"Mr. Bluedecker, throughout the will, there are many instances of overwritings, such as in *Las* in *Las Vegas*. Is it your opinion that since the forger didn't like the way he wrote it the first time, he decided to write it over several times and make it better, thinking that maybe nobody would notice that he had rewritten it several times?"

"That might have been the purpose of the forger. But, I want to suggest to you that it is possible that the forger intended this as a joke."

"As a what?"

"As a joke."

"In the 'Dear Chester and Bill' letter, are there any similar overwritings, which you suggest was used as a model by the forger?"

"There may be some."

"Look and show me one."

He looked. "I don't see any."

"Do you think that the supposed forger used the *Dear Chester and Bill* letter as a model from which to copy?"

"It is obvious from the many overwritings in the will that the forger couldn't have copied them from the published writing of the *Dear Chester and Bill* letter, because there aren't any in it. I don't know what he used as a model."

"You found pen lifts with blunt endings and blunt beginnings in illogical places in the will, didn't you?"

"Yes, I did, and these are always indications of forgery."

After showing him several exemplars, I asked, "Didn't you find the same thing in the exemplars?"

"It is true there are some. I admit this."

"What about the tremulous lines in the questioned will? Didn't you find the same tremulous lines in the exemplars?"

"Tremulous lines, yes, but not the same kind. You must remember that it is extremely important that we use contemporaneous exemplars. You can't compare the writings of Mr. Hughes in the 1940s or 1950s with his writing in 1968."

"But, Montgomery Bagby testified in his deposition for the contestants that it didn't make any difference when the exemplars were written. He said that all of them were of equal significance because Mr. Hughes wrote the same way throughout all his life. Do you agree with him?"

"I do not."

"What about the size of the letters in the will?"

"The letters in the will are smaller than those in the exemplars."

"In the *Dear Chester and Bill* letter you will notice a small *e* in the word *Dear*. Compare that *e* with the *e* in the word *memory* in the will. Which is larger?"

"Obviously, the *e* in *memory* in the will is much larger."

"We could take a day doing this, but, instead, will you admit that there are many letters in the questioned will which are much larger than the letters in many exemplars?"

"I'll save you the time. Yes, many are larger in the questioned will."

"From your examination of the samples of Melvin Dummar's handwriting, are you going to tell us that he wrote the will?"

"I have no opinion on that."

"Did you examine the Pitney Bowes imprint on the back of the envelope?"

"Under magnification, yes."

"Was the imprint made by a Pitney Bowes machine, or by a tattoo artist?"

"The imprint was not put there by hand."

"And your opinion is diametrically opposed to the opinion of Spencer Otis on this point, isn't it?"

"Yes."

The night after Bluedecker finished, I poured myself a brandy and walked out to the pool area to relax, and found Sam out there relaxing ahead of me. After two hours of reviewing the evidence, Sam said, "I wonder if all the questions'll ever be answered. You could examine the evidence and be forced to conclude that the will could not have been written by Howard Hughes. He'd never have wanted his will delivered to Melvin Dummar. That is, if he had ever met Melvin Dummar. And you could examine other evidence—the ink, the medical, the handwriting— and be forced to conclude that the will could not possibly be a forgery. And yet it's got to be one or the other! I wonder if all of the questions'll ever be answered."

I wondered with him. We wondered for another hour.

60. THE RAPIER

Earl Yoakum called the last of contestants' handwriting experts, Edwin Arledge of Chicago. Tall, grandfatherly, Edwin Arledge smiled when his name was called, and seemed to be a likable and gentle man. As Sam Mayerson watched Arledge walk to the witness stand, he whispered, "Be careful with this guy, the jurors are going to love him."

Edwin Arledge testified under Rex Clairbourne's direct that in November 1976, he was hired by Earl Yoakum to examine the original will in Las Vegas. He compared the will to exemplars 2 and 4, the originals of two memos Howard Hughes had written to his lawyer Bob Edison. The same day Arledge concluded that the will was a forgery. After that he saw other exemplars in Spencer Otis' office.

Dashes instead of periods in the will was one factor that led to his conclusion. And he found the evidence overwhelming that the forger had used as a model for his copying Hughes' *Dear Chester and Bill* letter published in either *Life* magazine or in the book *Hoax* or both.

During a recess in Arledge's testimony, Earl Yoakum, seated alone at his counsel table, stared at a closed file, then motioned for me to come over to him. "Hal, Ah want to tell you somethin'." He looked up at me without smiling. "Ah've really come to like you. Ah want you to know that."

"I like you too, Earl, but you must promise that you won't kiss me in front of the jurors. We don't want them to—"

"Ah mean this! Hal, Ah'm sorry for what's gonna happen. Ah want you to know when it happens, that Ah'm sorry for you personally. As a lawyer Ah'm gonna enjoy what it's gonna do to your case, but Ah'm not gonna enjoy what it's gonna do to you."

"What are you talking about, Earl?"

"Ah can tell you now because there's nothin' you can do to stop it. An' there's no way you can prepare for it. Ah'm not gonna tell you what it is, but Ah cain tell you that a long sharp rapier is goin' to be thrust straight into your belly up to the hilt, an' it's goin' to hurt like all hell!"

"When am I going to get it?"

"Sometime before the end of the day. An' when it happens, Hal, keep in mind, will you, that Ah'm sorry for you."

Earl Yoakum seemed to mean what he said. No grin, no chuckles, no wink. He seemed to mean it.

After the recess, Rex Clairbourne asked Edwin Arledge, "Did you find anything significant when you studied the first line of the questioned will where the words *I, Howard R. Hughes, being of* appear?"

"Yes, I did. Quite significant! I found that in the name *Howard R. Hughes,* the first name and the middle initial were traced. They were traced from a signature on page one of the Answers to Interrogatories published in the book *Hoax.*"

For the next fifteen minutes, there was no sound in the courtroom other than the voices of Rex Clairbourne and Edwin Arledge.

"First, how can a tracing be accomplished?"

"The forger places the model over a glass table with a light coming from underneath, tracing the signature by placing the paper on which the writing is traced over the copy."

"Was the last name also traced?"

"No, it was a freehand attempted imitation."

"Can you prove this to us?"

"Yes, I can."

Arledge then used a projector to show on a screen an enlargement of the two signatures made from a transparency of the *Howard R.* in the will, and *Howard R.* published in the book *Hoax.* Arledge used a pointer. "You will see that it is a very, very close superimposition. The length is very close. The height is very close. The *R,* I admit, is offset—it does not superimpose. I am convinced that this is because the paper slipped, and that is why the *R* does not match up and is not in its proper place. But when we match up the two *R*'s we again find a very, very close superimposition. It is true, however, that the original *R* contained in the signature in the book *Hoax* has a longer staff to it. That is because the forger was a careless tracer."

"Mr. Arledge, what do you conclude from all this?"

"This is overwhelming evidence that the portions of the signature that I've shown you were a traced forgery. You will note that the signature as reproduced in the book *Hoax* is a reduced copy. The original was much larger. And yet, the first name and the middle initial as they appear in the original of the will are practically the same size as the reduced size in the book. This smallness is a vital factor."

"Are you absolutely sure it is a tracing, Mr. Arledge?"

"Absolutely!"

It looked like a tracing to me, too.

Rex Clairbourne turned to me and smiled. "Do you wish to cross-examine, Mr. Rhoden?"

When Clairbourne turned Edward Arledge over for cross-examination, I felt like a fighter on the canvas hearing the nine count and praying for the bell, and the bell sounded as Judge Hayes said, "We'll take a ten-minute recess."

As soon as the jurors had filed out of the room, Sam said, "Don't cross-examine him! It's too risky!"

"I've got to! If I don't, this is the end of the case!"

"Hal, you can't match with him! Don't try! He's an expert—he's had a lifetime in this field—it'll only make it worse!"

"It can't be any worse, Sam. This is the ballgame!"

During the short recess, I examined the two transparencies made by Arledge, and when I finished and walked back to our counsel table I saw the grin on Rex Clairbourne's face and the look on Yoakum's face asking, See what I meant?"

I plopped down in my chair, because I was too weak to keep standing. For the first time since the trial had begun, six months earlier, I faced the prospect of losing. And I thought of what losing would mean.

"Hal," Sam said, "wave him off as though it weren't important! It's bad, but if you cross-examine, he may kill you."

"Sam, I don't have anything to lose."

"Mr. Arledge, on this sheet of paper tacked to this board, I'm going to draw in red, *Howard R.* as it appears on the questioned will. It won't be a perfect drawing—just an illustration of what you and I are going to talk about." I did. "Now, I'm going to draw, superimposed on the red—but this time with a blue crayon—*Howard R.* as it appears in the transparency you made from *Hoax*." As I did, Arledge shouted, "That is not an accurate drawing! And that's not the way the forger saw it!" The gentle grandfather had become a screeching sergeant.

"Please, Mr. Arledge, I didn't mean to offend you. I know that my drawing isn't perfect. It's only so that you and I can point to what you found to help the jurors better understand us. Now, Mr. Arledge—"

"I know what you're up to!" he hollered. "And I'm not going to comment on anything you've drawn on that board!"

"Mr. Arledge, I'm going to ask you questions, and you are going to give answers! If you say that what I've drawn on this board is not accurate, you can point that out to the jurors and we'll let them compare the transparencies to what I've drawn. Now, sir, don't tell me what you're not going to comment on!" I knew that I had overstepped my bounds by instructing the witness like that, but with the quicksand I was in, there was no way that Judge Hayes was going to order me to sink standing at attention.

I pointed out to Arledge the differences between *Howard R.* as it appeared on line two of the questioned will and as it appeared in the publication in *Hoax*. The first name and the initial *R* were wider in the questioned will than in the book *Hoax*. And taller in the will.

"That's because the forger was not a skillful tracer."

The initial stroke of the *H* in the will was different from and larger than the initial stroke in the *H* in the book.

The shape of the *o* and the lines leading to and from it were different in the two in their form and position.

I pointed out the differences in the form and position of the two *w*'s, the *a*'s, the *r*'s and the *d*'s, and in the ending strokes. And the two middle *R*'s were not only in the same place but had other obvious differences.

"Now, Mr. Arledge, why is it that of all the handwriting experts who have testified in this case—including the illustrious Spencer Otis, and ex-FBI agent Jeremy Bluedecker—you alone found that there was a tracing?"

"I don't know."

"If this were really a tracing, wouldn't the attorneys for the contestants have let their other handwriting experts in on this secret so that they could also testify to this and support you?"

"I don't know!" he snapped.

"Now, if this were really a tracing, that would be conclusive evidence of forgery and there wouldn't be any need for any other testimony on any other aspect of the handwriting. Isn't that true?"

"The tracing is itself conclusive! My other observations are in support of my opinion."

"As a matter of fact, if this were a tracing, there wouldn't be any need for the contestants to present any evidence on any other subject matter in this case, would there?"

"It is a tracing!"

"If it really were a tracing, why are there so many differences between what was traced and what you call the tracing in the offered will?"

"That signature is traced!" he shouted again.

"There are three signatures, one at the bottom of each page, and there's a fourth on the envelope in addition to the *Howard R.* on line two. Why do you suppose that a forger would have traced only the writing on line two—and not even the last name—and not any of the other three signatures in the will or the signature on the envelope or any of the other three hundred words in the will?"

"When he found that the tracing didn't work well on line two, he decided to use the freehand method for the rest."

"You mean, he decided not to continue tracing because the tracing was not a good tracing?"

"Ask the forger!"

"Mr. Arledge, what is your fee in this case?"

"Ten thousand dollars and expenses of five thousand."

"Come now, Mr. Arledge, surely you're going to bill Mr. Yoakum for a lot more than that for your superb work in this case, particularly for your work on the tracing."

"I've put in in excess of five hundred hours and I charge seventy dollars an hour. I suppose there may be a further bill of perhaps around thirty-five thousand more."

"That's more like it. Mr. Arledge, you said that one reason that you found the will to be a forgery was that the writing in this was smaller than the writing in Mr. Hughes' exemplars. If I were to show you writings from Mr. Hughes' exemplars that were smaller—smaller in letters and in words—than the writing in the will, would you be willing to admit as to just this one factor, that it was not significant?"

"I would not!"

"I have no further questions."

Could it be a tracing? My God, could I have been wrong about the whole case? About the evidence that made a forgery impossible, about the ink and the medical evidence and the handwriting, about the evidence that Forsythe could not have made up this story about knowing Hughes?

No, it couldn't possibly be a tracing.

Couldn't it?

No!

That evening in my apartment, Sam and Wilbur and Linda and I anguished over this testimony of tracing. There were good arguments against it, but Arledge's testimony and his demonstration could mean disaster. The jurors could be so impressed with Arledge's tracing testimony that they ignored all the evidence that the will was genuine.

"What do you do about it?" Sam asked. "If you call back your other handwriting experts to testify that it isn't a tracing, you know what you'll face."

"Sur-rebuttal."

"You can count on it! They'll recall Otis and Bluedecker back to testify that it's a tracing. Right now, you've got only Arledge against you on the tracing. None of their other experts backed him up, and the fact that they didn't, weakens Arledge's tracing opinion. But if you recall any of your experts to say it's not a tracing, the contestants are bound to recall Otis and Bluedecker and make it three against you instead of one."

"What do you think, Wil?"

"Ah need another drink!"

"I sat there in court today," Linda said, "listening to Arledge as the jurors did, and if I had to cast a vote right now, and I were going to be honest, I'd have to vote that it's a forgery."

Sam said, "How much time do you think you'll have before they rest and you've got to decide about rebuttal?"

"If Bittle and Yoakum are smart, they won't allow me any time to decide. They'll rest tomorrow morning and end their case with the only big punch they've had in it."

The morning headline in the *Las Vegas Sun* read:

BOMBSHELL EVIDENCE EXPLODES IN HUGHES' WILL TRIAL

The morning headline in the *Review Journal* read:

MORMON WILL TRACED

61. CONTESTANTS REST

On May 3, 1978, instead of resting their case at its dramatic peak after Edwin Arledge left the stand, Bittle and Yoakum read the deposition of Howard Hughes' live-in barber in the Desert Inn. On cross-examination, the barber testified that there were no scars around Mr. Hughes' eyes or cheeks, although the barber had said in a signed statement to me that Mr. Hughes had a scar on his left cheek about an inch long, and that every time he trimmed Mr. Hughes' beard, he was careful because Mr. Hughes did not want the scar to be left naked. This insignificant testimony was followed by the insignificant testimony of a few other witnesses who served only to dull the sting of the tracing testimony of Edwin Arledge.

The weekend following Arledge's testimony, Marvin Mitchelson flew in from Los Angeles to insist that I recall our experts to testify that what Arledge called a tracing was not a tracing. "I don't care what it costs, I'll pay it! This case can't be lost on some chickenshit point about a tracing that isn't a tracing!"

"Marvin, that it isn't a tracing can be argued and demonstrated in final summation."

"It can be argued in final summation a hell of a lot better if you have experts to back you up! A lawyer saying it isn't a tracing is one thing, a handwriting expert saying it isn't a tracing is another. You've got to recall our experts! At least one! Just one, for chrissakes!"

Sam calmly argued the other side. "Marvin, if we recall any of our experts in rebuttal, it'll be a sign to the jurors that we've been hurt by this evidence—hurt so badly we've had to recall an expert from Europe to rebut it. It'll give undue emphasis to the tracing. That's one problem with putting on a rebuttal."

"If we don't put on a rebuttal," Marvin said, "that tracing is going to remain a tracing that could kick all of us out of Las Vegas!"

"Marvin, it's good of you to offer to put up the money," I said, "but even if we had time to get an expert back here, what could he testify to? With any two signatures made by the same person—if they occupy approximately the same space on the paper, and are roughly the same length and height—it could be argued that one could have been traced from the other. Look here." I showed him two photographs of Hughes' signatures on the bottom of two pages of Answers to Interrogatories. The two signatures were almost exactly the same height and length. Each letter, each link, was different, but if one signature were superimposed on the other, it could be argued that one was traced from the other, and that the differences were the result of sloppy tracing by the forger, as Arledge argued. "If we recall an expert to testify that looking only at the two *Howard R*'s, he's positive that it's not a tracing, this would weaken his credibility on everything else because it is possible that what Arledge showed us was a bad tracing. On the other hand, if our expert says that while it's his opinion that the *Howard R.* in the will is not traced, it is possible that it was, of what value is he? Either way, all an expert can do is hurt us."

"Hal, I've got about a quarter of a million dollars stuck in this case! And this whole case may hinge on that fucking tracing testimony! You can't just argue it before a jury without evidence in rebuttal to back yourself up!"

"There are several arguments," Sam said, "that Arledge is as wrong about the tracing as Otis was wrong about the Pitney Bowes tattoo."

"Marvin, you may be right," I said. "But I'm inclined to agree with Sam. Throughout this trial, the contestants have insisted that Dummar used the book *Hoax* as a model for his hoax. I can take that argument and twist it back at them, and point out that in this courtroom, the jurors did, indeed, see an attempt to perpetrate a hoax. First by Spencer Otis with his certainty about a fake Pitney Bowes imprint—which they can see is ridiculous. And then the attempt by Edwin Arledge with his certainty that because two signatures are similar in size—despite differences in every letter and in every link—that one absolutely had to be traced from the other."

We had the rest of the weekend to talk about it.
We talked about nothing else.

On Sunday afternoon, Marvin said that he wanted to search through the eighty-two promissory notes with Hughes' signature to see if there were some where Hughes wrote his signature as small as it was when reproduced in the book *Hoax* and as small as *Howard R.* on line two of the will.

"Marvin, let's face it! The size of the signature in the book is small. When the original was photographed, it was made smaller to fit the page in the book. And that same reduced size is about the size of *Howard R.* on line two of the will! You aren't going to find any true-size signatures of Hughes that small. You're wasting your time!"

Marvin searched through the signatures while Sam and I talked it out at the pool. An hour later, Linda ran out and called us back in. Marvin had found five samples of Hughes' signatures: two almost the identical size of the *Howard R.* in the questioned will, two more only slightly larger, and one that was smaller than in the will.

"And I just got a call back from Verhaeren," Marvin said. "I asked him to look at the so-called tracing."

"What did he say?"

"He's still laughing. Hal, you've got to recall him to testify that it's not a tracing! Please! If you don't, you may regret it as long as you live!"

"If I do, Marvin, I may regret that as long as I live."

Contestants then presented the testimony of several more witnesses on minor matters, for a total of forty-one witnesses, thirteen by deposition, taking six weeks. On May 4, 1978, when Judge Hayes looked at Bittle and Yoakum and said, "Call your next witness," Phillip Bittle rose to say, "Contestants Cameron, DePould, and Roberts rest."

And Earl Yoakum said, "Contestant Annette Gano Lummis rests."

Judge Hayes looked at me, and I imagined that he was thinking, What have you decided?

"No rebuttal."

62. OPENING ARGUMENT

On May 23, 1978, at 9:30 A.M., as reported in volume ninety-seven beginning at page 11,928 of the official transcript, the opening argument for the proponent began:

"Howard Hughes wrote it.

"You know that.

"You know that from evidence about the ink. From evidence about Hughes' medical condition in 1968. From the opinion of our handwriting experts and from contestants' experts, and from what you could see with your own eyes.

"You know that Howard Hughes wrote it from the testimony—not of LeVane Forsythe—you wouldn't believe that man alone—but from the testimony of the many witnesses who corroborated him. Witnesses whose credibility you can't question.

"You know that Hughes wrote it—not from the testimony of Melvin Dummar—another man you wouldn't believe if you had heard only him—but from the testimony of the many witnesses who corroborated him. Including the three FBI agents."

"If Forsythe told the truth, Howard Hughes wrote the will. To find that this is a forgery, you've got to find that LeVane Forsythe was a liar. Let's look at one of the crucial statements by Forsythe which contestants will argue is a lie.

"Forsythe said that in the summer of 1972, he went to a room in the Bayshore Inn Hotel in Vancouver, Canada and received the will from Howard Hughes. There's no possibility of mistaken identity of the man in the Bayshore Inn. Forsythe said he had known Hughes for twenty-five years. Contestants will argue that Forsythe made up this lie after Melvin Dummar failed to confess in this courtroom in January 1977. Let's reason it out.

"How, in January 1977, could LeVane Forsythe have known where Howard Hughes was in the summer of 1972? If we assume that Forsythe did some research, he might have found some five-year-old newspaper story that Hughes was in the Bayshore Inn Hotel in Canada in 1972. But what if the story were inaccurate? What if, in fact, Hughes were in London that entire summer? Forsythe would have known that if that newspaper were wrong, he could easily be proven to be a perjurer. And that could mean prison. Who would risk so much on a lie that could so easily be exposed? Would you? Would anyone who wasn't crazy?

"I challenge opposing counsel to explain—if Forsythe's story is a lie—when he began the lie. If Forsythe began the lie before Hughes died, wouldn't Forsythe have planted evidence of a phony delivery on April 27, 1976, to make his story look good? Such as a Salt Lake City hotel bill? If Forsythe began the lie after January 1977, as contestants argue, how do they explain the twenty-eight one-hundred-dollar bills deposited by Forsythe the very day Hughes died, April 5, 1976? Bills which had been out of circulation since 1971. And how do they explain the hole in Forsythe's San Francisco hotel charge records on April 27, 1976?"

"Contestants will argue that Melvin Dummar made up the story about picking up an old man who said his name was Howard Hughes. Let's examine their argument. Is it reasonable that Melvin Dummar would have made up that story? If you were forging the will of a wealthy, eccentric recluse, and you wanted to concoct a story to explain your being named by him in his will, wouldn't there be two ingredients you'd be certain to put in your story? First, if it's a one-encounter story, wouldn't you make up something heroic? For example, that when you had found the old man alone in the desert being robbed and beaten by a couple of goons, you courageously fought them off at great risk to yourself, or frightened them away by pretending to have a gun? Something—anything—that would explain why the man you helped would have left you a couple of hundred million dollars in his will! Instead, what's Melvin's story? Nothing that would explain why he was named in the will of the man he said he had picked up. What does Melvin claim he did for the old man? A lift in a car to a place Melvin was driving to anyway.

"Wouldn't the second ingredient you'd put into your phony story be believability? Surely, you wouldn't invent a story that nobody would believe. Melvin's story is that in December, at midnight, off the main highway, he found an old man alone in the desert, at twenty degrees above zero, in his shirtsleeves. And Melvin gives us no explanation of what Howard Hughes could have been doing there. Would anyone wanting to be believed make up a story like that?

"You have a right to ask, 'Why would Howard Hughes have named Melvin Dummar in his will if all that happened was only what Dummar claimed had happened?' I'd like to tell you why. But I can't. I don't know why. I don't know why Howard Hughes named Dummar in his will, I don't know why Howard Hughes did any of the abnormal things he did in those last twenty years of his life. We do know from his memos that Hughes felt that everybody was out for his money. He wrote in one memo, *Nobody gives a damn about me, all they want is my money.* Here, perhaps, was one time when Hughes met a young man who was told that he was in the presence of the great Howard Hughes, but asked for nothing. Expected nothing. Received nothing. Not even a thank-you for the ride. A man who actually gave up something. A coin or two. Would you be so impressed by that that you'd leave that young man a fortune in your will? I doubt that you would. I wouldn't. But, because you and I wouldn't, does that mean that Howard Hughes wouldn't? I don't know why Howard Hughes named Dummar in his will. But he did.

"Is it reasonable that Howard Hughes would have entrusted his will to someone with instructions to deliver it to Melvin Dummar? No, it isn't reasonable. It's ridiculous. But the alternative is far more ridiculous. The alternative is that the will is a forgery by Melvin Dummar, either alone or with help. Now, all over the will you can see what the doctors saw. Scratches and pen jerks. A lack of motor control. In exemplars written by Hughes you can see the same scratches and pen jerks, the same lack of motor control caused by the kidney disease that took his life eight years later. How do contestants explain this same abnormality in the March 1968 exemplars and in the March 1968 will? Their explanation is that in April 1976, Melvin Dummar just happened to guess that in March 1968 in the Desert Inn in Las Vegas, Howard Hughes suffered from a kidney disease which caused a lack of motor control in his writing, and—without seeing any 1968 Hughes writings—Melvin was able to so perfectly duplicate that abnormality in his forgery as to fool not only handwriting experts but doctors into believing that the writer of the will suffered from a kidney disease. Hughes' personal aides didn't know that he had a kidney disease in 1968. Even Hughes' doctors didn't know. How did Melvin know?

"Impartial, uncontradicted medical testimony proved that in 1968 Howard Hughes had the kidney disease he died of in 1976. In the opinion of competent doctors—and with no contrary testimony—the will is filled with indications that it was written by someone with a kidney disease—uncontrolled strokes, the overwritings, the blatant misspellings, the telegraphic style. Are contestants going to argue that the forger just happened to have the same kidney disease that Howard Hughes had?

"You saw and you will be free to study in the jury room dozens of memos written by Howard Hughes in 1968 that show the identical abnormalities as those found in the writing on the will, evidencing the same disease. The same man wrote both."

After lunch, on the second day of my opening summation, I was sitting in the hall waiting for court to resume when Phillip Bittle walked over to me and asked if he could sit down. I told him he could and he did and said, "There's something I've wanted to tell you for a long time. I know I've said a lot of things I shouldn't have. Sometimes when I get excited, the words come out before I know it. I never meant anything personal. And if it ever came out that way, I want you to know it was unintended. I don't know exactly how to put this. I can't wish you good luck—I don't wish you good luck. But I would like to shake your hand."

We shook hands.

"Members of the jury, for you to bring in a verdict that this will is a forgery, there are certain things you've got to believe. Remember, it's Melvin or Howard. A forger unconnected with Melvin would never have put Melvin's name in the will. To believe that this is a forgery, you've got to believe that Melvin wrote it, or was in a conspiracy with whomever did. Let's examine contestants' theory and see where it will lead us. It will lead us down an alley of the absurd until we bump into a wall of the ridiculous!

"Here's what you have to believe to accept contestants' theory of a forgery. About ten days after Hughes died, there was publicity that he had not left a will. Hearing this, Melvin Dummar, working in his gas station in Willard, Utah, said to himself, 'I am going to pull off the greatest heist in history! I'm going to write a will, name myself in it, sign Howard Hughes' name to it, and get rich!'

"One of the first things Melvin decided, according to contestants, was to write a handwritten will. Not a typed will where Melvin had to forge only Hughes' signature and the names of two phony witnesses. No, Melvin decided to handwrite the whole thing. One whole page of handwriting? No, that'd be too easy. Melvin decided to forge three whole pages.

"Now, of course, Melvin had no knowledge that Howard Hughes even knew that wills could be handwritten. Would you have expected Howard Hughes to handwrite his own will? He'd have lawyers do it. But Melvin guessed that Howard Hughes had told his aides that his will was handwritten. And that Hughes had written this in one of his memos— one that Melvin could not possibly have seen. This was Melvin's first correct guess.

"Next, Melvin had to pick a date for his forged will. Everybody knows that it's the last will that gets in. Did Melvin pick a date a couple of months before Hughes died? This would have greatly lessened any chance of a later will cutting out Melvin's forgery. No, Melvin chose to date his will back to March 19, 1968, eight years earlier. And this choice of a date gave Melvin his first major problem. He had to know where Howard Hughes was on March 19, 1968. And how he was. Did Hughes have a broken hand that day leaving him unable to write? Was Hughes so busy with other matters that day that he could not have had time to write a will? What about records that might have shown that Howard Hughes was on a safari in Kenya that day? Melvin guessed that there was no proof available that Hughes could not have written a will the day Melvin selected. A second lucky guess. No doctor came in to say that Hughes was in an oxygen tent on March 19, 1968. No logs showed up to prove that Hughes could not have written a will that day.

"Next, Melvin had to know what kind of pen he ought to use. A right pen would be the kind Howard Hughes used in 1968, that is, if Hughes used any pens in 1968. Well, what kind of pen did Howard Hughes use in 1968? Whom could Melvin ask? If, in April 1976, Melvin bought a Paper Mate ballpoint pen with blue ink to forge a will dated 1968, his forgery would be laughable because that pen would have in it a type of ink which had not been manufactured until 1974. Melvin couldn't do that. But, first, Melvin had to know that he couldn't do that. How did Melvin know this? How could he possibly have known this? The ink used to write the will was Paper Mate's 307 PAGO, which was available in March 1968. How did Melvin know what ink he was using? How did he know that this was a safe selection? A safe selection? In fact, it was a brilliant selection, because this was the very ink which Howard Hughes used in March 1968 in many of his writings.

How did Melvin know what ink Howard Hughes used in his memos in March 1968? Melvin didn't have any of Hughes' memos. And Melvin couldn't have got any. And even if Melvin had borrowed or stolen one, no chemist outside the United States Treasury Department would have been able to determine what kind of ink was on it. And if Melvin had miraculously learned what kind of ink was on a March 1968 memo written by Hughes, where could Melvin have found that ink? It had been off the market for four years. And if he had found it, how would he have known it when he found it? How could Melvin Dummar have known Paper Mate's 307 PAGO from any of the thousands of other inks? How did Melvin solve this ink problem? What do counsel for contestants suggest? That Melvin went to the FBI Forgery Information Service for a little assistance?

"But, contestants will offer an alternative theory. Chance! Pure chance! That is, in 1976, Melvin Dummar just happened to pick—out of three thousand available inks—an ink which hadn't been on the market for four years, but which just happened to be the same kind of ink that Howard Hughes used to write memos in the month of March 1968 —the very month and year Dummar just happened to select as a date for his forged will!

"Let's look at the odds against a correct selection of Paper Mate's 307 PAGO by pure chance. In 1972 right before 307 PAGO went off the market, if that ink, along with every other available ink was poured in a different pen and the pens were dumped into a barrel, there would have been three thousand pens in the barrel. Suppose that Melvin reached into the barrel to select the right pen. Melvin wouldn't know what he was looking for, but he'd have to select the one pen that had ink in it that was available in 1968, and also the kind that Howard Hughes had used in 1968. What are the odds against Melvin selecting the one pen with Paper Mate's 307 PAGO? The answer is easy. Three thousand to one. But contestants contend that Melvin forged the will in 1976. What are the odds against Melvin, by pure chance, selecting the right pen out of the barrel in 1976? This time the answer is not quite so easy because the one pen out of three thousand which Melvin must select had been out of the barrel for four years.

"We know that Paper Mate's 307 PAGO ink is on the will dated March 19, 1968. We know that Hughes wrote memos with Paper Mate's 307 PAGO ink in March 1968. Surprising? Hardly. You'd expect that in the same month the same man would write his will and other memos with the same pen or with a similar pen out of the same batch. But if you are to conclude that the will was written by a forger, you must accept one of only two possible alternatives to explain the use of the same ink. Either the forger knew that he had to use Paper Mate's 307 PAGO ink, or he used it by pure chance. The first alternative is idiotic. The second is more so. And yet contestants must convince you to accept one of these two explanations if you are to conclude that this will is a forgery. I challenge them to offer you a third."

"Let's go on with what contestants expect you to believe in order to bring in a verdict that this will is a forgery. News that Hughes had apparently not left a will came out around April 15, 1976. The will showed up in the Mormon Church on April 27th. According to contestants, the will was forged within that twelve-day period. That gave Melvin twelve days to learn not only what ink to use, and what ink not to use, and what kind of paper to use, but also what to write in the will to make it pass, and to learn how Howard Hughes wrote each letter, and to learn all of Hughes' handwriting idiosyncrasies sufficient to fool some of the most renowned forgery detection experts in the world. All while pumping gas, going to school three nights a week, and fixing up those two apartment buildings in Ogden.

"Contestants argue that this is how speedy Melvin did it. Melvin went to the Weber State Library, took the book *Hoax*, and somehow, there in the library, lifted the section containing the photographs out of the book. But not by cutting the paper or the threads. No cut paper remains and the threads are still uncut. Melvin did that to copy the *Dear Chester and Bill* memo photographed on one of those stolen pages as his model. But after going to all this trouble to steal the model, Melvin decided not to copy his model. First, Melvin decided to use margins different from the margins on the model, but like other margins Hughes sometimes used in memos Melvin had never seen. There are no misspellings in the model. So Melvin decided to deliberately misspell words which he could spell, and to prove he could, he spelled them correctly in other parts of the same forgery. There are no dashes in the model. So Melvin decided to use a lot of dashes. There are no overwritings in the model. So Melvin decided to do a lot of overwriting in his forgery.

"Now it just so happens that each deviation from the model, was a deviation to be found in memos written by Howard Hughes in 1968. Opposing counsel expect you to conclude that each correct guess deviating from the so-called model was—are you ready for this—a coincidence!

"There's no telegraphic style in the model which contestants argue Melvin used. So Melvin decided to use a telegraphic style in places in his forged will. And, sure enough, in memo after memo written by Howard Hughes—memos which no forger could possibly have seen—Hughes used the identical telegraphic style. Nowhere in the model is a word incorrectly capitalized. But Melvin decided to write the word *my* in the middle of a sentence with a capital *M*, and again, Melvin guessed that in

many memos Howard Hughes improperly capitalized and put a capital
M on the word *my* in the middle of a sentence.

"Melvin decided to use in his forgery eight capital letters which
weren't in his model. How did Melvin know how Hughes wrote those
eight? Melvin exercised his psychic powers, and in a flash he was able to
write each of the eight capitals the odd way Hughes sometimes wrote
them, though Melvin had nothing to copy from. Amazing! Even Spencer
Otis, Mr. Bittle's chief handwriting expert, admitted that Melvin had
made some pretty good guesses when it came to those missing eight
capitals.

"What about the bequests to Hughes' aides? Melvin guessed that
Howard Hughes would have provided for his aides, not by name, but by
general category. And that is exactly what Hughes told his aides, and
that is what he wrote that he had done. Once again, lucky Melvin
guessed correctly. This is some of what you've got to believe to find that
this will is a forgery!"

"Next, Melvin decided to put a Pitney Bowes imprint on the back of
the envelope. For this, Melvin needed a Pitney Bowes imprint that had
on it 'Las Vegas, Nevada,' and for the date, March 19, 1968, or later and
the right cost to show that the imprint was actually made in 1968.
Where in Willard, Utah, could Melvin get a Las Vegas, Nevada, Pitney
Bowes machine? He had to get one in Las Vegas, Nevada. How did he
go there? When? The records show that he was at his gas station
whenever he wasn't in night school all during that April. But if Melvin
Dummar could forge a three-page will in the handwriting of Howard
Hughes, he could easily be in two places at the same time, and so,
perhaps by Magic Carpet Airlines, Melvin pops up in Las Vegas. Once
there, where was he going to get a Pitney Bowes machine? He had to
borrow one and ask that they don't look to see what he does with it.
Alone with the machine Melvin had to set the date back to March 19,
1968, and set it down to six cents. In 1976 a stamp was thirteen cents.
But when Melvin pulled his sealed envelope through the machine, he
could see that one thing he absolutely needed—the year to show that it's
old—didn't come out on the imprint. Does he put it back through the
machine a second time to get a clearer imprint? No, he goes back to
Willard with an imprint that doesn't give him one of the main things he
dashed to Las Vegas to get.

"Now if you aren't pleased with that theory of the Pitney Bowes
imprint, the contestants have an alternative for you that's even funnier.
Melvin didn't go to Las Vegas at all. Melvin, the fabulous forger, was also
a talented tattoo artist. He pecked the Pitney Bowes imprint on the
envelope by using a needle and red ink. Even under this theory that Mr.
Bittle and his handwriting expert expect you to buy, Melvin still had to
use a Pitney Bowes imprint to do the tattoo job. There he was in Willard,

Utah. How could he get a Pitney Bowes imprint with 'LAS VEGAS, NEVADA' and 'MAR' on it? By clapping for his genie? Melvin clapped for his genie, quickly acquired a copy of a Las Vegas Pitney Bows imprint and started tattooing. One thing he needed was the year 1968. So he tattooed the imprint and left off the year 1968.

"Each Pitney Bowes imprint has the machine's number on it. The number on the back of this envelope can't be seen by the naked eye. But under a high-powered microscope the FBI expert was able to read the last three digits. What a steady hand Melvin must have had! He was able to tattoo a number on that envelope which he himself could not see, but three digits of which could be seen under high-powered magnification. If our tattooing Titian had the genius to tattoo that well with his little needle, why didn't he tattoo the year 1968? He forgot. He got tired.

"This is just some of what you've got to believe to bring in a verdict that the will is a forgery! This is what contestants expect you to swallow! This is the theory with which they hope to hijack an empire!"

Throughout the four days of opening argument, I felt confident that the verdict would be that the will had been written by Howard Hughes. Sheila was confident of it, and while I worked evenings, she went house hunting to find a new home for us for our new life in Las Vegas. Sheila suggested that we name the orphanage "Hughes House." Members of the press told me that they could see that we had the verdict sewed up, and the word spread among the attachés in other courtrooms, among the guards, and among Las Vegas attorneys in the courthouse that the Mormon will was going to be admitted to probate.

63. CONTESTANTS' ARGUMENTS

On May 31, 1978, as reported in Volume 101 beginning at page 12,590, Earl Yoakum began his two-day argument chewing gum, standing behind the lectern, leaning on it to support his massive frame. "Ladies an' gentlemen of the jury, Ah'd bore you if Ah were to answer all those challenges by Mr. Rhoden. An' since Ah don't wanna bore you, Ah'm not gonna waste your valuable time answerin' him.

"This so-called Mormon will is garbage!

"A fraud! A forgery! That's evident in mah mind an' in mah heart, an' Ah believe this with every ounce of energy Ah can summon. Mr. Rhoden referred to an attempt to hijack this estate. Well, there's a hijacker in this courtroom, all right, but it's not us. It's him!" Without turning around to look at me, Earl Yoakum pointed his left thumb over his left shoulder. "It's him!"

"Now, there are a lot of things about this LeVane Forsythe—Ah cain't say his name without wantin' to vomit—that Ah know about, but Ah just cain't tell you about, because they're not in evidence. It's difficult to know things that Ah cain't tell you about, but Ah'm gonna stay within the rules.

"Friends, what we tried to do in our case is stick to the real issue. The forgery of the will. But what did Rhoden do? He began showin' a lotta things about Mr. Hughes' life, even the disgustin' details about his physical condition. This isn't a medical case! It's a forgery case. And Mr. Rhoden went into Mr. Hughes' tragic death. Why? To poison you against men who would testify that the will was a forgery—Mr. Hughes' loyal executive staff assistants—as Ah told y'all when the case began—good, God-fearin' decent Americans! But Ah'm gonna stick to the facts an' the real issues an' present the case to you fairly. Ah tell you that Dummar—whoops, that was a Freudian slip—Ah tend to confuse Rhoden and Dummar—Rhoden is saddled with two of the biggest liars in history. An' what does he do to try to take your attention away from the fact that his two star witnesses are liars? He attacks those fine men who devoted their lives to protectin' an' comfortin' an' aidin' Mr. Hughes. In comparison with Forsythe an' Dummar, Mr. Hughes' personal aides are saints.

"As for Forsythe, when Ah cross-examined that liar in his deposition in Alaska, an' proved that he was lyin' about that calendar entry on the 23rd of April 1976, Forsythe was finished. An' when Forsythe was finished, so was Rhoden. But Rhoden just doesn't know when he's finished, an' so he brings this phony case to trial at an enormous expense to this Court, to Clark County, to the citizens of Nevada, and to you!

"An' when Ah proved that Melvin Dummar's fingerprint was on the Mormon Church Visitors Center envelope, that completely destroyed Melvin Dummar, and there was no excuse after that for Rhoden continuin' with this case!

"An' after Dummar came here in January 1977 an' lied an' lied an' lied for three long days, up pops LeVane Forsythe to back him up. Mr. Rhoden then runs up to Anchorage, Alaska, anxious to find any ole witness who can save his case, an' presents in this courtroom to you jurors, the testimony of an obvious liar with a cock-an'-bull story that left so foul a stench in this courtroom that it may take years to fumigate it out!

"Nobody in the Hughes organization ever even heard of LeVane Forsythe! As to all this money that the accountant was shown by LeVane

Forsythe an' his father in the early sixties, Ah have a pretty good idea
how Forsythe came by that money, but Ah just cain't tell you what Ah
know, because it's not in evidence."

At this point, I had to object. "Your Honor, I didn't attempt to stop Mr.
Yoakum when he tried this cheap trick before, but this is enough! He
again tells the jurors that he knows of matters not in evidence. This is in
deliberate violation of the rules, and I ask that he be ordered to stop
cheating!"

Judge Hayes said, "Mr. Yoakum, I believe that Mr. Rhoden's observation is quite in order."

"Your Honor, Ah was through with the point anyway."

"And what does Rhoden say about Dummar? He admits to you that
Dummar lied an' lied an' lied, but then, Rhoden says, Mr. Dummar
suddenly decided he would lie no more. Hah! Ah tell you, if you catch a
man lyin' in somethin', you cain't believe anything he ever says. An'
Dummar is an admitted liar!

"Mr. Rhoden would have you believe that there was Mr. Hughes out
in the desert checking on his mines at midnight, in twenty-degree
weather, in his shirtsleeves, no flashlight, when up pops that guardian
angel Melvin Dummar to the rescue! Who does Rhoden think you
people are? Mindless idiots?

"If you don't swallow the desert pickup story hook, line, an' sinker,
there's no way you can find this will valid, because there's no way you
can accept it with Melvin Dummar in it as beneficiary because there's
no other reason for him to be there. Rhoden argues that because the
desert pickup story is unbelievable no liar would have made it up, an'
that's why you ought to believe it. That isn't a reason to believe it! That
it's unbelievable is a reason to not believe it!

"Dummar never picked up Hughes, an' that ought to be the end of the
case. Do you know how many, many, many times Ah've gone to people
an' Ah've asked them if they believed this story about Hughes bein'
picked up in the desert? They laugh at me when I ask them that. They
say it's the silliest thing they ever heard, an' they tell me that—"

I had to interrupt again. "Your Honor, again Mr. Yoakum is telling
these jurors about something someone said to him—matters not in
evidence—"

"Ah apologize, your Honor, Ah may have stepped a little bit outside
the record in my efforts to tell the jurors the whole truth."

"Now, as to Rhoden's handwritin' experts. Polly Jean Pfau simply
wasn't qualified. Why do you think Rhoden went to Europe? Because he
couldn't get any qualified American handwriting experts to testify for
him! An' behind it all, there was another insidious plan of Rhoden's in
bringin' two French experts here. It was because Rhoden knew it would

be extremely difficult for us to effectively cross-examine them because they had to testify through a translator.

"For Mr. Hughes to have written a will like this, he would have had to have been a nut. An' there isn't one ounce of evidence that Howard Hughes had ever lost one bit of the intellect he had had in his youth. True, he neglected himself. But this doesn't make him a nut.

"You wanna know who really wrote this will? All the evidence points to Melvin Dummar. When? About a week or so after Mr. Hughes died, an' Dummar heard that there was no will. What did Dummar use as a model? He went to the Weber State Library, an' without checkin' out the book, removed pages from it that had photographs of writin's by Howard Hughes. Dummar then dropped his forgery off at President Kimball's office in the Mormon Church Headquarters.

"An' Dummar's wife Bonnie is involved in it with him. Maybe I cain't prove it, but it's just one of those things you feel! You feel it in your soul!"

"Ladies an' gentlemen of the jury, in this case Ah haven't tried to hold any evidence back. Ah've wanted you to hear everything we knew about this case. Ah've tried to let it all hang out! This is not a case where anythin' should have been kept away from you.

"The evidence is overwhelming that Howard Hughes did not write this piece of garbage! Thank you."

After reviewing Judge Hayes' instructions to the jury for an hour, Rex Clairbourne argued that there was no reliable evidence that Mr. Hughes had a kidney disorder in March 1968.

"The model used by the forger was the *Dear Chester and Bill* letter written in 1970, and published in *Life* magazine in 1971 and later in the book *Hoax*. Mr. Rhoden's attempt to ridicule our fine American handwriting experts accomplished nothing. Mr. Rhoden said that our handwriting experts would have been better prepared if they had spent a little more time training with their seeing-eye dogs. But the integrity of these experts and their competence is not affected by Mr. Rhoden's sarcasm.

"As for the conclusive evidence of tracing, so brilliantly presented to you by Mr. Edwin Arledge of Chicago, it was absolutely devastating! Mr. Rhoden threw a challenge at me in his opening argument. He said, 'If Rex Clairbourne tells you that there are no exemplars of signatures of Mr. Hughes' where the writing is as small as that in *Howard R.* on the second line of the will, I will show you several, including at least one even smaller than that name in the will.' Well, I'm not interested in Mr. Rhoden's games. That it was a tracing was obvious when you saw it, and it's obvious now.

"I ask you, just take a look at the will, and at any one of the first ten exemplars in this case, and look at them side by side, and ask yourself, Did the same man write both? You will see by an arm's-length inspection of the so-called will with any of these exemplars, that the same man did not write both. Mr. Rhoden and his experts scoffed at a gross inspection, such as the kind I suggest to you. Let Mr. Rhoden and his experts scoff! Common sense tells you that when two handwritings don't look alike, they are not written by the same man.

"Since I'll have no opportunity to argue again, I urge that if Mr. Rhoden launches into a personal attack against me, or against Mr. Bittle or against Mr. Yoakum, that you make him stick to the evidence in this case. Let's not have any more smoke and diversions!

"I hope that after the trial I will be able to shake your hands. It would be inappropriate to do so now."

Phillip Bittle closed the argument for contestants as reported in Volume 104 beginning at page 12, 1915:

"Mr. Rhoden referred to phases. The ink phase. The medical phase. But I call it fiction. The ink fiction. The medical fiction. His whole case is one big fiction! And so, in reviewing it, I'll give titles for the chapters of his fiction.

"The first chapter I would entitle, 'Got Smart.'" Phillip Bittle then reviewed Melvin Dummar's admitted lies, and Forsythe's inconsistencies about his entry of airline flights on April 23, 1976.

"The next chapter I entitle, 'Why Was There No Weeping at Weber?' This chapter deals with why Melvin Dummar lied, why he first denied being in Weber State Library and then later, when he knew we had him cornered, admitted that he was there. I would call all of Dummar's testimony the four F's. Fiction, Fantasy, Fabrication, and Forgery.

"The next chapter I call 'Dietrich's Revenge.' Dietrich wanted revenge for having been fired by Mr. Hughes, and that's why we had all of this evidence about Mr. Hughes' bathroom and urinal habits and enemas. It was Mr. Dietrich's way to hurt Mr. Hughes in the one thing Mr. Hughes treasured above all else: privacy. And who is responsible for getting Mr. Dietrich his revenge? Mr. Rhoden.

"The next chapter is entitled 'Cadillac or Cab?' Now the handwriting experts we called, are they Cadillacs or cabs? Respected experts such as Spencer Otis, Jeremy Bluedecker, Edwin Arledge, Parker Saeta of the FBI, are they Cadillacs? Or are they cabs, such as the experts Mr. Rhoden called?

"Yes, Edwin Arledge, who proved to you that part of the offered will is nothing but an amateurish tracing, and Mr. Spencer Otis did get a little feisty when Mr. Rhoden launched into one of his sarcastic cross-examinations. I don't blame those experts for having turned on Mr. Rhoden! You would too, if your competence and integrity were ridiculed in that manner.

"We have in our church literature a little parable which might keep you from being misled by Mr. Rhoden. It's about five blind men in a remote village in India.

"In this village the elephant had been unknown. The five blind men would sit and hold discourses about things outside reality that they couldn't perceive without sight, and they tried to learn as much as they could by sharing their impressions to the extent they could get them in a tactile or sensory way other than through the eyes.

"So these blind men hear the word that an elephant is coming. What's an elephant? They didn't know! They're very excited! This is new knowledge that might be shared among people by the roadside in their day-to-day discussions. There was quite a commotion! They can hear the sound growing louder! Four of them get up and rush out to the roadside, and whoever is leading the elephant is making it run, so they get only a brief, very incomplete sensation.

"One of the blind men touches the trunk and thinks he's got a feel for what it is. Another one brushes his hand across the side. Another one grabs onto the tail and holds on a little bit. Another one touches the leg, or one of the legs. So these four men go back to where the fifth one is, who has chosen, for one reason or another, not to go out.

"The fifth happens to be the wise one. And they start debating. What is a true elephant? What is it like?

"One starts saying what a true elephant is—because he perceived it, and the truth is that it's like a snake. Another one says, No, it's truly like a rope—that is, the tail is like a rope and the trunk is like a snake, a snake with a big ball on it, the head. The other one says, No, it's like a walking wall, having touched the sides. And the fourth one said, It's like a tree.

"And while they're arguing so strenuously, the fifth one traces an outline of the true configuration, the whole picture of the elephant. That's his wisdom as we're told by the parable. And it's true, ladies and gentlemen.

"It's interrelated truth!

"So perspective—getting the right perspective—the right distance, is particularly true of handwriting. That is what Mr. Otis was talking about. I hope that this explanation will be of help to you."

"The next chapter, concerning Mr. Hughes' death in Acapulco, I call 'Death and Defamation.' Here, Mr. Rhoden tried to show you that all of the men around Mr. Hughes were vultures! Quacks! Murderers! What is this case about? Truth, not murder! And what is the truth? The truth is that you have seen fraud in this courtroom. The same kind of fraud that Bonnie Dummar was convicted of, and for which she spent ninety days in jail under our American judicial system.

"As to the ink evidence, how reliable are chemical tests to distinguish anything? Is it margarine or is it butter? You can tell by your taste. What does the color test tell you? Maybe nothing. They look awfully much the same. Then we go to the animal level. Then we get to persons and back to things. And I hope that some of my thoughts that I'm giving you might be helpful in terms of when you get into this push and shove, and whether this ink was identified or was not identified. Think also of this: I'll give you a little problem illustration. I think it will give you some perspective.

"You live in a neighborhood where a neighbor has a black-and-white cat. There is this racket every night. It's upsetting, and keeps you awake, and you are suspicious of the black-and-white cat. You complain to the neighbor. The neighbor says, 'I keep my tomcat in all the time.' So one night you take the flashbulb camera out and take a picture and you show it to your neighbor and you say, 'It's a black-and-white cat, it looks like your cat.' Well, guess what's coming! The neighbor still persists that the cat never leaves at night, and so you station yourself the next night near the trash barrel and then you conclude that he's right. It's no tomcat, it's a polecat.

"The commonality—this is something that deceives as much as educates.

"Then there's the matter of differentiation. If your neighbor's child runs away and gets to China, you could differentiate him from four million Chinese quickly. This is a problem some of you may remember following World War Two when identifications of persons, following the massive raids that we conducted on Japan, and when grave registration teams would go over the country trying to locate the graves of lost airmen who had been buried by the natives, we had the problem of identification. No dogtags. When you have ten airmen wearing the same kind of uniform, horribly mutilated, it becomes almost impossible to differentiate a person.

"What is representative and phony? Don't be fooled by commonality. The mere fact that there are certain things in the questioned will which can be found in some of the writings of Mr. Hughes does not mean that they were written by the same person.

"What I'm getting at is this: True, you can find perhaps some female d's in Mr. Hughes' writings in 1968, and certain d's in the questioned will might look like the female d, but you must remember that commonality is not conclusive.

"Back to the ink evidence, Mr. Lyter's testimony was confused because he was confused. I don't say that Mr. Lyter was unintelligent. Very smart people—Einstein might not be a proper photographer, but technique is developed through experience. And Mr. Peter Fitzrandolph, of Chemlabs in California, is a man of considerable experience, and you heard his testimony that he could not be sure, using thin-layer chromatography, what ink was on the questioned will. And these chemical tests can give you a false picture, like a picture of a body without a head, but they can be differentiated because of gross size or missing limbs or something. It's a matter of inadequate information, and we have inadequate information about the ink on the will."

During the morning recess, the first day of Phillip Bittle's two-day argument, Judge Hayes called us into chambers. "Mr. Bittle, I'm not going to interfere with your argument. But it's my duty to tell you, sir, that as to a lot of these analogies of yours, I haven't the faintest idea what you're talking about. Maybe the jurors do, but I doubt it. From the looks I see of almost everyone in the courtroom, I'm not the only one hopelessly lost by much of your argument. I urge you, please, no more missing heads, missing limbs, or mutilated corpses in Japan!"

Ten minutes after the second half of the morning session began, Mr. Bittle said to the jurors, "Now, about Caesar and the Industrial Empire, as a vague sort of reference point, I feel that the analogy might be of some help in understanding the tax problems explained to you by Mr. Hughes' tax attorney, Gilbert Boswell . . ."

"Who wrote the will? Consider the misspellings in the will. And a year later, Bonnie Dummar gave her deposition and misspelled 'companies,' 'divided,' and 'revoke' the same way they are misspelled in the will. Consider that and then you tell me, who wrote the will?

"Of course, you may conclude that the actual writing was by Melvin Dummar. It doesn't make any difference which one did the actual writing, they were both involved in it.

"And was there a third conspirator? You know who he was. The conspiracy was a triangle, and the third point of the triangle points up northwest to Alaska. And who lives in Alaska? You know. LeVane Forsythe.

"We know that Forsythe lied. His motive? I'll tell you what it is. He intends to claim under this will."

I addressed the Court. "Your Honor, there is not only no evidence that Mr. Forsythe intends to claim under this will, but the suggestion is nonsense! Mr. Forsythe was not one of Howard Hughes' personal aides! He was not one of the key men in Hughes' company!"

Bittle said, "I grant you, Mr. Forsythe may not have filed a claim under this will, but the jury is entitled to consider that possibility!"

Judge Hayes said, "Mr. Bittle, there isn't any evidence of any such thing, is there?"

"No, but there is a note written by Mr. Hughes which referred to a special, secret envoy in Los Angeles, someone who Mr. Hughes could trust to deliver sealed envelopes unopened, and Mr. Rhoden has suggested that that man was LeVane Forsythe."

I said, "What has that got to do with Forsythe's claiming under this will? There is no provision in the will for anything to go to any trusted secret envoy in Los Angeles!"

Judge Hayes said, "Mr. Bittle, the objection is well taken and will be sustained."

Bittle concluded. "The will is a rank forgery! Our families, and their effort to develop a morality, our churches and governments are all suspect in some degree. This Court is one of the last bastions where we feel we have a constitutionality that is still respected for the truth. I'm confident that you will bring in a verdict of the truth, that Dummar and Forsythe are frauds, and have abused you and this Court!

"And outside, I am sure that I will have the courage to shake your hand, if you don't see things the way I do, when this is over."

64. CLOSING ARGUMENT

". . . The best argument made in this courtroom that the offered will is genuine, was an argument made by counsel for the contestants. An eloquent argument made by eloquent silence. They were given the opportunity to explain to you how evidence, which no one disputed, could possibly be consistent with their theory of forgery. They didn't take that opportunity. They didn't because they couldn't. Mr. Yoakum said that he wouldn't because he didn't want to bore you. Mr. Bittle didn't because he was too busy feeding his elephants and tomcats, and searching for children missing in China."

In the men's room during a recess, standing next to me, Earl Yoakum said, "Do you want to make a prediction?"

"Earl, any lawyer who predicts a jury verdict is either inexperienced or a fool."

"That's true."

"Here's my prediction. The verdict is going to be that Hughes wrote it. You want to make a prediction?"

"Hal, any lawyer who predicts a jury verdict is either inexperienced or a fool. You really think Hughes wrote it, don't you?"

"I know he did. And you know it too, don't you?"

Earl chuckled.

The evening before the last day of my closing argument, Sam, Marvin, Linda, Wilbur, Sheila, and I celebrated our coming victory with dinner in the Regency Room of the Sands. After we ordered drinks, Wilbur asked Sam what he thought the verdict would be.

"There are questions nobody can answer, but a forgery is an absurdity. I don't see how the verdict can be anything but that the will was written by Howard Hughes."

"All right," Linda said, "I'm going to get this off my chest! I don't think Howard Hughes wrote it! I think Melvin Dummar did. Don't ask me to explain how or about the inks, I can't. I just think he wrote it. But I think it's going to be admitted to probate anyway. I think the jury is going to be for us."

Marvin Mitchelson said, "We're going to win and that's all that matters!"

"Yoakum made some points," Wilbur Dobbs said, "Some awful good points. But they just gotta give us that verdict!"

Everybody looked at me for my turn. "Hughes wrote it and that's why the verdict is going to admit it to probate."

We reminisced about the early problems in finding out if the will were genuine, and about the problems in getting the hundreds of thousands to finance the trial, and about the lies of Melvin Dummar that meant that the case had to stop and then the Forsythe saga and the FBI report that meant that it had to go on.

I thanked Wilbur for his loyalty and his work on the ink and medical phases that made our case, and I thanked Linda for her work seven days and seven nights a week for the last year and for finding those bits of evidence that gave us some of the best moments in the trial, and I thanked Sam for his support. And I reminded them of Eli's contributions working with the FBI and with some of the handwriting experts and with the Forsythe phase and the Utah witnesses. And everything blurred when I thanked Marvin for his faith in me.

Just one more day of closing argument, and all the work would be over. Two years, one month, and one week after it started that day in my office when I heard Joyce's jubilant voice on the telephone: "Hal, are you sitting down?"

My closing argument ended on June 5, 1978 at 4:30 P.M.:

"Is Howard Hughes going to be allowed to dispose of his wealth as he saw fit? True, he was eccentric. His life-style was bizarre. He wrote a bizarre will and did a bizarre thing with it. For this, is he to be deprived of the legal right guaranteed to all other men? The right to dispose as he wishes of what he leaves behind?

"It's ironic. After Howard Hughes' death, who was the one man to bring this case to court to protect that legal right for him? It was the one man who had served him so well for thirty-two years, only to quarrel with him and leave him twenty years ago. That one man came back to help his old boss just once more—for the last time. Noah Dietrich.

"Members of the jury, for the past two years I've held the responsibility of proposing this will for probate. It's been a heavy responsibility. Now, finally, I'm about to be free of it.

"I hand that responsibility to you."

65. THE VERDICT

On June 8, 1978, at 7:50 P.M., a moment after the phone rang, Sheila's calm voice from the living room—"They have a verdict!"—sprang me off the bed and dashed me to the dresser for a shirt, and pierced electric chills across my back and pounded a drum in my throat. It was too soon! The jury had come back too soon—no, they didn't have to spend any more time on it! There was no way—no way they could have reached a verdict for Yoakum and Bittle—I had won it! It was all over! The verdict was in and all that was left was for the clerk to read it. "Sheila, are you sure they said it was a verdict and not—"

"It's a verdict!"

"Phone Sam and Linda and ask her to phone Wilbur and Marvin!"

I ran into the closet, grabbed a tie, and wondered when the tension would ease off and why I had it. This was going to be a great night, a night we would remember always, and this was the hour of that night. That jury was mine! I had felt it in the voir dire, all during the trial, and in my closing argument I saw it in their faces. That jury was mine and their verdict was mine. But they were out for only one day.

In the warm Las Vegas night, five minutes after the phone call, Sheila and I walked fast to my car where tall Sam and tiny Linda were waiting. Sam gave me his hand and a smile that said, This is your night!

In the ten-minute drive to the courthouse, we must have hit every red light. I had sweated juries before, but the verdict we were driving to hear could have effects far beyond those of any verdict ever rendered anywhere. A jury verdict is like the gunshot that ends a football game, and like the final score, all that matters is that verdict, not how the case was tried. And a jury verdict decides not only which side won, but the worth of the lawyers, and is always taken by the winning lawyer as applause, and by the losing lawyer as a slap in the face. It had to be a verdict for me. It had to be. But they had come in so damned fast!

The hallway outside Department 9 was packed with newspeople shouldering cameras and holding lights and microphones, and with spectators waiting to get in. An ABC newscaster smiled and raised a thumb, and the tall blond girl of Channel 8 said, "Good luck," as the bailiff made a path for us to the door and let us into the courtroom. Sheila and Linda took seats in the front row. Wilbur and Marvin were waiting at our table, and as Sam and I joined them, I said, "Calm down, Wil, we've got it made!"

Marvin said, "Hal, remember? I get a crack at handling the scholarships."

"I made you that promise, and I'll keep it."

After a nod from the clerk, the bailiff let the mob burst in, and seconds later every seat was taken. At our table, flanked by Wilbur and Sam, I silently rehearsed my extemporaneous comments to be given after the verdict was read and the judge left the bench and I faced the cameras with my arm around Sheila's waist: *Without my wife's patience and love, I still would have won.*

Judge Hayes, in his black robe, entered from behind his chair and sat at the bench, and every sound stopped. "Mr. Bailiff, bring in the jury."

At contestants' table, Yoakum was tense and forced a grin. Bittle was tense and didn't pretend. In between them, Clairbourne seemed to be praying.

Juror number one walked in first, followed by number two, and then by five and six, and none of them looked at me—Jesus Christ! But, they didn't look at Yoakum or Bittle, either.

"Members of the jury, have you reached a verdict?" Judge Hayes asked.

Juror number five, the elected foreman answered, "We have."

"Hand the verdict to the bailiff."

The bailiff took the verdict envelope, walked fast across the courtroom and handed the envelope up to Hayes. Hayes opened it, pulled out the two verdict forms, read them, handed one to his clerk and said, "The clerk will read the verdict."

The clerk rose and faced the jury.

"We, the jury, find that the purported three-page will dated March 19, 1968, was not written by Howard R. Hughes."

The clerk's words "not written" spiked a long needle into my gut, shooting a sick chill up into my chest and out to my arms, and as I heard loud gasps from the contestants' table, I knew that I would never be able to forget how the words "not written" felt.

Judge Hayes ordered the jury polled. As each juror's name was called, he was to state if the verdict as read was his. Juror number one answered, "Yes." Juror number two answered, "Yes," and I wondered how it could have happened—it couldn't have! But it did! I had lost. I had lost it. I had lost the Howard Hughes will case.

I had expected at this moment to be ready to invite the press to the Sands for the champagne celebration Marvin had ordered. Instead, at this moment, I sat still with an emptiness sinking inside. I didn't want to look at Wilbur or Sam or Marvin, or back at Linda. Or at Sheila. I had failed them. I had failed all of them. How do I face my sons? How do I pay off those notes? Where do I go now? What do I do now?

The verdict was eight to nothing.

As Judge Hayes coolly thanked the jurors for their seven-month service to Clark County, they fixed their eyes on him and they seemed angry; and as Judge Hayes spoke to them, he seemed angry.

At the contestants' table, Bittle, emotionally exhausted, slouched in his chair and held his face in his hands. Yoakum and Clairbourne grinned at each other and shook hands. When Yoakum's eyes met mine, his grin broadened, and I forced a slight smile and threw him a soft salute the way Errol Flynn did to the German who shot him down in *The Dawn Patrol.*

The court reporter looked at me with tears, and I could see that the clerk would cry as soon as Judge Hayes left the bench. Judge Hayes announced, "Court is adjourned!" He slammed his pen on his desk and left the bench, and his clerk cried, and the courtroom thundered with reporters and their camera crews rushing to our tables. It hurt to hear the cheers from the contestants' side. I took a deep breath and made myself face Wilbur and Sam and Marvin. "Sorry, you guys."

Wilbur mumbled something about not believing it, Sam shook my hand and said that he was proud to be at the table with me, and Marvin said something about winning a few and losing a few. Still seated in the front row was loyal, little Linda like a frail bird too hurt to stand up, looking at me and saying nothing because there was nothing to say. Sheila tried to smile and reached out her hand; all I could say was, "Sorry, baby." The Judge's law clerk pushed his way through the crowd and said something to make me feel better but it didn't, and he added, "I'll never understand it!"

Long black microphones pointed at my face from all sides like vultures swooping in to record the last gasp of the carcass, and the bright lights seemed brighter than before. What the hell did they expect me to do, cry?

A girl's voice from behind one of the microphones asked, "How does it feel to lose?"

"Lousy."

"Word is that you are in debt a third of a million dollars, and that you personally will face a judgment for costs of another quarter of a million. There was speculation that if you lost, you'd file bankruptcy. Are you going into bankruptcy?"

"Why, do you want to recommend a good lawyer?"

"Aren't you too old to start all over again?"

"If you say so." I had had enough of her and turned to the tall, gruff-looking reporter from NBC.

"What was your first reaction to the verdict?"

"Stunned."

"Now that you've had a few minutes to reflect, how would you describe your reaction to the verdict?"

"Stunned."

"Would you say you are disappointed?"

"I am disappointed."

A young man's voice next to a bright light asked, "What are you going to do now?"

"Check the weather for a flight back to Los Angeles."

"Surely, you plan to appeal?"

"There'll be no appeal."

"Why not?"

"We had a fair trial before a fair judge. There's no reversible error. Nothing to cause an appellate court to order a new trial. There'll be no appeal."

"You mean you're going to let the verdict stand?"

"The verdict will stand."

"What'll happen to the Hughes Estate now?"

"Around eighty percent will be eaten up by inheritance taxes."

"And nothing will go to medical research or to—"

"Nothing."

"Then the case of the Mormon will is over?"

"It's over."

"Are you now willing to concede that it was a forgery?"

"Hell, no! That verdict doesn't change the writing on the will. It doesn't change the evidence. True, I lost. I failed as a lawyer to convince a jury that that will was written by Howard Hughes. But my failure doesn't change the fact that that will was written by Howard Hughes. Or make me blind to it. That will is genuine. I know it. I will always know it. And someday, perhaps, everyone will know it."

At the door, Yoakum was making his victory speech before the cameras, and in front of the contestants' table Bittle was smiling at the reporters, and I wanted to get out of there. I motioned for Sheila to follow me but I was stopped by a tall blond girl of Channel 8. "Please, Mr. Rhoden, just one more?"

I stopped for the last interview.

"Mr. Rhoden, you spent two years of your life on this case, you gave up your law practice for it, and you face financial disaster with this loss. Would you do it again?"

"Yes," I answered without thinking. Then I thought about it. "Oh, yes."

66. EPILOGUE

November 29, 1979, Las Vegas, Nevada.

In the modern, white-walled Church of Jesus Christ of Latter-day Saints on Tropicana Avenue, Governor Robert List, the Justices of the Nevada Supreme Court, the entire Clark County judiciary, the court-room staff of Department 9, the Las Vegas press, and several hundred attorneys and friends solemnly sat in respect for the memory of Judge Keith C. Hayes and for his family. One of the speakers at the service said:

"In his hospital room a few days ago, Keith discussed with me the hereafter life he knew he would soon begin. After I named the two souls I most looked forward to greeting in the next world, Keith said that his first was his mother. Then Howard Hughes. Keith said something about a question he wanted to ask him."